Blanco White

Frontispiece Goya: Pupils of the Pestalozzian Institute, Madrid, 1807 (see p. 39 and p. 214, note 15).

Blanco White
Self-banished Spaniard

Martin Murphy

Yale University Press
New Haven and London
1989

For my parents
Michael Francis and Angela Murphy

Designed by Ann Grindrod

Set in 11/12 Bembo by Textflow Services Limited, Belfast, and printed and bound in Great Britain at The Bath Press, Avon.

The publication of this book has been assisted by a subvention from the Program for Cultural Cooperation Between Spain's Ministry of Culture and United States Universities.

Library of of Congress Cataloging-in-Publication Data

Murphy, Martin, 1934–
  Blanco White.

  Bibliography: p.
  Includes index.
  1. White, Joseph Blanco, 1775–1841—Biography.
2. Authors, Spanish—19th century—Biography.
3. Intellectuals—Spain—Biography.   I. Title.
PQ6574.W5Z75   1989   861'.5 [B]   88-33835

ISBN 0–300–04458–5

Contents

List of Illustrations

Preface and Acknowledgements

No hay opiniones, sino opinantes
—Miguel de Unamuno

It was, I think, in Mark Pattison's *Memoirs* that I first came upon the name of Blanco White. Blanco was just leaving Oriel and Oxford as Pattison came up, but he lingered on in college memory as an exotic refugee from another culture and another century, for whom Oxford was only a transitory resting-place on his long quest, or flight. That is how he is still remembered—if he is remembered at all—in these islands: as a shadowy, even baleful, figure who played a formative part in the pre-history of the Oxford Movement.

It was only when I followed these tracks backwards in time from Oxford to London, Cadiz, Seville and Madrid, and forwards to Dublin and Liverpool, that I began to appreciate the variety of Blanco's metamorphoses, as poet, priest, novelist, political editor, literary critic, teacher and theologian. He was a man of rare gifts whose destiny it was to arrive where history was being made and to have a hand in its making. There was scarcely a major figure in the political and cultural world of Spain in the first quarter, and of England in the second quarter, of the nineteenth century with whom he did not come in contact, and on some he exercised a decisive influence.

The very disparateness of Blanco's life explains why he has hitherto lacked a full biography. There have been biographical sketches, and there have been monographs on separate aspects of his career—on his contribution to the early history of Spanish American independence, for instance, or on the part he played in the Catholic Emancipation controversy, or in his Spanish poetry (to name only three assorted examples)—but this is, as far as I know, the first full attempt to draw all these strands together into a single narrative whole.

Though I have often questioned my own capacity for the task, I have never doubted that it was worthwhile. The life of Blanco White, quite apart from its historical interest, has some of the elements of myth. It is the story of a quest: the progress of a rationalist Quixote in search of the transcendental. Or, as Gladstone put it, solemnly: 'His spirit was a battlefield upon which with fluctuating fortune and a singular intensity, the powers of belief and scepticism waged, from first to last, their unceasing war; and within the compass of his experience are presented to our view most of the great moral and spiritual problems that attach to the condition of our race'.[1]

The need for a biography of Blanco is all the greater in so far as the Works and the Life are in his case more than in most, inextricably linked. It might be argued that as far as the Works are concerned, Blanco never achieved, in any one of the genres he attempted, the complete success he promised (though he came nearest to it as a literary critic). But everything he wrote was, however indirectly, autobiographical—the product of experience, and of a hypersensitive and vulnerable mind and body. After reading Blanco's *Life*, Darwin is reported to have observed that 'It greatly took away from one's sympathy with a man's religious scruples to find that they were merely symptoms of a diseased liver'. His interlocutor, Lady Ashburton, replied wisely that 'Until the dominion of the liver was precisely ascertained, it was safer to speak respectfully of it'.[2]

The fact that Blanco wrote several versions of his own life is a mixed blessing for his biographer. Six of his works contain an autobiographical element. Four of these are more properly described as apologias, the author's aim being to present his life as cautionary evidence of the destructive effects of Catholic theocracy on individual character and conscience.[3] The 'Narrative of his Life in Spain and England'— later incorporated in the posthumously published *Life*—is at first sight more directly autobiographical but this, too, was written for his literary executor to present at the bar of English public opinion. Only in the unfinished, and unpublished, fragment 'The Examination of Blanco by White' did he begin to attempt a more candid and self-critical dialogue with himself. As we shall see, some of the most important episodes in his private life find no place in these writings, not out of any deliberate intention by the author to suppress the truth, but because it was too painful to record, or even to remember.

This work rests on foundations laid by others. The first conspectus of Blanco's life, based almost entirely on secondary sources, was that written by Leslie Stephen for the *Dictionary of National Biography* (1917), and though it gives insufficient attention to the Spanish years, it is still the best account available in English. If we leave aside the brilliant, highly tendentious, sketch by Marcelino Menéndez y Pelayo in his *Historia de los heterodoxos españoles* (1882), the pioneer work of Spanish scholarship was that of Mario Méndez Bejarano in his *Vida y obras de D. José María Blanco y Crespo* (1920). This is a book which has received far less than its due, when one considers the difficulty the author must have had in gaining access to sources. Méndez Bejarano was not content to write about Blanco's work (which he did, with remarkable objectivity and sympathy), he actually read it in its entirety in English as well as Spanish. These are solid merits which more than outweigh the book's defects of organisation and chronology.

The recent efflorescence in Spain of interest in Blanco White is due above all to the late Professor Vicente Llorens, himself an exile from Spain, who during the fifties and sixties published a series of seminal articles on different aspects of Blanco's career, based on his research in Spanish and British archives. Unfortunately Llorens did not live to bring his work to conclusion in the form of the biography he had planned, but the introduction to his anthology of Blanco's Spanish work is a fine piece of synthesis and the best available account of the life to date. I am greatly indebted to his work, as also to that of his pupil Professor Antonio Garnica, the translator into Spanish of *Letters from Spain*, who has done much to illuminate Blanco's early life in Seville.

In attempting to rescue from obscurity so complex, elusive and multi-faceted a figure I have strayed into much unfamiliar territory. I owe a great deal as an autodidact to the professional scholars who have given help and encouragement, and even more to friends and family. I am grateful to Dr Antonio Garnica for giving me the opportunity to spend a year at the University of Seville, and thus to get to know Blanco's native city. He also kindly translated into Spanish two articles which prepared the ground for the present work. Tony Cross, formerly Principal of Manchester College, Oxford, whose doctoral thesis on Blanco's theology is nearing completion, has been an expert and patient guide to matters Unitarian and an enthusiastic believer in the cause. During my stays in Seville, Baltasar Fra Molinero and Eduardo Varela Bravo gave much valued advice and support. More recently I have benefited from the erudition of Dr Manuel Moreno Alonso, indefatigable researcher, generous host and devotee of Andalucian history. I owe to our shared interest in Blanco, the valued friendship of André Pons, who in the course of a long correspondence has thrown much light on the American dimension of this story. At a critical stage in the writing, the support and encouragement of Professor Nigel Glendinning were decisive. Others whose help I gratefully acknowledge include Sir Raymond Carr; Professor Dorothy Sherman Severin; Miss Maria Victoria de Lara, *doyenne* of Blanconian studies in this country; Dr Miriam Hood, Cultural Counsellor at the Venezuelan Embassy in London, who encouraged my pursuit of Andrés Bello; Professor P. E. Russell; Professor John Lynch; Mr M. R. Perkin, Curator of Special Collections, and Mr J. Clegg, at Liverpool University Library; Jean F. Preston, Curator of Manuscripts at Princeton University Library; Mrs Barbara Smith, formerly librarian at Manchester College, Oxford; the late Fr Stephen Dessain of the Birmingham Oratory; Sir Philip de Zulueta; H. N. Blanco White, QC; the Rev Graham Murphy; John Hall; Francis Baden

Powell. I would also like to thank the British Council for a travel grant made under the Anglo-Spanish Joint Research Project, which made possible a visit to Seville in 1983. The Dr Williams Trust made a generous grant to cover the expenses of typing the manuscript, and for this I am indebted to the Trust's secretary, the Rev James McClelland. Finally, this book could never have been written without the facilities provided by the Bodleian and Taylorian libraries at Oxford which I have been privileged to enjoy.

Part I: Spain

Sombra hecha de luz,
Que templando repele,
Es fuego con nieve
El andaluz.

Enigma al trasluz,
Pues va entre gente solo,
Es amor con odio
El andaluz.

Oh hermano mío, tú.
Dios, que te crea,
Será quien comprenda
Al andaluz.

—Luis Cernuda

Chapter 1
Hortus conclusus

When, descending fast into the vale of years, I fix my mind's eye on those narrow, shady, silent streets, where the footsteps re-echoed from the clean, watered porches of the houses, and every object spoke of quiet contentment—of bare sufficiency of fortune enlarged by cheerfulness and moderation of wishes—modest gentility supporting its claims to respect, not by riches and power but by inherited nobleness and delicacy of feeling; the objects around me begin to fade into mere delusion, and not only the thoughts but the external sensations which I then experienced revive with a reality which makes me shudder; it has so much the character of a trance or vision! Alas, what is there left of the objects themselves but these mental traces, these deep and painful impressions which like unhealed wounds must in the heart of many an exile bleed anew whenever they are examined!

Thus at the age of 50, in Chelsea, Joseph Blanco White looked back at the birthplace of his original self, José María Blanco y Crespo. Throughout the vagaries of a life which took him from eighteenth-century Seville, a theocracy still living on the spiritual proceeds of the Counter-Reformation, to nineteenth-century Liverpool, a plutocracy built on the profits of steamships and railroads, this interior landscape remained the one abiding constant.

Seville in 1775, the year of Blanco's birth, was a city living on inherited capital, now fast diminishing. Despite its reputation for intolerance, it had, over the centuries, successfully absorbed differing cultures: Roman, Visigothic, Moorish. After the reconquest of Granada and the discovery of America it became in the late fifteenth and early sixteenth centuries the most prosperous centre of commerce and industry in Spain, a cosmopolitan focus of Mediterranean and Atlantic trade. Yet by the end of the sixteenth century the signs of future decay were already visible. Just as the expulsion of the Moriscos, in the name of racial and religious purity, had damaging effects on the agriculture of southern Spain, so the expulsion of the Jews deprived Seville of the very sources of enterprise and capital which were needed for survival in the face of international competition. In the seventeenth century Seville's population was decimated by a succession of plagues, its trade routes were disrupted by English buccaneers and it began to lose its long commercial battle with its rival Cadiz, more conveniently

3

situated on the Atlantic seaboard. In 1680 Cadiz replaced Seville as the
base of the Atlantic fleet, and Seville became merely the seat of the
bureaucracy which administered Spain's trade with her American
empire. It lost even this position when in 1717 the tribunals of the Casa
de Contratación and of the Consulado de Indias were transferred to
Cadiz. The magnificent Seville Exchange, La Lonja, once a centre of
international dealing, fell into disuse until the end of the century when
it became the repository of the imperial archives. While Cadiz looked
to the future, Seville lived on its past.[1]

Those who called the tune in late eighteenth-century Seville were its
patrician aristocracy, living off the rents of their country estates, and
its clergy. The tone was set by those who were, or who aspired to be,
hidalgos, and the true *hidalgo* regarded trade as an occupation beneath
his dignity. The effect of such attitudes was described by the reformer
Juan Pablo Forner: 'We want commerce yet we scorn the merchant,
we want agriculture yet we despise the farmer, we praise lavishly the
cloth from England while we refuse to speak to the cloth manufac-
turer'.[2] A census of the city taken not long after 1775 estimated the
population to be about 76,000. What is chiefly remarkable about the
figures is the low number of those engaged in active work. Over a
third of the population could be classified as being in a distressed state:
those without regular employment, beggars, prisoners and the sick.
What industry there was, mainly consisted of the production of craft
or luxury goods commissioned by the aristocracy or the Church.[3] The
largest single employer was the Royal Tobacco Factory, whose
magnificent buildings completed in 1758 were a triumph of rhetoric
over functionalism. The English traveller Joseph Townsend, on a visit
in 1787, noted that the workforce in the factory had recently fallen
from 3,000 to 1,700, on account of mismanagement.[4] In order to
establish new industries, the Spanish crown often had to bring in
foreigners, such as the English entrepreneur Nathan Wetherell, who
was given assistance in setting up a tannery in a disused convent.[5] Of
ecclesiastics there was a more than adequate supply. Seville—'Sevilla
la piadosa'—contained no less than eighty-four monasteries and convents and a clerical population of over four and a half thousand. Of
these, more than one half were regulars of whom as many as sixteen
hundred took part in the spectacular Holy Week processions. The
Cathedral supported a total establishment of two hundred and thirty
five, according to Townsend, including sixty canons. A Spanish
observer described the city some years earlier as an *imperium monacho-
rum*.[6]

Nevertheless the ruler of Spain in 1775, Charles III, was one of the
most enlightened monarchs in Europe, and able ministers such as
Aranda, Campomanes and Floridablanca, though encumbered by a
top-heavy, many-layered bureaucracy and constantly having to look

over their shoulders at a largely hostile Church, were dedicated to the cause of progress. Their reforms were, however, imposed paternalistically, from above, on a population which was indifferent and deeply conservative. The enlightenment put down few roots in the Spanish soil. The most daring of the Bourbon administrators, Pablo de Olavide, was appointed to Andalucia in 1767, and for the next eight years made Seville a centre of experiment. He was a pioneer in town planning and educational reform, but his most audacious venture was a utopian project which involved the establishment of model settlements, manned by German colonists, to reclaim and cultivate the waste lands of the Sierra Morena. But Olavide's free-thinking views and his attachment to foreign ideas antagonised the Church, and in 1776 his enemies succeeded in having him arrested by the Inquisition, brought to trial and imprisoned. It was a spectacular victory for the forces of conservatism. The progressives, or *ilustrados*, were put on the defensive.[7]

In 1781 Blanco, as a boy of six, saw the bundles of firewood piled on barrels of pitch for the last victim of the Seville Inquisition to be condemned to death. Since it throws so much light on the dark underside of the contemporary theocracy, the case deserves attention. The accused, known as the *beata ciega*, was a blind and deranged woman who was charged with having seduced a succession of spiritual directors and with claiming private revelations and dispensations from the moral law. For nine months she was interrogated and harangued in prison by theologians who tried to extract from her a confession of guilt, but even Fray Diego de Cadiz, the most famous preacher of the day, had to admit defeat. At last, on 24 August 1781 she was brought to the church of San Pablo for the *auto-de-fé*. The Oratorian priest P. Teodomiro Ignacio Díaz de la Vega—later to be Blanco's spiritual director—began by appealing to the *vox populi*, asking the packed crowd 'if they believed that all acts against the sixth commandment were wrong. To which all shouted out yes, that they were wrong and sinful'. When the woman protested her innocence, she was gagged 'to curb her blasphemous tongue'. The priest whom she was regarded as having seduced was sentenced to suspension and confinement in a monastery while she, still protesting the truth of her revelations, was sentenced to death by fire. It was only at the very end, in prison, that she broke down and signed a retraction, confessing that all the accusations were true and that 'since the age of six when she discovered evil, she had resolved to live without restraint'. Because of her last-minute repentance, instead of being burned alive she was garrotted inside the prison, her body then being burned on the pyre or *quemadero*. It was P. Díaz de la Vega who heard her last, terrified confession.[8]

The difference between Seville and Madrid is graphically illustrated

by Townsend's account of the *auto-de-fé* which took place in the capital
only three years after the case of the *beata ciega*. This concerned one
Ignacio Rodríguez, who was accused of making aphrodisiac powders.
The fashionables of Madrid thronged to the trial, held in the convent
of San Domingo, the nuns crowding to the grille to hear the intriguing
details. Rodríguez was sentenced to be whipped through the streets,
but in fact, Townsend reported, he was conducted through the capital
'without receiving any stripes; and as he proceeded, he was frequently
refreshed by his friends with biscuits and wine'.[9] The *madrileños*
regarded such goings-on with contemptuous amusement.

The fall of Olavide led to a re-establishment of ecclesiastical control
over intellectual life. His plan for the reorganisation of the university
curriculum was abandoned, and the theatre introduced to the city by
Olavide was suppressed.[10] Not that the *sevillanos* needed a theatre to
satisfy their appetite for spectacle. The Holy Week processions, with
their tableaux depicting the scenes of Christ's passion in all their
agonising detail, involved the whole city, street by street, in a vast and
corporate mystery play. As for actors, none could have been more
effective in arousing pity and fear than the histrionic revivalist preachers of the day such as Fray Diego de Cadiz. The evils of the theatre
were, ironically, Fray Diego's favourite theme. If scenery was
wanted, what more spectacular than the gilded retablos of every
church and chapel? There the poor could be transported by their
prayers into a baroque heaven crammed with free-floating apostles,
bishops and cherubs, defeating the laws of gravity by the power of
spiritual make-believe. One of the richest of these retablos, that of the
church of the Salvador, was completed as late as the 1770s—a last gasp
of the Counter-Reformation on the very eve of revolution.

The Revolution in France sent shock waves over the Pyrenees and
horrified all but a small circle of intellectuals. The central government
attempted to insulate Spain from infection and used the Inquisition to
prevent the entry of French books and French ideas. The politicians
who, a generation earlier, had opened the windows to let in European
air, now shut them tight.

Kingship in Spain was invested with an aura of semi-divinity, and
so the execution of Louis XVI in 1793 aroused incredulous revulsion.
A sumptuous requiem was held in Seville Cathedral, and in his
panegyric P. Teodomiro Díaz de la Vega denounced the godlessness
of the revolutionary Assembly which 'by its decrees allows the
Socinian, the Anabaptist, the Quaker, the Jew, the Musulman and the
Idolater to open their Temples, their Synagogues, their Mosques and
their Pagodas, while only Catholic churches are closed . . . A vast tide
is rising, alive with reptiles: *ibi reptilia quorum non est numerus*'.[11] The
outrage done to the monarchy in France brought Throne and Altar in
Spain even closer together.

From an Irish father and a Spanish mother Blanco, in his own words, inherited 'the unhesitating faith of persecuting Spain' along with 'the impassioned belief of persecuted Ireland'.[12] His paternal grandfather, William White, was one of the many Irish Catholic refugees from the penal laws who settled in Seville and Cadiz in the early eighteenth century and made a living in the shipping trade. The legend that the Irish exiles on the Continent were all wild geese and gallant soldiers of fortune is only now giving way to the realisation that a large proportion of them were hard-headed entrepreneurs who were quick to exploit the opportunities in Atlantic trade which their Spanish counterparts neglected or disdained. Their close commercial and family network extended from Malaga, Cadiz and Seville to the Canaries and out to America, and from the Bay of Biscay to Bordeaux, Nantes and St Malo. Irish Catholics had enjoyed privileged status in Spain since the early seventeenth century. An Irish College had been established in Seville in 1612 to train priests for the mission, and until its closure in 1767—following the expulsion of the Jesuits—it provided a focus for the Irish colony.[13] Among the more prominent members of this colony in the late eighteenth and early nineteenth centuries were the brothers James and Patrick Wiseman who like the Whites and indeed like most of the Irish community came from Waterford. The Wisemans had a hand in many enterprises, including a liquorice factory set up in association with the English entrepreneur Nathan Wetherell, and they acted as bankers and agents for Lord Holland during his two visits to Seville in 1803 and 1809. Their prosperity can be gauged from the size of their house, which still survives in what is now the calle Fabiola—renamed in honour of James Wiseman's eminent son Nicholas, Cardinal Wiseman, the author of a historical novel of that name. 'Paddys of the grave sort' was how Lady Holland inimitably described the Wisemans, and the same sobriety was characteristic also of their less prosperous neighbours the Whites.[14]

Most of the Irish married their own kind, but Guillermo Blanco, José María's father, married into an impoverished branch of the lesser Andalucian nobility. His wife, Doña Gertrudis Crespo y Neve could claim some distinguished connections. Her maternal uncle, Felipe de la Neve, was Governor of the Californias (1775–82) and founder of Los Angeles, while further back she was related to Don Justino de la Neve, Murillo's patron, a Canon of the cathedral and founder of the hospice of the Venerables. Murillo's portrait of him, now in the National Gallery in London, reveals a fastidious and cultivated man very like his descendant.[15]

Doña Gertrudis' gaiety complemented her husband's gravity. 'Under the influence of a happier country, her pleasing vivacity, the quickness of her apprehension and the exquisite degree of sensibility

which animated her words and actions, would have qualified her to
shine in the most elegant and refined circles'. Her natural talents had
not, however, been developed by education, and like many women of
her class and time all her energies came to be concentrated on her
devotional life, which took the form of an anxious scrupulosity and
turned her, in time, into a *mater dolorosa*. Don Guillermo was a
fundamentally unworldly man, the stuff of whom saints are made.
'Benevolence prompted all my father's actions', his son wrote;
'endued him, at times, with something like supernatural vigour, and
gave him, for the good of his fellow-creatures, the courage and
decision he wanted in whatever concerned himself. With hardly
anything to spare, I do not recollect a time when our house was not a
source of relief and consolation to some families of such as, by a
characteristic and feeling appellation, are called among us the *blushing
poor*'. As a young man Guillermo Blanco had visited his father's
relations in Ireland and had been sent on a continental tour, 'which
gave a polish to his manners which at that period was not easily found
even in the first ranks of the nobility'.[16] He had no training or aptitude
for commerce, so when the family business foundered after his
father's death he had to take a subordinate position in the new firm set
up after a rescue operation by his cousin Thomas Cahill.[17] He was for
a time (1783–99) the English vice-consul at Seville, an unpaid and
honorary post.

  Later, Blanco recalled being 'brought up without any distinct
impression of our being either rich or poor; yet with deeply inculcated
ideas of *gentility*'.[18] From the age of eight he was expected to work
long hours alongside the Irish clerks in the office, copying correspondence, but his mother had all the distaste of the *hidalgo* for
commerce, and this was to lead to some conflict between the Irish and
the Spanish sides of the family when it came to deciding his future. He
was shielded from contact from other boys of his own age, and since
his two sisters were educated away from home in a convent, he was
deprived even of their company. Fernando, his younger brother, was
eleven years his junior, so it was not until much later that they became
companions. He was, to use his own words, 'a solitary being'.

  The austerity of the house contrasted with the sensuality of the city,
which also played a part in Blanco's formation. In *Letters from Spain*,
written in a Berkshire vicarage, he evoked the sights and sounds
which surrounded his youth: the architectural and ritual grandeur of
the cathedral; the cool and fragrant gardens of the Alcazar, an oasis of
stillness in the heart of the city; the 'perpetual tinkling' of the bells
from the churches and convents; the languor and drowsiness of the
afternoon heat; the processions which filled the animated streets with a
year-long round of spectacle. The more heady excitements, such as
those of the bullfight, were out of bounds, but Blanco's childhood was

not devoid of other, more simple pleasures. 'The joy and delight of my childhood', he wrote, 'was centered in the house of four spinsters of the good old times who during a period of between fifty and sixty years . . . had waged the most successful war against melancholy, and were now the seasoned veterans of mirth. In a lofty drawing-room, hung around with tapestry, the faded remnants of ancient family pride, the good old ladies were ready, every evening after sunset, to welcome their friends, especially the young of both sexes, to whom they showed the most good-natured kindness. An ancient guitar, as large as a moderate violincello, stood up in a corner of the room, ready at a moment's notice, to stir up the young people into a dance of the Spanish *seguidillas*, or to accompany the songs which were often *forfeited* in the games that formed the staple merriment at this season'.[19]

Across the river, in the district of Triana, there was another Seville, the haunt of sailors and gypsies, where genteel respectability had no place. Solidarity, robust good humour, a keen appreciation of wit and physical beauty, an appetite for pleasure and intense religious faith rooted in experience of life—these were, as they still are, the marks of the Andalucian. Nowhere is religion so physically incarnate as in Seville, so built into the social fabric, so embedded in custom and fleshed out in visible signs and cult images. Every district and brotherhood has its own Virgin, to the outsider indistinguishable from any other Virgin, but to the initiate a unique focus of personal devotion and group loyalty. Seville, as well as being the city of Don Juan, was the city of Mary, and it prided itself on being the oldest and staunchest defender of the doctrine of the Immaculate Conception, long before it was accepted by Rome, Even the beggar calling at the door invoked the name of Mary with the greeting 'Ave María purísima', answered from within by the response 'Sin pecado concebida'. Every day began with the leader of the dawn procession singing out, street by street, his melodious call to join in the worship of the Mother of God.[20]

This popular religion ignored theology and bypassed the clergy, except perhaps the friars, who took human nature generally as they found it, and whose earthy style and waggish humour won them a receptive and tolerant following. Such was the pleasant young friar whom Joseph Townsend met on a boat trip down the Guadalquivir, who ogled the girls and played his guitar and at the end of the journey made off with Townsend's luggage.[21]

On Sunday, Don Guillermo would take his son with him on a round of devotions: first to confession at the Dominican church of San Pablo, on to the Cathedral for High Mass, after dinner to another church, and then to the hospital where he would spend two or three hours tending the sick, 'making the beds of the poor, taking the helpless in his arms and stooping to such services as even the menials in

attendance were often loth to perform'. He was regarded by the poor
as a saint, and at his death crowds thronged the house to honour his
memory.[22]

The self-mortifications of Spanish penitential religion are the
reverse side of a natural sensuality, but Don Guillermo's asceticism
was of the Irish sort—an attraction to the austere for its own sake.
Though with hindsight Blanco may have exaggerated the reaction of
his younger self, it would have been surprising if he did not chafe
against this round of duty and discipline. He found an escape in music
and literature. He learned the violin from his father's partner, and
before long was playing in the orchestra of the Oratorian church—'the
spiritual opera house of Seville'.[23] But it was literature which was his
chief source of liberation. A music master lent him *Quixote*, which he
devoured in secret, and Fénélon's *Télémaque*, in translation, gave even
more disturbing pleasure. Fénélon's Greek heroes seemed to inhabit a
guilt-free world and to have found the secret of happiness without the
benefit of Christianity. Their mythical world of beauty and light
contrasted with the images of suffering and death and the dark,
repressive aspect of Sevillan Catholicism. Here perhaps lie the seeds of
Blanco's later *aesthetic* revolt against the religion of life-denying
preoccupation with sin.[24]

It was Blanco's taste for literature which determined his choice of
career. His mother insisted that he should be released for a few hours
every day from the office to have Latin lessons. His aversion to the
drudgery of the office grew as his passion for study increased. 'Those
who wished me to be a merchant were jealous of every kind of
knowledge which could draw my attention from business. I myself
perceived the real state of the case; and though only twelve years old at
the time, and more ignorant of the world than an English child of
eight, hit, as it were instinctively, upon the only expedient that could
release me from my mercantile bondage. I declared I felt a strong
inclination to be a clergyman'.[25] The choice was natural for a boy who
was so evidently docile, ardent and gifted. He had also voiced his
mother's longing 'to have a son who shall daily hold in his hands the
real body of Christ'. The glamour of the Church and the dignity of its
priesthood were further powerful motives. So a love of study,
genuine piety, a desire to please, ahd childish vanity all combined to
determine Blanco's destiny.

Had he been born thirty years earlier, the boy would now have gone
to the Jesuits for his philosophy course, but the suppression of the
Jesuits had left a vacuum in higher education which was never
satisfactorily filled. The Dominican college of San Tomás, to which
he went first, followed a course of rigid Thomism. Blanco had already
been inoculated against scholasticism by reading, in his aunt's library,
the *Teatro Crítico* of the Benedictine Feijóo—a work which managed

to combine Catholic orthodoxy with the empirical spirit of the French encyclopaedists. The tediousness of the classes at San Tomás prompted Blanco, though frightened by his own boldness, to challenge his teacher. He then persuaded his mother to have him transferred to the University. This had only recently been established in one of the larger houses confiscated from the Jesuits. Olavide had drawn up ambitious plans for the reform of its curriculum, but these were cut short by his fall. The University was now firmly under the control of the cathedral chapter and though it included small faculties of law and medicine it was in effect a theological seminary.[26] Blanco and his contemporaries learned more from each other than from their official teachers. He himself came under the influence of a theological student, Manuel María del Mármol, who introduced him to Bacon's *Organum*. It was when he passed on to the theology class at the age of sixteen that he came into the orbit of an older contemporary who left a lasting mark on his life: Manuel María de Arjona. Arjona, a graduate of the University of Osuna, was now studying canon law at Seville and shared the reforming ideals of a small group of higher clergy. 'He was far above the common standard in point of learning and had few equals in natural abilities. He had a knowledge of literature uncommon in my country, was an excellent Poet, and well acquainted with Ecclesiastical History. He had, besides, a great desire of promoting that species of learning unknown in the Spanish universities—I mean, elegant Literature. His private servant who, as is often the case was intended for orders, had entered the first Divinity class with me, and being desired by his master to make him acquainted with some of his fellow-students whom he might think capable of profiting by his literary advice, he made choice of me'.[27] Arjona now became Blanco's literary mentor and spiritual guide. Two other students also attached themselves to Arjona: Alberto Lista and Félix-José Reinoso. Lista, the only son of a weaver, whose widowed mother kept a ribbon shop in Triana, became almost an adopted member of Blanco's family. It was Reinoso who took the initiative in drawing up a systematic programme of self-improvement. Braving the mockery of the frivolous, he formulated the constitution and rules of a youthful literary academy, the Academia de Letras Humanas, and with Arjona's help persuaded Seville's most eminent lawyer and man of letters, Juan Pablo Forner, to be its patron.[28]

The proceedings of the Academia were at first conducted in Latin, later in Spanish. Members were obliged to submit poetical or rhetorical compositions for criticism and discussion, and an annual prize was awarded by a judge appointed from outside. They set out to teach themselves the principles of criticism and taste, starting with Quintilian, then moving on to the Renaissance humanist Vives and finally to French and Italian critics such as Rollin, Batteux and Muratori. They

wrote epistles to each other in Latin. They learned French from
Racine, and Italian from Tasso and Petrarch. They composed pastorals in which they themselves appeared in Arcadian disguise (Blanco,
for instance, as Albino and Lista as Licio). If the odd 'Phyllis' and
'Dorila' also put in an appearance, they were as yet only figments of
the imagination. The prevailing tone of piety and neo-classical
earnestness is evident from the titles of their poems: 'To Apollo,
beseeching him to re-establish his altars in Seville', or 'To Charles III,
restorer of the sciences'. Blanco's first effort was an ode to the
Immaculate Conception.

He and his friends succeeded in giving each other the kind of
humane, refined education they would have received from the Jesuits,
had they still existed. His first published work was a translation into
Spanish of an edifying pastoral drama, *Alexis*, written in Latin by a
German Jesuit for college performance. This exercise in pious allegory
transposed the atonement into an imagined Arcady, where the king's
son, Alexis, gives his life to save his father's country from the plague.
'The characters of Agathocles [the king] and Alexis', the translator
claimed rather grandly, 'are surely worthy of Racine'.[29]

More interesting, because it touches on themes which were to
become a lifelong preoccupation, is a poem Blanco dedicated in 1796
to the Academy's patron J. P. Forner. In the poem Blanco contrasts
Forner's philanthropic humanism with the philistinism of those who
controlled higher education—idle, unproductive parasites who used
their false reputation for learning to lord it over the ignorant. For
Forner, education was a gift to be used in the service of one's
fellow-men; for these others, it was simply an instrument with which
to control and manipulate society. 'Theology' and 'theologians' are
not mentioned by name, but it is clear that these are the targets, from
the references to 'sterile dogmas', and to the 'baleful science' which
enables its sectaries only to hide their ignorance by airing their
prejudices as if they were 'infallible oracles'. 'What is learning but an
empty show, which unmakes those who could be useful to mankind?'
The poet compares Ignorance to a foul bird, polluting the altar of the
Muses, a loathsome incubus which keeps humanity in thrall. It was to
such as Forner that the Muses looked to defend their honour and to
expel the monster.[30] The poem shows how far, at the age of twenty-
one, Blanco had already become a man of the enlightenment. The
ideal of practical usefulness, the concern for education and the
aversion from dogma remained characteristic of him throughout his
life.

Forner had a seminal influence on Blanco's thinking, imbuing him
with the ideas and the ideals of the late enlightenment. He shared the
enthusiasm of the age for plans and projects but combined this
commitment to social and educational reform with orthodox belief.

Faith peacefully coexisted with reason in him as in many of the *ilustrados*, though none of them attempted a synthesis of the two. He was one of those who were aware that changes and reforms, if they were to be lasting, must be adapted to Spanish conditions: it was no good applying theory (usually French theory) without taking account of the history of the country, the character of its people and the limits of the possible. These views were shared by another Andalucian, José Cadalso, whose work Blanco knew. If a doctor wants to cure a sick man, Cadalso argued, he needs to be familiar not only with the theory of medicine but with the peculiar temperament of the patient. Both men advocated the kind of gradualism which Blanco was much later to encounter in the works of Burke. Forner's enlightened nationalism also took the form of a new interest in Spanish history. With other *ilustrados* he took the revisionist view that Spain had been most truly Spanish in the Middle Ages, when she had enjoyed her own liberties and laws. The Spain of Charles V and Philip II had, according to this view, been led astray from her true path: absolutism, far from being suited to the national character, was foreign to it, and the so-called 'Golden Age' had marked the beginning of decadence. These ideas had a profound if delayed effect on Forner's young followers. They are evident in Lista's later historical writing and prepared the ground for much of Blanco's political and literary criticism.[31]

The publication by the Academia in 1797 of a first collection of poems finally confounded its critics and established its reputation even beyond Seville. A new 'Sevillan School' was born. Its members often teetered on the edge of becoming a mutual admiration society, but their loyalty to each other was deeply rooted enough to last a lifetime. They had an appetite for knowledge which amounted to an *ivresse de savoir*, and a passion for clarity. 'It was the favourite amusement of myself and those constant associates of my youth that formed the knot of friends of whom [Arjona] was the centre and guide, to examine all our feelings, in order to resolve them into some general law, and trace them to their simple elements. This habit of analysis and generalisation extended itself to the habits and customs of the country, and the daily incidents of life, till in me it produced the deceitful, though not uncommon notion that all knowledge is the result of developed principles, and gave me a distaste for every book that was not cast into a general theory'.[32]

The pursuit of knowledge and the cult of friendship sublimated but did not extinguish the instincts of the flesh. After taking minor orders at the age of fourteen, Blanco was, he recalled, 'strictly kept from intercourse with young women, but my amorous disposition showed itself very clearly. My feelings, which I was obliged to lay constantly before my confessor, were a source of constant alarm'.[33] Nevertheless his docility to his parents and spiritual directors was absolute: 'No waywardness of disposition appeared in me to defeat or obstruct their labours. At the age of fourteen, all the seeds of devotion which had been assiduously sown in my heart sprung up, as it were, spontaneously. The pious practices which had hitherto been a task, were now the effect of my own choice'.[34]

His introduction to the world and first glimpse of its pleasures came in 1793 with his first visit to Cadiz, a city henceforward to be associated in his mind with light and freedom. To his father, Cadiz was a Babylon, a secular city fraught with moral danger. He would have been confirmed in his suspicions had he read the impressions of a German visitor at about this time: 'No where do the sexes seek each other with equal eagerness, in no part do the pleasures of sense seem so indispensable, in no part does the influence of the climate so easily disarm the severest of moralists. But it is when the *solano* blows that this impulse becomes most impetuous; for then the very air they breathe is on fire, and all the senses are voluntarily inebriated, the imagination is bewildered, and an irresistible instinct becomes authorised by example'.[35]

Blanco's first, and clandestine, visit to Cadiz at the age of eighteen was also his first venture into the outside world. He was invited to spend the summer at Sanlucar de Barrameda as the guest of a South American widow with four boys of his own age. His companions were to spend the last week of their holidays in Cadiz, but he was forbidden to accompany them there. When the end of the holiday came—a holiday Blanco was to describe as the beginning of 'a new era' in his life—'it was quite inhuman (so, I believe, the good old lady thought to herself) to keep me a prisoner and separate me from her own boys . . . Was it lawful to send me to Cadiz by stealth and against my father's wishes?' The question was put to the family's confessor. 'Fortunately for me, the priest was in favour of a mild interpretation, and I was allowed to proceed to Cadiz, as a parcel of smuggled goods. My father was not to hear of it; and to avoid all danger on that point, I was not to visit some relations of mine who lived in that city . . . One thing, however, in the opinion of my gentle keeper atoned for whatever guilt might attach to the deception. We were not to go to the Play. This was solemnly promised, and the promise was kept'.[36]

If this visit offered a first, innocent taste of forbidden fruit, the effects of a second visit the next year were more disturbing. Blanco was then on the eve of ordination to the subdiaconate—beyond which there was no turning back from an ecclesiastical career. On this occasion he stayed with relatives and there fell in love with a young cousin, to whom he was too timid to declare himself. It was on this occasion that he visited the theatre, which to his father was the seat of the city's licentiousness, but which gave him 'overwhelming pleasure'.[37] His brief introduction to society left him with the ambition of

becoming a man of the world and he returned to Seville fully
intending to extricate himself from his clerical career.

Back in Seville, however, the net was too tightly drawn for him to
escape so easily. If he was to withdraw from the Church, what other
career was open to a young man of limited means who at all costs was
determined to avoid the office desk? The law was too expensive and
medicine, as a profession, hardly counted. The only visible alternative
was the navy. He had reckoned, however, without the reaction of his
mother who, from the moment the question was mooted, 'never
raised her eyes to me without tears. It is not indeed in my own praise
(for I reckon it one of the inherent defects in my own character) that I
mention my utter helplessness, my absolute weakness, in cases where
I am called upon to give pain to any human being, and especially to
those whom I personally love . . . I am convinced that of the things
which I wish undone by myself, the greater part may be traced to that
weakness. What could then be expected of such a being at the age of
twenty and with less knowledge of life than an English schoolboy has
at twelve?' So when on the day before the ordination Blanco's father
uncharacteristically took him aside to assure him that he was still free
to turn back, he no longer had the will or the inclination to free
himself. 'I was under the spell of my mother's affection. To make her
happy was the only way, I conceived, of securing my own happiness.
She had besides gained over to her views any person, young and old,
who had any influence on me'.[38] These included Arjona and Lista.

The doubts and hesitations were also drowned, as on previous
occasions, in a wave of emotional piety induced by a retreat at the
Oratory of San Felipe Neri. The spiritual exercises were conducted
there by Blanco's own director and the most sought-after preacher in
Seville, Fr Teodomiro Díaz de la Vega. Blanco later depicted him as a
man whose combination of spiritual passion, insight into souls, love
of power and animal energy gave him an influence in society to which
no mere layman could ever have aspired. His remarkable physical
resemblance to Oliver Cromwell was noted by others besides Blanco.
'That he was sincere I have no doubt; but that he loved power, and
sought it with the most consummate and successful policy, is equally
clear to me. No eastern potentate could exceed him in that air of
habitual command which appals the most resolute minds when drawn
within its sphere'. In his autobiography Blanco masterfully evoked
the scene of the spiritual exercises: the darkened chapel with its
illuminated figure of Christ in agony; the charismatic presence of the
spiritual stage manager who had a full ten days in which to operate at
leisure on the emotions of his penitents; the preacher's 'wild luxu-
riance' of imagery; the 'graduated scale of spiritual terrors' by which
he annihilated the retreatants beneath the burden of their guilt before
allowing them a glimpse of redemption. In the second stage of the

proceedings, 'the object in view was a revulsion of feeling, consisting in . . . that devotional tenderness which renders the mental faculties powerless and reduces the moral being to the weakness of infancy'.

The result of this experience in Blanco's case was a victory of the emotions over the judgement, but it was a victory which brought with it a sense of violation and of self-betrayal. All Blanco's later revulsion from anything which smacked of what he called 'mysticism' or 'enthusiasm' may perhaps be traced to this experience. With his inherent fastidiousness he recoiled from the 'almost frantic strains of impassioned tenderness in which Father Vega addressed the Deity, in whose immediate *bodily* presence he conceived himself to be . . . The effect of this *mystic* discipline upon my mind and feelings was certainly powerful, but there was a secret source of resistance which fortunately opposed the direct tendency of that part of my education, else my warm temper might have made me a perfect visionary. With the most ready will to obey the impulse, and the most sincere desire to rise to that summit of devotional perfection which was so often and so forcibly marked out to me, I could never overcome my natural dislike to that cloying, that mawkish devotion. Though tears flowed from my eyes and convulsive sobs wrung my bosom, my natural taste recoiled from that mixture of animal affection (I do not know a more appropriate name) with spiritual matters, which is the very essence of mysticism'.[39]

It was on the tide of such feelings that Blanco was ordained to the subdiaconate. As a young man of talent but of no private means 'there were two roads to such preferment as my family wished for me, ie preferment above that of the parochial clergy: interest at court, and display of talent at the public trials of learning [*oposiciones*] for a certain number of places reserved in the Church for literary merit. By the first of these roads I had no chance: the second offered a better prospect'.[40] Arjona, Blanco's mentor, persuaded him to put in for a fellowship at the Colegio Mayor of Santa Maria de Jesús—the All Souls, *mutatis mutandis*, of Seville. The *colegios mayores* had been stripped of many of their privileges by Charles III's reforming ministers, but that of Seville, at least, retained considerable prestige as a nursery of talent, membership of which was a passport to positions of emolument. However, the fellows were jealous of their exclusive privileges and candidates had to undergo an exhaustive examination to prove their pedigrees as well as their intellectual talents. So commissioners were appointed to scrutinise every detail of the candidate's ancestry—a laborious process which involved the examination on oath of as many as thirty witnesses at the birthplace of both parents and all four grandparents, the purpose being to ensure that there was no taint of Jewish, Moorish or African blood in the candidate's veins, and no connection with menial servants, shopkeepers or mechanics.[41] Blanco's feelings on being elected a fellow of Santa Maria de Jesús were comparable with those of John Henry Newman on the day when he was elected to Oriel. In all the vicissitudes of the years that followed he never lost his devotion to his college. Years after he had left Seville he was still asking his brother for news of the fellows: 'All Anglicised as I am, I feel that I would still *vote* through thick and thin for my College'.[42]

1. José María Blanco y Crespo, c.1808. A portrait by an unknown artist, now in the Sala de Profesores of the University of Seville.

By his election Blanco became a member of the élite corps of higher clergy, a promotion which further set him apart not only from his father's family but also to some extent from those of his companions who had to soldier on in the clerical infantry. He was now an *abbé*, while they remained *curés*. The Colegio Mayor regarded the University of Seville disdainfully as an upstart, and so instead of continuing his theological studies there, like Lista and Reinoso, he transferred to the University of Osuna as an external student. It was Arjona, in fact, who directed his studies. Fellowship of the Colegio Mayor commanded social prestige also, and in his picturesque gown the newly elected fellow was expected to make the rounds of the salons or *tertulias*. 'It was understood that, when once thus introduced, you were to contribute to the never-ending round of small talk in which

the better class of Spaniards employ most of their time. Instead,
therefore, of increasing my knowledge by study, I much relaxed my
reading during the three or four years which I spent at College'.[43]

It was in the course of these social rounds that Blanco was introduced to, and fell in love with a young widow. Such attachments were
regarded with indulgence in a society which guarded its daughters
implacably but which allowed married women and widows a freedom
which often shocked outsiders. 'The state of my mind, the first time
when from my change of circumstances I was enabled to give way to
the passion of love which had very often before filled my whole fancy,
is absolutely indescribable. Imagine a boy of fourteen with the
passions of a young man of two and twenty, and you will form some
idea of my state and behaviour'.[44] But the influence of his mother and
his close friends whose help she enlisted, soon engineered a renunciation, and the lovesick young cleric left for a cooling-off period in
Cadiz.

There, staying with relatives, Blanco spent his time in what he later
called 'luxurious idleness', indulging 'all the pleasures of sensuality
which were within my reach'.[45] Bearing in mind that he wrote these
words as a newly-converted evangelical, and given his tenderness of
conscience, it is unlikely that the indulgence amounted to more than
theatre-going and flirtatious socialising. Nevertheless, this protracted
exposure to occasions of sin in what Sevillans regarded as the modern
Gomorrah, alarmed his friends and family. Reinoso sent him an
epistolary poem, warning him to beware of the snares laid by a
'seductive people' to entrap the innocent and guileless, and begging
him to reject the blandishments of a corrupt and self-interested society
and to return to his true friends. The poem is evidence of the intense
cult of friendship which characterised the members of the Academia.[46]

Even more revealing is the letter of restrained reproach which
Guillermo sent his son. 'In these present times, which give us cause
only to shed tears in the sight of God, I am continually troubled by the
thought of your long stay in Cadiz, leading a life of idleness and
dissipation which cannot be good for any Christian, still less for one in
your state, who is exhorted to be always occupied in good works and
frequent prayer. I beg you, consider these things'.[47] For the father, the
world was a vale of tears, a place in which to prepare for eternity by
penance and mortification. Though Blanco, like a good son, returned
home, he had now tasted the forbidden fruit.

The three years between the subdiaconate and the priesthood were
passed in this perpetual oscillation between pleasure—or at least a
yearning for pleasure—and remorse:

> A sincere and determined effort to resume the retired life of my early
> youth, and obtain some peace of mind by tearing myself away from the
> objects that had robbed me of it, succeeded long enough to allow me to take

Deacon's orders in a state of feeling not unsuitable to the occasion. I believed for some time that I had reconciled myself to my profession; but that happy delusion was soon dispelled. It revived, however, as the time approached when I was about to be ordained a priest. I had an awful sense of the dignity of the priestly office, and trembled at the idea of profaning it. Led by these feelings, I once more bent my whole soul upon being faithful to my duty.[48]

Years later, in a review of Blanco's life J. H. Newman concluded that 'he never found comfort in religion, not in childhood more than in manhood, or in old age. In his very first years, as in his last, it was a yoke and nothing more; a task without a recompense'.[49] If this was the impression which Blanco sought to make in his *Autobiography* it is totally contradicted by the passage in *Letters from Spain* in which he recreated his feelings on the day of his ordination to the priesthood. Coming as it does in a chapter which is otherwise a bitter indictment of Spanish clericalism, it is remarkable for its almost wistful evocation of devotional ecstasy:

When the consecrating rites had been performed—when my hands had been anointed—the sacred vesture, at first folded on my shoulders, let drop around me by the hands of the bishop—the sublime hymn to the all-creating Spirit uttered in solemn strains, and the power of restoring sinners to innocence conferred upon me—when, at length, raised to the dignity of a "fellow-worker with God", the bishop addressed me, in the name of the Saviour: "Henceforth I call you not servant . . . but I have called you friend"; I truly felt as if, freed from the material part of my being, I belonged to a higher rank of existence. I still had a heart, it is true—a heart ready to burst at the sight of my parents, on their knees, while impressing the first kiss of my newly-consecrated hands; but it was dead to the charms of beauty. Among the friendly crowd that surrounded me for the same purpose, were those lips which a few months before I would have died to press; yet I could but just mark their superior softness. In vain did I exert myself to check exuberance of feelings at my first mass. My tears bedewed the *corporals* on which, with the eyes of faith, I beheld the disguised lover of mankind whom I had drawn from heaven to my hands. These are dreams indeed—the illusions of an over-heated fancy; but dreams they are which some of the noblest minds have dreamt through life without waking—dreams which, while passing vividly before the mental eye, must entirely wrap up the soul of every one who is neither *more* nor *less* than a man.[50]

Chapter 2
Paradise Lost

Extraneus factus sum fratribus meis,
Et peregrinus filiis matris meae.
—Ps. 68, 9

Of the two years which followed his ordination, Blanco later wrote:
'To exercise the privileges of my office for the benefit of my fellow-
creatures was now my exclusive aim and purpose'.[1] As a member of
the higher clergy, however, he was not involved in pastoral or
parochial work, then regarded as a lower form of clerical existence.
Apart from his obligations to say Mass and recite the office, he was in
demand as a confessor to nuns. It is easy to see how his gifts of
compassion and sensitivity attracted the troubled and the scrupulous.
Even if later, in his polemical writings, he painted a one-sided picture
of convent life, making no mention of those who found in it serenity
and fulfilment, there is no reason to doubt what he says of the trapped
and despairing. The convent was a convenient receptacle for surplus
daughters, and while many of the conscripts accepted their fate it is not
surprising that others did not—particularly since the strict enclosure
offered little outlet for activity or practical service to society. Of the
victims of this system Blanco wrote that:

> in the dull monotony of their lives, in the agitated state of a soul troubled
> with all the fears of a morbid conscience—perhaps with the remorse of
> such guilt as can only increase their despair—they have no-one to whom
> they may confide their sorrows but the priest whom they choose as their
> confessor . . . When therefore a sensible woman thus confined for life,
> meets with a priest, who being on his guard against even the remotest risk
> of a hopeless and, in those circumstances, dishonourable affection, proves
> his real interest by listening patiently, and establishes his authority by
> deciding promptly and confidently; she cannot but look upon him as the
> last support of her wrecked happiness, or rather as the last help against
> complete misery.[2]

These duties could not but make a young priest painfully aware of the
blighting and frustrating effects of the system. Had Blanco been

allowed the practical satisfactions of ordinary pastoral work, his spiritual development might have been different. His friend Reinoso, for instance, as curate of a city parish, was active in the relief of poverty and later, in the war of independence, organised soup kitchens and hospitals for the victims of famine and pioneered a free vaccination service.[3] Lista, too, was already actively involved in teaching and had a widowed mother to support. Like them, Blanco yearned to be of practical service to society but was prevented from doing so by the dignity of his position.

In 1800, at the age of twenty-five, Blanco was elected Rector of the Colegio Mayor. His year of office coincided with the devastating plague of yellow fever which by the end of the year had killed fifteen thousand people—about one fifth of the city's population. Instead of taking practical measures to control the spread of the infection, the authorities had recourse to divine intervention. The solemn rogations reached an awesome climax when Dean and Chapter ascended to the top of the Giralda to bless the four winds with the Cathedral's precious relic of the true cross. But the crowding together in the August heat of the enormous number of people who witnessed this imposing ceremony only served to spread the infection. Blanco was at first unwilling to desert his college and, though ill with malaria, stayed there until he was physically removed by one of the fellows and taken to join his family in a neighbouring village. There, he wrote later: 'expecting hourly the infection . . . and fearing the final result of my complaint which the country practitioner who attended me thoroughly mismanaged, I gave up all hopes of life and resigned myself to an early death'.[4] By the autumn, however, he had recovered and in the last day of the year returned to the almost empty college to hand over the rectorship to his successor.

The disaster was seized upon by revivalist preachers as yet another sign of God's anger at contemporary immorality. Not only the plague but also recent droughts, famines and military defeats were all seen as divine visitations and warnings. Blanco's statement that the plague was interpreted from the pulpit 'as the punishment of the incorrigible perverseness of our females' is supported by a contemporary chronicler who describes how women whose hemlines revealed too much of the ankle were abused in the street by small boys, self-appointed guardians of morality, to the approval of bystanders. 'It was even declared in the pulpit that these were not boys, but angels'.[5]

Preachers adopted an apocalyptic tone, urging the faithful to escape the wrath of God by repentance and mortification. This was the message taken out into the countryside by travelling missioners. In the cities there was an increase in the number of pious associations dedicated to a strict rule of life. Such was the *Escuela de Cristo* of which Blanco became a member in 1800. He later wrote a memorable

description of the meetings of a similar sodality which he attended at
the church of La Cueva in Cadiz.[6]

Blanco now began the long and arduous process of submitting
himself to the open competitions or *oposiciones* which were the only
path to ecclesiastical preferment. In 1801 he was a candidate for a
canonry at Cadiz, and acquitted himself so well that although not
appointed he was made a diocesan examiner. The experience stood
him in good stead shortly afterwards when he successfully competed
for a vacancy in the Royal Chapel of St Ferdinand at Seville. The royal
chaplains were an anomalous body forming their own chapter under
the same roof as the cathedral canons but independent of them. The
long-standing rivalry between the two chapters was notorious. One
of the senior fellows of Blanco's college, a canon of the cathedral, at
first opposed his candidacy for the royal chapel on the grounds that the
position was beneath the dignity of a Fellow of the College of Santa
Maria de Jesús. But Blanco was allowed to proceed, and performed
with distinction in the scholastic disputations demanded by the occasion. The climax was an hour's sermon which had to be delivered
without notes before the assembled chapter, with only twenty-four
hours allowed for preparation. How victory was almost snatched
away from him by an old rival of dubious social origins, and how at
the last minute the latter's brilliant sermon was discovered to have
been plagiarised, and how Blanco successfully beat off the claims of a
third rival, 'a young man of no talent and of rather low connections'
who was a protégé of the Dean, is related in a revealing passage of the
Autobiography.[7] Blanco was elected, and at the age of 27 was now
established in status and security, able to look forward to steady
advancement in a career which offered the eventual prospect of a
bishopric. As *capellan magistral* of St Ferdinand he was now expected to
add literary lustre to the royal chapel, as a preacher and poet.

At this period all the evidence shows that Blanco was committed to
the ideals of the Jansenist party within the Spanish Church. Spanish
'Jansenism' was concerned not with theological doctrines of grace, but
rather with practical reform and opposition to Papal claims. It drew its
inspiration from the Italian bishop Scipione de Ricci and the Council
of Pistoia (1786), whose programme, though denounced by the
Papacy at the time, now looks very like that of the Second Vatican
Council: a return to biblical and patristic sources, translation of the
Bible into the vernacular, pastoral renewal, decentralisation, respect
for other denominations and religions, control of extravagant superstitious practices, and so on. Its ideal was a national church, on the
Gallican and regalist model, free from excessive Papal interference. It
was opposed to the Inquisition and wanted to curb the power of the
regular clergy. Its adherents occupied influential positions—
Jovellanos being the most distinguished example—but it remained

always restricted to an élite, who tended to show a lofty disdain for popular religion and dismissed as 'superstitious' what were authentic expressions of real faith. The people listened more readily to those who blamed current evils on human corruption, impiety and infidelity rather than on any institutional defects in the Church itself. With revolutionary ideas threatening to infiltrate Spain from across the Pyrenees, the traditionalists were on the lookout for enemies within, and tended to denounce would-be reformers as Deists in disguise. This goes some way to explain why the Jansenist movement failed ultimately to strike roots in Spanish soil—with lastingly disastrous consequences for the Church.[8]

The Jansenists were most strongly represented in Madrid, Valencia and Salamanca. Their austerity and distaste for the manifestations of popular religion prevented their making much headway in Seville. Nevertheless, through Arjona, his friend and spiritual director, Blanco was drawn into the movement, and a discourse he delivered in 1799 'On the advantages of reviving the preaching method of the Fathers' is evidence of this. In it Blanco deplored the process whereby sacred oratory had become a mere performance, for the entertainment of pious ladies. Instead he recommended the exegetical method of the Fathers: a free exposition of the text of the day, concentrating on moral precepts and the great truths of faith, couched in simple language and eschewing 'sterile speculations'. It was the parish clergy who must put these changes into practice, he declared, since the bishops were too occupied with other, and more worldly, cares. This concern for simplicity, this desire to remove the false mystique with which the professionals had surrounded religion, and to return it to the service of the people, is typical of the Jansenist spirit.[9]

Why, then, did Jansenism fail to satisfy Blanco? Part of the reason lies in his natural impatience with the *via media* and a propensity to take the 'all or nothing' view, but more importantly he rejected what he saw as the Jansenists' ascetical rigidity and their subordination of nature to grace. One of the more remarkable features of his later autobiographical writings is the admiring tone of his references to the Jesuits, who had just those qualities of flexibility and humaneness which the Jansenists, with their 'strict, unbending maxims . . . urging all characters and tempers to an imaginary goal of perfection', lacked. He was to single out the educational and cultural benefits the Jesuits contributed to Spanish society: 'The influence of the Jesuits on the [sic] Spanish morals . . . was undoubtedly favourable. Their kindness attracted the youth from the schools to their company and . . . contributed to the preservation of virtue in that slippery age, both by the ties of affection and the gentle check of example . . . Their conduct was correct, and their manners refined. They kept up a dignified intercourse with the middling and higher classes, and were always ready to help and instruct the poor, without descending to their level'.[10]

It could be argued that the expulsion of the Jesuits in 1767 removed from the scene the one organised Christian body capable of providing a moral and intellectual counter-attraction to the deism or unbelief which by the end of the century was pervading the Spanish intelligentsia. Blanco recalled how in his youth he regretted that the abolition of the Society had prevented his becoming a member of it. 'To identify myself with some one body of men devoted to useful pursuits, and acting according to a well-directed plan, I know from recollection to have been one of my earliest wishes . . . I perfectly recollect the points of attraction which that religious order had for me. It was its compactness, its effective but not individually oppressive discipline, its widely ramified connections in all parts of the world; in a word, it was its perfect unity that acted upon me like a charm'.[11]

By 1802 the truce between Blanco's piety and his reason was under intense strain, and Rousseau and Voltaire were winning the battle for his soul. Intellectually he had reached an *impasse* on the problem of authority: 'I believed the infallibility of the Church because the Scripture said she was infallible; while I had no better proof that the Scripture said so than the assertion of the Church'.[12] A genuinely impartial examination of the problem was impossible since this meant suspending judgement on matters of faith, which was in itself sinful, and he feared that once a part of the whole interrelated superstructure of dogma was weakened, the entire edifice would collapse around him. He turned for reassurance to the French apologists such as Bergier and Chateaubriand whose recent *Génie du Christianisme* had enlisted the imagination and the feelings to defend the Church against the attacks of reason, but this offered only a temporary palliative.

These intellectual difficulties were, however, secondary to the growing conviction that Christianity itself, in its Catholic, Spanish and specifically Sevillan form was a baleful force which, manipulated by a privileged theocracy, blighted human happiness and obstructed social progress. In his ode to Juan Pablo Forner he had already attacked the unproductive and parasitical theologians who used their monopoly of education not to serve society but to control it. He felt a kind of shame at being a member of this priestly caste. Through the confessional he had now seen at first hand the tragic human cost of the religious life, and the dark underside of clerical society. His semi-monastic upbringing and refined idealism had not prepared him to cope with these revelations. Within his own family his father had been, as he saw it, robbed of moral independence by his complete submission to his spiritual director. Spain, he later put it, was 'a country where every person's conscience is in the keeping of another, in an interminable succession of moral trusts'.[13] He had carried out his priestly obligations faithfully, but they had become a joyless burden. Perhaps the fault lay not in himself but in the system? These were thoughts which the reading of Rousseau's *Émile* could only exacerbate.

Something of the violent debate going on in Blanco's mind at this time is evident in his surviving sermons. In 1802, on the occasion of the Peace of Amiens, he was invited by the élite corps of Royal Carabineers to deliver a sermon in honour of their patron St Ferdinand, the warrior Christian king and liberator of Seville from the Moors. For the occasion, held in the Royal Chapel, the King granted special permission for the preserved body of the dead saint to be exposed before the high altar, and his sword was offered for public veneration. The congregation of splendidly uniformed officers, civic dignitaries, and their ladies looked—as their modern counterparts still look—for an oratorical display, and Blanco did not disappoint them. The sermon he delivered, modelled on Bossuet's *Oraisons Funèbres*, made his name as a fashionable preacher. Its florid style directly contradicted the principles he had advocated three years earlier in his Jansenist discourse. In an attempt to establish the link between natural and supernatural virtue, between the military hero and the Christian saint, the preacher began by arguing that Ferdinand's victory over the enemy was rooted in his victory over himself: his heroism was the direct result of this sanctity. Then turning devil's advocate, he voiced the objections which might be raised against this thesis by the 'vain philosophers of the age'. They would dismiss what had just been said as mere sophistry, designed to reconcile a military audience to a religion which was in fact directly opposed to worldly ideals of glory and ambition. The true Christian saint was concerned with renunciation rather than with achievement, with self-perfection rather than with working for the good of society: 'Its heroes flee the sight of men, ignore the ties which bind them to society, make the lairs of wild beasts their home, weaken their bodies with perpetual mortifications and submit their spirits to servile humiliation. Are these the men to grasp the sword and advance on the ranks of the enemy?'

The objector is Blanco himself, struggling with the gathering conviction that Christianity in its authentic form was fundamentally unnatural and anti-social, dedicated to self-annihilation rather than to self-fulfilment. Yet at this stage the orthodox arguments still carried just enough weight with him to hold the balance. In answer to his own objections he pointed to Ferdinand as evidence that the Christian saint, far from being concerned exclusively with his own soul, had a heightened sense of his duty to his fellowmen as a consequence of his duty to their common Creator and Father. The secret both of Christian living and of social justice lay, paradoxically, in the fear of God: 'The Christian worthy of that name fears nothing on this earth. He fears only the author of his existence. This freedom from fear does

not make him independent, however, for he is bound by his respect
for God to respect all those in whom God's authority resides on earth,
by fulfilling all the duties which God's law requires and by carrying
out all the obligations to which he is bound by nature, God's creation'.
Then Blanco continued, with words directed more at himself than at
his hearers: 'God's gaze reaches your inmost heart. Beware of being
content with an outward show of submission and obedience. Beware
of entertaining even the most secret thought against your sacred
obligations'.[14]

In this final struggle Blanco in his sermons brought to bear on
himself all the traditional arguments against unbelief, attributing it to
intellectual pride and to the distorting effects of sensuality. 'I have
observed in the course of my life', he wrote later, 'that on the approach
of some great change in my religious opinions I have clung with
increased eagerness to the tenets from which I felt I was forcibly
drawn'.[15]

It was an event within his own family which tipped the scales. In
1802 his elder sister died in a convent at the age of twenty-two and as a
priest he attended her deathbed. His beloved younger sister was still at
home, but the next year, under the influence of her confessor, she
announced her intention to leave her ageing and sick parents and to
enter the severely penitential convent of the Poor Clares. To Blanco
this seemed an abandonment of natural obligations, an act of perverse
self-immolation, a turning aside 'from the path of practical usefulness
into the wilderness of visionary perfection'.[16] What is more, he knew
that she was acting under the influence of a spiritual director who was
secretly unfaithful to his vow of chastity, a hypocrite seeking vicariously to atone for his own sins by the sacrifice of another. He could
not bring himself to attend his sister's reception as a novice, but a year
later—when he had rejected all that his priesthood stood for—he
celebrated the High Mass at her solemn profession, with Arjona
preaching the sermon. By that time Arjona

'my early, my valuable friend, the most successful instructor of my
opening mind had . . . fallen into habitual and reckless immorality.
Whether he had rejected all religion in his heart I knew not, for to the last
day of our acquaintance he was reserved to all his most intimate friends
upon that subject—but I was well aware of the utter wreck which his
morals had made both in *theory* and in practice. He wrote the greatest part
of the Sermon he was to preach at the approaching ceremony in a state
bordering on intoxication . . . The ceremony of Profession, including the
sermon of High Mass, lasted three hours, during which the heart of the
officiating Priest was in a state which only the infinite mercy, as well as the
infinite knowledge of Him who can unravel its secrets, and distinguish the
effects of anguish from those of wickedness, could endure and forgive'.[17]

As a confessor, Blanco had been made aware of the gap which
existed between theory and practice in all that related to clerical

celibacy. Arjona was not the only one of his friends who had discovered the temptations of the flesh, and he now saw as a tyranny the law that compelled them to dissemble their natural feelings: 'A more blameless, ingenuous, religious set of youths than that in the enjoyment of whose friendship I passed the best years of my life, the world cannot boast of . . . Of this knot of friends not one was tainted by the breath of gross vice till the Church had doomed them to a life of celibacy and turned the best affections of the hearts into crime'.[18] Blanco himself, by his own account, was still faithful to his vows, but Arjona—now Canon Penitentiary of Cordoba—underwent a moral collapse which was as complete as it was sudden.

Serious though Blanco's intellectual difficulties were (and he had an unerring eye for singling out the most unresolvable of theological dilemmas in order to impale himself on their horns), his was a loss of hope as much as of faith. 'The portentous mass of moral evil which I perceived around me . . . made all the *Metaphysical* arguments for the existence of the Deity (the only proofs with which I was acquainted) fly up as light as the dust in the balance'.[19] It was all very well for a calm and comfortable Englishman to look around at his well-ordered society and conclude that since all was well with the world, God must be in his heaven. In Spain the argument from design worked in reverse. The moral corruption of society seemed to indicate that the religion on which it was based was an imposture, and that the world was not under the direction of an intelligent moral agent. Blanco was to spend the next ten years of his life nursing this growing conviction. It was not in his nature to do things by halves, to reserve judgment or make qualifications: once the spell had been broken, the whole edifice of faith, previously kept up by an act of the will, tumbled to the ground. 'Having burst my chains I could not bear the shadow of control. Nothing short of demonstration would satisfy my mind. I was determined not to believe anything while there remained an objection unanswered'.[20]

Blanco was now in the position of professing a priesthood which he believed to be an imposture, yet to acknowledge that fact was impossible without putting himself outside the pale of society. In addition there were his parents to think of—above all his mother, who with her quick intuition had already perhaps guessed his secret. For a time he even considered the idea of emigration to the United States, to try his luck there as a musician. In the memoir he wrote in 1830 he represented himself as having come to a *modus vivendi* which enabled him to make a truce with his conscience: 'I will not put myself forward in the Church. I will not affect zeal; whatever trust is put in me as a confessor, I will conscientiously prove myself worthy of. I will urge people to observe every moral duty. I will give them the best advice in their difficulties, and comfort them in their distresses'.[21] Perhaps, in hindsight, Blanco was over-anxious here, as elsewhere, to put himself

in the best possible light, but what he says of his sense of duty is borne
out by the evidence of his conduct.

Having plucked up courage to confide in others, he began to
discover an underground confraternity of kindred spirits. After the
first risk of self-disclosure came the release of long stored-up
resentments and frustrations, impassioned denunciation of 'prejudice'
and 'superstition', 'monks, ecclesiastical encroachments, extravagant
devotion'.

He found these *esprits forts* in unexpected places, as in the Char-
terhouse at Seville, where he discovered a young admirer of Voltaire.
He was introduced to an older cleric who offered him the use of his
secret library of prohibited French works:

> 'With indefatigable industry I now gave myself up to that kind of reading.
> The danger in which we were from the Inquisition only gave a relish to the
> stolen waters of which I was drinking so deep. We once had reason to
> suspect that a search was intended by the *Holy Tribunal*; and as the books
> could not be entrusted to servants, we ourselves conveyed a great number
> of volumes from the house of my younger friend to my own, repeatedly
> walking from one house to another in the course of the same day in our
> Canonicals, in the large folds of which we concealed the works which, if
> discovered, would have exposed us to the greatest danger'.[22]

How far was Blanco justified in claiming, as he did later, that the
majority of the Spanish clergy were, like him, secret atheists or deists?
'Among my numerous acquaintances in the Spanish clergy, I have
never met with anyone, possessed of bold talents, who has not, sooner
or later, changed from the most sincere piety to a state of unbelief'.[23]
Blanco based his judgment on his experience of Seville, and Seville
was where the ideas of the Jansenist reformers had least influence. The
gap there between the vast majority of poorly educated clergy and the
minority of clerics such as himself—highly cultivated but
déracinés—was at its widest.[24] Yet his evidence is not to be dismissed
lightly. It is corroborated by that of another convert to Protestantism,
Juan Calderón, who entered the Franciscan order in 1806. There, he
asserts, his superiors had long since become reconciled to the fact that
nearly all their young students of theology and philosophy were
unbelievers, and it was the very universality of the scandal that made it
tolerable. 'Revelations of this kind' wrote Calderón, 'should only be
made deliberately, with one's gaze fixed on God. Those who make
them are generally reviled by the world at large. It seems at first sight
more plausible to suppose that the few who speak out are impostors,
than to believe that such a degree of corruption could pervade so
respected an institution. The very scale of the disorder makes it
incredible'.[25]

Within this freemasonry of unbelievers Blanco could vent his spleen against what he saw as the follies and indignities of the established orthodoxy. He and his friends spent their time, he later wrote, 'scoffing and railing'.[26] It was in such circles and during these years that there grew up within the educated professional classes, even within the higher clergy, that bitter and doctrinaire spirit which was to characterise the liberalism of nineteenth century Spain. The later extremism of these enragés was the product of their earlier frustrated impotence. Their contempt for Spanish and Catholic tradition was only matched by their enthusiasm for Voltaire, Rousseau and the ideas of the French Revolution: France stood for the forces of light, Spain for the forces of darkness, and France could do no wrong. Later, in his English incarnation, Blanco came to repudiate his addiction to French 'theory', but he never lost that sense of shame for his country which was the result of these years.[27] Outwardly he was the dapper, culti-vated cleric, in much demand as a confessor and preacher, making his way daily to the Cathedral to recite the office in the choir of the Royal Chapel, saying Mass for his parents in their private oratory. Inwardly he was consumed by despairing rage. Gladstone was right to see in these years the key to all Blanco's later development: 'The moral consequences of maintaining a Christian profession for eight years upon a basis of Atheism—the Breviary on the table and the anti-Christian writers of France in the closet—may have been fatal to the solidity and consistency of his inward life thereafter'.[28] Above all it was Blanco's self-esteem which suffered. Dissimulation was repug-nant to him. His later obsessive concern to make public every change in his convictions—in spite of his essential distaste for self-revelation—was an attempt to recapture that correspondence between his public position and his private thoughts which he lost in Seville.

Only friendship and pleasure offered a distraction from the strains of leading this double life. Blanco increasingly sought escape from Seville, where he had to live under the silent but reproachful scrutiny of his parents. In the summer of 1803 he accompanied Arjona on horseback through the bandit country of the Sierra de Ronda—a journey which later provided material for the most picaresque epi-sodes in *Letters from Spain*. He and Arjona had put refinement behind them and revelled in experience of low life, carousing in country inns after hunting expeditions. Arjona was now installed in Cordoba as Canon Penitentiary of the Cathedral. 'I heard him boast that the night before the solemn procession of *Corpus Christi*, where he appeared nearly at the head of his chapter, one of two children had been born which his two concubines brought to light within a few days of each other'.[29] Arjona, who had once led the way in self-improvement, now did so in self-destruction.

Recalling this period of his life Blanco wrote later, 'My dislike of

every thing grossly immoral was, I may say, born with me. Yet I have
to blush at the recollection of the orgies in which I used to join, and
which were always preceded and followed by a feeling of unhappi-
ness'.[30] He was now on terms of easy companionship with his
younger brother, who was discovering the pleasures of literature and
study. The wit and high spirits revealed in his letters to Fernando are a
useful correction to the gloomy self-portrait he painted of himself
later. At the same time he could not help envying his brother,
discovering *Quixote* for the first time as he had done, and paying his
first visit to Cadiz. With the touching world-weariness of premature
middle-age, he wrote: 'Like two plums on the tree at harvest time, you
continue to mature while I shrivel: you make progress with the flute,
while I have forgotten how to play—I have hardly touched the violin
all summer; you study, while I scarcely look at a book. It won't be
long before I turn into a prune'.[31]

The Academia de Letras Humanas had by now been formally
dissolved, as its members went their separate ways. Reinoso was
preoccupied with his parish duties, Lista was professor of mathematics at the naval college of San Telmo. The old association survived,
however, in a looser form, and widened out. Among the newer
members of the circle were Manuel López de Cepero, later Dean of the
Cathedral, Ceán Bermúdez, then curator of the Archivo de Indias and
later to distinguish himself as an art historian, and Sebastian Miñano y
Bedoya. The latter was, like Blanco, a cleric in secret revolt against his
profession who arrived in Seville in 1799 as secretary to the 23-year-
old Cardinal Archbishop, Luis de Borbón. Along with the rest of the
group (with the exception of Blanco and López Cepero) he sided with
the French during the war of independence, after which he was to
make his name as an anti-clerical satirist and journalist. He would
almost certainly have been one of those 'possessed of bold talents' who
shared Blanco's secret.[32]

Education was the only field where Blanco could place his talents at
the disposal of society. In his Ode to Juan Pablo Forner he had already
attacked the exclusive monopoly which the theologians exercised
over higher education. Forner himself had called for the provision of
basic technical education to train young people in the skills needed to
promote industry and trade. Forner's views were shared by others in
influential positions in late eighteenth-century Spain who came
together to form economic and friendly societies. It was the Real
Sociedad Económica in Seville which, like its fellow societies in other
major Spanish towns, founded elementary vocational schools for
boys and girls, and started teacher training. It also supplied the need
for scientific education at a higher level, by appointing a Frenchman to
give public classes in mathematics. Until that date, 1780, the only
institution in Seville which made provision for mathematical or

scientific education was the naval college.[33] Encouraged by the success of this initiative the Society then broadened its scope to take in the Humanities. Hitherto instruction in the Humanities had been restricted to future theologians, but now for the first time it was taken out of clerical control and made available to the public at large (or rather, to those young men of good family who had the leisure to attend).

In 1804, Blanco was appointed, without salary, to teach a course in rhetoric and poetry. The prospectus he wrote for the course offers a valuable insight into his ideas on education. The creation of an educated middle class was, he maintained, the one area in which the Sociedad Económica could achieve progress. It was no good their trying to improve agriculture (as they had originally planned), because the peasants would only be interested in new methods if they had a positive stake in the land, instead of working as day labourers for the benefit of absentee landlords. Nor was there any point in trying to educate the lowest class of society. They were, he declared, 'the dregs of humanity . . . essentially beyond improvement'. The way ahead lay in extending into secondary education the benefits already visible at the primary level. Children were already emerging from the Society's primary schools with a better general knowledge than that of the so-called learned. At the higher level, now that mathematics was provided for, he proposed to teach the laws of good taste—for laws they were, 'based on reason', universal and immutable. The unprecedented feature of the course was that it did not require Latin as a condition of admission, and the ancient classics could be studied in French translation. The course textbook was French, and the poetic or rhetorical models recommended for imitation were French also: Racine, Corneille, Bossuet, Massillon.[34]

Now for the first time Blanco discovered his talents as a teacher, and his ability to inspire. Later, looking back, he found his youthful francomania embarrassing and deplored the 'destructive' effects of French literature and philosophy which tended 'to produce a superficial character, incapable of patient investigation, rash in inference, despondent in difficulties and ready to settle into a sardonic laugh as the ultimate result of all moral and political enquiries'. He also adopted the view that the policy of the Sociedades Económicas in despairing of university reform, and promoting a separate education system exclusively concerned with modern studies, had ultimately been divisive, and had helped to widen the breach between the two Spains of reactionary clericalism and rootless liberalism. It would have been more far-sighted to have concentrated first on reviving classical studies in the universities and to have required all prospective students of philosophy and theology to pass a preliminary examination in Latin and Greek, thus 'humanising' and reconciling the clergy rather than abandoning them to their obscurantism to be a permanent obstacle to all attempts at progress.[35]

By the end of 1805 the strain of leading a life of dissimulation had become intolerable, and was taking its toll on Blanco's health. What compounded his misery was that he had 'conceived an attachment' (his own words) for a married woman.[36] There was no way out of the impasse except to leave Seville, however much this would give pain to his parents. The statutes of the Chapel Royal allowed for three months' absence a year, and he obtained this on health grounds, to be spent in Madrid. There he hoped to find a sinecure which would carry with it a longer residence permit. The arrangements were made in little more than a week. He explained the move to his family as a career decision: only by going to Madrid could he hope to get further preferment. His real motive was more negative: he wanted to escape.

Chapter 3
Limbo

In Pleasure's lap
I looked for rest and deep oblivion,
But rest was none for me.[1]

In the middle of 1807 one of the founder-members of the Academia de
Letras Humanas wrote from Madrid to Reinoso in Seville: 'Arjona
and Blanco are now at large in this Limbo, from which the latter is
unlikely ever to emerge. The former has more chance of being taken
up into what he imagines is a higher existence, but who knows if he
will get there? This place is a Babylon, and no artist, however gifted,
could do anything like justice to the original'.[2] There was in fact just
such an artist already at work, recording his vision of a society which
hid its despair behind a mask of frivolity. Goya's world is one of
contrasts: on the one hand, amorous dalliance and *déjeuners sur l'herbe*;
on the other, vacant or grinning faces of madmen, shrunken inquisitors sitting in judgment over their humiliated victims, a procession of
flagellants absorbed in self-torment—a mob bent on darkness and
overhung with doom. The prose sketches which are to be found in the
Madrid chapters of Blanco's *Letters from Spain* are characterised by the
same savage indignation which pervades Goya's work.

When Blanco arrived in Madrid in 1805, Charles IV had been on the
throne for seventeen years, and for almost all that time power had
been in the hands of the royal favourite Manuel de Godoy. Godoy,
who had emerged from the obscurity of Extremadura, was barely out
of his teens and a member of the Royal Guard when he caught the eye
of Queen Maria Luisa by falling off his horse. Before long he had
become the trusted and indispensable confidant not only of the Queen
but also of her husband, an ingenuous and good-natured man who
appears to have been innocently unaware of his wife's infidelities.
Portraits of the period chart Godoy's transformation over the years
from slim youth to fleshy potentate, reclining at his ease in the seat of
power.

The years since Charles IV's accession in 1788 had seen a steady
erosion of the consensus which had marked his father's reign. Opti-

mism turned to pessimism. The French Revolution put the government on the defensive and made it less receptive to new ideas from
outside. Not that the mass of the Spanish people were susceptible to
the siren voices of liberty which came from across the Pyrenees. They
rallied to a holy war against the French infidel, in defence of God,
King and Country. When the French invaded Catalonia in 1794 they
met solid resistance from the people, led by their priests. But the
government, under its new chief minister Godoy, was forced to come
to terms. To the list of Godoy's many titles was now added that of
Prince of the Peace. No sooner, however, had the country extricated
itself from the costly war with France than it was involved in war
with Britain, and the disruption this caused to communications with
Spanish America and to trade further damaged the economy and
increased inflation.

Although Godoy was a well-meaning ruler who supported economic and educational reform, he succeeded in pleasing nobody. The
aristocracy resented him as an upstart, the clergy suspected him of
irreligion, the intellectuals were irked by his monopoly of patronage,
and the common people blamed him for their economic hardships.
Charles III had possessed the authority and prestige to unite these
different sectors of society, but under a king who had the reputation
of a cuckold and a booby the nation began to fall apart. However
enlightened Godoy's despotism might be, it was felt to be a yoke.
Besides, the younger intelligentsia were no longer prepared to accept
the assumption of their elders that enlightenment and reform must be
handed down from above. Revolutionary ideas were gaining cur-
rency and young men eager for change increasingly looked to France
for liberation. Madrid, ever the slave of fashion, flirted with radical
chic: fashionable youths sported Phrygian caps or guillotine
waistcoats, and theatre-goers displayed fans inscribed with revolutionary slogans.

Meanwhile the conservative and ultramontane party in the Spanish
Church had mounted a successful counter-offensive against the Jansenist reformers. Charles IV turned to the altar to defend his throne. In
December 1800 he endorsed Pope Pius VI's condemnation of the
'Jansenist' Council of Pistoia and authorised the Inquisition to enforce
compliance. Prominent Jansenists were banished from court, and the
great Jovellanos was deported to prison in Mallorca. Godoy, who
knew that the Inquisition had him also in their sights, was obliged to
acquiesce. All this served to drive a deeper wedge between reformers
and conservatives. The latter had the advantage of being able to rely
on the mass of the rural population who looked for leadership to their
clergy, not their politicians. The battle-lines were already being
drawn for the conflict between radicals and conservatives which was
to tear Spain apart for almost two centuries. Meanwhile, over the

Pyrenees Napoleon was waiting for an opportunity to intervene and settle the 'Spanish problem'. The fruit was ready to fall into his lap.[3]

Madrid in 1805 was an artificial enclave of courtiers, bureaucrats and hangers-on, surrounded by a vast and deeply conservative country which belonged in spirit to an earlier century. Blanco later sketched some brilliant impressions of the scene: the 'Chinese ceremonial' of the court within which the royal family was imprisoned; the levées to which aspirants to office brought their pretty wives or daughters in the hope of their catching the eye of the Prince of the Peace; the cafés, filled with cigar smoke, in which the latest gossip was retailed to the accompaniment of 'an eternal giggling and bantering'.[4] Madrid was the centre which attracted successive waves of place-hunters, or *pretendientes*, who would spend as much as three or four years in the profession of what he described as 'toad-eating'. There were ecclesiastics in search of a prebend, for which they had to have the support of a privy councillor; lawyers hoping for magistracies in Spain or the colonies; businessmen looking for a tax-collecting contract. Like Roman *clientes* hanging about their patron's door they waited on ministers with petitions or a printed list of their qualifications, or attended evening receptions hoping to catch the eye of a well-placed lady by 'a handsome figure or some pleasing accomplishment'.[5]

The *pretendientes* followed the court out to its summer palace at Aranjuez, thirty miles from Madrid, set in formal gardens which rivalled those of Versailles. Charles IV had taken a leaf out of Marie Antoinette's book by constructing a 'labourer's cottage' where the royal family could lead the simple life, equipped with sculpture gallery (its ceiling decorated with allegorical figures of Trade and Agriculture), billiard room and ball room. The *pretendientes* meanwhile, were to be found in the lodging-houses of the town, where a visitor might have found

'a large paved court surrounded by apartments, each filled by a different set of lodgers, with three or four wretched beds, and not so many chairs for all the furniture; here one of the party blacking his shoes; there another darning his stockings; a third brushing the court dress he is to wear at the minister's levée; while a fourth lies still in bed, resting, as well as he can, from the last night's ball. As hackney coaches are not known either at Madrid or the Sitios, there is something both pitiable and ludicrous in the appearance of these judges, intendants and governors in embryo, sallying forth in full dress, after their laborious toilet, to pick their way through the mud, often casting an anxious look on the lace frills and ruffles which, artfully attached to the sleeves and waistcoat, might by some untoward accident betray the coarse and discoloured shirt which they meant to conceal. Thus they trudge to the palace, to walk up and down the galleries for hours till they have succeeded in making a bow to the minister, or any other great personage, on whom their hopes depend'.[6]

Twenty years later Blanco recalled witnessing at Aranjuez the
solemn ritual of the King's dinner. He was in the corridor of the palace
when he saw two halberdiers clearing a path and raising the cry
'Vianda, vianda!':

> All the bystanders had to take their hats off to a tureen which was about to
> have the honour of delivering its contents to the king's stomach, and as
> such, according to Spanish protocol, had to be considered an integral part
> of the royal person. The indignation with which, in my passionate youth, I
> witnessed this degradation of the nation, deprived me of any further wish
> to walk in the palace, for who knew how far such respect could be carried,
> or whether one would have to doff one's hat to any utensil that had a
> connection with the sacred person of the Spanish monarch.[7]

The anecdote says as much about the writer as about the quaint
custom. The ossified ceremonial of the court symbolised for Blanco
and his circle the backwardness of the nation itself. They were
ashamed to be Spanish.

In an attempt to curb the influx of *pretendientes*, a permit was
required for prolonged residence at Madrid, and in the summer of
1806 Blanco made his application from temporary quarters in Salamanca. He had an introduction there to the liberal lawyer and poet
Juan Meléndez Valdés (later Minister of Education under Joseph
Bonaparte) and was introduced by him to the Bishop of Salamanca,
Antonio Tavira, the leader of the Jansenists, whom Jovellanos called
'our Bossuet'. Blanco wrote to his father that the Bishop was
'kindness itself', and during his stay regularly dined at his table and
attended his evening gatherings.[8] Tavira had been a resolute opponent
of the Inquisition and was officially out of favour. He was a model
bishop with a high, austere ideal of pastoral responsibility and an
unpretentious style—a living contradiction of Blanco's later sweeping
allegations about the higher clergy. Soon after this date he was
demoted to the see of Las Palmas in the Canaries. Blanco expressed
surprise that 'a man with his taste and information' should accept the
bishopric of a 'semi-barbarous portion of the Spanish domains'.[9] It is a
revealing comment. It was Blanco, not the bishop, who rated dignity
above pastoral vocation.

Having obtained a residence permit, on health grounds, Blanco
found lodgings in Madrid, which he shared with Arjona. Thus began
what until now has been the least documented period of his life: two
years of poverty, freedom from responsibility, outward gaiety and
inner despair. His correspondence with his father was almost
exclusively concerned with money matters. With only a meagre
allowance from Seville to live on, he was reduced to writing home for
a mattress, and he and Arjona shared one cassock between them for
appearances at official occasions. He was determined not to practise as

a priest, and so could not supplement his income by mass stipends or chaplaincy fees. Such was his horror of everything connected with the priesthood that he would not enter a church, even to see a work of art. Yet in spite of the discomforts, 'such was the intoxication of pleasure (for I cannot find a more appropriate name for what I felt) which was produced on my mind by the enjoyment of liberty from the restraints of my town and family, that I was always in the highest spirits'.[10] He revelled in the anonymity of the metropolis. Eventually he would have to find a job, but he seems to have regarded this more as a way of prolonging his stay in Madrid than as the stepping-stone to a career. At one time he tried to obtain an honorary post in a recently established botanical institution, and later made enquiries in a still more unexpected quarter. In October 1806, he wrote to his brother: 'If you see Señor Monzón, find out if he will recommend me to someone here in the Inquisition . . . I am casting around on all sides for a nook which will provide me with a *requiem aeternam*'.[11] The Inquisition in Madrid was little more than a branch of the Civil Service, but that does not lessen the irony of the request, and it is not surprising that the episode does not figure in Blanco's memoirs. In his defence it should perhaps be added that his contemporary Juan Antonio Llorente was an official of the Inquisition at this time and put the experience to good use by gathering materials to be used in his History.

Meanwhile he became a member of the literary circle of the poet and dramatist Manuel José Quintana, a liberal lawyer with a social con-science, who had attracted round him a group of younger intellectuals who chafed at the petty restrictions of Godoy's regime and the sycophancy which surrounded it. Quintana's combination of poetic sensibility and sense of the writer's responsibility to promote social justice and civic harmony, struck an answering chord in Blanco.[12] It was to Quintana that he addressed the most personal and deeply felt of all his poems, which reveals more of his inner life at this time than any of his autobiographical writings. The unpublished *Elegía a D. Manuel José Quintana* is a tortured expression of romantic agony, but the rhetoric and the romantic imagery are, for once, equal to the emotion. The poet represents himself as a wanderer and outcast, unable to escape the pain of the poisoned arrow that has lodged in his breast. The world is a prison, in which he is condemned to a lifetime's suffering, condemned to eternal restlessness by his sensibility and his yearning for unattainable love. His life is like a bud that has withered at the very point of opening to the light. He can only be understood by those like him who are victims of their own tender feelings, however far removed they may be in time and place. Perhaps even now there is one such as he, wandering along the banks of the Mississippi. Nature is indifferent to him, and he is doomed to flight from everything to which he is most deeply attached: family, friends, country: 'Why do I flee from you? Why do I flee from all that I love, from all that beckons me towards the happiness which I have always sought but which has eluded me since infancy?' The poet's heart, born for love, has been denied it, and he is sentenced to solitude. 'Happiness exists on earth, but not for you. "No, not for you": I hear the words re-echo, and the bitterness of that eternal "No" runs through my veins and quenches the well-spring of my life'. As it stands, the poem is evidence of how far Blanco already saw alienation as his destiny. Another longer version of it, which he later suppressed, also contains a violent attack on social injustice, though this was by now a commonplace in the poetry of the pre-romantics. Blanco's sentiments and language are very close to those already used not only by Quintana but by Jovellanos—a writer not normally associated with calls for social revolution. The additional verses depict a poor labourer refused entrance at the gate of his disdainful master—a scene illustrative of a world where the good man suffers and the wicked prospers. In such a world, the poet declares, given the indifference of the haves, the have-nots are justified in recourse to violence. 'Go to it, then: let crime supply the remedy that fate denies you! Shed blood, shed blood, let all cry out in pain! Let the innocent suffer along with the guilty! Flood the earth with blood and tears!' Since men are forced to choose between being sheep or wolves, he concludes 'Let us be wolves!' The cry sounds incongruous coming from one who was not by nature a predator.[13]

In spite of his association with Quintana, Blanco allowed himself also to be drawn into the orbit of Godoy. He shared an interest in the violin with an *ilustrado* army officer named Amorós, who in 1806 persuaded Godoy to give his official support and patronage to a new progressive military school at Madrid organized along the lines advocated by Pestalozzi. The Pestalozzian system, European, not Spanish, in inspiration, was what would now be called 'pupil-centred', and there was an emphasis on mathematics and on the principle of *mens sana in corpore sano* which was quite new in Spain. In his *Memoirs*, Godoy took some pride in what the school achieved: 'It was the first time in Spain that physical and spiritual education were seen to go hand-in-hand'.[14] He took a risk in supporting the school in the face of ecclesiastical opposition, but the modernity of the educational philosophy and the good results which the school soon produced made it fashionable. Amorós became its first director in 1807 and he used his influence with Godoy to get Blanco appointed to the literary committee which supervised the choice of textbooks. The post was an unpaid sinecure, but it brought with it an impressive-sounding title and a 'position' which guaranteed Blanco's continued residence in Madrid. He also had the satisfaction of being associated with a progressive educational experiment with which he was fully in

sympathy. The freshness and idealism of the school was captured by
Goya in the allegorical portrait which he painted to mark its foundation. The picture was partially destroyed in the wave of destruction
which followed Godoy's fall, but an attractive fragment survives,
depicting some of the pupils engaged in *al fresco* mathematical study.[15]

What appealed to Blanco in Pestalozzi's philosophy was the idea
that learning should be a joyful release of the child's natural capacities,
and that it involved the education of the heart as well as of the mind. In
some unpublished notes on Pestalozzi's school at Yverdun he
described the 'moral spectacles' staged there on festival days to delight
and instruct the pupils. Thinking doubtless of his own lonely and
repressed childhood he went on: 'In education, pleasure should
precede instruction just as in nature the blossom precedes the fruit. Let
the child's imagination be roused by pleasurable sensations associated
with ideas of moral goodness: let them enjoy spectacles such as these in
order that love of the social virtues may be engendered and strengthened in their hearts'.[16]

In November 1807 it was Blanco who was invited to deliver an
address to mark the anniversary of the school's foundation. Instead of
a progress report, what the fashionable audience got—and what they
no doubt expected—was a 'Discourse on whether the educational
method of Henri Pestalozzi discourages genius, in particular that
which is required for the imitative arts'. The discourse set out to
answer the objection that Pestalozzi's emphasis on mathematics
would detract from the humanities, and that the average pupil would
be favoured at the expense of the artistically gifted. Blanco answered
the objections by invoking Bacon, Locke, Descartes and 'the
incomparable Newton', but he also found an Athenian parallel for the
current educational debate. Pestalozzi, he claimed, belonged to the
tradition of Plato, who had required a grounding in geometry as a
condition of entry to the Academy, and gave his pupils vigorous,
methodical training in analytical thought—unlike his opponents the
sophists who, despite their claims to universal knowledge, taught
their pupils nothing but the art of juggling with words. As for genius,
Blanco argued, that could take care of itself, for unlike the power of
reasoning it was not a skill which could be acquired or lost: it was an
innate gift. 'There is no danger to be feared in training the nascent
powers of reason; let us further its progress . . . and rejoice in a
generation which will not have to suffer as we did from the malign
influence of evil institutions'.[17]

At a later date Blanco felt sufficiently embarrassed by his association
with Godoy to excise the title page from his copy of the printed
discourse, which carried his name and a dedication to the Prince of the
Peace. He must have been far more embarrassed by the existence of an
Ode, 'La Verdad', in which two months later at a public recitation he

REAL INSTITUTO MILITAR PESTALOZZIANO
ESTABLECIDO POR S. M.
BAXO LA PROTECCION DEL S.ᵐᵒ S.ᵒʳ
PRINCIPE GENERALISIMO
ALMIRANTE.

2. An engraving of the allegorical *escudo*, or coat of arms, designed and painted by Goya to adorn the entrance of the Pestalozzian Institute. Following a precise brief from his patron Godoy, the artist depicted a cadet in carabineer's uniform, his right hand resting on Pestalozzi's geometric table. In the background a ray of heavenly light illuminates the glad faces of the pupils; other children hasten to take advantage of the enlightenment. The original *escudo* was destroyed in the anti-Godoy riots of 1808 (see the article by J. Milicua, in *Goya*, no. 34, 1960, pp. 332–34).

eulogised Godoy as the champion of Truth. The unpublished poem (of which only one manuscript copy survives) is a hymn to the triumph of truth over error, of reason over superstition, of light over darkness. The poet represents Truth as a goddess whose light has for centuries been dimmed in his native land but who has now found her liberator and her 'hero': 'From his cradle I breathed my spirit into him', Truth declares, 'and dwelt in his heart: it was I that wove the immortal crown of lustrous olive and shining laurel with which victory and peace have adorned his brow. Now victory and peace are joined with Truth. Look, Spain, upon his mettle! Time and his cruel scythe have no power over you, my Prince'. The Ode concludes with a prayer for the young pupils in whom lie the future hopes of their country, trained in an academy which future generations would look back to as a 'temple of Truth' guarded by an 'illustrious warrior'. Given Blanco's passionate commitment to the educational cause to which Godoy had lent his patronage, his admiration was not insincere. Besides, other much more distinguished writers had showered similar compliments. But Blanco chose the wrong moment, for the star of the Prince of the Peace was already waning. Furthermore, in pleasing the Prince, he displeased Quintana and his friends, in whom he now detected 'a degree of coldness and something like suspicion'.[18]

Some valuable light is thrown on this milieu by the historian and scholar Antonio de Capmany who, though considerably older than Quintana, was on the fringe of his circle. Both men later followed the Central Junta to Seville and Cadiz. There Quintana's fame eclipsed that of Capmany, who vented his injured feelings in an attacking pamphlet calculated to discredit Quintana by making insinuations about the company he had kept. His imputations, though prompted mainly by *amour-propre*, reflect on Quintana's *tertulia* in Madrid:

'There I came to know many a man behind his mask . . . There one night I met a priest who abused his mother for persuading him into the Church. At which a friend chaffed him, saying: "Does your profession not bring you in an income of 20,000 reals? You don't say Mass, or recite the breviary; you put on your frock-coat and boots and go out to the promenade, the café, the theatre, the ball, the drawing-room, the—no matter. So where are the bars your poor mother put you behind?" Another night I saw two other clerics who acted out for our amusement a scene never before witnessed by human eyes: one of them paced up and down, striking tragi-comical attitudes, declaiming a defence of suicide, while the other, a man well-read in the Greek and Latin classics, lolled back on a couch extolling the virtues of sodomy. There I met the wise and the would-be wise, the foolish and the sensible, ignorant and learned, men of sound heart and others (all poets) of corrupt soul, who protested their hatred of tyranny one day and flattered the tyrant the next. One of them bought the tyrant's protection by presenting him with a little poem entitled *El incordio*; another dedicated to him a comedy called *The Nun's Labyrinth*, in which he sacrilegiously betrayed the confidences entrusted to him as confessor and apostolic visitor of the convents of Cordoba, where he was Canon Penitentiary of the Cathedral. This was the same cleric who later came out to greet the usurper with a Pindaric ode. There I heard the notorious exhibitionist Amorós being sniggered at by the very men who had just being been paying him court, in order to please the host, who hated him as cordially as I did. It was from there that two *literati* believed to be unbelievers sallied forth to seek appointment as teachers of doctrine in the Pestalozzian school. One of them, on the anniversary of that bizarre institution, delivered himself before a crowded and distinguished audience of such blasphemies as: "O gentle Truth, that came down from heaven to rest on the lips of His Highness!" '[19]

The *literati* are, of course, Arjona and Blanco. (Was it Blanco who extolled suicide, and Arjona sodomy, or vice versa?) The Pindaric ode was that which Arjona composed two years later to celebrate Joseph Bonaparte's entry into Cordoba. His shamelessness on that occasion was compounded by the fact that it was the same ode he had written earlier to celebrate the entry of Charles IV into Seville.

More important is the reference to Blanco's poem *El incordio*, written for the amusement of Godoy, which still survives in its original autograph manuscript and which provides the other key to the author's mood at this time. *El incordio* ('The Tumour') is a burlesque miniature epic which owes its effect to a comic incongruity between its high-flown neo-classical form and its low-life subject matter. It purports to celebrate the discovery of a new remedy for syphilis, the 'French disease' (hence the sub-title 'Poema epi-gálico'). The poet tells us that he has himself just undergone the painful removal of a tumour at the hands of the surgeon. From the very beginning he strikes a note of bathos. He will not be invoking any muses, he tells us—though if they are obligatory, he will make do with some good-hearted ladies of the night. He then launches into an account of a dream in which the messenger of the gods appeared to him to summon him aloft for an interview with the god of love. To his surprise, the message is delivered not by a beautiful maiden—the Iris of his imagination—but a worm-eaten old hag dressed in a friar's habit. She has some disconcerting news about recent events on Olympus. All the old gods have been swept away in a proletarian revolution: Mercury has been given the sack, and Cupid has been packed off to boarding school to have some morals and manners beaten into him by the brothers. More shocks are in store when he reaches his heavenly destination. The Olympians carry on like a rabble at a bullfight, and the new god of Love turns out to be a swaggering, street-wise *majo*, dressed to kill and speaking in a strong Andalucian accent. Love, he tells the poet, has completely changed its style under his régime: sighs, agitations and jealousies have taken early retirement and gone into a monastery, and if Love still has its pains, they are of a more down-to-earth kind. Mystery is out, and realism is in, for 'here, although not spotless, Love is frank'.

The wit and inventiveness of *El incordio* mask a profound disillusion. The revolution on Olympus is an image not only of the earthly revolution which the *enragés* of Madrid longed for, but also of the revolution which had taken place within Blanco himself. Innocence and supernatural virtue, once a beautiful dream, had become an intolerable burden. Henceforward honesty, not purity, would be his watchword: he would be a man, not an angel. Nevertheless, this mood of disillusioned realism was not one which he was likely to sustain for long. He was too fastidious to feel quite at home in low company, nor was he a natural cynic. Much later, after his conversion to Anglicanism, he would refer to *El incordio* briefly and indirectly as verse of which he was 'morally ashamed'.[20] There is no reason to suppose that the poem is autobiographical in the sense that Blanco himself contracted syphilis.

It was at this period that he formed an association with the woman, Magdalena Esquaya, who after his departure from Madrid was to bear him a son. Little is known of her save that she was poor and in ill-health. Her social condition may be deduced from the fact that her sister Felipa, a wet-nurse, was illiterate. Blanco mentioned her by name only in letters to his brother. He excised the passage referring to her in his earliest self-examination, on the grounds that it 'might give needless pain', and in a later autobiographical narration wrote obliquely: 'When I was on the point of yielding to the influence of those laws [the Church's laws on celibacy] which impelled me to boundless dissipation, the sight of utter destitution, in a long and dangerous sickness, instantly reclaimed me to the course of benevolence, even beyond my pecuniary means. Thus was my attachment *exclusively* fixed on the person whom I had been the means of rescuing from death'. When Felipa wrote to him in London in 1816 to tell him that Magdalena was dying, he sent money to his brother for her relief. 'She was a woman of some very excellent qualities', he wrote, 'whom circumstances had plunged into wretchedness and degradation'. The relationship was not an equal one—nor could it be, given Blanco's fastidious class-consciousness, but it involved, if not love, then at least tenderness and affection. The episode was later to be shamefully exploited by his denigrators.[21]

Blanco was just on the point of emerging from obscurity when the first tremors were felt of the earthquake which brought down the decaying structure of the *ancien régime*.[22] By the beginning of 1808 Godoy was under pressure from within and without. Bowing to pressure from Napoleon he was forced by the terms of the Treaty of

Fontainebleau in the autumn of 1807 to allow French troops to pass through Spanish territory in order to attack Portugal. Thus Napoleon already had his Trojan horse installed within the Iberian peninsula. At home, Godoy was blamed for all Spain's troubles, and he had also to contend with the intrigues mounted against him by the Prince of the Asturias, the odious Ferdinand. The latter, disliked by his father and excluded from power, had long been jealous of Godoy's influence, and his frustration and resentment was fuelled by the disaffected nobles who used him for their own purposes. In October 1807 Ferdinand was arrested on his father's orders on a charge of conspiracy. It was on this occasion that Blanco narrowly escaped being involved in the fate of the royal family. The tutor of Ferdinand's younger brother, the Infante Don Francisco de Paula, whom the King was now thinking of making his heir, was suspected of complicity in the plot, and Blanco was summoned to the Escorial as a possible replacement. In the event the tutor was exonerated.[23]

Events were playing into Napoleon's hands. He saw Ferdinand as a useful puppet whom he could manipulate in order to dislodge the King and Godoy. Meanwhile the latter, aware of Napoleon's ambitions, was laying plans to move the King and the royal family away from Madrid to the safety of Seville or (if the worst came to the worst) America. Rumours that something was afoot inflamed the popular mood. It was even put about that Godoy was planning to declare himelf Regent. His enemies in the ranks of the aristocracy and the army now brought things to a head by engineering a mob attack on his house in Aranjuez on 17 March 1808. Having unleashed the dogs of revolution, they were no longer able to control the momentum of events. All the suppressed discontents of recent months exploded in an outburst of hatred against the Prince of the Peace. In Madrid crowds paraded the streets with cries of 'Long live King Ferdinand!' and 'Death to Godoy'. On 18 March Godoy was relieved of his military commands, and was only saved from the fury of the mob by Ferdinand's intervention. The houses of his supporters were sacked. Faced with anarchy, and deprived of his right-hand man, Charles IV abdicated in favour of his son, who now entered Madrid in triumph. Blanco witnessed the scene:

> Never did monarch meet with a more loyal and affectionate welcome from his subjects; yet never did subjects behold a more vacant and unmeaning countenance, even among the long faces of the Spanish Bourbons. To features not at all prepossessing, either shyness or awkwardness had added a stiffness which, but for the motion of the body, might induce a suspicion that we were wasting our greetings on a wax figure.[24]

Ferdinand had been preceded into the city by Murat and his French troops who were seen as liberators. The general enthusiasm for the

French at this juncture was later conveniently forgotten by patriotic Spanish propagandists who found it, in retrospect, embarrassing. The French had apparently manoeuvred themselves into a perfect position. They had won the gratitude of the people by expelling the 'tyrant' and putting a popular young prince on the throne. The educated class saw them as a guarantee of reform without disorder. Even the clergy was well-disposed. After all, Napoleon was no revolutionary now, but the man who had recently made a Concordat with the Pope. Yet, having won these advantages without shedding a drop of Spanish blood, the French were to throw them away in a matter of days.

The one loser in all these confused events was the Spanish monarchy. A king who had forced his father's abdication and come to the throne as the result of street rioting and popular agitation could no longer claim the mystique and inviolability which hitherto had attached to his office. The spell of the Catholic monarchy was broken. Besides, what had the revolution—if it was a revolution—achieved? Nobody was sure. Everybody could claim to be the winner: Ferdinand VII, the French, the mob, the nobility, the advocates of reform and the forces of reaction. What few realised was that in getting rid of Godoy they had lost the one man who was not taken in by Napoleon and had determined, belatedly, to resist him.

It was not long before French intentions became clear. Ferdinand and his father were both persuaded to leave the capital and to go north to meet Napoleon—a journey from which Charles never returned and which for Ferdinand was the beginning of six years of exile. If Napoleon had kept him in place as a figurehead he could have done what he liked, but he had already decided to impose his brother Joseph on the unsuspecting nation as their new monarch, having persuaded Ferdinand to abdicate. Bourbons gave way to Bonapartes. When the news reached Madrid and the people realised how they had been duped, their mood changed to one of savage fury. Having got wind of Murat's plans to remove the remaining members of the royal family from Madrid, they gathered at the royal palace to prevent it. It was the Second of May—the day made internationally famous by Goya. Blanco's house was not far from the palace, and he later recalled the scene:

A rush of people crying 'To arms!' conveyed to us the first notice of the tumult. I heard that the French troops were firing on the people, but the outrage appeared to me both so impolitic and so enormous that I could not rest until I went out to ascertain the truth. I had just arrived at an opening named Plazuela de Santo Domingo, the meeting point of four large streets, one of which leads to the Palace, when, hearing the sound of a French drum in that direction, I stopped with a considerable number of decent and quiet people, whom curiosity kept riveted to the spot. Though a strong piquet of infantry was fast advancing upon us, we could not imagine that

we stood in any kind of danger. Under this mistaken notion we awaited
their approach; but, seeing the soldiers halt and prepare their arms, we
began instantly to disperse. A discharge of musketry followed in a few
moments, and a man fell at the entrance to the street, through which I was,
with a great throng, retreating from the fire. The fear of an indiscriminate
massacre arose so naturally from this unprovoked assault, that every one
tried to look for safety in the narrow cross streets on both sides of the way.
I hastened on towards my house, and having shut the front door, could
think of no better expedient than to make ball pieces for a fowling-piece
which I kept.[25]

The French troops now moved into the city and occupied all the
strategic positions, and as the main corps marched through the *Calle
Mayor* 'such as had guns, fired through the windows; while tiles,
bricks and heavy articles of furniture were thrown by others upon the
heads of the soldiers'. In spite of an amnesty, Murat used the pretext of
a ban on the bearing of arms to carry out a series of reprisals, and as
many as four hundred civilians—all of the lower class—were summa-
rily executed. The streets emptied, Madrid overnight took on the
appearance of a ghost town.

> The dead silence of the streets since the first approach of night, only broken
> by the trampling of horses which now and then were heard passing along
> in large parties, had something exceedingly dismal in a populous town,
> where we were accustomed to an incessant and enlivening bustle. The
> *Madrid cries*, the loudest and most varied in Spain, were missed early next
> morning, and it was ten o'clock before a single street door had been
> opened. Nothing but absolute necessity could induce the people to venture
> out.

By the action of 2 May Murat succeeded only in dealing a death
blow to French hopes of winning the hearts and minds of the Spanish.
It was a disastrously bungled affair. He had entered Madrid as the
protector of Ferdinand, the people's hero, and had he continued in this
role, with Ferdinand installed as an instrument of French policy, Spain
would have fallen to Napoleon without a shot fired. The majority of
intellectuals were already disposed in favour of Napoleon, whom they
regarded as a standard-bearer of progress and reform. Now the French
were seen unmistakeably as a brutal foreign oppressor, and the shock
waves of their action in Madrid were soon felt throughout Spain. The
Spanish people was united, as never before, in a mood of violent
anger.

Blanco himself was now faced with a dilemma. As a radical and
francophile he had been, like many of his class, disposed in favour of
the French, believing that they would draw Spain at last into the
mainstream of modern Europe and impose those reforms which no
native administration could achieve without dividing the country.

From a purely selfish point of view, also, he saw in the destruction by the French of the existing régime the only prospect of escaping from his personal *impasse*. However he had now seen the ugly face of the 'liberators' and shared the instinctive patriotic reaction of the masses. Not for the first time, his head was at odds with his heart. Was it not madness to contemplate resistance to the French? 'To declare war against an army of veterans already in the heart of Spain, might be, indeed, an act of sublime patriotism; but was it not too, a provocation more likely to bring ruin and permanent slavery on the country than the admission of a new King [Joseph Bonaparte] who though a foreigner, had not been educated a despot, and who, for want of any constitutional claims, would be anxious to ground his rights on the acknowledgement of the nation?'[26] This was the attitude adopted by Blanco's Seville friends, *afrancesados* almost to a man, who collaborated with King Joseph in the belief that under his enlightened monarchy Spain would retain some measure of self-government and would be freed from the Inquisition and from the 'degradation' of the *ancien régime*. (Quintana and his associates on the other hand put patriotism before ideology. So did Jovellanos, though only after some hesitation. King Joseph was so sure of his support that he had already published his nomination as Minister of the Interior.) At this point news reached Madrid that Andalucia had risen against the French and that a revolutionary junta had been formed there which claimed to be the legitimate representative of King Ferdinand, now Napoleon's captive. It took Blanco six weeks to make up his mind. If he stayed in Madrid, he would be branded a traitor by the patriots. To return to Seville, however, meant taking on again the ecclesiastical role he had discarded in Madrid, resuming the 'detested and long-discontinued task of acting the hierophant'.[27] By every rational argument Blanco leant towards the *afrancesados* and yet he chose the opposite side. On 15 June he slipped through the military cordon around Madrid and began the dangerous journey south.

Chapter 4
The Junta Chica

Recedant vetera, nova sint omnia
—St Thomas Aquinas

Since the French army under Dupont had cut off the main road south
through La Mancha, Blanco and his companion were obliged to take a
more circuitous route south-west through Extremadura. 'The notice
we attracted at the approach of every village, the threats of the
labourers whom we met near the road, and the accounts we heard at
every inn, fully convinced us that we could not reach our journey's
end without considerable danger'. As an example of the uncontrolled
fury now sweeping the provinces and what he called, for the benefit of
the genteel English reader, 'the unfortunate propensity to shed blood,
which tarnishes many a noble quality in the southern Spaniards',
Blanco described the scene at a typical small town in the region,
Almaráz. There a mob gathered before the Alcalde's house, armed
with whatever weapons they could find.

> Having with no small difficulty obtained a hearing, the Alcalde desired to
> be informed of their designs and wishes. The answer seems to me
> unparalleled in the history of mobs. "We wish, Sir, to kill somebody", said
> the spokesman of the insurgents. "Someone has been killed at Truxillo;
> one or two others at Badajóz, another at Mérida, and we will not be behind
> our neighbours. Sir, we will kill a traitor". As this commodity could not
> be procured in the village it was fortunate for us that we did not make our
> appearance at a time when the good people of Almaráz might have made us
> a substitute on whom to display their loyalty.

The travellers were eyewitnesses of a similar scene at Mérida, where
an angry mob of about two thousand surrounded their inn when they
heard that a French prisoner had been brought there under custody.
Blanco and his companion found sanctuary in the Bishop's palace,
while the Frenchman was with difficulty escorted to prison. 'But
neither the soldiers nor the magistrates could fully protect him from
the savage fierceness of the peasants, who crowding upon him, as half
dead with terror, he was slowly dragged to the town gaol, stuck the
points of their knives into several parts of his body'.[1]

There had been tumultuous scenes at Seville, too. When news of the Aranjuez riot had reached the city in March, a mob had forced its way into a church, seized a portrait of Godoy which had been installed there only five months earlier amid general adulation, borne it off to the main square and torn it to shreds before committing it to the flames. In May the news of the French atrocities in Madrid had sparked off a popular rising led by the demagogue friar Padre Gil and the Conde de Tilly. The aristocratic representative of the old order in Seville, the Conde del Águila, was murdered and his dead body, tied to a chair, exposed to public insult. Scenes such as this could not fail to alarm the establishment, fearful of mob rule. By the time Blanco arrived in Seville, a Provincial Junta, including Gil and Tilly, had been set up under the presidency of the former minister Saavedra, who had difficulty in preventing the situation from degenerating into anarchy.

On his arrival, Blanco presented himself to the Junta. Though he was received courteously by Saavedra, he discovered that his recent past had caught up with him, when Padre Gil openly charged him with having been one of the 'flatterers' of the Prince of the Peace. It was a time when rumours of treachery and espionage were widespread, and since it was already known that some of his associates at Madrid had come out in favour of King Joseph, Blanco himself came under suspicion of being a French agent. These experiences on the journey and after his arrival must have caused him to doubt the wisdom of his political choice. This was not the revolution he and his friends had dreamed of, led and controlled by educated idealists, but a movement of raw patriotic and religious fervour which brought the lower clergy and the proletariat—the forces Blanco most despised—into formidable coalition. It was only with difficulty that the local nobility and gentry gradually brought these forces under their control.

That summer there were delirious celebrations at Seville when news arrived of the defeat of General Dupont's army at Bailén by the Spanish general Castaños. Soon afterwards the victor entered Seville in triumph, to the accompaniment of the pealing bells of the Giralda, and proceeded to the Royal Chapel where the body of St Ferdinand was solemnly exposed for thanksgiving. Bailén was followed by the flight of King Joseph from Madrid (1 August), and for a brief period the loyalists believed in their own invincibility. Elated by victory, the provincial juntas patched up their differences sufficiently to set up a national government, the Central Junta, which invested itself with the royal authority. Charles III's former chief minister, Floridablanca, was brought out of retirement to be its President, and another of its members was the even more distinguished veteran Jovellanos, recently released after seven years of political imprisonment. To mark the installation of the Central Junta, Blanco published an Ode in

which, in tones of exalted patriotism, he depicted the tyrant Napoleon
trembling on his throne at the resounding shout of defiance echoing
over the Pyrenees.[2] But the euphoria was short-lived. In December
Napoleon himself led his troops back into Madrid, Joseph was
reinstated, and the Central Junta, along with a train of refugees, made
its way south to Seville, which now became the seat of legitimate
government and the centre of resistance.

The crisis called for a strong executive authority with emergency
powers and a unified military command, but what the nation got was
a prolonged political debate. The Central Junta had neither the means
nor the will to enforce its authority on the different provincial juntas,
with which communication was difficult, and it was composed of
veteran politicans and conservative churchmen who had an innate
distrust of innovation. Lord Holland, who saw them in action,
described them as 'too much occupied with the ceremonies, forms and
patronage of the new government', even the best of them, including
his admired Jovellanos, 'being somewhat too scrupulously observant
of technical rules inapplicable to the exigency of circumstances and too
readily alarmed at those vigorous measures of innovation which a
state of revolution and civil war demands'.[3] The vacillation and
timidity of the Central Junta alienated the young Turks like Blanco
who saw resistance to the French not as an end in itself but as a unique
opportunity to bring about revolutionary reform. The group of
intellectuals which had centred round Quintana in Madrid now
re-formed itself in Seville. Nicknamed the 'junta chica', it was the
nucleus of the party of liberals who later came to power in Cadiz.
Blanco was regarded as one of the rising stars of this group.

Meanwhile he had resumed his duties in the Royal Chapel. The
chaplains had to take turns in celebrating daily mass for the members
of the Junta Central in the palace of the Reales Alcázares, and the
chapter minutes reveal that it was Blanco who insisted that he and his
colleagues should be paid extra for their professional services.[4]
However much he later protested his dislike of 'acting the hierophant',
it seems that his attitude at the time was less detached. Along with the
rest of the royal chaplains he officiated at the solemn funeral and burial
of Count Floridablanca which took place in the royal chapel on the last
day of the year. The passing of Floridablanca symbolised the end of his
periwigged and seigneurial century.

It was at this point that Blanco first made the acquaintance of Lord
and Lady Holland. The Hollands had discovered Spain on an earlier
visit in 1802, when they met everyone who was anyone in Spanish
political, social and literary life. In Jovellanos, above all, Lord Holland
found an aristocratic, enlightened and benevolent statesman after his
own eighteenth-century heart—a Spanish Whig whose principles
could compare with 'those of Cicero and Mr Fox'.[5] Spain, in fact,

came near to replacing France in the Hollands' affections, for they were not only Francophiles but admirers of Bonaparte—an attitude which consigned them to the political wilderness in England during the war years. Lord Holland had, however, welcomed the news of the Spanish rising with enthusiasm, seeing it as Spain's opportunity to free itself from the bonds of absolutism and to establish the mixed constitution which he advocated so tirelessly—a constitution in which the aristocracy had a key role to play in holding the balance between despotism and demagogy. There was no immediate prospect of putting these ideas into practice in England, but circumstances now seemed to present Spain as an ideal laboratory in which to produce a political model.

There was, in fact, general enthusiasm in Britain for the Spanish cause at this time. The provincial juntas lost no time in appealing to the British government for support. When the delegation from the Asturias arrived in London in June, it was given an enthusiastic popular reception. The Spanish really wanted British money and arms, but what they got was a British expeditionary force, and this was to be the cause of later tensions. In July a British force embarked for La Coruña under the command of Wellesley, and he was followed by Sir John Moore. Much to the embarrassment of the British government, the Hollands embarked in October 1808 on one of the troopships carrying reinforcements for La Coruña. Once in Spain they roamed in and out of the theatre of war in ambassadorial style. Since Lord Holland knew everybody of importance in Spain and had a network of aristocratic friends and relations in the British expeditionary force, he would indeed have made a splendid ambassador— except that in his eyes Spain could do no wrong, an attitude which was not shared by the military. Their attitude was summed up in an outburst from Lord Paget, who indignantly rejected Holland's criticism of British tactics: 'You are the most prejudiced man alive. You talk to a parcel of people snug upon the sea coast, and who, knowing your enthusiasm for the Spanish cause, flatter your misconceptions of the state of the country . . . 'Tis one not worth saving. Such ignorance, such deceit, such apathy, such pusillanimity, such cruelty, was [sic] never both united. There is not one army that has fought at all. There is not one general who has exerted himself, there is not one province that has made any sacrifice whatever'.[6]

This is an extreme example of the view of the Spanish held by most British officers. For them the war was a British war carried on against Napoleon on Spanish soil, with little help and much obstruction from their allies. For the Spanish, on the other hand, this was a people's war, a war of independence, carried on with inadequate and half-hearted assistance from the perfidious English. It was the conduct of General Sir John Moore and his retreat to La Coruña in January 1809 (while the

Hollands were at Seville) which most starkly polarised the two opposing mythologies. According to the one, Moore, the victim of Spanish intrigues and disunity, had carried out a brilliant withdrawal. According to the other, he had run away. Lord Holland shared the latter view.

In January 1809 the Hollands and their retinue—whose progress was once compared by Sydney Smith to 'the march of Alexander or Bacchus over India'—reached Seville. The panache and lordliness of their operations went down well in a city which can recognise a grandee when it sees one—and they found appropriate quarters in the splendid Casa Liria, the palace of the Dukes of Berwick and Alba. Once installed in these magnificent surroundings they set about recreating Holland House, as it were, on Andalucian soil. Elder statesmen were invited to dinner, and bright young men—of whom Blanco was one—were summoned to show off their paces. With the Hollands was John Allen, their physician, unofficial secretary of state and constitutional expert, and their sixteen-year-old protegé, Lord John Russell. Allen was supposed to be tutoring Russell in Latin and Mathematics, but in fact was giving him an incomparable introduction to constitutional and political history in the making. He was at work on a draft constitution for the proposed Cortes, and it has been remarked that many of its provisions have a striking resemblance to those later embodied in the Whig Reform Bill of 1831.[7] If that is so, then Lord John Russell, its proposer, learned his lessons well in Spain.

The Hollands were in Seville for four months. Shortly before their departure, Blanco was appointed joint editor of the *Semanario Patrió-tico*, a weekly journal which had originally been published at Madrid by Manuel Quintana during the brief interregnum between the first and second French occupations. The Central Junta had now appointed Quintana under-secretary with responsibility for information and propaganda, and so he handed over the editorship of the revived *Semanario* to Blanco and a colleague, Isidoro Antillón.

Quintana's rival Antonio Capmany later made much fun of the self-important manifesto which the new editors published to advertise their journal. They represented themselves and their companions as having been marked out by providence for the defence of truth and the enlightenment of the nation. The Madrid *Semanario*, they declared, had been the only journal worthy of Spain, and all were agreed that the new editors were uniquely qualified to take up the pen again in order to given the people the benefit of their 'wise guidance'. Both were at pains to establish their patriotic credentials. Without mentioning himself by name, Blanco described his flight to Seville as a journey 'across mountain and ravine', in which he had been 'ever guided by his star towards Seville'.[8]

When allowance is made for youthful vanity, the *Semanario Patrió-tico* may be said to have earned a place in history as the first free, or semi-free, journal of political opinion to be published in Spain, and as such it achieved considerable fame, its views being hotly debated in the cafés of Seville and Cadiz. Without attacking the Central Junta directly, it urged radical measures of reform. Resistance to the French, it argued, was not enough by itself: there was also an enemy within to be reckoned with—the 'egoists' who 'shivered at the name of reform'. On two essential points the *Semanario* differed from the government. Blanco and his colleagues, whose thinking had been shaped by Rousseau and Montesquieu, believed that in the absence of the King, sovereignty had reverted to the people, whereas the members of the Central Junta thought of themselves as having inherited the mantle of an absolute, albeit an enlightened and benevolent, monarch. The Junta was committed, rather uneasily, to the convocation of a Cortes, but what they had in mind was something on the medieval, corporatist model and representing the estates of the realm, whereas the *Semanario* wanted a democratically elected national assembly representing every section of the community. 'If this great enterprise is to be carried through, it must involve the whole nation: nobles, plebeians, churchmen, peasants, tradesmen and artists'. If the government failed to take advantage of the new mood in the country, if it attempted simply to preserve the *status quo*, then it would be sowing the seeds of a terrible vengeance: 'A nation in which the poor man has no secure home, in which the day-worker is ignored and the artisan frustrated, in which one class abounds in wealth while others lack the very means of existence—such a nation is close to total destruction'.[9] If in the pages of the *Semanario* Blanco was obliged to moderate his opinions, in private he was less restrained. In June he wrote to Lord Holland, now in Cadiz: 'Though I acknowledge the advantages of that conci-liating manner of writing which you recommend to me, I must own that I cannot temperate [sic] my indignation when I consider this hideous crowd of Grandees, Hidalgos and Churchmen, who will never be gained to anything favourable to the good principles'. He also voiced his suspicions that the Central Junta was only interested in perpetuating its power and was going to rig the Cortes accordingly. Lord Holland pinned his hopes on the presence within the Junta of the enlightened Jovellanos, but Blanco was less sure of him: 'I pay the greatest respect to the knowledge and virtues of this honourable man, but I cannot trust to him alone the defence of our liberty'.[10]

It is evident that Holland was impressed from the beginning by Blanco's ability and saw him as a useful convert to the cause, if his Jacobin hot headedness could be moderated. The junta chica alarmed him with their disregard for tradition and their doctrinaire and provocative style. It was composed, he later wrote, of young men of more ardour and imagination than experience or prudence, who had imbibed their notions of freedom from the encyclopaedists of France rather than from the history of their ancient institutions or from the immediate wants of their own country. They were perhaps more competent to exhibit their own contempt of superstition and disdain of abuses than to reconcile either the Church or the nobility to a rational correction of them.[11]

He asked Jovellanos to pass on to Blanco his copy of the *Letters of Peter Plymley*—that powerful and witty plea for Catholic Emancipation—hoping, perhaps, that it might teach him a lesson in religious toleration. 'It seems to me it would be very useful for those who write in this excellent periodical [the *Semanario*] to inform themselves about English affairs and to acquire a flavour of the way constitutional matters are handled in England—which I may say, without national vanity, is much wiser than that which obtains in France'. He was also anxious that Blanco should read Blackstone, from whom he might learn a 'very sensible and *non-French* approach to questions of freedom and the constitution'.[12] Blanco was a ready learner, but he could not share Lord Holland's unrealistic hopes of the Spanish aristocracy. Meanwhile, the Hollands were as critical of their own government as Blanco and his colleagues were of theirs. John Allen warned Blanco against the British ambassador, Marquess Wellesley, whom he represented as a despotic and reactionary Nabob, 'an enemy of popular government and public discussion, and above all a hater of the liberty of the press', who would consider the Spanish as 'mere instruments for the destruction of Bonaparte'. Wellesley's brother (the future Duke of Wellington) was accustomed to defer to him in everything, Allen declared, so he would be able to dictate military as well as political strategy.[13] Wellesley must have heaved a sigh of relief when the Hollands finally left Spain in June 1809.

It was inevitable that the *Semanario* should fall foul of the conservatives of the Central Junta. Blanco's co-editor Isidoro Antillón was publishing in serial form a military account of the war, but when he approached that section of the campaign which covered the generalship of the Duke of Infantado, he was summoned to the latter's presence and given to understand that the Duke 'would not endure any remarks upon his conduct'.[14] Quintana, Blanco's patron, was not strong enough to resist the mounting pressure. When the Junta formally recommended greater moderation, the editors took umbrage and insisted not only on resigning but on going out with a flourish. The final issue contained a veiled defence by the editors of the principle of press freedom. The affair caused considerable éclat, and when Blanco visited Cadiz about a month afterwards he found himself acclaimed as a champion of free speech: 'The impression of my parting words was still so fresh that on my entering one of the Cafés, which was frequented by the principal inhabitants, a person unknown to me addressed the whole company, pointing to me, and thanking me for the uncompromising spirit I had shown'.[15] Uncompromising stands on principle were a luxury which the nation could ill afford with an invader to be dealt with. Blanco himself later found fault with his own inexperience and 'ignorance': 'I had read something on political liberty and popular rights, but my notions were too crude and speculative: all therefore which I could produce were well-turned phrases against tyranny and abuse of power'.[16]

After the obscurity of his years in Madrid, Blanco was now a celebrity, a rising hope of the new generation of revolutionary liberals. When the University of Seville was asked by Jovellanos to submit its recommendations for the new Cortes, it was Blanco who was entrusted with the preparation of a report. In it he again opposed Jovellanos' historical constitutionalism. Spain could not afford the luxury in the present crisis of investigating the ancient privileges of the medieval Cortes, which in any case, he declared, were never a genuine national or representative congress, nor could they wait upon the King. 'Our kings do not have the right to change the constitutional basis of the nation'. In other words, the King was subject to the law and held authority only because it was conferred upon him by the people. In the absence of the King, authority had reverted to the people, and the role of the Cortes was to give the people a voice. 'If we believe in a Cortes, it is because it can rouse public opinion . . . because it can revive the flame of the original revolution, because it can give the Spanish people a feeling of nationhood. The Cortes will be a school for patriots'.[17]

Lord Holland was not the only Englishman to visit Seville during this critical period. The Spanish struggle had caught the romantic imagination of England, and the adventurous—deprived by the war of opportunities for travelling in France and Italy—made their way to the centre of action. As in 1936, so in 1809 Spain was suddenly fashionable. Blanco was the ideal *cicerone* for these visitors in Seville and, safe in their company, could freely vent his scorn on the Inquisition and all its works. William Jacob met him in November 1809 at the house of Dean Cepero, 'the most intellectual of all the Tertullas [sic] of Seville'. 'Padre Blanco, so well known throughout Spain as the author of the patriotico seminario [sic] frequently joins this circle', he wrote. 'If there be a priest without bigotry, a philosopher without vanity, or a politician without prejudice, Padre Blanco is that man: whenever he is of the party he enlightens it by his knowledge and animates it by his patriotism'.[18]

Jacob gives a vivid account of the régime at Seville on the eve of its collapse. Instead of organising for the impending French onslaught, 'His Majesty the Junta' frittered away its time on ceremonial duties.

Jacob attended a lengthy review when an entire regiment went on
parade to mark the solemn declaration of war against—Denmark.
Instead of alerting the population to danger, they kept it in a false sense
of security. On 20 January French troops broke through the passes of
the Sierra Morena into Andalucia and met little resistance as they
advanced on Seville. Even then the Junta did not release the full facts,
no doubt fearing the violence of the popular reaction when the scale of
the collapse was known. On 23 January they slipped out of Seville and
made their way to Cadiz.

In the few days of unnatural stillness which followed, Blanco found
himself at a critical turning-point. His parents, who were strongly
anti-French, wanted him to follow the Junta to Cadiz. Yet he himself
had no confidence in the Junta and indeed no real confidence in the
effectiveness of further resistance. No-one could have predicted at this
stage that Cadiz would successfully hold out for over two years or that
a combined Anglo-Spanish force would eventually achieve the
impossible: the defeat of a Napoleonic army. Defeatism was in the air.
Besides, what would he do,in Cadiz? Whatever he did, he would have
to continue the outward profession of his priesthood, and this was a
prospect he shrank from. It was at this point, almost by accident, that
the idea occurred to him of leaving Spain altogether for England.
Once the idea had been suggested he took it up with characteristic
fervour: 'Mental freedom attracted me with irresistible power: I now
saw it within my reach, and there was nothing in the whole Universe
which could allure me from it'.

He kept his parents in ignorance of these intentions. If there was one
thing which held him back it was the thought of their frailty.
Fernando, his younger brother, had been captured the previous year at
the fall of Madrid and was a prisoner-of-war in France. Doña Gertrudis was now permanently bedridden, and Don Guillermo an old man.
Though anxious for their son's safety, they could not have contemplated a permanent separation. As for Blanco's friends, they were
already preparing to collaborate with the French. On the eve of his
departure Lista begged him not to leave: 'A person whom he did not
name, had acknowledged to him that he was in direct communication
wih the government of King Joseph. By the desire of that agent, my
friend came to promise me not only protection but also especial
favour. My friend was convinced that the military struggle was now
at an end; and that the duty of every honest man was to contribute to
the establishment of a new dynasty which, supported as it was by
many of the most enlightened Spaniards, would raise the country out
of its moral degradation'.[19]

However pessimistic these arguments, Blanco could not have
become a collaborator without dealing a death blow to his father. At
the same time he knew, as his father did not, that he was leaving

Seville probably for good. At about nine o'clock on the morning of 29 January 1810, with his cousin Luke Beck and two other relations, he embarked for Sanlucar and Cadiz. He never forgot the last glimpse of his father's bent figure still standing on the quayside as the boat wound out of sight at the first turn of the Guadalquivir.[20]

Blanco and his companions were the first refugees to arrive at Sanlucar and they avoided the town rather than risk the wrath which might be vented on the bringers of bad news (as was the fate of the hapless members of the Central Junta when they reached Cadiz). After a night spent in an open boat at the mouth of the river, the party embarked for Cadiz in an English boat which took on board a consignment of wool from the house of Cahill and White. 'Loud explosions were heard in the distance, and when darkness came on we saw flashes of light precede them. This continued the whole night. The Captain assured us they were not discharges of artillery; and rightly conjectured that some forts on the coast were being destroyed before the expected approach of the French'.[21] The French, meanwhile, had entered Seville to an ecstatic welcome.

Cadiz was in the midst of political turmoil. On 31 January, the day before Blanco's arrival, the Central Junta had resigned and been replaced by a Regency. 'His Majesty the Junta' suddenly found itself treated like a common criminal, and even Jovellanos was publicly humiliated. The new Regency was a weak body, and real power now lay with the local junta which represented the political and commercial interests of the Cadiz merchant class.

During the three weeks he remained in Cadiz, waiting for a passage, Blanco's relations there tried to persuade him to change his mind. It would have been uncharacteristic of him not to have hesitated, even at this late stage. What counted in the end was the prospect of personal escape. He knew what he wanted to escape *from*, but had no clear idea of what he was escaping *to*. On 23 February 1810 he sailed for Falmouth in an English frigate, the *Lord Howard*. The shimmering white skyline of Cadiz, gradually disappearing like a mirage beneath the horizon, was his last sight of Spain.

Part II: England

'Quid terras alio calentis
sole mutamus? Patriae quis exsul

—Horace, *Odes* 2.16

Por que otro sol buscando y otras tierras
Inquieto, dí, te agitas?
Si de la amada patria te destierras
A tí jamás te evitas.
—Alberto Lista, *A Albino. La felicidad
consiste en la moderación de los deseos* (1808)

Chapter 5
The Language of Freedom

Barbarus hic ego sum quia non intelligor illis
—Ovid. *Tristia*

After a stormy journey, on the morning of 3 March 1810, the *Lord Howard* approached the coast of Cornwall in thick fog.[1] When it anchored in Falmouth harbour, Blanco recalled,

> a chill, such as I had never experienced, seized my whole frame. I thought I was breathing in death with the fog. . . Unacquainted with every thing about me, and fearful to an absurd excess of that kind of ridicule and disrespect which a foreigner, especially a Spaniard, apprehends in England, I stood motionless, waiting for the last turn and perfectly indifferent whether I passed the remaining part of the day and the ensuing night in the packet. A strong persuasion that the climate would kill me in a short time took possession of my mind; and I felt as if I were going to land in the grave.[2]

Within an hour, however, the weather—and Blanco's mood—had changed. The green and soft Cornish landscape was a revelation to one who had never yet been beyond Andalucia, Extremadura and Castile. Throughout his years in England he was to be subject to this oscillation between euphoria and melancholy—between a determination to admire every feature of English life and the sense of being a stranger.

On the long journey by post-chaise across the southern counties there were glimpses of English prosperity. Blanco was an observant traveller and quick to leap from the particular to the general. He later recalled being struck, as they approached London, by the numerous signs marked 'nursery', which prompted indignant reflections on the heartlessness of English mothers who could entrust their babes-in-arms on such a vast scale to the tender mercies of wet-nurses.[3] Though he told the joke against himself, he managed to turn it against one of his favourite targets, the theorizing Frenchman, who would confidently run up some philosophical reflections on the state of the nation on the basis of a fortnight's tour.

One of his fellow passengers was a young artist whose acquaintance he had made in Seville, Lascelles Hoppner, the younger son of the eminent portrait painter. Hoppner had been recalled home by news of his father's illness but arrived too late. When they reached the Hoppners' house in St James's, Blanco found himself the impotent and bewildered spectator of a scene of family grief. It was not an auspicious beginning to his life in England, nor was his first glimpse of London the next morning, seen from the window of his lodgings in the warren of dingy streets near Carlton House.

> I jumped out of bed and ran to the window to enjoy as I supposed, a scene of splendour such I had never conceived. . . Dirt, smoke and darkness seemed to have undisturbed possession of every thing I saw. Even the Palace wanted all the circumstances which give to public buildings their power of cheering and exalting the feelings. It lay behind a screen of columns, which seemed to suggest that it had been built in a fit of sulkiness, to allow the occupier to skulk away from the world. But nothing offended me more than the sooty appearance of the buildings. The whole town looked as though built of coal and cinders.[4]

If Blanco had no idea as yet of how he was to make a living in London, he was fortunate in the social connections he had made in Seville. Among them was the naturalist J. G. Children, who not long before had sent his 'ever-to-be-remembered kind friend' a set of works of Shakespeare, Gibbon and Hume. For the first month of his stay he dined daily with the Childrens and was conducted on a round of dinners, plays, concerts and exhibitions. The dinner party, especially, struck him as a baffling phenomenon, and he noted what little pleasure the English seemed to derive from their social gatherings. As he wrote later in *Letters from England*,

> There are houses of quality in which the unfortunate guest who does not console himself with the bottle has to put up with two hours of languid and tedious conversation, until about eleven o'clock at night, numbed in body and mind by the inactivity which both have had to endure for such a stretch, he stirs himself with a cup of coffee and another of tea, and if he has no cab, must wade through a sea of mud in his silk stockings and thin shoes, breathing a sigh of relief when at length he regains his lodgings.

Even worse than the dinners were the 'parties':

> During the 'season', or the period when every body is in London, your fashionables see it as their solemn duty to advertise their importance by the number of people they can assemble in their house at one time. For that is the real object of the parade at which every society hostess reviews her troops of acquaintances at least once a year. It is on the same principle, but with less expense (one person excepted) that the good citizens of Seville send out five or six hundred funeral invitations, measuring their social importance by the number of mourners who come to offer condolences to

the bereaved. . . And what do people do at these parties? Why, the same as at a funeral in Seville: they put in an appearance. The hosts stand at the door of the drawing-room and spend two or three hours shaking the hand of those who manage to reach them through the throng, 'very pleased to see you' and hoping you will go as soon as possible.

At the theatre Blanco was struck by the contrast between the refinement of the ladies in the lower seats and the 'vicious degradation' of the prostitutes in the galleries. English family life was a model of virtuous respectability, but it was difficult to reconcile this with the 'lubricious bacchanale' of London street life at night. The pace and crush of the streets were another shock, conducted as it was on the principle of *sauve qui peut*. He noted the Englishman's bullish determination to resist all encroachments on his person: 'Every Englishman, before attending a public function, must make his composition of place on the supposition that he is going to have to flatten—or, to use the technical expression—"floor" someone in the throng'.[5]

At this early stage, Blanco did not voice these thoughts. His main feeling was that of being 'a peasant at court':

> This constant intercourse with society was attended with a growing perception of that most painful deficiency—the want of power to express oneself satisfactorily in the language of the country. Accustomed in my childhood to the Irish pronunciation of English, I found at first a difficulty even in catching the words of the company. The more I gained in the knowledge of the language, the clearer was my perception of the inadequacy of my words to express my thoughts. The retired manner in which I was brought up had made me extremely sensitive to every apprehension of the ridiculous.[6]

This was the feeling which he never quite lost, even when in all outward appearances he could pass for an Englishman. The self-confidence of the English filled him with a mixture of admiration and resentment. As yet, he was only prepared to admit to the former.

At Holland House he had a mixed reception. Lord Holland received him with typical cordiality, but his wife intimated that in her view Blanco had no business to have left his country in its hour of crisis. Indeed, since his motives in leaving Spain were not entirely clear in his own mind, he had difficulty in explaining them to others. It was only later that he fashioned an image of himself as a political refugee, flying from the Inquisition to the land of freedom. He dined at Holland House for the first time on 16 March, along with Andrés de la Vega, the envoy in London of the Provincial Junta of Asturias, an Anglophile liberal who later, on his return to Cadiz, became his most trusted correspondent, and Manuel Abella of the Spanish Embassy.[7]

Perhaps it was at this meeting that the idea of *El Español* was first mooted. Blanco had arrived in London without any clear idea of how

3. Holland House in 1810.

he was going to earn his living. When on the point of leaving Spain, he
had entertained the romantic notion of playing the violin in a London
theatre, but this idea was soon abandoned in the light of reality. His
next idea was to try to obtain employment in the Foreign Office, and
to this end he called on another acquaintance he had made in Seville,
Richard Wellesley, the son of the Foreign Secretary. Wellesley did not
make the hoped-for offer but suggested that he should set up a
Spanish-language journal in London, and gave him an introduction to
a French emigré publisher. Lord Holland had first hand knowledge of
Blanco's journalistic talent, so was likely to have encouraged the
project. The original idea was that Blanco and Abella should collaborate on the journal, to be entitled *El Español*. However, the various
parties all had different interests and expectations. Abella no doubt
wanted a journal which would reflect the views of the Cadiz government (little understood in London), Lord Holland wanted a means of
disseminating his ideas for the future of Spain, and the Foreign Office
wanted a Spanish-language journal which would interpret British
policy to Spain and Spanish America. However, the Foreign Office
preferred not to be too closely associated with the venture, for fear of
provoking Spanish suspicions. Blanco was left to take the initiative

and to bear the financial responsibility. The collaboration with Abella foundered at an early stage, when it became clear that they differed fundamentally on editorial policy.[8]

Blanco was no businessman, and the contract he made with his printer, a French emigré priest named Juigné, was to involve him in a great deal of drudgery at little profit. The journal—entitled *El Español*—was to be published once a month, for which he was to receive a monthly advance of £15, though this would be forfeited if the journal made a loss. All the work of writing, editing and proof-reading fell to him alone, yet the copyright was in the hands of Juigné. Since the printers were ignorant of Spanish, the proof-reading alone was a laborious and painful task, so it is not surprising that during the four years of the *Español*'s existence, he should have complained so often of the drudgery and its effect on his health. As editor of the *Semanario Patriótico* he had cut a figure in society, but in London he was just another statusless emigré endeavouring to earn a living on the fringes of Grub Street. In Seville he had enjoyed leisure and domestic comfort, whereas in London he was thrown back on his own company in lodgings which served also as an office. Whereas in Seville there had been a readership at hand—a visible and audible readership whose reactions could be taken into account—in London he was like the castaway on a desert island who sends off his message to the outside world in a bottle. Consequently the *Español* was a monologue, albeit an eloquent, passionate and brilliantly argued monologue, unique in the history of Spanish journalism.[9]

The first number, published on 30 April 1810—less than two months after Blanco's arrival in England—contained a statement of policy by the editor, who signed himself as 'Mr White, known in Spain by the translated form of his surname, Blanco, of an Irish family settled in Seville'. This anglicisation of his name was to prove a significant factor in alienating opinion at Cadiz, since it seemed to indicate that he had abjured his Spanish nationality. The periodical was to appear once a month, and would contain political articles, news of the war in Spain and Europe, extracts from official documents and literary contributions. Besides being able to translate material (extracts from military despatches and parliamentary debates, etc) published in the official gazettes, Blanco was also given access to Foreign Office reports, particularly on American affairs, and could draw on Lord Holland's private correspondence with his highly-placed Spanish friends. The title-page carried a somewhat pessimistic quotation from the Aeneid: *At trahere, atque moras tantis licet addere rebus*. Decoded, it meant that if Napoleon could not be defeated, he might at least be delayed.

The leading article of the first number, 'Reflexiones generales sobre la revolución española', set *El Español* off to a storm of controversy.

Reviewing developments in Spain since May 1808, Blanco fiercely
criticised the Central Junta for its failure to seize its opportunities.
Both the provincial and the central juntas, he declared, had simply
reinstated the old despotism in a new guise, and in damping down the
spontaneous revolutionary ardour of the people, had extinguished the
one force which was capable of ensuring military victory. He was by
turns scornful and provocative, and his peroration was a call to arms:
'Let all be allowed to think, to speak, to write, and do not use any
other force but that of persuasion. Uproot everything that reminds
you of your former government. If the ardour of the revolution
alarms you, if your anxieties make you fear the very idea of liberty,
then know that you are doomed to everlasting slavery'.

For Blanco this was the first time in his life when he had the
opportunity to express himself with complete freedom, without
qualifications or conventional courtesies. There was no attempt to
take account of his readers' susceptibilities, to accommodate his
language or to adjust to changing circumstances. The article made
grave charges against the Central Junta, but apart from the fact that
accusations of bad faith were unlikely to bring about a change of
policy, the target had disappeared.

The article was not only provocative, therefore, it had also been
overtaken by events. The Foreign Office was alarmed by Blanco's
tone. On 12 May the Under-Secretary of State for Foreign Affairs sent
a hundred copies of the first number of the *Español* to Charles
Vaughan, the British minister at Cadiz with a nervous covering note:

> Since it has come out, we have some questions of conscience, or, if you
> will, prudence, in respect to a few passages in this number, which appear
> rather too acrimonious—and may possibly do more harm than good
> among the friends we still have [in Spain]. . . The succeeding numbers
> will be revised, and of course no very exceptional passages be allowed to
> remain.[10]

In the event, such censorship did not have to be exercised, since
Blanco, under the tactful guidance of Lord Holland, gradually became
his own moderator. However, by then the harm had been done, for
the first number alienated even Blanco's former friends and colleagues. The surprising thing is that neither Lord Holland nor his friend
John Allen seem to have anticipated the storm of protest that the article
on the Junta would arouse, even though their familiarity with the
Spanish political scene and their extensive correspondence with its
leading figures should have led them to anticipate trouble. Lord
Holland's initial reaction to the first number was enthusiastic. He
wrote to commend Blanco's 'diligence, judgment, argument and
wit', and continued: 'If you continue to write so you will have readers
everywhere, and . . . even in England the sale of your work will

increase prodigiously'.[11] Both Holland and Allen failed to appreciate that it was one thing for Blanco to criticize Spanish government policy in Cadiz, but quite another for him to do so in London under an English name. It was not so much the language of the article which was found offensive in Cadiz (it was mild compared with most of the press there) as the public criticism of Spanish policy in London at a sensitive period in Anglo-Spanish relations. The reaction from Cadiz seems to have taken Holland House by surprise. The most indignant letter came from Quintana, Blanco's friend and former protector.

On 7 May Quintana wrote to Lord Holland:

> For all the will in the world I would not wish any friend of mine to have written such an article. What does he hope to achieve with this scornful sarcasm which he uses to describe all our proceedings?. . . It is galling, and more than galling, for one who is thoroughly familiar with the course our affairs have taken and with the spirit which has informed us, to see this poisonous picture in which truth is distorted, motives misrepresented and old wives' tales of Cadiz and Seville retailed as if they were facts—all to discredit a government which no longer exists . . . I do not know if Blanco will achieve his purpose, because the general tone of his article is that of a malcontent rather than an impartial witness, but whatever result he obtains, we honest Spaniards will forever resent his imprudent publication, for the blows he so rancorously strikes at the Central Junta are not so well-aimed that they do not rebound on the nation as a whole.

At a time when Spain needed the support and understanding of public opinion in England, Blanco had represented her government as dishonourable and incompetent. 'Finally, as his countrymen and friends we will always regret that he attaches so much importance to an Irish name and origin, thereby, so to speak, disowning us'.[12]

This was a devastating rebuke from the man who had been Blanco's intimate confidant and protector. Because of the slow communications between London and Cadiz, the full force of the reaction there to the first number of the *Español* had not yet been felt when at the end of July an even more controversial article provoked another delayed, but even more violent, explosion.

In his first number Blanco had addressed himself not just to Cadiz but to the other Spain which still remained free, across the Atlantic. Since it was generally believed that Cadiz would not hold out for long, the attention of all interested parties turned to Spanish America. Both London and Cadiz feared a situation in which the American colonies, infiltrated by republican propaganda from France and the United States, would fall into the lap of Napoleon. Even before the French invasion of Spain, the ideas of the French enlightenment and the revolution were circulating in America, as in Spain, among the intelligentsia. However, colonial America in this, its final, phase remained surprisingly stable. Separatist and republican ideas were confined to a small minority of the educated Creole élite. Beyond the few urban centres, the vast native population of the interior lay like a sleeping giant, profoundly indifferent to political change. The individual provinces had better lines of communication with the mother-country than with each other and so remained politically isolated.[13]

The events of 1808–1810 in Spain—the collapse of the monarchy followed by the disintegration of the Junta Central's authority—had a profound effect in America and created a power vacuum which it was imperative to fill. The provinces of the mother-country had acted on the principle that in the absence of the monarch, sovereign power had reverted to the people, and so they had set up juntas to govern provisionally in the King's name. Why should not the provinces of America do the same? The first to take this initiative was the province of Caracas which on 19 April 1810 procalimed a provisional Junta to exercise power in the name of Ferdinand VII. It deposed the Captain-General and rejected the authority of the Cadiz Regency as illegitimate. Though this Junta contained some radical elements, which were eventually to gain the upper hand, at this stage it was a very un-revolutionary body, concerned to act according to law and precedent. Quite independently, another Junta was formed the following month in Buenos Aires. (The rebellion in Mexico in September was a different affair altogether, a violent and spontaneous rising of the native peasantry, led by the clergy, against their colonial masters.)

London had much better lines of communication with South America than Cadiz—this was to be one of the great advantages of the *Español* in gathering and disseminating news—and Blanco published his first reactions to the Caracas coup at the end of July. He welcomed it, and endorsed the right of the *caraqueños* to do what other regions of the Spanish mother country had done—namely to reclaim the sovereignty which the people normally invested in the King and which, in his absence, reverted to them by right. The *caraqueños*, he maintained, were not rebels or separatists: 'They are concerned only for their security, and to do what every region in Spain has done, namely to form a temporary government during the absence of the monarch . . . The Americans will never think of separating themselves from the Spanish Crown unless they are forced to do so by ill-advised measures'. The Regency viewed things differently. As the central government of Spain they saw themselves as having inherited the absolute power of the monarch over the Spanish empire. Blanco prophesied that unless this policy was reversed, the Americans would be driven into abandoning their moderation. In an eloquent passage he attacked the injustice and crippling effects of the Spanish monopoly on American trade, and championed the Americans' right to buy and sell freely and to their own advantage.[14]

In Cadiz, the Caracas rising was regarded as a cowardly and

ungrateful stab in the back of the mother country, at a time when she was engaged in a life and death struggle with Napoleon. The *caraqueños* were rebels against the legitimate authority. Those who called the tune at Cadiz were the merchants who had a vested interest in maintaining their monopoly of American trade. It was this 'mercantile party' which was the object of Blanco's attacks, and which, in turn, denounced him as a fomenter of sedition and as a tool of British interests. Anti-British feeling was deeply rooted in Cadiz, and the overnight transformation of the British from enemies into allies in 1808 had not changed traditional attitudes. The Cadiz traders were suspicious of British designs to move into the lucrative South American market, and they had not forgotten the episode only a few years earlier when a British expeditionary force attempted to 'free' the citizens of Montevideo and Buenos Aires from Spanish 'tyranny'. Moreover, Britain had for some years now been giving political asylum to revolutionary agitators such as General Miranda, who was using London as a base from which to prepare a Venezuelan republic. All the fine words in the *Español* about political rights for the Americans were, in their eyes, simply a cover for the advancement of British commercial interests. Moreover, the British colonial record was not so blameless that they could preach altruism to Spain. They had not given up North America without a struggle. And, nearer home, what political rights were enjoyed by the Catholic Irish?[15]

Blanco's views on the American question may have coincided with British interests, but they were his own views, independently held. In the remarkable article 'Integridad de la monarquía española', published in August 1810, he set out his vision of a Spanish commonwealth of nations, based on partnership instead of exploitation. The present crisis, he argued, offered an unique opportunity for the metropolis to ensure the future of the empire by allowing the Americans a measure of autonomy under the Spanish Crown. Together, he declared, they could 'lay the foundations of the most glorious empire the world has ever seen'.[16] Privately, he was more realistic, admitting to Lord Holland that the 'pride and ambition' of the Spanish government would very probably militate against a scheme which could only be carried through by 'moderation and forbearance'. He knew also that men like Miranda (who was soon to return home to join the revolution) and his sympathisers in Caracas would ultimately be satisfied with nothing less than complete independence. 'In praising the moderation of the Revolutionists of Caracas, I only had in view to *recommend* that virtue', he told Lord Holland. In other words, by calling them moderate he hoped to make them moderate. It was a dangerous game to play, and one which in the end earned him the vituperation of both sides. If he made the attempt it was because he anticipated, with remarkable prescience, the effects of a civil war. 'If it ever takes place among people so discordant in manners, opinions and political situation, amongst numbers who will delight in carnage and plunder, it never will be quenched but in floods of blood'.[17]

Immediately, however, the furious reaction at Cadiz was matched by the delight in Caracas. *El Español* was printed on the same press in London as Miranda's journal *El Colombiano*, and Blanco's articles were reprinted there and in the Caracas press.[18] He was made an honorary citizen of Caracas and hailed as the only Spaniard who had supported its cause. Meanwhile, even before the American crisis burst, the Regency had begun to take counter-measures. After the publication of the first number of *El Español*, the Spanish ambassador in London had denounced Blanco as a subversive. Now steps were taken to prevent the journal getting into Spain. On 18 August the Regency sent a directive to the authorities in Mexico to prevent the ciruclation there of *El Español*. It was deliberately couched in insulting language, referring simply to 'Blanco' (without the conventional honorifics), and branding him as a malignant and as Godoy's syco-phant.[19] To the insults of the Regency were now added those of the Cadiz press. In September an unsigned article in *El Observador* branded Blanco as an unnatural son of Spain, a public enemy and an outlaw. A subsequent, even more savage attack a week later was signed by his former friend and colleague, Manuel López Cepero, branding him as a 'monster' and hypocrite who was dressing up his personal rancour towards his native country under a cloak of philanthropic principle. 'The man who once composed a pompous ode to celebrate the installation of the Junta Central now, disappointed in his prophecies, runs off to London to blacken its name, transforms himself into a *man of the world* and turns his back on Spain'. 'My prevalent feeling', Blanco wrote to Lord Holland when he read the article, 'is a kind of stupefaction, considering how has it been possible that my name should be published in Cadiz with the epithets of a monster, and a corrupter of the public morals, in a town crowded with my former friends. But now I am practically convinced that I had not one among them'. For one so sensitive on points of honour and with so high an ideal of friendship, this experience was overwhelming.[20]

The Regency was so worried by the adverse publicity they were receiving from *El Español*, and by the possible effect this might have on British public opinion and policy, that they sent an envoy to London with the specific task of writing counter-propaganda. This was the poet J. B. Arriaza, a former acquaintance of Blanco from Madrid days when they both belonged to the circle of Quintana. Arriaza also had the advantage of an entrée to Holland House, though he made no headway there with his campaign. He lost no time in setting to work. In the preface to his *Poemas patrióticas*, published in London in 1810, he did not mention Blanco by name but criticised those who belittled the Spanish war effort and sowed the seeds of suspicion between the allies. The same year he published a hard-hitting pamphlet in which as a 'Spanish patriot' he directly attacked *El Español* and its editor, whom he castigated as a know-all intellectual with a facile gift for destructive criticism, a callow product of the sacrsity who lacked experience of political reality and was concerned only to release his bile and display his rhetoric. (Curiously, these were in part the charges Blanco himself was later to bring against the Cadiz liberals.) He mocked Blanco's complaints at having been libelled and betrayed by his former friends. Had he not himself libelled his own country? It was childish, Arriaza declared, to talk of friendships when national survival was at stake. He made much of Blanco's change of name, seeing it as an attempt on his part to disown or disguise his Spanish origins, and went on to denounce him as a 'quasi-Spaniard', who dared to express himself freely only where and when it was safe to do so. He even accused his adversary of being in the pay of the American *criollos*.[21] Because this onslaught was written in Spanish, it had little effect in London. It was not until the following year that Arriaza extended his campaign to the British press. But the attacks at such close range from so sharp an adversary heightened Blanco's sense of insecurity.

His unpopularity in Cadiz was further increased by the support he gave to the Duke of Alburquerque in the latter's acrimonious dispute with the Cadiz junta. At the time of the French invasion of Andalucia, Alburquerque, by rapidly marching his army across country, had undoubtedly saved Cadiz from capture, but his subsequent differences with the Cadiz junta had led eventually to his removal from the scene as ambassador extraordinary to London. There he set about vindicating his reputation, and recruited Blanco to help draft his apologia. The junta issued a riposte in which they described its author as an enemy of his country. The Duke, whose sense of honour was developed to a pitch rare even in a Spanish grandee, and whose mind was already unhinged, now fell into a paroxysm and attempted to throw himself off the balcony of the Clarendon Hotel. Two days later on 18 February 1811 he died of inflammation of the brain, aged only 37. His magnificent cortège was followed through the streets of London by the entire British cabinet and most of the Lords, and he was given a hero's funeral in Westminster Abbey. The Spanish emigré community turned out in force but Blanco, the Duke's confidant and defender, received no invitation.[22]

The Regency had already asked the embassy in London to prepare a secret report on Blanco and to see what it could do to have him silenced. In his report the ambassador took the view that Blanco was a maverick whose views were too idiosyncratic to have any lasting impact. In his opinion, the Foreign Office found it convenient to allow

El Español to continue, and to use it as a stalking horse. He had registered a protest with the Foreign Secretary, but the latter pointed out that England had a free press and that even he and his ministerial colleagues were pilloried in the press every day. Cobbett had recently been imprisoned on a charge, but continued to write articles there for his paper, which as a result was in even greater demand.[23]

It was at this time also that Blanco received a warning letter which made him fear for his life. He had taken lodgings for the summer in Bayswater—then separated from the end of Oxford Street by open fields—and to protect himself on his walk home late at night bought a brace of pistols. Years later he discovered that the warning had come from a former friend at Seville who belonged to a secret society in Cadiz and had taken advantage of inside information to put him on his guard.[24]

Blanco evidently feared that the British government might yield to pressure from Cadiz and possibly deport him, and took steps to establish his rights to British citizenship. He was also anxious to prove his editorial integrity. From the start, the Foreign Office had supported *El Español* by buying one hundred copies of each issue for distribution in Cadiz. He now wrote to the Foreign Secretary offering to forego this subscription. Lord Holland persuaded him not to go ahead with this quixotic gesture, which would have put the future of the journal at risk, and also urged him to adopt a more moderate tone:

> Though it is essential to your independence not to say anything you do *not* think in your journal, it is quite consistent with it to regulate the mode of saying what you do think to the taste and wishes of those in power. . . Your journal is doing much good, and I cannot but apprehend that were our Government to become actually hostile to it, its circulation would be diminished, if not stopped, and all that good consequently defeated. . . What you preach so well to Spain and America, I am very anxious to preach to you, viz, conciliation and forbearance.

The last point was particularly apt, but Holland's advocacy of the doctrine of reserve must have been difficult for Blanco to swallow. He had resigned from the *Semanario* on just that issue, and it was even more galling for him to have to restrain his freedom of speech in England, since he had come there precisely to escape such restrictions.[25]

Nevertheless, the influence of English moderation was already at work in Blanco's mind, as he declared to Lord Holland: 'I assure you that I have done [sic] every effort in my power to conquer my former propensity to theoretical principles of reform, in which I was rather too much imbibed to be cured entirely in the space of five months, that I have been studying and admiring the practical wisdom of the English system of politics'.[26] With the fervour of the convert, Blanco now began to preach the virtues of pragmatism and compromise.

Having persuaded Blanco to persevere, Lord Holland and John Allen began to play a more active role in *El Español*. The former suggested a number of topics which were of prior importance. On the American question, he declared that

> the distinction between the mother country and the colonies must be done away with in reality as well as words. Ready recognition of such juntas and authorities as the South Americans may appoint, and as ready acquiescence in such demands as are consistent with the connection, seem absolutely necessary in order to prevent their separation and to persuade them to acknowledge in return the supremacy of some government resident in Spain in all imperial questions of peace and war.

Next in importance was the Cortes, and here he urged Blanco to acquaint his Spanish readers with British parliamentary procedures as a model for their own. (A translated extract from Sir Samuel Romilly's treatise on House of Commons procedure was published in no. 6 of *El Español*). The Cortes, he believed, should address itself pragmatically to immediate problems—the reform of the army, the civil service and the judicial system—rather than to debating a Utopian constitution. The Cortes was a subject close to his heart, and he was particularly anxious that a bi-cameral system should be established, with an Upper House to act as a safeguard against impetuous legislation: 'I recollect the emphatic observation of Mr Fox that any government which could make a law in half an hour was despotic, whether its forms were monarchical, aristocratical or democratical'. An Upper House would also bring the aristocracy and the higher clergy into the democratic system. The recent debates at Cadiz on the rules of the Cortes had not been encouraging, however. 'I was sorry to hear the President had a bell—it is not only a French custom, but a very bad one'. He urged Blanco to 'depreciate the custom of reading speeches', as being likely to militate against genuine debate. Likewise, the practice of delivering speeches from a tribune (rather than, in British fashion, from the benches) would deprive the assembly of the 'short, unpremeditated speeches of less active and ambitious members' and result in oratorical harangues. As for the proposal to debar deputies from holding office, this was nothing less than 'absurd', and likely to perpetuate the gulf between governors and governed which had been so disastrous a feature of the old régime. 'We all expected', he declared, 'that the Cortes would serve to familiarise a large body of men with the routine of public affairs and acquaint public opinion with the character, zeal and talents of persons to whom they could entrust affairs'.[27]

Blanco was a ready and willing convert to this common sense, and Lord Holland's principles were further reinforced by reading Burke and studying the British parliamentary system. 'Notwithstanding my

former objection to the two Chambers', he wrote to Lord Holland in
October, 'I am pretty well cured of my *bona fide* Jacobinism to agree
upon the great use of this separation of the representatives of the
people, in order to avoid the evils of precipitation and surprise. I
further acknowledge the injustice done to the grandees, in not allowing them a representation in the Cortes'.[28] Under Lord Holland's
influence, Blanco also checked his more irreverent sallies at the
expense of practices such as the appointment of the Virgin Mary to
military commands.

It was already clear that the Cortes were to proceed on diametrically
opposed principles, ideological rather than pragmatic. The younger
generation of Spanish politicians was out of sympathy with the ideas
of Holland House. If they looked eventually to England for inspiration, it was to the more radical republicanism of Jeremy Bentham,
who was opposed to the two-chamber system.[29] By the end of 1811,
Blanco was referring privately to the Cortes as a mere 'tertulia', and it
was not long before his contempt became evident in *El Español*.
Increasingly he concentrated his attacks on the small and unrepresentative group of intellectuals who now dominated the Cortes—the class
of 'pettifogging lawyers', clerics and literati, their heads filled with
French political theory, to which Blanco himself had belonged but
from which he now saw himself as having been rescued. As far as such
men were concerned, he knew that his message was likely to fall on
deaf ears, so he began to address himself over their heads to the
'people' of Spain, the silent majority untainted by foreign ideology
who were the real source of resistance to Napoleon and whose
guerrilla successes had already shown up the incompetence of the
official government forces:

> Poor Spaniards! Unhappy nation! I cannot recall it without sorrow. There
> is not a better people in the whole world: more courageous, more willing,
> more stout-hearted, more trusty. . . My good friend, the health of Spain
> lies in its poor: it is the official class which is rotten, and there is no way of
> isolating the disease since it pervades the whole body.[30]

This was part of a letter published in *El Español* of April 1811, signed
Juan Sintierra: John Lackland. The pseudonym was symbolic, for
Blanco now felt himself to be a stateless exile, disowned by Spain and
an outsider in England. That same number of *El Español* contained
what purported to be a letter to the editor by Antonio Joaquín Pérez,
leader of the American delegation to the Cortes, strongly criticising
the Regency and praising the policy of *El Español*. In fact the letter was
a hoax, and Blanco was accused in Cadiz of having forged it. In a
debate on 24 May in the Cortes the epithets rained down on him from
all sides: 'an enemy of his country, worse than Napoleon himself',
'infamous', 'unnatural'. One deputy demanded that he should be

stripped of his Spanish citizenship and that representations in the strongest terms should be made to the British government to silence *El Español*. None of his former friends spoke in his defence, and some of them joined in the attack.[31]

What had enraged opinion in Cadiz above all was Juan Sintierra's castigation of the egoism and incompetence of its government, particularly in the conduct of the war. 'The Cortes are a wet blanket' he declared, 'sovereign in name, but slaves of whatever shadows confront them—the Regency, the merchants of Cadiz, the clergy and the friars'. Even more provocative was his attack on the short-sightedness of the Cortes' policy towards America, which he compared with that of Napoleon towards Spain. The Cortes were given to invoking the rights of the parent country, but 'if a father loses his reason and requires his son to sacrifice himself to his errors, and if the son has a wife and children to look after and is loth to remain in perpetual minority, what will the son do but pity the poor old man in his madness, and try to restrain his chastising arm?'[32]

Blanco should by now have been aware what kind of reaction would be aroused by such language, but his contempt for the 'philosophers' of Cadiz made him reckless of the consequences. As far as his own standing went, he had nothing to lose, but there was another, perhaps more important consequence: from now on, however penetrating his political analysis, however compelling his reasoning, *El Español* could no longer hope to influence Spanish government policy. Years later, Robert Southey wrote that 'no writer ever gave more unequivocal proofs of political sagacity than Blanco did in the *Español*'.[33] Tragically, the controversy surrounding the man obscured the good sense of his message.

His sense of isolation was mitigated by the close and lasting friendships which he formed at this time. Before leaving Spain he had read the despatches of General Sir John Moore edited by his younger brother and apologist Dr James Moore. Its strictures on the moral state of Spain and on the 'intrigues' of the Central Junta coincided with his own views, and he became an ardent admirer of the 'noble and brave victim', the hero of Corunna. Through the Hoppners he was introduced to James Moore and through him to the General's old mother, and the rest of the numerous family. Mrs Moore took a maternal interest in his welfare and comfort.[34]

A rather different new friend was Robert Southey, who was already at work on his history of the Peninsular War. Having been in his youth a supporter of the French Revolution, Southey was now an aggressively Protestant Tory who saw the war against Napoleon in terms of a Christian crusade against the infidel. This was a conviction shared by the Spanish guerrillas—which is why he took up their cause with such enthusiasm. Southey's travels in Spain before the war had

paradoxically confirmed him in his patriotism ('I have learned to
thank God I am an Englishman') while at the same time making him
an ardent Hispanophile—though his idealization of the Spanish people
was matched by an obsessive hatred for the Spanish church. The
levantamiento against the French caught his imagination because he saw
it as a genuinely spontaneous, popular movement of national self-
assertion, untainted by ideology: the Spanish, in fact, had behaved like
true Britons. He was anxious to be introduced to Blanco in order to
glean first hand information from him for his history, but was
dismayed to find him associating with the 'anti-Spanish' James
Moore: 'I confess that house is the last place in London where I should
expect to meet a Spanish patriot'.[35]

In the autumn of 1811 Southey enlisted the help of his friend Henry
Crabb Robinson to defend Blanco from a campaign against him in
The Times orchestrated from the Spanish embassy by J. B. Arriaza,
who had been sent to London by the Regency the previous year to
conduct a propaganda counter-offensive against *El Español*. At his
instigation, *The Times* published a series of articles about Blanco
translated from the Cadiz press, which Southey described as 'abominable calumnies'. Robinson used his influence with the editor, John
Walter, to halt the campaign.[36]

Southey found his new friend disappointingly despondent about
the prospects for Spain—a defect which he attributed partly to
'complection', partly to 'ill-usage' and partly to the company he kept.
He described him to Crabb Robinson as 'not so staunch a hoper as I
am. . . The best atmosphere which he breathes in this country, that of
Holland House, is not likely to steady his nerves. The little hope
which he finds there is not, like yours and mine, founded upon what is
inward and imperishable'.[37] For Southey, Holland House was the
embodiment of irreligion and Whiggery: one could not be a true
Englishman and a patriot if one was not a Tory and a member of the
Church of England. This was a conclusion which Blanco himself was
about to reach.

Chapter 6
Juan Sintierra

Quomodo cantabimus canticum Domini
In terra aliena?

—Ps. 136, 4

The England of Blanco's imagination, the England he had pictured from his reading of Gibbon and Hume and which to some extent was embodied in Lord Holland, had been the sceptical and enlightened England of the eighteenth century. He had been surprised, therefore, to find on arrival in London that among educated Englishmen, Christian belief and observance were the rule rather than the exception. The Madrid intellectual tended to regard orthodox religion with contempt, but in London it was atheism that was unfashionable. Blanco arrived in England at a time when the Evangelicals were beginning to wield a powerful influence in political and social life. Organisations such as the British and Foreign Bible Society and the Church Missionary Society were expanding rapidly, the anti-slavery campaign was moving towards a successful conclusion and Prime Ministers such as Spencer Perceval and Lord Liverpool set an example of god-fearing virtue at the highest level. If the British public still believed, against all the odds, that Napoleon could still be overcome, it was in part due to the conviction that the godly would ultimately prevail against the godless.[1]

Blanco was beginning to feel a tension between his loyalty to Lord Holland and his growing desire to identify with the more central and prevailing English tradition of Protestant Toryism. Southey embodied this tradition in the world of literature, but he also encountered it in the living context of family life. Soon after arriving in London he was introduced by the Hoppners to James Christie, who in 1803 had succeeded his father as head of the now famous firm of art dealers and auctioneers. The Christies were committed Evangelicals, and through them Blanco began to feel the attraction of the values of Protestant Christianity—a philanthropic, refined Christianity committed to the improvement of society. The example of virtuous family life presented by the Christies and the Moores could not but remind him of his

77

own family, from whom he was now cut off by the war, and when he
contrasted it with the life of 'dissipation' he had led so recently in
Madrid he felt shame and remorse. Thus the ground was prepared for
his conversion. He had already lighted upon a copy of Paley's *Natural
Theology*, and the 'feelings of piety' which this inspired had begun 'to
thaw the unnatural Frost which misery . . . had produced in a heart
not formed to be ungrateful'. It was in this state of mind that he
wandered one Sunday into St James's, Piccadilly.

> I had not for many years entered a church without feelings of irritation and
> hostility, arising from the ideas of oppressive tyranny which it called up in
> my mind; but here was nothing that could check sympathy or smother the
> reviving sentiments of natural religion which Paley had awakened. It
> happened that before the address was given, Addison's beautiful hymn:
>
> > When all thy mercies, O my God,
> >   My rising soul surveys,
> > Transported with the view, I'm lost
> >   In wonder, love and praise.
>
> At the end of the second verse, my eyes were streaming with tears, and I
> believe that from that day I never passed one [sic] without some ardent
> aspirations towards the author of my life and existence.[2]

This religious conversion had important repercussions on Blanco's
political thought, for Burke reinforced politically what Paley taught
theologically. From Burke, Blanco learned a new reverence for
tradition and for the principle of organic growth in preference to
sudden change. In *El Español* he began like Burke to invoke metaphors
of nature in his political language. In urging moderation on the
Americans, for instance, he describes liberty as 'a delicate plant': those
who seek it may have to spend many years 'cultivating the field'.

Blanco's name was now indissolubly linked with his policy on
America. America, he wrote later, 'is my proprietary interest, an
interest with which I am personally identified and because of which I
find myself persecuted, insulted and now almost outlawed'.[3] For
many in Spain who had never read a word of *El Español*, Blanco was
the fomenter of the American rebellion. His notoriety may be gauged
by the tone of a letter which the normally charitable Jovellanos sent to
Lord Holland in August 1811: 'I have not seen a copy of his journal,
but if what I hear of his speeches is true, I cannot find words strong
enough to characterize his conduct. For a stranger to fan these fires
would be an act of rashness, for a Spaniard to do so is a cruel outrage'.
He dismissed Blanco's appeal to 'principles of justice' where the
Americans were concerned as an irrelevance: 'Politics is not a science,
and therefore principles do not apply'. Like most of his fellow-
countrymen he thought that the Caracas revolution was the work of
an unrepresentative minority of urban *criollos* who used 'principles' as

a cloak for their own material self-interest and who really wanted the freedom to exploit the Indians unchecked. He foresaw the dreadful prospect of civil war—race against race, class against class, continent against continent: 'Ambition will lead to fragmentation of power, and then will raise up a second Bonaparte who will first devastate his dominions and then unite them under an iron yoke'. In his reply, Lord Holland begged Jovellanos not to judge Blanco on hearsay: *El Español* was 'full of political wisdom, prompted by a genuine patriotism, written with much good sense and eloquence, and remarkably dispassionate considering that it is written by one who has been insulted in the most disgusting manner . . . by the Cádiz press'.[4]

The circulation of *El Español* in Spain was small, being almost entirely limited to the copies which arrived in Cadiz by the British diplomatic bag, but this was more than compensated for by its success in the colonies. It was circulated in Mexico, the Caribbean, the Canaries, Buenos Aires and Caracas. Blanco built up a wide network of informants in all these places, and since these centres often had easier communications with England than with each other, *El Español* played an important linking role. For instance it was through *El Español* that news of the revolutions at Caracas and Mexico first reached Buenos Aires and that the Argentinians first learned the details of the 1812 Constitution which the Cadiz government—its author— withheld as being too dangerous for them. *El Español* helped to make the separate colonies aware of their unity and to develop a wider and specifically American consciousness.[5]

However, alarmed by what he considered the dangerous radicalism emerging at Caracas, Blanco was now urging moderation. In July 1811 he published an exchange of letters with the Secretary of Foreign Relations at Caracas in which he preached the gradualism he had learned in England: 'Spanish America has not yet served its novitiate in liberty, and to seek to achieve it at one fell swoop is to run the risk of constructing an edifice of no substance, which will fall apart at the first breath. Spanish America will have to become independent one day (I cannot say when) but if the Americans do not wish to prolong this period, they must not be precipitate'. When the *caraqueños* did proclaim full independence, *El Español* reported the event in October 1811 with the solemn warning: 'Peoples of America! Liberty is not won by savagery. Those who need to employ proscriptions and terror exhibit all the signs of the most dreadful tyranny'. Blanco did not mention Miranda by name, but he was the target of the warning.[6]

Meanwhile he urged the metropolitan government not to over-react, but to win over the silent majority of moderates in America by magnanimity and conciliation. He recommended that Britain should be asked to mediate in the dispute, but this was advice which had little chance of acceptance in Cadiz, where the British were seen as having

too much of a vested interest to qualify as impartial arbitrators. As
Blanco commented ironically, 'Some cast the English in the role of the
wicked fairy to whom every mischief is attributed, others as the
slippery customer from whom it is not safe even to take holy water'.[7]

In 1812 Blanco developed his American policy in an important
exchange with the Mexican priest-patriot Fray Servando de Mier.
Mier's stay in London between 1811 and 1816 was a relatively calm
interlude in a tempestuous career. He originally joined the Dominican
order in his native Mexico and was already a well-known preacher
when in 1797 he was chosen to deliver the annual sermon at Guadalupe
to commemorate the apparition of the Virgin in 1531. The centre of
the great national shrine at Guadalupe was the sacred relic of a cape on
which the Virgin's image was miraculously imprinted. Fray Servando
electrified his audience—which included the Viceroy and the
Archbishop—by declaring that the cape pre-dated the Spanish conquest and was in fact a relic of a far earlier evangelization of Mexico by
none other than the apostle St Thomas, who—he claimed—had
survived in Indian folk memory as the hero Quetzalcoatl. This
startling theory knocked away the foundation stone on which the
Spanish claim to a divine imperial mission rested—namely the identification of conquest with evangelization—and gave Mexican nationalism the driving force of a powerful religious myth. Not surprisingly
Mier was arrested, banished to Spain, and imprisoned by the Inquisition. In 1801 he escaped to France where he imbibed the Gallican and
Jansenist ideas of Bishop Grégoire, the leader of the constitutionalist
clergy. After further picaresque adventures, which included a second
spell in a clerical prison at Seville, escape to Rome and promotion to a
domestic prelacy by Pius VII, he joined the Spanish resistance in 1808,
spent a brief period in Cadiz and was now in London working for
Mexican independence. In particular he set himself to write the story
of the heroic but ill-fated Mexican revolution of 1810–11 led by
Miguel Hidalgo.[8]

Mier and Blanco, though temperamentally different, were of one
mind on almost all the main issues. Mier admired what he called
Blanco's 'clarity of judgment, rectitude and disinterestedness of heart,
and thorough-going combination of principle and sagacity', and he
was influenced by Blanco towards adopting the English rather than
the French constitutional model. Both were scathingly critical of the
illiberality of the Cadiz liberals who, while professing theories of
popular sovereignty and equality, denied representation in the Cortes
to anyone with an admixture of African blood (thereby disenfranchis-
ing the vast majority of the population of Spanish America, for
mestizos were disqualified as well as mulattos). For Mier, this exempli-
fied the 'arrogance of the white Caucasian'.

Where the two men differed was on the question of independence.

Blanco took the line that America was not yet ready for full political independence: it needed a long transitional period of peace and stability in which to develop its own identity and serve its political apprenticeship. Liberty was insecure unless it was supported by economic prosperity and social solidarity: when these were achieved then political independence would follow naturally and spontaneously. In other words, Spanish colonial rule had arrested the development of the Americans, who were not yet mature enough for full self-government. Like Jovellanos, Blanco now believed also that independence would serve the interests not of the majority Indian population—who did not want it—but of the urban *criollos*, the oligarchy of merchants and lawyers whose heads were full of French revolutionary theory and the Rights of Man but who were motivated at heart by economic self-interest. As in Spain, so in America, Blanco appealed to the silent majority who, he believed, wanted only a limited measure of home rule under the Spanish Monarchy, and urged them to accept British mediation in their dispute with Spain. Premature independence, he argued, could only result in anarchy, bloodshed and—eventually—military dictatorship.[9] Mier challenged this policy in two public letters to Blanco published in London between 1811 and 1812. First of all he rebutted the thesis that America was not yet 'ready' for independence. On the contrary, he asserted, America was *ahead* of Spain in political maturity: the representatives from America were among the most enlightened of the deputies in the Cortes, and the newly promulgated Venezuelan constitution, for instance, was far more pragmatic than the doctrinaire constitution of Cadiz. To counter what he evidently considered to be Blanco's rather patronising and paternalistic arguments he quoted the Spanish proverb: 'The mad man knows more about his own house than the wise man next door'. He went on, 'Have no fear, then, for America. There is no better school for developing a nation than a revolution'. Mier (who rested his case for independence on historical and legal arguments rather than on republican ideology) also challenged Blanco's contention that the independence movement was animated by Jacobin principles, and was able to back this up with the evidence of the spontaneous mass movement in Mexico led by Hidalgo. (Mexico, Blanco might have replied, was a special case.) The atrocities which the Spanish had committed in crushing this rising made it impossible now for the Americans to consider compromise; and in any case the Spanish had already made it clear that nothing would satisfy them except a restoration of absolute authority. 'It is insulting to talk to us of compromise: there is not and there cannot be a compromise with such damnable tyrants'.[10]

This much publicised exchange, which ended with expressions of mutual regard between Mier and Blanco, shows to what extent the latter was now in danger, like many would-be arbitrators, of being caught between two fires. But he had no doubt that it was the Cortes which bore the main responsibility for the coming colonial war. In spite of having failed to mount an effective campaign against the French on their own doorstep, they were now preparing to waste their energies on a punitive expedition across the Atlantic in order to impose their 'liberal' will on the Caracas rebels. Having chosen the path of violence, they must now face the consequences: 'Let the sword and the god of justice decide'.[11]

Later in 1812 when the Caracas revolution collapsed in the aftermath of a disastrous earthquake, Blanco attempted in a further letter to Mier to draw some lessons for the future. He attributed the failure of the 'revolutionists' to their addiction to the destructive principles of French political philosophy, their want of practical common sense, and their lack of grass roots support: 'To put oneself at the head of a revolution knowing nothing save some crude and undigested principles derived from the reading of a few vague and declamatory treatises on natural law and politics is as insane as to take the helm of a ship in a storm without ever having seen the sea, on the strength of having read the odd navigation manual in one's cabin'.[12]

In his *Memoria de Cartagena*, written two months after the publication of this article, Bolívar drew exactly the same conclusions and made the same criticisms of the first Venezuelan constitution. It had, he declared, been framed by 'visionaries', with the result that they had had 'philosophers instead of leaders, philanthropy instead of legislation, dialectic instead of tactics and sophists instead of soldiers'. If America was to achieve independence, he argued, it needed strong and unified leadership and an apprenticeship in practical politics.

The similarities between Blanco's second letter to Mier and Bolívar's *Memoria de Cartagena* are too strong to be a mere coincidence. Nor did the debt end here. When Bolívar made his second bid for power in 1814 Blanco, in *El Español*, did not disguise his distaste for the Liberator's dictatorial style. Nevertheless Bolívar was to refer approvingly in his *Jamaica Letter* (1815) to *El Español's* indictment of Spanish colonialism, and his political testament, the *Angostura Manifesto* (1819) adopted the central demands of *El Español* which the Spanish constitutionalists rejected, proposing Britain rather than France as a political model and advocating a second chamber to act as a guardian of individual liberties. It was by means of *El Español* that the message of Burke found its way to the mind of Bolívar.

Blanco's first published article in English—his style was described by Southey as 'wonderfully free of anything which could betray the foreigner'—was an attempt to interpret recent developments in Spanish America to the British public. It is an indication of his shift of loyalties that the article was published not in *The Edinburgh Review*, the organ of Holland House, but in the pages of its rival *The Quarterly*, with which Southey was closely identified. It contained a harsh indictment of the Spanish colonial system, applying to it Montesquieu's simile of the savage who, to pick the fruit, first cuts down the tree. However, he argued, if the men 'of jacobinical hue', 'hot-brained philosophists' like Miranda, were allowed to prevail, they might well open the door to the French. The mass of the people were loyal and moderate, 'trembling between the dread of American democracy and of Spanish revenge', and would welcome British arbitration with open arms.[13] This was, perhaps, wishful thinking.

The publication of the new Spanish constitution at Cadiz in 1812 confirmed Blanco's and Lord Holland's worst suspicions. Instead of addressing themselves pragmatically to urgent reforms, the Cortes had produced a Utopia which they now proposed to establish as sacrosanct. Blanco not only castigated the Cortes as shallow, narcissistic and doctrinaire, he attacked their competence in the direction of the war. By the middle of 1812 the tide had begun to turn, and in April *El Español* was able to announce Wellington's victory at Badajoz and the news of Ballesteros' entry into Seville. However it maintained that these victories had been achieved in spite of, not because of, Spanish military organisation. It had already made the suggestion that the Spanish army should be put under the command of English officers, and it now demanded that Wellington should be appointed commander-in-chief of the combined forces. In August 1812 it went so far as to call on the Cortes to make Wellington Regent of Spain.[14] Blanco, so susceptible himself, was insensitive to the susceptibilities of others. He did his Spanish reputation no good by simply reflecting the British view that the Spanish military command was incompetent. The fact that he was now quite out of touch with Spanish opinion is confirmed by his proposal in September 1812 that the Cortes should hand back to Britain the works of art originally belonging to Charles I which the Commonwealth had sold off to the Spanish Crown.[15]

By the middle of 1812, the measures taken by the Spanish government to prevent the circulation of *El Español* in America were taking effect, and since America was its main subscriber, the possibility of bankruptcy was becoming a reality. It was kept going only by the substantial regular subscription from the firm of Gordon and Murphy, which had interests in British trade with Spanish America. One of its partners, Blanco's friend Colonel Juan Murphy, used his influence to try to get him an appointment in the Foreign Office, but without success.

In August 1812, therefore, Blanco wrote to Andrés de la Vega in Cadiz asking him to use his good offices with Sir Henry Wellesley, the British ambassador, and Charles Vaughan, the embassy secretary, to persuade them to recommend an increase in the Foreign Office's subscription to *El Español*.[16] Vaughan was enthusiastic in his support, and on 8 September wrote to the Under-Secretary of State: 'We have long felt at Cadiz the importance of a Press that should speak of Spanish affairs as Englishmen feel about them'. He mentioned his unsuccessful attempts to bring one of the newspapers at Cadiz under English influence, and a later scheme whereby Blanco was to have been set up as editor of a British-inspired Spanish-language newspaper at Gibraltar. These schemes had fallen through, which made it all the more important that *El Español* should continue. 'Blanco', he went on, 'writes very clearly and forcibly, and himself and his friend Vega are the only two Spaniards I ever met who looked into Spanish affairs like Englishmen. . . I strenuously recommend it to you to lay an embargo upon Blanco for the Foreign Office and to keep him regularly attached to you with a good salary'. This was in line with his general recommendation that 'Great Britain must interfere more directly in all the concerns of Spain than she has hitherto chosen to do'.[17]

As a result of this appeal, the Foreign Office decided to give Blanco an annual grant of £250, to be paid out of secret funds in order to protect the recipient. This was a bitter pill for Blanco to swallow. An indirect subsidy, in the form of an increased subscription to *El Español*, would have left him his pride, but his independence was now compromised. He wrote to Robert Southey at the end of October,

> I cannot divest myself of some feelings which embitter the good which has been done me. I am paid out of the secret service money just as those who betray their country, and should this be known to my enemies, it would be a settled point with them that I would do anything for money. I would prefer a pension of one hundred pounds for past services to four times that money in this way. But this, I know, could not be done without flying in the face of the Spanish government. I must be contented, and so I am, upon my word.[18]

Blanco was never again to face the realities of this episode so directly. It became a secret concealed not only from his enemies but even, to some extent, from himself. Even before the grant was made he was undertaking reports and translations for the Foreign Office, and the archives contain about thirty documents written by him between 1811 and 1814: abstracts of the American press, translations and reports.[19] When he came to write his autobiography in 1830 he had edited out of his memory the extent of his work for the British government: 'At one time, many years ago, I received from the Foreign Office some rather laborious commissions, in the shape of translations; but this took place only once or twice'.[20] In fact, most of the work did take the form of translations or abstracts of the Spanish-American press: a passing on of information which came Blanco's way as editor of *El Español*, nearly all of it relating to developments in America. There were policy recommendations, too, in which Blanco continually urged that the British government should support what he believed to be the majority in America which wanted neither a return to viceregal government nor independent republics but self-government under the Spanish Crown. From this it is evident that it was not the nature of his work for the Foreign Office of which Blanco was ashamed—for that was perfectly innocent—but rather the secrecy of his remuneration.

The news of the liberation of Seville on 27 August 1812 meant that after nearly three years Blanco could re-establish contact with his family. From news received in London he was able to tell them that his brother Fernando was safe and well. Blanco also had to bring his parents up to date with his own history since his departure from Seville at the end of January 1810. He was at pains to reassure them about his health and financial circumstances, even though this meant disguising his difficulties. Knowing that the reopening of communications between Seville and Cadiz would lead to his family being exposed to rumours of his recent conduct, he went on,

> These are the good parts of my fortune. Of the bad, I shall say very little. The injustice with which my fellow-countrymen have treated me caused me unbearable pain at first, but they have repeated it so often and with so little cause, and I am so sure that my conduct appears in its true light to impartial witnesses that now I am impervious to their attacks. But this is a business which should not be spoken of with loved ones. The world of politics knows nothing of friendship, or love, or any kind of virtue, and those who possess such qualities cannot do better than close their ears and eyes to it, unless they are forced by necessity to enter its labyrinth.[21]

Soon afterwards Blanco received his first letter from his father, who at the end of his wife's postscript wrote some lines which must have pierced to the heart: 'My dear son, If you could have seen your poor mother when she wrote you this first message—the pen falls from my hand and my heart seems to be torn from me. That I should have to lose for ever the two treasures of my soul, you especially, who I had hoped, because of your state, would keep me company until the hour of my death!'.[22]

Most of Blanco's former university friends, having collaborated with the French, were now political and social outcasts, victims of the witch-hunt which followed the reoccupation of Andalucia. The full picture emerged from a letter which he received from Reinoso in November 1812: 'Nearly all your old friends came out for King Joseph. It could not have been otherwise. He was skilful enough to win over to his side everybody in the country who was on the side of progress, to the extent that apart from the few who found refuge in

4. The sea front at Cadiz – 'sweet Cadiz', as Byron described it, 'the first spot in creation'.

5. Interior of Seville Cathedral, during the ceremony of Corpus Christi, 1833, by David Roberts. On the left, in front of the choir screen, is the celebrated silver *custodia* by Juan de Arfe. For Blanco, the Cathedral was 'the first temple in Christendom'.

Cadiz there was hardly a man left of any merit who was not of his party'. Lista had been editor of the pro-Josephite *Gaceta de Sevilla*, and had fled with the French. Arjona—'more mad every day'—was now a prisoner. The others were all 'hiding in their corners, not daring to let out a squeak, frightened of being swept away by the whirlwind that has come out of Cadiz'. Reinoso bitterly contrasted the conduct of the French, who after their entry into Seville had declared a general amnesty, with that of the liberals who 'proclaim freedom of thought and authorise the freedom of the press under a constitution which protects the rights of the individual—and all the time there are people who have been in prison for two months without being told why'.[23] Evidently Blanco's parents were anxious that he should sever his connections with Lista, but that would have been quite foreign to his nature. His reply is revealing for the light it throws on his deepest loyalities.

> Although I abhor the French, I love the only true friends who are left to me, friends almost from the cradle, irrespective of political party. If one of them made the mistake of joining the oppressors, I believe that he must have done so on the mistaken principle that resistance would make things worse. How am I to believe that those who all their lives have been models of uprightness should suddenly turn into scoundrels?

He was indignant that the fact that he had corresponded with Lista should be exploited by malignants in Seville to embarrass his parents. In *El Español* he courageously attacked the vengeful persecution of the *afrancesados* by those who claimed to stand for liberalism and toleration. The liberals, he declared, had no monopoly of patriotism: 'There may be *Patriots* who are inspired by base motives, and *Traitors* whose "treason" is the result of very painful circumstances'.[24]

There was other news from Spain which affected Blanco even more personally. It was in September 1812, after the liberation of Madrid, that he learned that Magdalena Esquaya had given birth to a son—his son—four years earlier, and that she was in distress. He at once shouldered his responsibilities as a father. Money was sent to support the mother, and arrangements were made to bring the boy, Ferdinand, to London the following year. The emotional and religious effect of this discovery of his fatherhood can only be guessed at. Some pride there may have been, but there was also shame at not being able openly (for reasons of respectability) to acknowledge the relationship, and remorse for the 'follies' of his youth, of which Ferdinand was now to be a permanent and living reminder.[25]

Very soon after his arrival in England he had begun the painful process of spiritual self-reconstruction. The domestic and public virtues which he so admired in the Christies and Moores seemed so intimately bound up with their Christian beliefs that he longed to be a part of their religious, as well as social, fellowship, and Paley's *Natural Theology* which he read with enthusiasm appeared in the context of well-ordered England to offer him at last a justification for professing himself again a Christian. Yet on the day when he formally took that step by receiving communion in the church of St Martin-in-the-Fields, he did so almost shamefacedly, concealing the fact from all but one of his closest friends. His private journal of the time, and the later *Examination of Blanco by White* show that he was uneasily aware of mixed motives. In his anxiety as to whether he was entitled to British citizenship through his grandfather he seems to have believed that membership of the Church of England would provide him with an alternative, *de facto*, method of naturalization. By becoming an Anglican, therefore, he was becoming fully and definitively English. Though he was uneasily conscious that he had taken this step before he was intellectually and spiritually ready for it, though the unregenerate sceptic in him distrusted this surrender to religious emotions, though he even suspected his own sincerity, he hoped that inward faith would follow its outward profession: 'My faith is but weak', he wrote in his journal, 'but it is better to foster it and ask the increase of it from God, than to smother its seeds by negligence and unthoughtfulness. I verily believe in Christ; I submit my understanding to his authority, as expressed in the Gospel. I say, *adjuva increduli-tatem meam*, and I hope that my prayer will be granted'.[26] 'I propose to myself two objects in keeping this journal', Blanco had written six days earlier. 'The principal one is to improve my mind and heart by obliging myself to examine my thoughts and affections, as closely as writing them down requires; and the second (though secondary, a very important object to me) to accustom myself to think in the language of the country which I intend to make my own till death'. He had decided to become an Englishman internally as well as externally. It was not just a question of citizenship: it meant remodelling his mind. But from the very beginning of this process the worm of doubt was at work.

It was a political as much as a religious conversion. A glance at *El Español* of December 1812 shows that Blanco had reached a position diametrically opposed to his early radicalism. In an article on the Russian victories he asked why the Russians—so often regarded as spiritless slaves—should have defeated Napoleon so crushingly, when the Spanish, who prided themselves on their freedom, had failed to do so. The answer, he suggested, was that 'in Russia there is government, and in Spain there is not: in Russia there is unanimity, and in Spain it has been lacking'. Spain, he declared, had soldiers, but not an army, and one of the main reasons for this lack of *esprit de corps* was that in the absence of a monarch there was no focus of military loyalty and national unity.[27]

Aware, perhaps, of the need to account for the startling discrepancies between his past and present opinions, Blanco wrote a spirited and telling apologia in *El Español* of January 1813. It was a recantation by one who had seen the folly of his doctrinaire ways and saw no reason to apologise for changing his opinions. If he had remained in Spain, he declared, he would probably never have done so, since like all the liberals he would have been preserved from contact with political reality. He described them (and he might have included himself) sarcastically as a generation of ex-seminarists whose only knowledge of the world was derived from books. The heady effect on them of French political philosophy was 'such as *La Nouvelle Héloïse* might have had on a Capuchin novice: short of quitting the habit, he would have set fire to the monastery'. Their facile and simplistic theories were nourished on works such as the *Rights of Man* and the *Social Contract*, which offered quick and ready-made political panaceas at no personal cost, feeding the dissatisfaction and flattering the vanity of young intellectuals such as he had been himself. 'Such a man', he went on, 'believing that he has won a complete victory over the enemies of the *people*, may one day discover that he has destroyed all the supports of subordination and law, and has reduced the *society* in which he lived to a mere multitude'. Of all the liberal dogmas, the most pernicious, he maintained, was the doctrine of popular sovereignty, which in practice meant the domination of one half of the nation over the other at the expense of national solidarity. Unity, he argued, would be guaranteed far more effectively by a strong monarchy than by an unalterable constitution. Elsewhere he had argued that in making the monarch subordinate to the sovereignty of the 'people', the authors of the constitution were storing up trouble for the future, since no monarch would tolerate such humiliation for long. Only if the monarchy were restored to its proper status, and only if an upper chamber were created to provide a balanced representation of interests, would there be real liberty in Spain. The Cortes had used its powers to divide, not to reconcile, and there would be a day of reckoning.[28]

Much to Blanco's disgust, the Constitution of Cadiz had for motives of expediency re-established Catholicism as the state religion: 'The religion of the Spanish nation is and will always be the one true religion, catholic, apostolic and Roman. The nation will protect it by wise and just laws and will forbid the practice of any other'. Such legalised intolerance was not only unjust, Blanco argued, but ineffective and, in the last resort, socially corrosive, since it bred hypocrisy and resentment: force could not produce faith. When in 1813 the Cortes abolished the Inquisition, one might therefore have expected *El Español* to raise a cheer, but in fact it attacked the measure as doubly mistaken. First of all the Cortes had replaced the Inquisition by laws

restricting the free expression of religious opinions, which would
have exactly the same damaging effects, and secondly the tactically
hamfisted way in which the reform had been presented (the clergy, for
instance, being obliged to announce it from the pulpit) had unnecessa-
rily provoked the traditionalists. The principle of *suaviter in modo,
fortiter in re* was one which Blanco also applied to the question of the
religious orders. 'The war of satire and sarcasm which is being waged
in Cadiz against the Frayles can do no good whatever', he declared.
No one was more aware of the evils of the system. He had been forced
to witness young novices making vows 'to overcome passions which
they hardly knew, to suppress emotions which they had not yet
experienced and to make sacrifices of which they had almost no
conception'. On such occasions, 'in the painful agitation which took
possession of me I wished I had rather been born among the savages of
America than to have to witness the terrible anomaly which such an
institution represented in the heart of a civilized society'. However, he
went on, though in theory it would be better if such institutions did
not exist, those already in the religious life should be treated with
justice and compassion. The indiscriminate suppression of the religious orders at a stroke would achieve nothing constructive apart
from satisfying the prejudices of the anti-clericals. Instead, he recommended that the number of religious houses should be restricted.
Reduced in quantity and improved in quality they could do much
good in society, not least in the education of the poor.[29] Blanco's
proposals, though typically *dirigiste*, compare favourably with the
purely destructive policy of the *liberales*, whose provocations were
now creating a politico–religious schism destined to divide Spain for
over a century. His main case against the *liberales* rested on the charge
that their political system was too artificial and foreign a growth to
take root in a country where monarchical and religious tradition went
so deep. In the spirit of Burke and Jovellanos he argued that reforms, if
they were to be lasting, had to be grafted on to existing institutions.

As the inevitability of the allied victory became clearer, so *El
Español* devoted more time to the post-war problems which Spain
would face. These articles on social, educational and religious questions have been unjustly neglected. On education, for instance,
Blanco argued in the tradition of Forner and Jovellanos that instead of
creating prestige institutions of higher education, the government
should concentrate on basic technical education. Given the lack of
qualified teachers available for this type of school, he proposed the
adoption of the system recently popularised in England by the Bell
and Lancaster schools, whereby older pupils were employed to teach
the junior classes.[30] (The system was later taken up by Bolívar in
South America and used there with some success.)

The most deeply-felt of all these contributions, however, was concerned with the subject of clerical celibacy. The two 'Algerian Dialogues, or Conversations between a Clergyman and an Arab on the Law and Vow of Celibacy' are important not just because they deal with a question of deep personal importance to Blanco but because they are an early example of his skill in elaborate literary self-disguise and mystification. To have argued against celibacy in his own name would have been to lose the case before it was heard. (There was also the necessity of not giving pain to his parents.) Blanco's solution was to adopt the method originated by Cadalso in his *Cartas marruecas* and later imitated by Southey in his *Letters of Don Manuel Espriella*—namely to put criticism of one's own institutions into the mouth of a foreigner. Blanco characteristically covered his tracks still further by using the fiction-within-a-fiction device (familiar from Cervantes), pretending that the *Dialogues* had been sent to him from Spain by a Catholic theologian and that they were the record of conversations between this correspondent and a mysterious Arab, remarkably well-read in Catholic theology (an *alias* of Blanco himself). 'I was convinced', the narrator declares, 'that the outward dress concealed a man whose opinions, interests or misfortunes had forced him to adopt a mask'. As on other occasions, the pseudonymous disguise allowed Blanco to get away from the subjective and the self-justifying, and to argue his case more dispassionately, basing himself on theological principle. As a result, the *Dialogues* present the classic arguments against enforced clerical celibacy with passion but without the sectarian bitterness that was to mar Blanco's later religious polemic. It was the human cost of celibacy which moved him to indignation, as he thought of all those whose power for good had gone to waste because they had been compelled to lead a double life: 'Rome, Rome, what answer will you give to the Redeemer when he lays these things to your charge on the Day of Judgment? When he asks you to account for all the souls who have been driven into mischief—for the blood of his redemption which has been allowed to run to waste?'[31]

Blanco also took the opportunity in the later numbers of *El Español* to denounce the evils of the slave trade. The Spanish government was under pressure from its British allies to abolish the slave trade in its dominions, but there were powerful interests at Havana which were intent on maintaining the traffic. In 1814 he was commissioned by the African Association to undertake a translation into Spanish of Wilberforce's *Letter on the Slave Trade*. In fact he wrote a new pamphlet, drawing on the additional evidence of Mungo Park and, more importantly for his Spanish readership, on a circumstantial report relating to the Cuban slave trade made available to him by an informant in Havana. The resulting 'Bosquejo del comercio en esclavos, y reflexiones sobre este trafico, considerado moral, política y cristianamente' is one of his most eloquent and closely reasoned

works. The apologists of slavery claimed that its cargo consisted of
semi-brutes, but Blanco demanded, 'Who has tried to civilize the
Africans? Europe, which had this responsibility, has done no more
than brutalize them'. Man was by nature free, he roundly declared,
and to deprive any man of that freedom was an injustice. Moreover,
he predicted the 'terrible consequences which must one day result in
the colonies from the existence of vast numbers of degraded men and
women, resentful of the crushing injustice which condemns them to
perpetual subjection'. The sophistries of his opponents were exposed
with devastating power, but Blanco also named names—specifying
the agents used by the Havana merchants—and gave harrowing
details of the African raids and subsequent transportations.[32]

In Spain the political tide was now turning against the *liberales*. The
conservative opposition, so muted in the first Cortes, was gaining in
strength and confidence, under clerical leadership. Blanco attributed
the development to the vanity of the *liberales* and their failure to
maintain contact with the pulse of the nation:

> They seem to have been unaware of how limited was the number of those
> who thought as they did, how small the circle of the *liberales*. . . They
> imagined that the nation was ready to transfer its respect, its trust and its
> reverence from the surpliced priest to the trousered lawyer. Intoxicated by
> applause, they deluded themselves into thinking that the whole of Spain
> shared the prejudices of those who parade the calle Ancha in Cadiz, and
> that the provinces thought like the 'sovereign people' who packed the
> gallery of the Cortes. Such an illusion could not last long.[33]

Not that the new Cortes of 1814, with the balance of power shifted
to the right, impressed Blanco any better. 'To tell the truth', he wrote
to Vaughan in Madrid, 'I think worse of them than of their
predecessors—less spirit (if possible) and as great pretensions. I really
wish it were possible to have a Cortes chosen out of the peasantry of
Spain, all people of good common sense and no book-learning
knowledge, for nothing is so bad as those *demi-sçavants* who are called
literatos in Spain'.[34] In what was a disturbing development, the
liberales, finding themselves in a minority in the Cortes, were
attempting to influence events by organising street demonstrations.
'Spain is at present in the hands of the *mob*; for under this term I include
all those who seek to intimidate the authorities by disorder'.[35]

In March 1814, *El Español* appeared under a new motto: *Nunc sinite,
et placitum laeti componite foedus*—the words with which, at the end of
the Aeneid, Jupiter commanded the Trojans and the Latins to settle
their differences and to work together in creating a united people.
Blanco's warnings were not directed only towards the *liberales* but
towards the King who was now returning to Madrid. However on 4
May the King repudiated the 1812 Constitution in a decree which was

published in the last number of *El Español* the following month. In his concluding article, Blanco had little hope to offer: 'I have one overriding impression: an improvement in Spain's situation is well-nigh impossible'.[36] While again attributing a large share of the blame to the *liberales* and their insistence on making the King bind himself to preserve the Constitution unchanged, he prophesied that the reimposition of politico-religious absolutism would in time produce another violent revolution.

Taken together, Blanco's contributions to *El Español* are an astounding single-handed achievement—eloquent, prophetic and persuasive. Yet from its beginning he antagonised almost everyone who might have benefited from the good sense which he preached. As Lord Holland wrote to the Duke of Infantado,

> His [Blanco's] fate has been as the fate of all men of moderate principles is apt to be, to offend both parties and to be misrepresented by both—
>
> > In Moderation placing all his glory
> > While Tories call him Whig, and Whigs a Tory.
>
> Argüelles and Quintana no doubt think him *servil*, and the Inquisition were it re-established would very likely burn him if they could catch him. The South Americans regard him as the enemy of their rights and independence—the Spanish as the fomenter of their rebellion.[37]

Beneath Blanco's scathing ironies there lay a passionate devotion to Spain and to the Spanish people—or rather to an idealised notion of the people—but just as the scornful tone often cancelled out the moderation of the message, so his denunciations of the government often looked like a slur on the nation itself. In a sense, indeed, he was ashamed of being Spanish, in so far as Spain was associated (and Blanco's mind always worked by association) with religious oppression. One of the most frequent criticisms he levelled against the politicians was that they were more concerned with theory than with practice. As he put it, in politics the difficulty lies not in devising wings, but in making them work.[38] This was his own weakness too, since the solutions he proposed often failed to take account of circumstances. Yet, in its intuitive brilliance and its sustained persuasiveness, *El Español* at its best rises above the level of ephemeral journalism, and its political analyses have a timelessness which make them not irrelevant even today.

Chapter 7
Fides Quaerens Intellectum

To choose thy Time and Place did Fate allow,
Wise choice would be this England and this Now.
—R Southey, *The Poet's Pilgrimage to Waterloo* (1816)

The gulf which now lay between Blanco and his compatriots must have been brought home to him by the letter he received in July from the writer Frasquita Larrea, whose literary salon he had once frequented in Cadiz. After spending the first years of the war in Germany with her husband, Nicholas Böhl de Faber, she had recently returned to Cadiz, where her monarchist sympathies aroused the hostility of the *liberales*. Encouraged by the pro-monarchical tone of the *Español* she appealed to Blanco to continue: 'I cannot believe that the finest journalist of whom Spain can boast should abandon her at a time when in similar circumstances France and Louis XVIII have found their Bonald and their Chateaubriand'. She went on to declare her misplaced confidence that Ferdinand VII intended to establish a moderate government, and urged, 'Your duty is to continue to enlighten us'. Evidently Blanco had written to her of his religious problems, for she continued:

> You tell me that you have returned from the dark abyss of unbelief to that middle ground which is concerned with what *is*, rather than with what *may be*. I, on the other hand, after a period of sinful indifference, have thrown myself *à corps perdu* into that *may be* which perhaps lacks *being*. You are afraid to cross the line of truth, whereas I love that *luxe de croyance* (as Mme de Stahl calls it) which you perhaps reject. In short, on this subject you *think* where I *feel*.[1]

The letter sounds the note of religious romanticism which was now to become fashionable in post-enlightenment Europe. As far as Blanco was concerned, the appeal fell on deaf ears.

The valedictory number of *El Español* was published in May 1814. That same month Ferdinand VII re-entered his kingdom and, secure in the backing of the army and the *serviles*, repudiated the Constitution of Cadiz and restored a regime of theocratic absolutism. The cry 'Up

94

with the Inquisition!' was heard in the streets of Madrid. 'Religion', exclaimed a preacher in the cathedral of Seville, 'has triumphed over the horrendous monster of impiety'.[2]

On 23 and 24 August there was a *fiesta* at Seville to mark the re-establishment of the Inquisition, during which the cathedral was illuminated and sumptuously adorned, and a solemn Te Deum sung in the Royal Chapel of St Ferdinand.[3] One of the chaplains was missing. Four days earlier José Maria Blanco y Crespo had signed the Thirty-Nine Articles in the presence of the Bishop of London, thereby becoming a clergyman of the Church of England, the Reverend Joseph Blanco White. To convalidate his orders, he needed only to present his former titles and sign the articles. It was a decision which he had been contemplating for some time, but, he later told Southey, 'the fear that while I was involved in political disputes, one of my enemies might give a death blow to my parents by publishing in the Spanish papers what they would call my open apostasy, made me retard this step until I had retired from the sight of my countrymen'.[4] As so often, mixed and even conflicting motives were at work. Now that he had turned his back on Spain, his options of making a livelihood were limited. The Church offered the prospect of a life of study and service which would satisfy his ineradicable sense of vocation. It also offered status and security. Blanco felt about the Church of England what once he had felt about the Jesuits. 'To identify myself with some one body of men devoted to useful pursuits, and acting according to a well-directed plan, I know from recollection to have been one of my earliest wishes. . . I gave full scope to my social feeling in regard to the English clergy. My desire to identify myself with that body of men was vehement'.[5] It is as if he were being drawn irresistibly into a re-enactment of the past, ignoring the lesson of experience.

Writing about his plans to William Hamilton at the Foreign Office, he explained his decision to abandon journalism: 'There is no party in my native country which a well meaning writer may support with the least prospect of success'. He went on to ask whether he could hope to receive his government allowance for another two years while he looked for a situation in the Church. His intention was to spend the two years in Oxford 'to qualify myself for the discharge of my duties in my resumed profession of a clergyman'.[6] His motives in going to Oxford were, in fact, twofold. First he wanted to make up for his want of a classical education. To be on a par with educated Englishmen and with his fellow-clergy he must become a Greek scholar. Secondly, and more importantly, he wanted to devote himself to theological study in order to construct a rational basis for his conversion of the heart and will. Yet by taking orders before, rather than after, this period of study he was yet again anticipating its conclusion.

He was entering a theological labyrinth in which at every turn he would be confronted with a fresh quandary.

Blanco's introduction to Oxford came through Philip Shuttleworth, Lord Holland's tame cleric, tutor to his son and Fellow of New College.[7] Shuttleworth found lodgings for Blanco in Holywell, close to the college, and introduced him to a select scholarly circle which included the Hebraists Alexander Nicoll and James Parsons, the brothers John and Philip Duncan (later Keepers of the Ashmolean), and R. D. Hampden, recently elected Fellow of Oriel. Through Seville friends, the Wetherells, he was also introduced to a Dr Bishop of Holywell and his sons William (a Fellow of Oriel), Henry and Charles. This was the beginning of a friendship which lasted until the end of his life, surviving even his abandonment of the Church of England. 'If when proudest of my connection with England', he wrote, 'I was asked for a sample of the highest worth which the land can produce, I would point to the family of the Bishops, of Holywell, Oxford'.[8] It was in William Bishop's country vicarage near Reading that he was to enjoy the most tranquil and creative period of his life in England. The Bishops were middle-of-the-road churchmen, and their moderate and commonsensical approach to religion exercised a calming and reassuring influence on his mind.

However, the fact that Blanco had no attachment to a college did nothing to diminish his sense of isolation and inferiority. Like other foreign visitors he was entranced by Oxford's rural calm and impressed by the grandeur of its buildings. The quadrangle at Christ Church, he wrote to his parents, was as big as the Plaza de San Francisco at Seville. However to an outsider such as Blanco the mystery of the University remained impenetrable. He might be invited to dine at college tables—learning, like other visitors, that the conversation did not always match the quality of the port—but the inner sanctum of college life, of corporate fellowship, was closed to him. He was impressed by the tradition of classical scholarship—so lacking in Spain—but in other ways he might have concluded that Oxford was more backward than Seville. To become a Fellow of S María de Jesús he had had to submit himself, like all candidates, to an open competition, but New College in 1814 still gave preference in awarding Fellowships to 'founder's kin' and jealously guarded the privilege whereby its undergraduates could be presented for their degrees without having to submit to public University examinations. There were schoolboys in the fourth form at Winchester who could sit back in their desks in the comfortable knowledge that their Wykehamist nest was feathered for life. Other anachronisms were more picturesque. For instance, Fellows and undergraduates were still summoned to dinner by two choristers who perambulated the college chanting 'Tempus est vocandi à manger, seigneurs'.[9]

In the Oxford of 1814, high Toryism reigned. The University had only just recovered from the celebrations held earlier in the summer to mark the visit of the Prince Regent, accompanied by Wellington, Marshal Blücher, the King of Prussia and the Czar of Russia—an occasion when, to quote a contemporary account, 'in the sacred swell of enthusiasm, every bosom heaved'.[10] However, behind the facade of tradition which foreign dignitaries so admired, intellectual and social life was dull and stagnant. Blanco might have felt inferior to the Fellows of New College in his knowledge of Greek and Hebrew, but in general culture and even in knowledge of church history and the Fathers, he and his Seville contemporaries were infinitely better read. The tone of university society at the time was later recalled by one who had observed the scene with the honest eye of a child:

> Two facts struck me, young as I was, during our residence in Oxford: the ultra-Tory politics, and the stupidity and frivolity of the society. . . The Christian pastor, humble and gentle, and considerate and self-sacrificing, occupied with his duties and filled with the charity of his master, had no representative, as far as I could see, among these dealers in old wines, rich dinners, fine china and massive plate. The religion of Oxford appeared in those days to consist in honouring the King and his *ministers* and in perpetually popping in and out of chapel.[11]

Blanco had escaped from the land of Throne and Altar only to find himself in that of Church and King.

Echoes of Spain still disturbed his Oxford retreat. Early in 1814 his brother Fernando arrived in London after being liberated from detention in France. Don Guillermo and Doña Gertrudis were now old and ill and isolated. Their only surviving daughter Maria Fernanda had died in her convent the year before—news which was kept from Blanco for a full two years—and they were anxious to have Fernando back. Blanco urged them that it would be in his brother's interests to delay his return for a year while he gained commercial experience in London, and to this they reluctantly agreed. Even at a distance he was still the elder brother and family adviser, decisive in everything except his own affairs.[12]

In Spain it was now the turn of the *liberales* to suffer persecution. Some of them took refuge in France, where they joined their former victims, the *afrancesados*, but England was a politically more congenial haven. Writing from his Oxford retreat to his friend Andrés Bello, Blanco enquired ironically, 'How are the Greeks and Trojans of this world? . . . I suppose that from time to time in London you meet the cream of Spanish politics, that is to say those persecuted persecutros, the *liberales*?'[13] The studied detachment does not altogether conceal Blanco's curiosity about the world on which he had turned his back.

Bello was a man to whom Blanco could unburden himself with

complete freedom—something which was impossible with the
Oxford clergymen he was now trying so hard to emulate. The two
men spoke the same language. Bello, who as a very young man had
been Bolívar's tutor, had come to London in 1810 as a member of the
Caracas delegation, studying and writing, preparing himself for the
service of his fellow-countrymen. In fact he never saw Venezuela again.
It was from Chile that the call came in 1829, and the last thirty-
six years of his life were spent there. He founded the University of
Chile, drafted a civil code which became the model for other Spanish
American states and directed Chilean foreign policy. As well as being
a jurist and philologist, he was a philosopher and poet. The foundations for this later life of active public service were laid during the
nineteen years he spent in London, in obscurity and poverty. Blanco
was instrumental in getting a government subsidy for Bello, through
the influence of Lady Holland, and in 1816 he got him a job tutoring
the sons of William Hamilton, his former patron at the Foreign Office.
Since Bello had a wife and children to support, he would not have
survived without this help. Blanco never failed a friend, and no friend
was more deserving.[14]

It is at this period that one finds in Blanco's journals and correspondence the first mentions of that mysterious intestinal complaint
which increasingly undermined his health and lowered his spirits,
even though it seems, paradoxically, to have actively stimulated his
intellect. Blanco himself traced its origins to the strain and overwork
involved in editing *El Español*, but there may have been more profound causes at work. The tension and conflict in Blanco's inner life
were at their most intense during these years. He had ceased outwardly to be Spanish without having succeeded in becoming wholly
English; his heart had led him back to Christianity, but his intellect
remained unregenerate; his position in the Church of England was
anomalous, and he could not help feeling the contrast between his
present isolation on the outer fringes of English society and his former
status in Spain. Above all, he craved the emotional consolations and
security of marriage, but his lack of financial means and his natural
timidity meant that his affections were denied their full expression.[15]

The theological problem to which Blanco addressed himself in
Oxford was the fundamental question of inspiration. He had been
attracted to the Church of England for emotional and moral, not for
intellectual reasons. He was now a member of a Church which based
its faith upon the authority of the inspired Scriptures, but the more he
investigated, the more he was led to the conclusion that the infallibility
of the Bible was as difficult to prove as the infallibility of the Church.
Yet, as he argued later, 'the foundation of certainty must be *certain*. . .
If God had intended to dwell *miraculously* among men in a BOOK, as
in an Oracle, from which we might obtain *infallible* answers, he would

not have left that first foundation of the intended certainty, to probability and conjecture'.[16] This line of thought led to the conclusion that since in fact the Scriptures have yielded conflicting and contradictory interpretations on all questions relating to faith rather than morals, they could never have been intended by divine Providence to be an infallible source of theological truth. The Bible could only be a *moral* guide. These were conclusions which Blanco was too nervous to confide to his acquaintances at Oxford, seemingly so secure in their orthodox certainties. They were safe to admit only in the privacy of his journal.

It was at this time that Blanco first allowed himself to be persuaded to officiate in an Anglican church. Later he wrote,

> After a long struggle with myself, and encouraged by that most excellent man, my dear friend the Revd William Bishop, then Vicar of St Mary's, Oxford, I determined to read prayers in his Church on a weekday, when there were scarcely half a dozen persons in attendance. I can hardly describe the state of agitation in which I went to St Mary's. . . My dear friend Bishop, seeing me so deeply agitated, offered to relieve me: but I would not give way. My voice must have been nearly inaudible. When I returned to my lodgings, my mind, free from the agitation which had kept it so long on the stretch, took a direction entirely devotional. . . With tears and sobs I recollected the day when I performed my first Mass.

In August 1815 Blanco was contemplating the possibility of entering an Oxford college as what would now be termed a mature student. At this point Lord Holland came to the rescue by extending an unexpected invitation to return to Holland House as tutor to his son Henry. It had not been easy to find a tutor who would be a match for the sophisticated and precocious youth, who was already a man of the world. Sydney Smith was consulted on the matter and wrote of the 'sense, firmness and judgement necessary to manage such a clever and suprafine boy'. By tradition, the tutor had to be a clergyman, but an English clergyman 'would require a great deal of attention' and 'would be troublesome from the jealousy of being slighted'. On the whole he favoured a Scotsman, but: 'Will he command the respect of Henry? Will he acquire an ascendancy over him? Will he be a man of sound sense and firmness?' If Blanco lacked schoolmasterly solidity, he was a man of wide culture and endearing personality. In urging him to accept the post, Lord Holland argued that it would give him the opportunity 'to improve yourself in your profession and the habit of writing and speaking English' and that the occupation in itself would raise his spirits. Blanco pleaded unfitness for the task, but the Hollands would not take no for an answer.[17]

In spite of all his diffidence he succeeded in winning the respect and affection of Henry and his younger sister Georgina, but from the

beginning his position was anomalous. Holland House was unusual
among the seats of the aristocracy in not having a chapel, and though
Lord Holland followed convention in employing a clergyman as a
tutor, the tone of the house was one of scepticism. Lord Holland
himself was mildly benevolent in his attitude to Christianity, but John
Allen, who at Holland House combined the duties of physician,
librarian, adviser, constitutional expert, carver of the joint and keeper
of the Whig conscience, was a confessed atheist. Having known
Blanco in unregenerate days, he must have regarded his conversion
with scant sympathy. It is not surprising that Blanco felt threatened
and ill-at-ease, the sole representative of Christianity in what was
mission territory. 'My knowledge of the opinions prevailing in that
family produced a feeling of danger and alarm, lest I should be shaken
in my faith and practice'.[18]

What irked him even more was the loss of independence, and being
at the mercy of Lady Holland's whims and snubs. 'She exercised', one
of her circle wrote, 'a singular and seemingly capricious tyranny even
over guests of the highest rank and position'.[19] Holland House was the
best club in London, but there was a price to be paid for admission.
Most of the distinguished guests were ready good-humouredly to
oblige the mistress and scurry around at her bidding, but she had a

6. The Library at Holland House, 1838. Mezzotint after the painting by
C. R. Leslie. (*left to right*) Lord Holland, John Allen, Lady Holland, the
librarian W. Doggett.

devastating effect on weaker spirits. Sydney Smith floated the fancy that there were apothecaries in London who specialised in the manufacture of pills to tranquillise those who had been unnerved by the ordeal. If such apothecaries had existed, Blanco would have been a regular customer. His pride was affronted by having to run errands. During her stay in Seville, Lady Holland had taken a liking to the incense used in the Cathedral, and Blanco—much to his embarrassment—was deputed to obtain supplies through his relations. The unpredictable changes in his mistress's emotional temperature kept him in a state of agitation which even the agreeable and civilised Lord Holland could not calm. In the words of the Spanish proverb, as he put it to his brother, their angels were back to back.[20]

During his editorship of *El Español* Blanco had been given the run of the library at Holland House, with its magnificent collection of Spanish literature, and had been a frequent dinner guest. At the Holland House table he met, over the years, the most distinguished men of his time from the worlds of politics and literature: Sydney Smith, Thomas Malthus, Samuel Rogers, Thomas Moore, Ugo Foscolo, Washington Irving, Pozzo di Borgo, Lord John Russell, John Philip Kemble, General Mina.[21] But as a mere usher he no longer felt on equal terms with his fellow-guests and he was conscious of the social ambiguity of his position.

As part of the Holland House ménage, Blanco did the round of the great Whig houses. In November 1816 he was at Brighton, where Lady Holland sent him along with John Allen and another guest to entertain the aged Lady Sarah Lennox, who recorded having 'these agreeable men added to our evening tea-drinking'.[22] He also accompanied the Hollands to Woburn Abbey as the guests of Lord John Russell—a visit which furnished the material for some devastating impressions of country house life. In one of the *Letters from England* written for a Spanish American readership he contrasted the magnificence and luxury of the surroundings with the emptiness and frigidity of the social intercourse: desultory conversation at dinner followed by an exchange of banalities in the drawing room where the ladies leafed through books of engravings they had seen many times before. He could not help comparing the sarcasm of the society 'wit', who delivered his carefully rehearsed epigrams with expressionless nonchalance, with the spontaneous geniality and animation of the Sevillan *chistoso*. These gatherings were unenlivened by music, and any sign of enthusiasm was regarded as betraying a lack of breeding. 'The fundamental principle of English manners amounts to this', he concluded: 'Avoid causing or suffering inconvenience'.[23]

In the summer of 1816 he accompanied the Hollands northwards on a pilgrimage to Edinburgh, their philosophical home and the shrine of the Scottish enlightenment. They took in York, Ripon, Bolton Abbey and Lambton House on the way, putting up at the great Whig houses. From Edinburgh they made an excursion into the Trossachs to visit the philosopher Dugald Stewart. Blanco noted the bare-legged women in the country and was pleasantly surprised by the taste of whisky. More oddly, he observed: 'In the course of my journey I scarcely saw man or woman riding or walking, barefooted or shod, without an umbrella under their arm. I was going to communicate my observation to Mr Stewart when the moment before he asked me whether I had remarked the rage of the Scotch people for umbrellas. He observed that they were scarcely known in the country sixty or seventy years ago'.[24]

In spite of the tensions between himself and Lady Holland, it was she who persuaded Blanco while he was at Holland House to realise the first draft of a project he had conceived some years earlier: a series of letters which would paint a portrait of pre-revolutionary Seville. It was a subject first suggested in 1811 by Robert Southey. But Lady Holland now provided the spur, and Blanco's draft (abandoned for the moment but later to be used by him as the basis for *Letters from Spain*) is accompanied by many scrawled suggestions from her. She reminded him how she had been turned out of the Cathedral at Seville for wearing too extravagant a mantilla (even Lady Holland was no match for a Spanish beadle), and on another occasion had been reprimanded for holding Mr Allen's arm. All these details added piquancy to the narrative, even though its publication was for the moment shelved— probably due to Blanco's reluctance to publish any personal reminiscences of Seville while his father was still alive.[25]

It was at Holland House, early in 1816, that Blanco heard the news of his father's death the previous November. It was a double blow, for his mother took the opportunity also to break the news of his sister Maria Fernanda's death two years before. It was now imperative that Fernando should return from London to Seville to support and comfort his mother. In his isolation, grief and self-reproach Blanco turned increasingly to the consolations of religion, and his journals of the time reflect his painful efforts to lead a devout life. Later that year he heard from Felipa Esquaya in Madrid that her sister was dying, and sent money through Fernando to relieve her distress. Meanwhile their little son, young Ferdinand, was at a boarding-school in London. It was a long time before Blanco acknowledged his paternity, either to the boy himself or to the world at large, though his closest friends were told, and Ferdinand stayed with them in the holidays.

Overwhelmed by these personal losses and by a sense of guilt, Blanco now had to screw up his courage to disengage himself from Holland House. In January 1817 he wrote to Lady Holland to broach the subject of his going. He must, he said, establish himself in a house of his own 'where I can live with my little boy, and inspire him with an affection the want of which might produce the misery of my old age'. Evidently at this time he contemplated the idea of marriage. But the Hollands were loth to let him go and months of agitation and agonizing were to pass before Blanco, in his own words, 'broke his chains'. He could not, of course, mention to Lady Holland the part that her own personality played in his longing to be free, but in his journals Blanco complained of her 'uneven, harassing manner. . . Her behaviour has been that mixture of kind words and suppressed anger which always leaves me in doubt whether she esteems or hates me'. Nevertheless, the lengths to which the Hollands went in trying to retain Blanco's services testify to the genuine esteem and affection which they and their children felt for him. When the moment of parting eventually came in the summer of 1817, Lord Holland wrote: 'If it is any relief to you to know that you have left behind you, in Lady Holland and myself, two old friends, who have now the additional motives of gratitude to their former good wishes to you, and in your pupil Harry, a boy much improved both in learning and intelligence, and sincerely attached to you, that comfort you really have'.[26] In the years that followed, Lord Holland repeatedly tried to persuade Blanco to return to his post as tutor, and Blanco himself found the parting from his 'little friends in the nursery' a painful one. He had reached a stage of inner agitation in which any decision tore him apart, a state of mind which was exacerbated by religious scruples and relentless self-examination. It was a trait which Blanco himself was inclined to believe he had inherited from his father. As he recorded in his journal for 8 February 1817, 'My absolute unfitness for the common dealings of life is very painful to me; but no previous resolution of mine is enough to prevent the silly awkwardness that seizes me as soon as I enter on business in which I have to contend with the interest of another. My excellent father was as unfit for making a bargain as myself. Whether such dispositions are hereditary, or whether (as I believe) the early impressions produced by early example transmit themselves from father to son, is a question I will not stop to discuss. I have, however, to lament that a ridiculous delicacy for the feelings of people who have no claim to it, as being in all probability perfect strangers to the impression I am anxious to spare them, makes me a most helpless man in the daily business of life.[27]

Given what he considered to be his unfitness for the task of tutor, Blanco could not understand why the Hollands should go to such lengths to keep him while his friend Andrés Bello—'a man who certainly exceeds me in the knowledge of those branches of literature which we have both undertaken to teach, a man of perfect humour and integrity'—had just been perfunctorily dismissed from a similar post. The truth may be that he never understood his own power to inspire affection, especially in the young.[28]

Chapter 8
White versus Blanco

Defienda me Dios de my
—Spanish proverb

The period that immediately followed Blanco's departure from Holland House brought him to the verge of a complete breakdown. At the beginning of 1818 he took rooms in Pall Mall, above those of his friend James Christie. The idea of marriage, it would seem, was now abandoned. In spite of poor health he followed a régime of almost monastic severity, rising at five in order to study the Scriptures, and carrying out an arduous course of theological and devotional reading. Without an occupation and without the social distractions he had enjoyed at Holland House, he was thrown back on himself. He was tormented by remorse for his dissipated and irreligious life in Madrid, and by the thought that he might have led others to spiritual ruin. 'It is my daily prayer to God', he wrote in his private journal, 'that their blood may not be found on my hands. Can I, who have so actively taken a part with the Devil, refuse any work, shrink from any labour, that may conduce to the extension of the benefits of the Gospel?' Even if he had wanted to forget the past, it was present to him in human form. 'I have been to see little Ferdinand', he recorded in January 1818. 'How dearly I pay for the follies of my youth!'[1]

To atone for past infidelity by undertaking a missionary apostolate: this was the scheme which now began to take shape in his mind. Once again he looked towards Spanish America, now at last successfully freeing itself from Spanish domination. 1816 was the year in which Bolívar successfully began the work of liberation with his epic march up the Orinoco, and in 1817 San Martín led the army of the Andes from Argentina into Chile.

As editor of *El Español* Blanco had identified himself with the American cause and had seen himself as a political missionary, preaching the virtues of moderation and common sense. Now, he imagined, Providence was calling him to a far higher task, a task (to use his own words) of 'transcendental utility': that of liberating Spanish America from the yoke of 'superstition'. It even seemed to have a suitable site on hand for a missionary starting-point: Trinidad, an island with a Spanish-speaking population recently ceded to Britain and conveniently situated off the coast of Venezuela.

'I was suddenly struck with the thought that it might be the proper place to lay the foundations of a Spanish Protestant Church', he confided to his journal. 'I really think that there is no other Spaniard in the world who is both a Clergyman and a Protestant'. Perhaps there he could sow the seeds of a religious reformation which would spread into the newly liberated territories of Spanish America and from there even back to Spain itself?[2]

Fortunately for all concerned, this chimerical scheme, the product of Blanco's heated imagination, soon ran aground on reality. Wilberforce, when approached again, was wary and the Bishop of London suspicious. It was finally quashed by the Colonial Secretary Lord Bathurst who realised that the problems of reconciling the Spanish-speaking population of Trinidad to British rule were difficult enough politically without provoking sectarian conflict. Blanco registered his private disgust at what he saw as moral cowardice on the part of the authorities but only two years later, when the fever had cooled, was able to admit to himself that the whole scheme had been a delusion— an unconscious attempt on his part to strengthen by activity a faith which in spite of all his efforts had not converted his reason.[3]

In fact this was not the first attempt by Blanco to proselytise in America, though on the earlier occasion he took some pains to cover his tracks. In the autumn of 1817 Fray Servando de Mier, the revolutionary Dominican, returned to Mexico after an eventful absence of more than twenty years, as part of the expedition led by the former Spanish guerrilla leader General Mina. The expedition failed, Mier was captured, and his large collection of books and papers was seized by the Mexican Inquisition. His library, as the Inquisitors reported to the Viceroy, included a work entitled *Inconvenientes del celibato eclesiástico*, translated from the French and published in London in 1815 for shipment to Buenos Aires. Under interrogation Mier revealed that the translation was the work of another turbulent priest, Vicente Pazos Kanki, a Bolivian by birth and Argentinian by adoption, who lived in London from 1812 to 1816 and like Blanco had become an Anglican. However the book also carried a preface and final chapter written specially (but anonymously) by Blanco who had widened the target of criticism to include not just priestly celibacy but also the infallibility of the Church, the primacy of Rome, and the doctrine of apostolic succession. Evidently this had been too much for Mier, who, though Gallican, was a loyal Catholic. Among his papers the Inquisitors found the manuscript of an open letter to Blanco which Mier had intended to have sent to Buenos Aires for publication, in order to counter the ill-effects of the book. In the course of an able defence of

Catholic tradition Mier made some telling points. How, he asked, could Blanco criticise him, Mier, for stirring up political discord when, by publishing such inflammatory material, he was exposing America to what was far more divisive—a war of religion? In any case, he went on, Blanco showed little understanding of the Americans if he thought that they could be so easily dislodged from their attachment to their traditional religion. They would prefer even Ferdinand VII to that. As to apologetics, he predicted shrewdly that Blanco would find the infallibility of the bible no less difficult to justify rationally than the infallibility of the Church. He regretted that Blanco had not been able to resist that urge to proselytise which was characteristic of recent converts.[4]

Later Blanco was to look back on this period of morbid enthusiasm with distaste, embarrassed by the written record of his attempts to force himself into the sentiments appropriate to a converted sinner. It is painful to read in his journals for 1818 the record of a daily struggle to overcome doubt. 'The spirit of unbelief is at work within me', reads the entry for 27 January 1818: 'I have prayed to God in fervent ejaculations to preserve me from this painful state of mind, and to increase my faith'.[5] He was fighting all over again the battle of fourteen years earlier, accusing his intellect now of pride, now of cowardice. Being the man he was, he had to follow through his own relentless logic. The more he investigated, the more convinced he became not only that the central doctrines of Christian revelation—the Trinity, the Atonement, Original Sin—were *unreasonable* (in the exact sense of that word) but also that they had never, in fact, been *revealed* at all. The logic went as follows: whatever has been revealed by God as necessary for salvation must have been *clearly* revealed (for God could not hold us to account for failing to see that which is obscure); but the fact that these doctrines have been capable of quite different, indeed opposing, interpretations shows that they were not *clearly* revealed; therefore they were never 'revealed' at all. Revealed Christianity, the argument went on, could consist only of those teachings which were self-evident to and accepted by all Christians, which in practice meant the moral precepts of the gospel.

Spiritually if not intellectually, Blanco remained a fervent evangelical, as his journal shows. In November 1818 after a visit to friends in the country, he confessed to having 'entered a good deal into the sort of domestic mirth which consists in laughing at very unmeaning things. . . My behaviour has not been what pious people, of the *Evangelical* sort, would call *quite so serious* as that of the summer before. I have not, however, neglected any opportunity of enforcing religious truths in my walks and in conversation at home; as well as of showing in my attention to religious duties, the serious and Christian disposition which I strive to keep up in my heart and mind'.[6]

By the end of the year he had reached the point of crisis. On 20 December 1818 he wrote in his journal: 'I am going to write down a full examination of myself, which has occurred to me this morning to be the best means to unravel my ideas on the subject of Religion'. This was to be his most searching and painful attempt at self-understanding: *The Examination of Blanco by White concerning his religious notions.* Its form was suggested by Rousseau's dialogue, *Rousseau juge de Jean-Jacques.* This work had been prompted by Rousseau's inability to recognise himself in the monster whom his enemies called 'Jean-Jacques'. It took the form of a dialogue between a representative of the common man, who voiced the commonplace charges against 'Jean-Jacques', and Rousseau who answered them.[7] Blanco too had been unable to recognise himself in the 'monster' and 'public enemy' which his enemies in Cadiz had made him out to be. But his problem went deeper than Rousseau's because he himself was unsure of his identity. To the Spanish he was now an Englishman, to his English friends he was still Spanish. He was a clergyman without a benefice, a father who could not acknowledge his son, a missionary who doubted his own faith. The dialogue form offered the man he was, White, to interrogate the man he had been, Blanco. Ultimately the dialogue form proved too difficult to sustain and lapsed into straight autobiography but free of the self-justifacatory tone which mars the later apologias. Blanco was frank with himself, as he could never have been with the public, about his early emotional development: his hypersensitivity, the 'amorous dispositions' which kept his feelings 'in a state of constant alarm', and the vanity which was his 'strongest passion'. He was later to excise several pages in the narrative relating to the Madrid years, on the grounds that they might give 'needless pain'. It can only be supposed that he described in these pages his relationship with Magdalena Esquaya, and that the person whom he wished not to hurt was his son. When he came to deal with his precipitate conversion to the Church of England he admitted to being embarrassed by his mixed motives: 'the conduct of a truly philosophical mind would have been more circumspect'. As for explaining his state of mind of only two years before when he was agitating to become a missionary in Trinidad while doubting the Trinity, he confessed to finding himself an enigma, better unravelled by one 'more versed in the recesses of the heart'.[8]

At the same time, Blanco faced up to his unorthodoxy. Just before Christmas he wrote out a statement of belief in which he admitted to himself his inability to assent to the doctrines of the divinity of Christ, of the Atonement, and of Biblical Inspiration as dogmatically formulated, while at the same time renewing his whole-hearted commitment to the gospel: 'I most solemnly declare myself a subject of the kingdom which God has given to Christ'.[9]

This clarification had practical consequences. William Bishop, a Fellow of Oriel College, had been trying to pave the way for an honorary degree which would have allowed Blanco to take up residence at Oxford. But this would have meant subscribing to the Thirty-Nine Articles, and this he could no longer bring himself to do. Yet he shrank from revealing his unorthodoxy even to the tolerant Bishop and least of all to the very shockable Christie. He could not unburden himself to any of his English friends for fear of scandalising them or of jeopardising the place in respectable society which he had struggled so hard to achieve. The only man he could trust with his secret was Andrés Bello.

Blanco had known Bello ever since the latter's arrival in London late in 1810 as a junior member of the revolutionary delegation from Caracas. Bello had stayed on in London after his colleagues returned, and since 1812 had been living a precarious existence, trying to support a wife and children while at the same time pursuing his studies and preparing himself for the call back to America. Blanco came to his rescue by putting his own social contacts at his disposal, obtaining him a government subsidy in 1815 and rescuing him from the brink of starvation the following year by finding him a job as tutor to the sons of William Hamilton, his former Foreign Office contact.[10] (Blanco, who always shrank from asking favours for himself, was tireless in seeking help for his fellow-countrymen whatever their political affiliations, whether they were *afrancesados* like the writers Moratín, Llorente and Reinoso, Americans like Bello and Mier, or the liberals of the 1823 exodus from Spain to Somers Town. These acts of charity were always done with self-effacing tact.) Blanco greatly admired Bello's qualities of mind and heart. Both men were idealistic, scholarly, diffident, unworldly and deeply serious. Both were natural teachers, with an insatiable appetite for knowledge and a belief in the saving power of reason. Both were products of the Spanish enlightenment and as such had experienced the shock of being suddenly exposed, after an early religious and scholastic training, to the heady excitements of Voltaire and Rousseau. Bello had the greater solidity, deriving from his marriage the emotional stability which Blanco lacked.

The latter had earlier presumed his friend to be, like most of the progressive American intelligentsia, an unbeliever or at least indifferent to religion, but a chance conversation proved him wrong: 'I had done him great injustice. He is what I should call a *devout* Deist. . . His faith in God was to me a matter of deep humiliation'.[11] So it was Bello to whom Blanco entrusted the manuscript 'Facts and Inferences relating to Articles of Faith' which he shrank from showing to Bishop. Like the earlier statement of faith it is a key document because it proves that Blanco was a Unitarian at heart a full seventeen years before he became a Unitarian in name.[12]

Bello, then, repaid Blanco's friendship over the next five years by acting as a confidant. In more senses than one, he spoke the same language. To find his true voice, Blanco needed to speak his mother tongue to one whose mind was attuned to his own. With his English friends he had continually to make mental reservations or accommodations, but with Bello these were not necessary. His letters to Bello are entirely free from the strained attitudes and forced sentiments which are to be found even in the private journal he kept in English. Some of his English friends understood a part of him, but Bello came closest to understanding the whole.

Though admitting to his heterodoxy, Blanco saw no need to sever his connection with the Church of England, since he held no official position in it. In a letter to Bishop—never sent—explaining his determination to avoid further subscription to the Thirty-Nine Articles, he wrote that his inability to accept orthodoxy did not imply that he had found a satisfactory alternative:

> As to communion with the Church in which it has pleased God to call me to the hopes of salvation through his Son, I not only think that I may continue in it without hypocrisy, but am convinced that unless the most clear reasons should compel me to a separation, it is my duty not to expose my *Faith in Christ* to the obloquy which any external change would produce. Besides I do not at present know a Church which I should prefer to that of which I have subscribed myself a member.[13]

The Oxford scheme was given up, and for the time being Blanco called a truce with theology.

It was immediately after this crisis that the news of his mother's death reached him from his brother in Seville. The letter he wrote to Fernando on that occasion is a moving revelation of his human heart and Christian soul:

> The admirable system which Providence has established to lead us to eternal happiness consists chiefly in gradually detaching us from external pleasures, and bringing us by means of suffering and affliction administered by a fatherly hand and mingled with manifold consolations, to a practical realization that even our legitimate and purely mental pleasures are imperfect and incapable of making us eternally happy . . . The spirit of the Gospel and all its lessons, as well as the example of Jesus Christ, have no other object than to make us see that God is our Father, and that 'if we, being evil, know how to give good gifts unto our children, how much more shall our Father, who is in heaven, give good things to those who ask him?' How often, when reading this passage, I have thought of the love of our dear parents! Is there anything they would have refused us, had we asked for it? So, too, the divine Father from whom their love took its source will grant us in abundance what we ask, if only it is for our good.[14]

In March 1819 Blanco accepted an invitation from his friends Francis and Charlotte Carleton to come and live with them at Little

Gaddesden, Hertfordshire. His health was improved by the country air, and he began to relax in affectionate and amusing company. Charlotte Carleton's teasing letters to 'Brother Joseph' show how much she succeeded in restoring his spirits. She took him to task for his 'surly liver', and urged him to leave all his 'facts' and wander 'in the gay fields of the imagination'. It was when staying earlier with the Carletons that he had found fault with himself for excess of that 'domestic mirth which consists in laughing at very unmeaning things'. There was, fortunately, a lot of mirth to be had in Little Gaddesden, where the world of Blanco White met the world of Jane Austen. Francis Carleton was a gentleman of modest means and unlimited leisure, and the family's hope of future wealth rested with the aged Irish peer, Lord Carleton, on whom they danced attendance. No one in Little Gaddesden quite measured up to the grandeur of the Earl of Bridgwater, whose magnificent Gothic pile, Ashridge House, had only recently been completed by Sir Jeffrey Wyatville. But Blanco soon made the acquaintance of the local gentry and as a violinist was a welcome addition to musical evenings. He and Charlotte had much fun at the expense of the rector's wife, Mrs Horseman, who loomed large in Little Gaddesden. Young Miss Horseman was once taken by her mother to see a craniologist who, after examining the shape of her head, opined that she had 'the organ of unbelief'. 'I could not help laughing in my sleeve', Charlotte wrote, 'that Miss Horseman should have the same lump as Brother Joseph'. While in London she had had Ferdinand White to stay during his school holidays, but she was prevented from inviting him to Little Gaddesden by fear of gossip. Mrs Horseman, she told Blanco, 'would surely have blazoned your prowess throughout the neighbourhood, and made all eyes stare'.[15]

The previous year Blanco had told his brother that Ferdinand was growing into a fine boy, but owned sadly that his son did not feel towards him that attachment 'which ought to have arisen from an early knowledge of the relation in which he stands to me'. This would suggest that Ferdinand, now eleven, had not yet been told the truth. In 1821 he was sent to a Pestalozzian school in Switzerland but his holidays were spent in the fond care of the Christies.[16]

Blanco's retrospect of this year, written in January 1820, recorded the improvement in his health and spirits, though he was as indefatigable as ever in intellectual self-improvement. In the intervals of tutoring the son of the house, Hugh Carleton, he had read the whole of Herodotus in Greek, Aristotle's *Ethics*, Cicero *de Officiis* and most of Gibbon, had started Thucydides and was studying the principles of harmony. In addition he was still working on the Spanish prayer book and on the edition of Scio's Bible which he had undertaken in collaboration with Bello.[17]

It was at Little Gaddesden early in 1820 that he heard the news of the revolution in Spain which led to the re-establishment of a liberal government, based on the Constitution of 1812. From the beginning he was sceptical about the long-term prospects of the liberals who, he believed, had learned nothing from experience. 'The struggle seems to be for *places* rather than for liberty', he wrote to Lord Holland, contemptuously dismissing the mass of the liberals as 'people of little respectability . . . ignorant, rash and insolent'.[18] There was no question, he told Fernando, of his returning to Spain. 'Those who enquire about my return are little aware of the great gulph fixed between us . . . Generations must pass before a man branded with the *spiritual* mark of slavery which it is my misfortune to bear can dwell free from oppression and insult among his deluded countrymen'. Nevertheless the sleeping Spaniard within him was re-awoken: 'The Revolution has caused my Spanish thoughts to burst their banks, and hardly a day passes without my writing something in our beautiful though neglected language'.[19]

The fall of tyranny, he wrote in his journal, had revived in him 'feelings of nationality' and the desire to be of service to his fellow-countrymen with the only weapon at his command—his pen. 'The only way in which I could write with some effect would be to establish myself at Gibraltar, as it was at one time proposed to me by Mr Vaughan during the French war'. This being ruled out, he decided to write for a Spanish readership a description of English society 'conveying a clear and popular idea of the present state of this great Empire, with a view to exciting the emulation of the Spaniards to follow (although it must be *non passibus aequis*) the steps of this country'.[20] This series of sketches, 'the vehicle both of instruction and amusement', was to be published five years later in the periodical *Variedades* under the title 'Cartas sobre Inglaterra'.

The 'Cartas sobre Inglaterra' show to what extent Blanco had lost contact with Spanish opinion. He was describing an idealised England for the benefit of idealised Spanish readers. During his ten years of exile, Spain had moved on, and his prescriptions took no account of these changed circumstances. This emerges even more plainly from his exchange of letters at this time with Manuel Quintana. In March 1820 at Lord Holland's suggestion Blanco re-established contact with his old friend, now restored to a position of influence, in order to voice his fears for the new régime. He was, he declared, reluctant to proffer advice, 'but long residence in this great metropolis—the centre, so to speak, of the world—and intercourse with its wisest and most experienced luminaries, give me some claim to share my reflections with you without appearing vain or arrogant'. Nothing could be more fatal for the future, he declared, than for the *liberales* to seek to re-establish the 1812 Constitution. That would only divide the nation again into two irreconcilable factions. Nor should they delude themselves that

the popular reaction against the absolutist regime was inspired by any
positive attachment to liberal principles: 'The lower classes, which—
in a poor and oppressed country—are always discontented and prone
to attribute their misfortunes to the government of the day, have
raised their cry in favour of the *liberales*—the same cry that was raised a
short while since in favour of the Inquisition, the cry that will be raised
in favour of absolutism when they realise that the change of government is doing nothing to alleviate their own needs'. The *liberales*
should seek rather to reconcile the *serviles* by giving them their proper
representation in an Upper Chamber, which would serve at the same
time as a check and balance between monarch and people. This was
the old lesson learned from Lord Holland and voiced in the pages of *El
Español*, but the *liberales* were even less receptive to this lesson in 1820
than they had been ten years earlier. If they looked to England for their
political ideas, it was not to Lord Holland that they turned now but to
the far more radical Jeremy Bentham, who was opposed to an Upper
House. Quintana's reply, while personally affectionate, delicately
suggested that Blanco was out of touch: 'As a patriotic Spaniard, I am
grateful for the interest you take in your old country, and appreciate
the advice you give us . . . Frankly we do not agree on all the points
you raise, and I feel that if you were here and could examine the local
circumstances you would alter your opinion. But this in no way
diminishes the respect which we all owe to the good sense which
prompted your reflections and the noble intentions which inspired
them'.[21]

In a letter to his brother, Blanco declared that if only he could
disguise himself, nothing would give him greater satisfaction than to
return to Seville and devote himself to teaching the younger generation. Since he could not fulfil that vocation personally, he resolved to
do so by the written word. In order to instruct the Spanish in the
merits of the English judicial and political system, he began a translation of Cottu's *De l'administration de la justice criminelle en Angleterre*,
eventually published in 1824. In his preface Blanco recalled the
patriotic motives which had prompted him: 'Only one means of
serving his country remained to the author, and that was to take up his
pen and write in his native language. But weakened as he was by an
internal complaint of many years, the mere sound of that language
was enough to raise a whirlwind of thoughts which for a long time
disturbed his hard-won mental repose'.[22]

If Blanco's political advice went unheeded in Spain, it still counted
for something in Latin America. In April 1820, Andrés Bello con-
fidentially sought his reaction to a proposal from a Chilean representative in London that a constitutional monarchy should be established
there, and a candidate found from one of the European royal houses.
'It seems to me', wrote Bello, 'that no proposal is more likely to satisfy

at one and the same time the interests of the Americans themselves (who, as you know, are not republican-minded), the anti-democratic principles of the Holy Alliance, the interests of the commercial and industrial nations of Europe (which want peace) . . . and even the interests of Spain itself which now has less prospect than ever of defeating the rebels'. Blanco's reply shows that he had lost nothing of his sagacity. In principle, he was in favour of the idea: 'The only means, in my opinion, which can secure the basis of American prosperity and put an end to the frightful war which is laying it waste, is the abandonment of the republican ideas which up to now have prevailed in those countries'. However, he believed 'that a monarchy would only work if it were demanded by a popular majority, not just by a minority faction, and no European prince would be likely to accept the offer unless there was a formal constitutional charter agreed by all parties'.[23] Blanco's caution was vindicated much later by the ill-starred attempt to establish a monarch in Mexico.

The agitation produced in Blanco's mind by the revival of his Spanish loyalties was exacerbated by the growing feeling that he was a burden to the Carleton household. Charlotte Carleton tried to laugh him out of these imaginary scruples: 'Mettez votre délicatesse espagnole dans votre poche, car nous ne savons qu'en faire'. But the instinct for independence was too strong to resist, and in December he accepted an invitation from his friend William Bishop to share his country rectory at Ufton Nervet, near Reading. Since Bishop was a bachelor, Blanco felt that he would put no strain on the domestic arrangements. In December the Carletons begged him to return ('We had hoped to share our mutton chop with you for the rest of our lives', Francis wrote) but by then he had settled into the more peaceful routine of undistracted study. Ufton provided him with just that tranquillity which was needed to regenerate his creative powers. His happiest and most productive period in England was about to begin.

Chapter 9
Paradise Regained

Tus muros no los veo
Con estos ojos mios,
Ni mis manos los tocan.
Estan aquí, dentro de mí, tan claros
Que con su luz borran la sombra
Nórdica donde estoy.

(I cannot see your walls, or touch them with my hands:
They are here, within me—bathed in a light so clear
It overwhelms this northern darkness of my banishment.)
—Luis Cernuda

William Bishop, Fellow of Oriel College and Rector of Ufton Nervet, embodied all that Blanco looked for in the Church of England: benevolent, refined, commonsensical, tolerant Christianity. 'Were [such] men to be removed from amidst the rural population of England, were the labouring classes left entirely to the influence of fanatical preachers,. . . that part of the population which is at present the soundest limb of the political body would soon be degraded to the lowest stage of depravity and barbarism'.[1] As a pastor, Bishop fulfilled the civilising, elevating and socially useful role which Blanco, like the reformers of the Spanish enlightenment, saw as the proper function of religion. Whereas the *cura* in Spanish villages was, in education and manners, scarcely distinguishable from his flock, clergymen like Bishop were the leaven in the lump of English rural society. Blanco dreamed of an Andalucia planted with Ufton Nervets and William Bishops.

It was at Ufton, in February 1821, that he received an invitation from Thomas Campbell, the newly appointed editor of the *New Monthly Magazine*, to write a series of articles on Spanish life and customs. With Bishop's daily encouragement he began re-working the sketches written at Holland House some years earlier. The quiet Berkshire rectory, with its view over the churchyard to the meadows beyond, was an unlikely setting in which to evoke the colour and tumult of Spain. Rarely can emotion have been recorded in such tranquillity.

114

The success of *Letters from Spain* owes much to the elaborate literary disguise which allowed the author, in the main body of the work, to distance himself from his subject and so to avoid the self-justificatory tone which distorts so much of his autobiographical writing. Under the pseudonym 'Don Leucadio Doblado'—a Greek-Spanish pun on his own name, 'Double White'—he posed as a Spaniard, long resident in England, who on a visit to his native country records his impressions in a series of letters to English friends. Blanco retained the lingering prejudice of the Spanish intellectual that the aim of mere entertainment was unworthy of the serious man of letters, but the pseudonym allowed him to give free rein to his wit and fancy, untroubled by such scruples. Safe behind his mask, he could even allow himself to indulge a Sevillan's pride in his Cathedral: 'our Church', 'the first temple in Christendom'. The description of the *Fasti Hispalenses*—the cycle of festivals which animated the Sevillan year—and of the scenes of street and bullring, achieves brilliantly that colourful and detailed 'life-painting' which Southey had recommended to him ten years earlier as essential for capturing the attention of the English reader. The later chapters contain vivid impressions of the *ancien régime* at Madrid, and its mummified court, an eyewitness account of the events leading up to the Dos de Mayo and anecdotes which convey the anarchic savagery of the popular uprising against the French.

The best passages in *Letters from Spain* are those where Blanco's more tender emotions come to the fore, as in the passage in praise of Andalucian women. His delicacy of style is perfectly adapted to the description, for instance, of the communicative power of the fan ('An Andalucian woman might as well want her tongue as her fan'). The *Letters* are seasoned also with a wit which Blanco indulged more often in conversation than in print. There is the story, for instance, of the grave Jesuit who in his youth was once prevailed upon, in a moment of 'transient gaiety' at a family gathering in Granada, to tread a few token steps of the dance out of courtesy to the ladies. Years passed, and in due time his friends expected to see him chosen as Jesuit Provincial in Andalucia. But Rome chose an inferior man, and in answer to protests 'the General desired his secretary to return a written answer. It was conceived in these words: "It cannot be: he danced at Granada"'.[2]

As soon as it touches on the subject of 'ecclesiastical tyranny' and 'monkish superstition', however, the tone of *Letters from Spain* changes to the atrabilious. 'Laugh, my dear reader, if you will, at what you call my *monachophobia; you* may do so, who have never lived within range of any of these European *jungles*, where lurks everything that is hideous and venomous'. Blanco had come to lay all Spain's ills—social, moral and political—at the door of theocratic Catholicism, and more personally he saw himself and the friends of his youth as the victims of this 'Church system' which had frustrated their idealism, obstructed their intellectual development and blighted their natural affections. The Catholic system in Spain was 'productive of exquisite misery in the amiable and good, and of gross depravity in the unfeeling and the thoughtless'. This was the theme of the third Letter, 'A Few Facts connected with the Formation of the Intellectual and Moral Character of a Spanish Clergyman', in which Blanco presented his early life as typical. 'Mine', he declared, 'is the lot of thousands'.[3]

Here again Blanco tells his story from behind a mask, since the autobiographical narrative is attributed to a 'friend' of Don Leucadio Doblado. The disguise made the self-revelation more tolerable. It has been observed that, though the Spanish will tell their life story to the merest stranger, they are generally reluctant to commit it to the printed word—unlike the English, who say little but write all. Blanco had an innate squeamishness which made him shrink even more from baring his soul in print. If he did so, it was because he had persuaded himself that he had a duty to donate his life as a specimen, as it were, of religious pathology, for preventive purposes. 'I do not possess the cynical habits of mind which would enable me, like Rousseau, to expose my heart naked to the gaze of the world . . . and as I must overcome no small reluctance and fear of impropriety to enter upon the task of writing an account of the working of my mind and heart, I have some reason to believe that I am led to do so by a sincere desire of being useful to others'.[4] He was also motivated by the desire to justify and explain what even some of his English acquaintances regarded as his desertion of Spain.

The narrative of 'A Few Facts' contains the essential features of what was to become the official version of Blanco's autobiography. The self-criticism which marked 'The Examination of Blanco by White' is absent in this portrait of the author as victim. There are passages of almost wistful nostalgia, but cumulatively the narrative was a bitter indictment of Spanish Catholicism. As such, it offered valuable ammunition to the opponents of Catholic Emancipation in England, now gathering their forces for a last stand. Sydney Smith, the veteran campaigner for Emancipation, was quick to see this. 'I hope you have read and admired *Doblado*', he wrote to Lady Grey. 'To get a Catholic priest who would turn King's Evidence is a prodigious piece of good luck, but it may damage the Catholic question'.[5] If Blanco did not yet draw the explicit moral, that once admitted inside the walls of the British constitution, theocratic Catholicism would soon work the malignant poisons that had destroyed Spain, there were those like Southey who were only too ready to persuade him that he was marked out by providence to do so.

As on other occasions, Blanco failed to take the wise advice he gave others. In 1821 Andrés Bello suffered the loss of his wife and youngest son. It was a desolating blow, which threw him back on his remaining reserves of faith. Blanco wrote him a letter which offered no easy formulas of comfort but an honest statement of his own experience. It shows again how in writing to an intimate in his native language he could achieve a spiritual clear-sightedness and balance which deserted him in his role of apologist. He wrote,

> The firm faith which you have in a benevolent God, and the power of reason which tells us that it is our duty and to our advantage to face adversity with courage—these, it seems to me, are the most effective resources you have in your present situation. Do not give way to superstitious fears, or force your mind to examine intricate and insoluble questions. The proofs that the Christian religion did not originate in mere imposture are very strong, but nothing is more difficult than to verify its abstract doctrines. The moral lesson of the Gospel is clear, and where it admits of doubt, the experience of human society serves as its interpreter. But where shall we find an infallible rule to interpret those passages which concern what they call matters of faith? No one who reads the story of Jesus Christ and forms from it his conclusions on his character, can fail to love him, and no one who considers his practical precepts can fail to follow them, as the best rule of life. For the rest, our future destiny is in the hands of our Creator, who cannot call us to account for not understanding the unintelligible, or for rejecting explanations which make the obscure yet more obscure. I have devoted ten years of my life to the study of theology and the Scriptures. For a short time, I thought I saw light, but in the end I found myself in darkness. I am a Christian, and I endeavour to follow the path prescribed by the Gospel in all that relates to practical morality. As for mysteries, not only do I not understand them (as was to be expected), I cannot even discover which ones have in fact been revealed. What I have acquired from my painful studies is the habit of not making assertions, either for or against, and of not seeking to convert others to my ignorance. Recourse to God is the only remedy I can recommend to you. But do not involve yourself in controversy.

It was not Bello who needed this advice.[6]

With the success of *Letters from Spain* Blanco found himself suddenly a celebrity. Now he could take his place at the Holland House table in his own right as an English man of letters. An entry in Henry Fox's diary records how at one such dinner party, Sydney Smith's drollery made his old tutor 'ill from laughing'.[7] With the fame went modest financial prosperity, which helped towards Ferdinand's education in Neuchâtel. In the spring of 1821 Blanco returned to London and rented his own house in Chelsea, first in Hemus Terrace and then in Paradise Row, near the Royal Hospital and just round the corner from the Christie family. With his new-found affluence he allowed himself the extravagance of buying a Guarnerius violin. His letters to Fernando during this period are full of high spirits, mingled with longing for old friends in Seville: 'How old I am getting, and how

7. Paradise Row, from a watercolour by G. Munson. Blanco lived from 1821 to 1826 at no. 7. The row, on the north side of what is now Royal Hospital Road, Chelsea, was demolished in 1906.

8. Major Ferdinand White, CB, of the 8th (The King's) Regiment of Foot, c.1845.

lonely I feel, separated from all who are dear to me! If you have an opportunity to remember me to Pepe Arjona, please do so; and to Lista, and to Marmol, and to all, all of them'.[8]

The English reading public was avid for Spanish colour, as the success of *Letters from Spain* showed. The romantic potential of Spanish legend had been discovered even before the war by Robert Southey, but the war produced a flood of poetry on heroic Spanish themes. There were obvious parallels between the ancient, epic stand against the Moors and the more recent stand against the French. A favourite subject was the story of the patriot King Pelayo who, when Spain seemed to have been almost totally conquered, kept the flame of liberty alive in his mountain stronghold of the Asturias, from which it was to spread until all Spain was liberated. Though the politicians of Cadiz did not fit this heroic mould, the guerrilla leaders such as Mina and Torrijos could easily be seen as modern-day Pelayos. Scott in his *Vision of Don Roderick* (1811), Landor in *Count Julian* (1812) and Southey in *Roderick, the last of the Goths* (1814) all attempted variations on the same theme. Southey, as already shown, made contact with Blanco soon after his arrival in England, used him as a source for his history of the Peninsular War, and now consulted him frequently on matters of Hispanic scholarship when preparing the learned footnotes which always accompanied, and sometimes threatened to submerge, his poetry. Southey's hispanomania, mocked by *The Edinburgh Review*, was rather too excessive for Blanco's taste. Acknowledging a presentation copy of Southey's *History of the Peninsular War*, he ventured to suggest that its picture of the national character was over-idealised due to over-reliance on Spanish sources: 'You do not suspect Spaniards enough where their vanity is concerned'.[9] He was far more scathing about his fellow-countrymen than any English writer would have dared to be. This is evident in the long article on 'Spain' which he was commissioned to write for the 1823–4 Supplement to the Encyclopaedia Britannica. In this, for instance, he described the eighteenth century project to build a waterway linking the Atlantic with the Mediterranean as 'one of those gigantic plans with which the Spanish government have often amused their vanity, providing as it were in the magnitude of their enterprise a ready excuse for inactivity'.[10]

Blanco however caught the English romantic enthusiasm for mediaeval romance. He read Scott and Froissart and began to discover the old Spanish chronicles and romances, so long neglected. Like the English romantics he searched through this vivid, unaffected litera-ture for the primitive aboriginal spirit of the nation before it had been corrupted by the foreign and the artificial. He began to collect materials for a history of King John II of Aragon, and translated the fourteenth century chronicle by Ruy González de Clavijo, relating his diplomatic mission from Cadiz to Samarkand. The history was never completed, but all these pioneering studies were to bear fruit in due course.[11]

Blanco was prodigal of his time in helping other scholars: Southey, Bello, the antiquarian Francis Douce, the philologist Richard Garnett and the poet and translator J. H. Wiffen. The latter was librarian at Woburn Abbey to Lord John Russell, with whom Blanco had maintained contact through Lord and Lady Holland since their first meeting in Seville in 1809. Lord John had remained strongly hispanophile and his Spanish tragedy *Don Carlos; or, Persecution*, published in 1822, went into five editions. He had also published anonymously a poem, *The Nun of Arrouca*, on the very Blanconian theme of the evil effects of enforced chastity. Wiffen, his young librarian, was an amateur of Italian and Spanish poetry, and consulted Blanco in 1822–3 when engaged on a translation of the poems of Garcilaso de la Vega. Italianate pastorals had been Blanco's model in his youth, and although they did not accord with his changed literary tastes, he relished the opportunity to put his knowledge and critical faculties at Wiffen's disposal.[12]

Blanco was less patient with the books on Spanish travels for which there seemed to be an insatiable demand, though if plagiarism is a form of flattery he might have been flattered by the way they pillaged *Letters from Spain*. The English dilettante tended to treat as picturesque aspects of Spanish life which as an enlightened progressive he regarded as downright superstitious or degrading. For the same reason he was irritated by artists like David Roberts who treated real people and places like artistic props to be rearranged—a friar here, a beggar there—to suit the artist's fancy or to satisfy the demand of the market.[13]

Blanco's most intriguing literary production at this period was one which he never acknowledged. In fact, so thorough was he in covering his tracks and disguising its very existence that it even evaded the notice of most contemporaries. The novel *Vargas: A Tale of Spain* was published anonymously in three volumes in 1822. The only journal which appears to have reviewed it was *Blackwood's Edinburgh Magazine*, whose editor J. G. Lockhart (himself an author of some versions of Spanish ballads) significantly began his notice by praising Doblado's *Letters*:

> Whether the novel that now lies on our table be the production of the same accomplished gentleman or not, we have no means of ascertaining. Be whose it may, it is deserving of much more attention than even nowadays is commonly bestowed on work of this species. It evinces an accurate knowledge of old Spanish manners and feelings and characters; and although the author displays little skill in the construction of a fable, he

writes with a spirit that carries one through his volumes with unflagging interest. In a word, had this book appeared ten years ago, it would have produced a *sensation*.

The point Lockhart was making was that *Vargas* was unlucky to appear in the wake of a wave of imitations of Scott, since it had distinct merits of its own, the scene being laid in a 'fresh and fertile soil', the characters 'strongly drawn', and the style 'clear, nervous and muscular'.[14]

Though Blanco succeeded in strangling the book at birth, out of anxiety to disguise his authorship (for reasons which will be suggested later), the very elaborateness of the disguise betrays his hand. In his preface the 'editor' claims that the manuscript he is publishing is the work of his deceased friend Cornelius Villiers, an Englishman with a long experience of Spain. (This fiction-within-a-fiction device was made popular by Cervantes.) The work opens with an exchange of letters between Villiers and his friend Don Juan Beamonte of Seville, in which the former deplores the general ignorance of Spain prevalent among educated Englishmen (a frequent complaint of Blanco's): 'You will hardly believe that whole crowds of young English gentlemen have marched and counter-marched from the Pillars of Hercules to the Pyrenees, without gaining even a tolerable knowledge of the Spanish language and, what is worse, without being ashamed of their ignorance'. To remedy this state of affairs, Beamonte suggests to Villiers that he should give the English public the authentic story of Antonio Pérez, the minister of Philip II whose flight from the Inquisition to Zaragoza provoked the Aragonese rising of 1590. 'Thou art destined', Beamonte tells his friend, 'to be the telescope through which England shall examine the stars of Spain'.

The true story of Antonio Pérez is interwoven by Villiers with the fictional story of Bartolomé Vargas (Blanco himself, thinly disguised in doublet and hose), a young man brought up at Seville in the household of the Marques de Bohorquia, with whose daughter, Cornelia, he is in love. Originally intended for the church, he goes into exile in England and there embraces Protestantism. Recalled to Seville by the Marquis, he marries Cornelia in secret but when he is told by the Archbishop of Seville that he is really her brother, he flees to Zaragoza. There he witnesses the rescue of Antonio Pérez from the Inquisition. Then, hearing that Cornelia is also the prisoner of the Inquisition at Seville, he goes back to rescue her but the lustful Archbishop has ordered her imprisonment so that he can have his dishonourable way with her. With the assistance of some picaresque gipsies, Cornelia and the Archbishop are kidnapped and spirited out of Seville—the latter being dumped on the way in a remote village gaol where the locals take his frenzied claims to be what he is as the ravings

of a madman. Vargas (who by now has discovered himself to be, not
Cornelia's brother, but the long-lost heir to an ancient title) escapes
with Cornelia to France. The Archbishop succeeds in making his way
back to Seville, but his reappearance is embarrassing for the Inquisition which has put it about that he has been assumed into heaven, and
so decides that he must be kept in custody, lest the truth be known.
Understandably he bursts a blood vessel, and dies in torment.

There are enough sub-plots in *Vargas* to make half-a-dozen novels.
In writing it, Blanco interwove the plot and characters of the anonymous anti-clerical novel *Cornelia Bororquia*, written in Spain over
twenty years before, with the Memoirs of Antonio Pérez and other
original sources, treating the whole in the manner of Walter Scott,
with a varied and colourful cast and many changes of scenery. It is the
Archbishop who steals the show—a Gothic monster on whom the
author vents the full force of his bile. He is a 'toad-like creature', a
'loathsome spider' who tries to entrap Cornelia into his web, only to
be met with her defiant: 'Hold—pollute not the air with one word
more, thou livid mass of carrion corruption!' In the last volume the
author hardly disguises his sadistic pleasure at the prelate's discomfi-
ture as he is gagged and bound, tied to a mule, doused with a stable
syringe and then left to a madman's fate. It is as if Blanco were
concentrating on his prelatical punch-bag all the pent-up rage and
frustration of a lifetime. The lengths to which he went in dissociating
himself from the book suggest that he was embarrassed by his own
violence. He never again completed a full-length novel.[15]

In 1823 the brief three-year interval of liberal government in Spain
came to an end when a French army—the 'sons of St Louis'—crossed
the Pyrenees to restore the alliance of throne and altar. Blanco
regarded the French intervention as 'unjustifiable', but he had little
sympathy with the radicals who, in his view, had courted self-
destruction by flouting tradition and condoning anarchy. The moderate liberals—those he had attacked in *El Español*—had now been
overtaken by a more ferocious breed of *exaltados* who exercised power
through secret societies and street agitation. Their attacks on the
Church divided the nation even more deeply and succeeded only in
making the 1812 Constitution more unpopular. When the French
invaded, in April 1823, they met little resistance and much support. In
1813 there had been a massive exodus of the *afrancesados*, ten thousand
of whom had followed the retreating French army to France. Now,
with yet another swing of the political pendulum, it was the turn of the
liberales to go into exile. With most of Europe under the control of the
Holy Alliance, England was the only country which offered them
asylum.

Blanco was as generous now to the liberals as he had been earlier to
their victims, the *afrancesados*. They began to arrive in London in the

summer of 1823, most of them crowding into the tenements of Somers Town only recently vacated by French emigrés of the previous generation. On their first arrival the refugees aroused great public sympathy, and their leaders, Generals Mina and Torrijos, were given a hero's welcome of the kind later afforded to Kossuth and Garibaldi. After the nine days' wonder, however, they settled down to the life of the ghetto, trying to exist on the small pension they were granted by the British government. Politicians, army officers and clerics learned new trades as cobblers, tailors, booksellers and confectioners. Blanco's journals and accounts reveal how often he helped individuals out of his own pocket. When a fund was launched by the Lord Mayor of London for the relief of the refugees, he lent eloquent support to the appeal in a letter to *The New Times* which sought to allay any lingering prejudice which the British public might retain against the Spanish constitutional party. While not withdrawing his criticisms of the constitutionalists, Blanco contrasted their restraint, when in power, with the vindictiveness of the royalists. 'When I consider', he went on, 'this most essential difference between the two Spanish parties, it grieves me to think of the severity with which I have exposed the errors and mismanagement of the popular government; and I should find it difficult to forgive myself were it not for the consciousness that the love of Spain . . . had actuated my mind and directed my pen'.[16a]

These were the 'unfortunate Spaniards' Carlyle remembered from his early days in London: 'Daily in the cold spring air, under skies so unlike their own, you could see a group of fifty or a hundred stately, tragic figures in proud, threadbare cloaks perambulating the broad pavements of Euston Square and the regions about St Pancras New Church. They spoke little or no English; knew nobody, could employ themselves on nothing in this new scene. Old, steel-grey heads, most of them; the shaggy, thick, blue-black hair of others struck you; their brown complexion, dusky look of suppressed fire, in general their tragic condition, as of caged Numidian lions'. Many of them were Basques, and the tree round which they congregated in Somers Town was re-christened the 'tree of Guernica'.[16b]

In spite of his contacts with individuals, Blanco stood aloof from the exiled politicians, the older generation of whom still remembered him as Juan Sintierra, the scourge of the *liberales*. The exiles had their own journal, *Ocios de Emigrados Españoles*, which published a revealing series of impressions of English life as seen from Somers Town. They are written in the same tone of mingled admiration and resentment which marks Blanco's *Letters from England*, and the objects of wonder are the same: the fog, the cold, the dreariness of English Sundays, gaslighting, billboard men, the 'lubricious bacchanale' of London by night, the shocking habit of burying the dead in the middle of the city, corsets (which 'over-emphasise features which are wont to provoke violent sensations'), and the salaciousness of the popular press.[17]

In two unsigned articles for *The Quarterly Review*, Blanco showed that he had not lost his ability to offend Spanish susceptibilities. He reviewed two novels written in English by Valentin Llanos, the husband of Fanny Keats, which he castigated as crude, tendentious caricatures. The first, *Don Esteban*, he described as marked by a tone of 'vaingloriousness'—a fault to which the Spanish seemed to be more given 'in these their days of national wretchedness than even at the period of their dazzling and transient glory . . . Never were the metaphysics of vanity, the abstracting powers of pride, carried to such lengths as in Spain. It is this national faculty of flying off from reality to imagination, of forgetting what they are, and glorying in what they have been and ought to be, that makes the Spaniards such a peculiar people'. Other references to Spain as a 'retrograde nation', and to its language as ossified and inflexible, offended his fellow-emigrés. In his review of the second novel, *Sandoval*, he poured scorn on Llanos' crude anti-clericalism, his 'atrocious libels' on the King and his 'glowing descriptions' of Spanish freemasonry. Llanos had titillated his English readers with Inquisition scenes, complete with thumbs-crews, racks and the rest of the apparatus of Gothic horror, and in protesting against the historical distortion, Blanco—the author of *Vargas*—found himself defending the (contemporary) Inquisition against charges of 'wanton cruelty'. The review as a whole presents the astounding spectacle of Blanco championing the despotic and discredited Ferdinand VII and even excusing French intervention in Spain on the grounds that it was the only means of saving the Spanish from themselves. This was too much for the liberal exile Antonio Alcalá Galiano, who in *The Westminster Review*, without mentioning Blanco by name, rejected his 'absurd reasoning' in arguing that the Spanish 'must be kept in bondage until they acquire those capabilities of which the same bondage is said to deprive them'. Blanco laid the blame for Spain's troubles at the door of the constitutionalists, but Alcalá Galiano argued that the excesses of this party were the effect of the national malaise, not its cause. The truth is that Blanco had despaired of Spain, which he now saw as doomed to lurch for ever between the extremes of sans-culottes and sycophants.[18]

All his hopes were now pinned on America and on the possibility of nurturing there a new Spain which would redress the balance of the old. The liberation movement in America was now irreversible. In 1822 the forces of Bolívar and San Martin converged; in the following year Bolívar took over in Peru and prepared the way for the final offensive in South America. Mexico, which had been slower to declare its independence, broke away in 1822 under Agustin Itúrbide who reigned briefly and grandiosely as 'Emperor' until he was replaced by a republican regime the following year. New national boundaries were beginning to take shape and new constitutions were being framed. Blanco had long since come to accept that nothing less than full political independence for America was now possible, and he saw these developments as a unique opportunity to realise his old dream of serving America. In the days of *El Español* he had once written to Lord Holland of his vision of a time 'when the Arts, Sciences and Happiness which are about to be banished from Europe will take shelter in the Spanish colonies of America and there thrive to the most glorious state of prosperity'.[19] This wildly utopian dream now seemed a possibility.

The British government had so far been reluctant to recognise the American republics, but British merchants and financiers were eager to move into this vast new market released from the Spanish monopoly. Among them was Rudolph Ackermann, the publishing entrepreneur whose colour-plate books, illustrated magazines and topographical prints had by the mid-1820s become part of the English national furniture. In 1822 it was he who printed the bond certificates for the first of the major south American government loans raised on the London money market, and he himself invested heavily in the mining companies and land settlement schemes of what looked like a new Eldorado. He also realised the publishing opportunities opening up in territories where the suppression of censorship had stimulated demand for education and the printed word. Years earlier, in *El Español*, Blanco had urged the Spanish government after the war of independence to lay the foundations of economic prosperity by promoting elementary education in literacy, numeracy and practical skills, and he had the idea of editing a series of elementary school manuals which could be used for the purpose. Now a chance meeting with Ackermann was to make this project a reality. If the idea was Blanco's, it was Ackermann who put it into action. Between 1823 and 1829 he published nearly a hundred Spanish titles in London, to be distributed through outlets in Caracas, Bogotá, Lima, Mexico and Buenos Aires, and these included about thirty elementary 'catechisms' on everything from agriculture to moral education. Many of these publications were adapted by the new republics as official textbooks. One happy side-effect of the scheme was that it provided employment for the Spanish *literatos* of Somers Town. The poet José Joaquín de Mora, for instance, was the improbable author (under a safe pseudonym) of a handbook on 'gymnastics for the fair sex'. Collectively, these publications had a formative influence on the intellectual and moral development of the generations who grew to maturity in the first decades of independence, and in that sense the project came close to realising Blanco's dream.[20]

His own direct contribution to the scheme of educating America

was as editor of a quarterly journal, *Variedades*, published by Ackermann in London for distribution in America. From the beginning
there was a certain discrepancy between the publisher and his editor as
to the tone the journal should adopt. In Blanco's words, Ackermann
'wished to get up a periodical somewhat in the style of *The Ladies'
Magazine*. He had a great number of plates of Glens, Cascades, Villas,
public buildings and fine ladies which, by the change of the lettering
into Spanish, would answer wonderfully well in the New World.
They were to form part of every number, and the idea of degrading
myself into a literary *Gallantee-show* man revolted me'. His own idea
on the other hand, as he told Bello, was to produce something which
would be 'useful to the Americans, giving them ideas which will
stimulate their curiosity and make them read and think'. In other
words he saw himself not as an entertainer but as an intellectual
missionary, and he appealed to Bello for advice on how he could 'do
most good for America'. After the publication of the first number in
January 1823 there was a temporary crisis when he felt it incumbent on
his literary dignity to resign, but at the end of the year he was
persuaded to return after insisting that the fashion plates should be
banished to the back pages where he could ignore their existence.[21]

In his prospectus the editor declared: 'In this miscellany, everything
that can tend to excite party spirit will be carefully avoided in order
that it may be equally adapted to the circulation in Old Spain and in her
American colonies'.[22] This was written before the restoration in Spain
of an absolutist regime which reimposed censorship, but in any case
America was the principal market.

The life of *Variedades* (1823–5) coincided with a crucial epoch in the
history of Spanish America and its relations with England. In 1824 the
battle of Ayacucho marked the end of Spanish colonial power in the
sub-continent, and in 1825 Canning formally recognised the newly
independent states. Though *Variedades* carried biographical notices of
the liberators and reported the major events just mentioned, it was
primarily concerned with literature and ideas. Nevertheless there was
a political dimension to its literary criticism. Blanco believed that
there would be no political stability in America unless there were an
educated, discriminating, enlightened middle class to lead public
opinion. The free exchange of ideas, he maintained, was the indispensable precondition of political reform, and no amount of constitution-
making would serve any purpose if—as he put it—the mind was still in
chains. The Constitution of 1812 had failed in Spain because it had
attempted to impose democracy on the country without first tilling
the cultural soil. This was the mistake from which Blanco wanted to
save America.

Variedades was true to its name. Its contents included extracts from
old Spanish chronicles and romances, translated specimens of Scott

and Shakespeare, articles on Spanish and English history, tales of travel and the supernatural, sketches of English social life and brilliant appraisals of neglected classics such as *La Celestina* and *El Conde Lucanor*. The second number contained a key article on Spanish intellectual history in which Blanco's political, literary and theological ideas came together. He argued that the so-called Golden Age of Spanish literature in fact marked the beginning of its decadence, resulting from the imposition of a monolithic, intolerant theocracy which suppressed intellectual and imaginative freedom. Spontaneity, originality and simplicity had given way to formality, imitation and mannerism. Spanish writers, as he observed earlier in his review of *Don Esteban*, had become accustomed 'always to act by rule and precedent', to accept French and Italian canons of taste, to be nervous of taking risks. Though a great admirer of Cervantes, he was to argue that *Don Quixote*, by its ridicule, had had the unfortunate effect of making Spanish writers wary of indulging their fantasy: 'The Spaniards of the seventeenth century lost their gift for what could be called the noble and generous *quixotism* of the earlier time'. But Blanco's romanticism was not merely backward-looking. He advocated a return to pre-Golden Age literature as a source of renewal for the future, because it involved a rediscovery of spiritual identity, and native genius, stripping away the artificial and formal to find the natural and the spontaneous. But any attempt to discover the native genius of Spain must, he urged, take as much account of its Arabic as of its Christian heritage. Here again politics and literature came together. He argued that Spain had begun to lose its intellectual vitality when under Philip II it became intolerant and exclusive, narrowly equating Spanishness with Catholicism. Imagination and thought could only work in conditions of political and religious freedom—which was why poetry was alive in contemporary England and dead in Spain.[23]

Though the editor himself characteristically regarded *Variedades* as something of a diversion from his serious mission, it was in fact his most successful attempt to break out of the strait-jacket of rationalism which inhibited his creative powers. He found it difficult to put pen to paper without asking himself the question 'Is this true?', or 'Will it do good?', but in *Variedades* he worked out a new aesthetic based on the idea of figurative, rather than literal, truth. The magazine included a number of tales of the supernatural, including the story of the Dean of Santiago from *El Conde Lucanor*. In his introduction Blanco defended the imagination against the 'philosophers' who would reduce art to mere literal imitation of life. 'The artist', he declared, 'addresses our feelings, not our intellect, and the representation he aims at is moral, not material'. In place of the gods and heroes of Greek mythology which neo-classical art and poetry had used as a paradigm but whose power to move the emotions had now been exhausted, he commended the European heritage of folklore, fantasy and romance, which opened a fresh new world of the imagination, not as a means of escape from reality but as a coded, emotionally heightened re-presentation of it.[24]

Blanco himself wrote a story in which he put this new aesthetic into practice. In 'The Alcazar of Seville', published in both the Spanish and English versions of Ackermann's popular Christmas album, *Forget-Me-Not*, he succeeded memorably in transmuting his experience into an imaginative fiction, thereby escaping from the tyranny of autobiographical 'fact'. It begins with a memorable evocation of the cool, fragrant gardens of the Alcazar, in the heart of Seville, where he pictures his youthful self dreaming away the afternoons in a silence broken only by the play of the fountains and the clipping of the gardeners' shears. The other habitué of the gardens is an ancient nobleman, who falls to telling stories of the Alcazar's past. The 'Tale of the Green Taper' relates how Fatima, the daughter of a *morisco* expelled from Spain at the end of the seventeenth century, secretly returns to Seville with her own daughter to recover the treasure buried beneath their former home. At midnight, as the Cathedral bell echoes through the empty streets, they return to their ancestral house and approach the vault with a lighted taper; it opens magically, and the daughter descends the steps with a basket while her mother mounts guard above. At the last moment the taper flickers and is extinguished, the spell is broken and the vault closes on the girl below. Fatima is left alone, listening to the faint and desperate cry below: 'Mother! Dear Mother! Leave me not in the dark!' Here, in this imagined world Blanco's deepest emotions found expression. The oriental atmosphere, the element of magic and the supernatural, the romantic vision of the past, are all managed with delicate sureness of touch. In the secret garden of the Alcazar he discovered a lost identity, and the cry which ends the story is the voice of his own buried self.

Vicente Llorens has suggested that the composition of this story may have been inspired by Blanco's meeting in London with the musician and singer Manuel García—the Manolito with whom he had played the violin as a boy in the orchestra of the Seville Oratory, and who was now, with his two daughters, taking the London musical world by storm. The emotional reunion, in such different circumstances, awakened precious but disturbing memories.[25]

As the year 1824 drew to a close, superficially Blanco appeared at last to have reached harbour. He enjoyed celebrity as an English writer, and the editorship of *Variedades* had given him financial security, creative fulfilment and above all the chance to be useful, if not to Spain, then at least to Spanish America. Even in theology he seemed to be freeing himself from the iron grip of rationalism: 'I am deeply convinced', he wrote to Bello in October 1824, 'that although the reason is preparatory to assent in religious matters, it is not the direct cause of religious conviction. The truly religious man is one who opens his heart, ready to welcome Truth wherever and however he finds it, with the help of his Creator. Such a man will surely, sooner or later, reap the reward of this humble hope . . . in that mysterious operation which we call *Christian faith*'.[26]

Yet all was not well. In 1814 he had turned his back on Spain, with the intention of beginning a new life as an English clergyman. Though that had not gone according to plan, *Letters from Spain* had given him a respected place in society. At that point, when he not only wrote but thought as an Englishman, he had reverted to his original identity and to his native language as editor of *Variedades*. The effort of writing in Spanish for an unseen readership while leading the social life of an English gentleman was disorientating. In wrestling with Spanish, after nearly ten years of disuse, he felt himself to be wrestling with a language which inhibited the free and flexible expression of ideas, and which was, for him, inextricably associated with political and religious absolutism. In struggling with the language he was struggling with invisible chains. The writing of *Letters from Spain* had also left him emotionally vulnerable. In 1823 he received from Alberto Lista an inscribed copy of the latter's collected poems, which included the sonnet dedicated to him as 'Albino', the name by which he had been known to the members of the Academia de Letras Humanas. It ended:

> You taught me feeling; it was from you
> I learned the language of the gods, and generosity of
>   heart.
> My verse is yours: that is my only boast.[27]

Blanco told his brother that he could scarcely control his emotion on reading these lines.

What compounded this malaise was that *Variedades* failed to satisfy Blanco's ideal of 'transcendental utility'. He wanted a mission, and he was now to receive just that, at the hands of Robert Southey.

Chapter 10
King's Evidence

Infandum, regina, iubes renovare dolorem
—Vergil, *Aeneid* 2.3

Southey, like Blanco, was a convert from Jacobinism and unbelief who, having seen the light, now preached his Tory Protestantism with the zeal of a missionary: 'Like you', Southey wrote, 'I have a duty to perform. The French Revolution led me astray from that Church for which I was designed in childhood'.[1] He had assumed the role of defender of the Church of England for reasons which were more political than theological. If he had any doctrinal views he tended in fact towards Unitarianism, but he regarded the reformed Church of England as the guardian of the nation's spiritual identity, and therefore as essential to the continuity of the English tradition. 'My endeavours', he declared, 'are to strengthen the moral and religious feelings, and to uphold those institutions upon which the welfare of society depends'.[2] His travels in Spain and Portugal had reinforced his antipathy to Catholicism, and so he became one of the most impassioned opponents of Catholic Emancipation when that issue came to a head in the 1820s. Like Blanco he was a man who, once astride his hobby-horse, charged at the imagined enemy with disproportionate ferocity.

J. S. Mill once described him, in terms which are equally applicable to Blanco, as 'a man of gentle feelings and bitter opinions. His opinions make him think a great many things abominable which are not so; against which accordingly he thinks it right and suitable to the fitness of things to express great indignation; but if he really feels this indignation it is only by a voluntary act of the imagination that he conjures it up, by representing the thing to his own mind in colours suited to that passion'.[3] Such a man was bound to exacerbate all Blanco's latent acrimony.

The correspondence between the two had hitherto largely been concerned with literature and politics. If Blanco had been tempted to enter the controversy over Catholic Emancipation earlier he was prevented from doing so by his association with Holland House.

Nevertheless he revealed his colours to Southey as early as 1812, when he declared that 'if [the Catholics] of Great Britain are not dangerous to the constitution, it must be because they *are not* what Catholics have been hitherto. The Pope and the Universities may make a thousand disavowals of their former characteristic principles, but I know that a true Catholic will go by the reverse the moment after'.[4] Moderate Catholics, who supported religious toleration and claimed that their spiritual allegiance to the Pope in no way interfered with their temporal allegiance to the monarch, were on this reckoning not 'true' Catholics at all: they must either be secret unbelievers or else wolves in sheep's clothing. A 'true' Catholic, Blanco maintained, had in fact a *duty* to be intolerant since he belonged to a Church which was committed to the extinction of heresy. It was inconsistent, he argued, for members of such a church to claim rights of toleration when they were in a minority (as in Britain) since they denied these rights to others when they were in a majority (in Spain). Such was the chain of reasoning whereby the preacher of toleration to America now became the opponent of toleration in the United Kingdom.

In 1822 Southey told Blanco that he was working on a religious history 'written for the purpose of making the rising generation feel and understand what they owe to the Church of England'.[5] This was the *Book of the Church*, published in 1824, which represented English Protestantism as the mother of enlightenment and freedom, and warned of the dangers of admitting the Trojan horse of Romanism within the walls of Parliament. 'The British Constitution', he declared, 'consists of Church and State, and it is an absurdity in politics to give those persons power in the *State* whose duty it is to subvert the *Church*'.[6]

This provoked a reply the same year from the lawyer Charles Butler who in his *Book of the Roman Catholic Church* denied the existence of any such 'duty' and vindicated the loyalty and patriotism of his fellow-Catholics. It was at this stage that Blanco was drawn into the controversy, persuaded that it was his 'duty' to answer Butler's 'fallacies and misrepresentations'. He was persuaded to do so by Southey's friend E. H. Locker and his wife. Southey, Locker and Richard Garnett were all hispanophiles and all active polemicists in the campaign against Emancipation, under the political leadership of Lord Liverpool. It was later alleged by Blanco's opponents that he had been 'bribed' by the Liverpool faction, but the rumour was of course absurd. He was capable of self-deception but not of dishonesty. He was totally ignorant—culpably ignorant—of the politics of Emancipation and took his stand on abstract principle. Locker, by appealing to his sense of 'duty' had revived in him that sense of providential mission and that desire to be useful which he most needed to satisfy. He was encouraged by Southey himself, who wrote of the 'great

utility' of the task which he had undertaken.[7] In making himself useful
he was also allowing himself to be used.

The 'answer' to Charles Butler was completed in the first few
months of 1825. The title was carefully chosen: *Practical and Internal
Evidence against Catholicism, with occasional strictures on Mr Butler's Book
of the Roman Catholic Church in six letters addressed to the impartial among
the Roman Catholics of Great Britain and Ireland.*[8] The evidence was
'practical' in so far as it dealt not with abstract theology but with the
concrete effects of the Roman Catholic 'system' on society and on the
individual; it was 'internal' because the author was exhibiting the
wounds inflicted by this same system on his own person. His claim to
speak with authority was announced on the title page, which gave his
name as 'The Reverend Joseph Blanco White, MA, BD in the
University of Seville; Licentiate of Divinity in the University of
Osuna; formerly Chaplain Magistral (Preacher) to the King of Spain
in the Royal Chapel at Seville; Fellow, and once Rector, of the College
of Sta María a Jesu of the same town; Synodal Examiner of the
Dioceses of Cordoba and Cadiz; Member of the Royal Academy of
Belles-Lettres, etc, etc; now a clergyman of the Church of England'.
There is an incongruous note of pride in this roll-call of titles, as if
Blanco, besides stating his credentials, were also anxious to remind
English readers of his former status.

Evidence purported to be addressed to the Roman Catholics themselves, with the object of persuading them that even if they were
admitted to Parliament they could not in conscience carry out their
duties since these would involve legislating on the affairs of a church
which they were bound to regard as heretical. In the preliminary
dedication addressed to Edward Coplestone, Provost of Oriel College
and leader of the anti-emancipation party at Oxford, he claimed that
he was not concerned with the parliamentary or political question,
only with establishing 'the important and to me indubitable fact that
sincere Roman Catholics cannot conscientiously be tolerant'.

If the book was really intended to convince Catholics, its tone was
singularly misjudged. In the course of his 'evidence' Blanco touched
on his own most painful memories, and the indignation this revived in
him was vented on Butler, whose very moderation acted as an irritant.
'I can easily conceive', he wrote of Butler, 'how galling it must be for a
modernized Roman Catholic, in this country, to be constantly suspected of being Roman Catholic in deed, and according to the Pope's own
heart. His case is as deplorable as that of a man of fashion, who should
be compelled to frequent the higher circles in company with an old,
fantastic, half-crazed mother, who daily and hourly exposed herself to
contempt and ridicule, in spite of the filial efforts to hide her absurdi-
ties'.[9] This violence of language is characteristic of the work as a
whole. Scholasticism is dismissed as 'intellectual garbage', and

'monkish' devotional practices denounced as 'drivelling imbecility'. The section on credulity and superstition is characterised by a Voltairean sarcasm. The writing of the book seems to have revived all the rage of Blanco's young manhood. *Evidence* is essentially an autobiographical work in which he accuses the Church of the moral ruin of himself, his contemporaries and Spain itself. It is also the work of a rationalist of the enlightenment outraged by the fact that the whole apparatus of monks and medievalism which he disdained as part of a dark, barbaric age was now, in England, coming into romantic fashion. For Southey the book was all that he had hoped, and he wrote to thank Blanco 'as an Englishman and a Protestant'.[10]

Charles Butler's reaction was characteristically dignified. 'Why', he asked, 'should Mr Blanco White write a book, the evident tendency of which is to raise popular prejudice against us; to perpetuate the laws under which we suffer; and thus to eternize the depression of a large proportion of his fellow-men, of his brother Christians; of those with whom, not many years since, he walked in union in the house of God?'[11] Other reactions were less restrained. Irish Catholics, in particular, saw Blanco as a renegade who had sold his services to a party intent on denying them their rights. At a crowded meeting of the British Catholic Association in January 1826, Daniel O'Connell's London agent Eneas McDonnell delivered a ribald attack which contained some innuendoes about Blanco's private life evidently based on information gleaned from Spanish emigrés in London. 'So far from his flying from his native city to avoid an enemy', McDonnell declared, 'he marched out like a good recruit to the tune of "The Girl I left Behind Me"'.[12]

These imputations—and the further charge that he had broken his parents' heart—touched Blanco's sense of honour at its rawest point. In a renewed attack on Charles Butler he sounded an almost frantic note, denouncing the 'filth-engines' of the Catholic Association and accusing Butler (who had been present at the meeting) of having connived at the slander by his silence. He saw Butler's very mildness of manner as a cloak for more sinister designs: 'It is more difficult to discover [the Church's] wiles when she has grown weak and artful in proportion to her weakness. She formerly took the field against heretics with all the pomp and clamour of a *battue* prepared for an eastern Prince; now she glides silently, like the degraded beings pursued by the game laws, setting her gins and traps in the dark'.[13]

Blanco must have known what the reaction at Holland House would be to his *Evidence*. Lady Holland was offended by what she called a 'want of taste in attacking old Mother Church so vehemently'. John Allen's rebuke was magisterial: 'I believed you a sincere friend of religious liberty, but I now find that after all your efforts to divest yourself of the rags of Popery, the mantle of Torquemada still clings to you like the shirt of Nessus'.[14]

Though Blanco now regarded himself as one 'entirely devoted to the cause of religious truth' he was to forfeit any claim to be non-political in agreeing to write a simplified version of *Evidence* for the benefit of the working man. The suggestion came from John Duke Coleridge, nephew of the poet, who wanted a tract which could be read by the country yeomanry, 'to have weight with them in their choice of a candidate for a seat in the commons';[15] in other words to dispose Tory selection committees in favour of anti-emancipationist candidates. Blanco duly obliged with *The Poor Man's Preservative against Popery*, in which the message of *Evidence* was condensed into a series of 'conversations' between the author and 'a representative of that numerous and respectable class who cannot afford to employ a great part of their time in reading'.[16]

The most devastating indictment of Blanco's evidence came not from a Catholic source but from an anomymous pamphleteer, evidently a member of the Church of England, possessed of Whig sympathies, little love for the University of Oxford, and a wit and eloquence worthy of Sydney Smith. After condemning the 'ignorance' of Blanco in attributing the evils of Catholic Spain to Catholic Ireland, he went on:

> But perhaps Mr White's is an interested ignorance:—he arrives trembling from Spain, and like a runaway schoolboy longing to complain of his master, rushes among men as terrified and vindictive as himself, to foster each other's ignorance and inflame each other's bigotry. Without religion to tranquillise his mind, without scepticism to teach him philosophy, he believes all he hears and trembles at all he believes: he takes men steeped in port and prejudice as his political guides and believes all accounts of Ireland given him by those who have never quitted their cloisters and seen nothing more of that country than a few drunken Orange gentlemen commoners and a few naked labourers on the Holyhead road. . . He has contributed to fix the badge of slavery upon those men whom he calls slaves;—he has dared to use an eloquence derived from Irish Catholic blood against Irish Catholic claims, and the curse of six millions of his relations and fellow-subjects hovers over his head'.[17]

Stung by the attacks on his personal honour, above all by McDonnell's taunts, Blanco appealed to his patrons to vindicate his integrity. Lord Holland readily obliged but at the same time advised his old friend 'not to be too susceptible to attacks, however coarse, virulent or unjust, for there is no meddling with the brambles of controversy without exposing oneself to be scratched by the thorns with which they are beset'.[18] The prudent advice went unheeded. Blanco was more susceptible to the kind of language with which, at about the same time, Southey summoned him to a holy war with all the gusto of a Protestant Chesterbelloc. He declared,

A greater struggle is at hand than has taken place since the first age of the Reformation. In Ireland it will be decided by fire and the sword; here, thank God, the warfare will be of a different kind;—but you and I must be in the front of the battle, and smite them we will, as that good Christian,—that perfect one with the shaven crown, the bishop Don Hieronymo, did the Moors,—for the love of charity and with a hearty good will.[19]

Nothing could better illustrate the contradictions in Southey's character than this use of the language of medieval romance and Catholic crusade in aid of a Protestant cause.

Blanco's entry into the emancipation controversy was a watershed in his life, for it marked his final abandonment of the Hispanic world. His editorship of *Variedades* did not long survive the publication of *Evidence*. Ackermann had stipulated that he should keep off contentious subjects such as religion, but increasingly Blanco chafed at this restriction. The new republics of Spanish America were now framing their Constitutions, and he regarded it as vitally important that these should include clauses guaranteeing religious toleration and freedom of conscience. In the May 1825 number of *Variedades* he broke his silence with a deeply felt article 'Important advice on intolerance addressed to the Spanish Americans', prompted by the recent publication of the new Mexican constitution. He described this as admirable in every respect other than its recognition of Catholicism as the religion of the state. He pleaded with the Americans not to go down the same path as Spain, all of whose social and moral ills he attributed to the stifling effects of state-enforced Catholicism. The atheism prevalent in intellectual circles in Spain was, he argued, the direct result of a system which forced men to choose between believing everything and believing nothing:

> Belief in a particular religious system is an act of the understanding in which no government can intervene. Where the law maintains one religious party in a position of privilege, in such a way that the man who does not believe its dogmas is forced to dissemble and learn to play the hypocrite, this engenders an implacable hatred against the religion which causes this degradation of man's freedom and rationality. . . Religion is of the utmost importance to public happiness, but if it is to produce its beneficial effects, belief must be the result of conviction.[20]

This eloquent plea summed up the message implicit in *Variedades* as a whole. It was the message, for instance, of the 'Cartas sobre Inglaterra', in which Blanco held up English social and political institutions as a model for the Spanish Americans. It was the message, above all, of the two letters 'On the Moral and Religious State of England', in which he sought to demonstrate that religious pluralism, far from undermining society (as the Spanish feared) was a liberator of moral energy.[21]

There is ample evidence that the effect of Blanco's 'important advice' was felt throughout Spanish America, being denounced by traditionalists and invoked by progressives.[22] But the strain involved in combining the roles of Spanish journalist and English clergyman was now proving too much for him. Besides, the revival of his native Spanish had proved emotionally disturbing because of its associations: 'To write and speak in my native language is always painful to me. The sound of that beautiful and ill-fated language carries with it to my ear the distant echo, as it were, of a dungeon in which I have suffered imprisonment and in which I have left my dearest friends to endure the same sufferings without hope or remedy'.[23]

Having decided to resign the editorship of *Variedades*, Blanco took his leave of his readers in October 1825 with one last appeal. This valediction, 'The Editor's Farewell to the Spanish Americans', was in fact another of Blanco's essays in autobiography and an adaptation of *Evidence* for an American readership. It was a final plea for religious pluralism in which the writer exhibited the destructive effects of institutionalised intolerance on the life of one individual: himself. What did the drawing-rooms of Caracas and Mexico City make of this painful self-revelation by one who described himself as a useful specimen for research in the field of religious pathology? In writing for a Hispanic readership Blanco was frank in avowing the vehemence of his former atheism. Guilt as well as anger motivated him in this apologia which was directed as much to Spanish as to American readers: 'I cannot doubt that my opinions and example during my youth have contributed to some extent to confirm the anti-religious ideas of many people and to sow doubts about my sincerity, now, among those who have never at any time known me well'.[24]

In resigning from *Variedades* Blanco had opted definitively for an English identity. It is significant that he now, for the first time, began writing poetry in English. Poetry had always been for him the language of the heart, and so the attempt marked the completeness of his intended transformation. It was Coleridge who guided his first steps. Coleridge had read *Evidence* with admiration, describing it to a friend as having 'inflicted a deeper wound on Anti-Christ and his scarlet *prima donna* than they have received since our Revolution'.[25] Blanco for his part had read Coleridge's *Aids to Reflection*, published the same year, and found it much to his taste, particularly its distinction between material belief and spiritual faith. Coleridge shared with him the conviction that Christianity was concerned not with assent to or belief in a 'system of doctrines', but with faith: 'fealty to the SPIRITUAL in our humanity, to that which contra-distinguishes us as human'.[26] Blanco may have found this language rather vaporous, but he certainly agreed with Coleridge as to what Christianity *was not*. Their first meeting at Highgate took place in July 1825 and lasted eight-and-a-half hours, which tends to confirm Carlyle's description of Coleridge's talk as 'not flowing anywhither like a river, but spreading everywhither in inextricable currents and regurgitations, like a lake or sea'.[27] If theologically the two men came to no firm conclusions, Coleridge more importantly sowed the seed in Blanco's mind which bore fruit at the end of that year in the sonnet 'Night and Death' (see Appendix). Coleridge, to whom it was dedicated, described it as 'the finest and most grandly conceived sonnet in the language'. Even if that praise is thought excessive, the poem remains Blanco's most enduring spiritual testament, the summation of his lifelong preoccupation with the themes of light and darkness.

Blanco wrote at least seven poems in English between December 1825 and April 1826, nearly all of them in the peaceful surroundings of William Bishop's rectory at Ufton. They were not originally intended for publication, and it caused some embarrassment to Coleridge when the manuscript of *Night and Death* was passed by a friend of his to the editor of *The Bijou* and published in that magazine. None of the other poems is the equal of *Night and Death*, though their recent translation into Spanish has revealed a beauty of imagery which in the English version is disguised by a derivativeness of language and rhyme. One theme is dominant: that of death and rebirth.[28]

One of Blanco's motives for accepting the editorship of *Variedades* in 1823 had been the need to provide for his son. In 1824 Ferdinand returned from school in Switzerland to live with his father and the Christies in Chelsea and to complete his education with a view to a career. Though he gratified his father by his affectionate and manly character, he showed no leaning towards literature. This ruled out the university, and Blanco lacked the money to purchase a commission in the army. There was no alternative but to work in an office—a fate which the boy, to his father's puzzlement, seemed positively to welcome. A clerkship was found for him in the city broking firm of Goldschmidt, with which Ackermann was connected and which at the time was heavily involved in raising loans for speculation ventures in South America. Ferdinand found himself handling business which amounted to as much as £300,000 in a week. But in 1825 the bubble burst, the London money market collapsed, and with it the house of Goldschmidt. Ferdinand had to be found a cadetship in the army, and his father used all his connections to solicit patronage. There is some evidence to suggest that the poet Samuel Rogers, whom Blanco knew through the Hollands, provided the financial help needed.[29] Ferdinand got his cadetship in 1826, and the following year left for Madras on his first twelve-year tour of duty as an ensign. His touching loyalty was to be the great consolation of Blanco's last years. The circumstances of his upbringing might, in a weaker character, have aroused feelings of resentment and self-pity, but though Ferdinand inherited

what his uncle called 'the loving melancholy of the Blanco Whites' he
also had his father's moral courage, along with his social grace and
tender heart.

With his son's prospects settled Blanco was freed from the necessity
of drudging for a living. He was now 51, in poor health, bruised by
controversy and eager for retirement. In annotating his copy of
Evidence Coleridge had written that it would be 'worse than cowardice' if the Church of England did not show her gratitude to its author
by conferring on him one of her dignities. Blanco had in fact decided
much earlier to refuse any such preferment, but the revival of the
proposal that he should take up residence at Oxford, as an honorary
MA and member of Oriel College, was now irresistible. Under the
influence of the Christies and in the heat of controversy his reservations about subscription to the Thirty-Nine Articles had evapo-
rated. Coplestone, the Provost of Oriel, to whom *Evidence* had been
dedicated, formally proposed to Convocation on 24 April 1826 that
the degree of master of arts be conferred on Blanco 'in consideration of
his eminent talents and learning, and of his exemplary conduct during
his residence at Oxford, but more especially on account of those able
and well-timed publications by which he has powerfully exposed the
errors and corruptions of the Church of Rome'.[30] The overtly politcial
tone of the proposal was not to everyone's taste, but Coplestone
forestalled any opposition.[31] Blanco received his degree at the end of
April, and in October came up to Oxford to take his place at Oriel. 'It
is my intention', he wrote to his brother, 'to retire to that seat of
learning for the rest of my life'.[32]

Chapter 11
Dear Oriel

This is my park, my pleasaunce
—Gerard Manley Hopkins, *To Oxford*

After years of social isolation in England Blanco was at last an insider, part of an academic community which satisfied to the full his need for corporate fellowship. 'I had brought to Oxford', he wrote later, 'the *ideal* of a College—a place for the education of youth, for the improvement and completion of early learning during the vigour of life, and of external repose and internal activity for a few old votaries of knowledge who, probably in consequence of that devotion, had continued an unmarried life till age had left them with only a few friends or distant companions'.[1] His arrival at Oriel was, in a sense, a homecoming. He had never lost his devotion to his own college of Santa María de Jesus in Seville, and soon after his arrival at Oxford he wrote to its Rector with a gift of Greek books. His dearest wish, he told the Rector, was that his *alma mater* should become the equal of an Oriel: 'What pleasure it would give me if my College were to become a seedbed of Greek studies in Andalucia, and that my memory should be preserved there in such a way!'[2]

Some things in Oxford had not changed since 1815. The Bishop family was still in Holywell, a token of permanence and solid friendship. Shuttleworth was now Warden of New College, still waiting for the Whigs to return to power and put him in the way of a bishopric. Blanco had kept up with other old friends from Holywell days such as the Duncan brothers, John and Philip, successive Keepers of the Ashmolean Museum, who were now playing an important part in the revival of scientific studies in the University. In the ten years since Blanco had observed it from the outside, Oxford had stirred to vigorous intellectual life. The centre of this renaissance was Oriel, to which Coplestone had attracted a formidable array of talent. Collectively the 'Noetics' of Oriel seemed to Blanco a living proof that Christianity and logic, faith and reason, could live together in harmony.

It was the Noetic *par excellence*, Richard Whately, who took Blanco under his protective wing. His hearty, vigorous, uncomplicated good humour was just the restorative which the latter's nervous temperament needed. His daughter wrote of him that he took a particular delight in encouraging diffident and despondent characters. If he had a tendency to use his friends as anvils on which to pound out his thoughts, he also had a Socratic gift for drawing out the shy, as his pupil J. H. Newman was to testify. To Blanco he seemed to be John Bull incarnate, all common sense and rough kindness. Though they were polar opposites in temperament and background, the two men found that theologically they occupied the same ground. Whately stood for a Christianity that was tolerant, enlightened and rational. Revelation, in his view, was intended to provide man with a practical, moral guide, not to be a source of speculative knowledge. His hatred of intolerance was instinctive and deep-seated. Religious persecution, he observed humorously, was one of the first lessons learned by rhyme in the English nursery:

> Old Daddy Longlegs won't say his prayers—
> Take him by the left leg and throw him downstairs![3]

Like Blanco he was opposed to the enforcement of religious orthodoxy by the state and even went so far as to advocate disestablishment, on the grounds that it would leave the Church free to require compliance with its rules like any other voluntary association, without incurring the charge of persecution or coercion.[4]

These views were shared by Whately's closest allies in the Oriel common-room: Baden Powell, R. D. Hampden and Edward Hawkins. Powell, who became Savilian Professor of Geometry in 1827, was a theologian as well as a mathematician and physicist. His recently published book *Rational Religion Examined*, which sought to provide a philosophical basis for Christian apologetics, put forward ideas which were remarkably similar to those which Blanco had expressed in his *Facts and Inferences*. In it he argued that creeds and articles were 'symbols' or 'tokens', *representing* scriptural truth but not invested with the authority of revelation.[5] This was also the view of his colleague R. D. Hampden. 'Strictly to speak', he was to write, 'in the Scripture itself there are no doctrines. What we read there is matter of fact'.[6] This distinction between 'fact' and 'interpretation' was very much in line with Blanco's thinking, and in the Oxford of the 1820s these ideas could still be put forward without incurring the charge of heterodoxy.

All these were men of wide intellectual interests and with a marked utilitarian streak. They were interested in economics as well as science. Whately's pupil Nassau Senior had been appointed in 1825 as the first Professor of Political Economy at Oxford, a post in which he was followed by Whately himself. The group was further linked by ties of marriage and common background. Baden Powell and Whately were to become brothers-in-law, and Hampden was Senior's cousin. Their influence in Oriel was consolidated when, in 1828, Edward Hawkins was chosen to succeed Coplestone as Provost.

It was rare for a foreigner to penetrate to the inner sanctum of college life. Oxford's knowledge of the continent was generally restricted to the anecdotes of the few Fellows, like Dornford of Oriel, who had seen service in the Peninsular War. Blanco was therefore regarded with some curiosity, as an exotic. Thomas Mozley was later to remember him as a latter-day wandering scholar, 'recalling similar incidents in past ages when marvellous personages, specially endowed with a migratory instinct, roamed about connecting the centres of knowledge'. Mozley remarked on the coincidence that Blanco's lodgings in Merton Street were on the site of those traditionally assigned to Duns Scotus.[7] Blanco, as a man of the enlightenment, would not have been pleased at being compared with a medieval scholastic. It was as a preacher that he attracted most attention. He had preached his first English sermon at Ufton in March 1826 and soon found himself in demand at Oxford. H. H. Milman, delivering the Bampton Lectures in 1826, found that on one occasion the ladies were 'drawn away to have their tender hearts melted by Blanco White's Charity Sermon'.[8] These Oxford sermons, like those of Seville, are often psychologically revealing. Sometimes the texts chosen have an autobiographical resonance: 'If thou hadst known, even thou, at least in this thy day, the things which belong even unto thy peace! but now they are hid from thy eyes'. On other occasions one can hear the preacher wrestling with his doubts, as when, on the text 'We must all appear before the judgement seat of Christ' he confides, 'I have indeed, since I proposed to address you on this text, often asked myself "Do I really believe these things?"'. Preaching at the reopening of Burford church in 1826 he delivered a prophetic warning on the dangers of ritualism. 'To worship in truth', he declared, 'is to avoid in the externals of religion everything which gratifies the imagination. . . Let the devout Protestant cast no longing eyes on the zealous Romanist while at his task of practices and ceremonies'.[9]

For Oriel, Blanco was a living source of information on everything connected with Catholic theology, philosophy, history and ritual. When Whately published his *Errors of Romanism* some years later, he dedicated the book to Blanco with these words:

I am indebted to you for such an insight into the peculiarities of the Church of Rome as I could never have gained from anyone who was not originally, or from anyone who still continued a member of that Church. . . You have learned to recognise in all, of whatever country or persuasion, the tendency towards each of those Romish errors which you have seen

7. Paradise Row, Chelsea
June 9th 1826.

Reverend Sir,

When I learnt the great honour which that University had conferred upon me, by a Diploma of Master of Arts; my most ardent wish was to signify my gratitude. But, being informed that it is not customary to address the University, on such occasions, I longed for the moment when I might personally return my thanks to you, & the other Heads of Houses. I have, however, in the mean time found it necessary to appear before the public, in the little work, which I enclose together with this letter; & as I have to request that you will honour it with your acceptance, I take this opportunity of expressing

my feelings on that event which I reckon the most gratifying of my life. Those only who have experienced the power of early Academic habits, & Collegiate attachments; those who recollect the value which youth gives to literary distinctions, & the agreeable recollections which they are capable of transmitting through the longest life: those alone can conceive the regrets, which during a long residence among you, I must have keenly felt; & such alone can imagine the delight which the adoption into your noble University has given me.

I am, with most sincere gratitude & respect
Reverend Sir,
Your most obedient humble Servant
J. Blanco White

To the Reverend
Richard Jenkyns, D.D. Vice-Chancellor of the University
of Oxford &c &c

To the Reverend
the Vice-Chancellor of the
University of
Oxford.

J. BLANCO WHITE

9. Letter from Blanco White to the Vice Chancellor of the University of Oxford.

magnified or exaggerated in that Church: to detect the minutest drop, in the most disguised mixture, of those poisons which you have seen in their rectified and concentrated form.[10]

Blanco was soon to sniff out Romish proclivities where he least expected to find them, in Oriel itself. His knowledge of Catholic practice was destined to be put to uses which he never imagined. In view of later history, his diary entry for 31 October 1827 is pregnant with irony. It reads: 'Pusey, Wilberforce and Froude came in the evening to learn the order of the RC Service of the Breviary'.[11]

The future rift between the generation represented by these three young men, and their Noetic elders, was at this stage scarcely detectable. Pusey in fact was generally considered to be theologically liberal. He had just returned from Germany where he had come into contact with modern Protestant scholarship. The following year he published a book in which he dealt sympathetically with the new German theology and developed the thesis that its excesses were a reaction against an inflexible 'orthodoxism' which the reformed churches had imposed in direct contradiction to Luther's intentions.[12] The tolerant and anti-doctrinaire tone of this book delighted Blanco, and his praise was ecstatic. 'I have employed the whole of this day in reading your Essay', he told Pusey, 'and feel confident that few days of my life have been employed more profitably . . . I should be proud of being a member of Oriel College if it had produced no other work of extensive usefulness besides yours, or reckoned no other master-mind among its members'.[13]

Hurrell Froude, Blanco's other visitor on this occasion, was a very different young man: a romantic Tory in love with the knightly and ascetic ideals of an imagined medieval past. 'Woe to anyone who dropped in his hearing such phrases as the dark ages, superstition, bigotry, right of private judgment, enlightenment, march of mind or progress'.[14] This was a species of young Englishman which was new to Blanco, and alarming.

Another name appeared in Blanco's diary for the first time on 18 February 1827: 'Newman drank tea with me'. John Henry Newman was then twenty-six years old, twenty-seven years younger than Blanco, and just beginning to come out from under the shadow of his mentor, Whately. In contrast with men like Whately, Powell and Hampden, who were made of worthy but prosaic stuff, Blanco found in Newman a young man whose refinement, sensitivity and piety reminded him of his youthful self and of his companions in the Academia de Letras Humanas. Newman for his part felt an immediate sympathy for Blanco, whom he described to a friend as 'well-read, well-informed, quick, lively, ingenious, sensible, modest and of a most ardent and affectionate mind—there is a character! I wish you

knew him—and the circumstances of his life invest him both with
mystery and with deep interest'.[15]

In February 1828 Blanco suggested to Newman that together with
Froude and Robert Wilberforce they should start a round robin
correspondence 'on subjects moral and religious'. The letter shows
Blanco tentatively testing the water, anxious to communicate with
young and sympathetic minds and yet unsure how they would react.
'It seems to me', he wrote,

> that few men (especially divines who have been brought up with little or
> no free communication with others) have any notion of the free variety of
> intellect which exists in mankind. . . [They] are not satisfied with ortho-
> doxy or conformity in *results*; they demand, for the most part, conformity
> and orthodoxy of *arguments*. It is this spirit which has consecrated the most
> questionable proofs of many an unquestionable Christian truth, and
> which, in the eyes of unbelievers, gives to Christianity the character of a
> mighty edifice, borne by an unsound foundation and made up of the most
> heterogeneous materials. Are we then to pull it to pieces in the spirit of
> German rationalism? God forbid! I feel under a considerable alarm lest . . .
> I should become a snare to any one of you.

Blanco must have been encouraged by the first part of Newman's
reply, in which he agreed that Christians might hold the same truths in
different ways: 'Accordingly I trust I shall always be very slow to
quarrel with persons differing from me in matters of opinion'.
Newman went on, however, to state his conviction that in religious
matters, 'intellect seems to be but the attendant and servant of right
moral feeling in this our weak and dark state of being—defending it
when attacked, accounting for it and explaining it in a poor way to
others'. Though he had Froude's support 'for lowering the intellectual
powers into handmaids of our moral nature', he was not sure that
either Froude or Wilberforce shared to the full his instinct that
intellectual deviation was the result of moral deficiency: 'Let me then
challenge W. or F. to give us some account of the connection (how far)
of speculative error with bad $\mathring{\eta}\theta os$—eg *in what is a consistent Socinian a
worse man than an orthodox believer? I* think him to be worse, but I wish
my mind clear upon the subject, which it is not at present'.[16]

Newman had touched on what was to become in time the crux of
the issue between him and Blanco. The latter was ready to concede
that rational arguments could not produce assent to religious truths
unless the heart was first disposed to receive them, but it was one thing
to say that belief stemmed from moral disposition, and quite another
to say that unbelief stemmed from moral indisposition. In writing to
congratulate Blanco on the publication of *Evidence*, Coleridge had
commended the 'manliness' with which he had opposed 'that current
illiberal dogma that infidelity always arises from vice or corrupt
affections'.[17]

To discover that Newman subscribed to this dogma must have caused Blanco unease. Nevertheless personal sympathy as yet far outweighed these latent theological differences. There is no better evidence of Blanco's moral charm than the affectionate, solicitous letter Newman wrote to him in the summer of 1828:

> I so regret you are banished to Hastings—I shall be at Brighton the latter end of July—my plan is to run along the coast and kidnap you . . . I wish I could express to you in words how very much I feel interested in all your movements and plans, and in every variation of your health. Indeed, whenever I think of you, your name is connected with so many grand and beautiful visions that I quite wonder how it is that having known you so short a time I seem so at home with you. And then I feel that my manner has often been cold, and seemed different from what it was meant to be. I would do everything to make you more happy than your health lets you be.[18]

Blanco's health was not improved by a feeling of being under-employed. Unlike the other members of the Oriel common-room, he had no official post in the college or in the university. Whately found him a private pupil or two, but cramming Livy and Thucydides into the heads of pleasant but dim young gentlemen was not enough to satisfy his need to feel useful. There was no one in Oxford who had a fraction of his knowledge of European literature and history, but these were subjects of which Oxford knew, and wished to know, nothing.[19]

At this point, providence seemed to intervene. In the summer of 1828 Whately's close friend and former pupil Nassau Senior was planning the launch of a new periodical. The Tory *Quarterly* and the radical *Westminster* had recently undergone changes of editor, and Senior judged the time ripe for a journal which would seize the middle ground and pursue a non-partisan line, as well as bridge the gap between the academic world of Oxford and the political world of London. Senior was aware of Blanco's ill-health and diffidence but thought that this was outweighed by his experience of journalism and his extensive literary contacts at home and abroad. Blanco's medical adviser, Dr Mayo, another Oriel man and member of the Whately circle, persuaded him to accept the offer. 'I really lament the necessity which forces me away from Oxford', he told Newman, 'but it is my lot not to be allowed to take root anywhere. Perpetually transplanted, perpetually torn up, and never without pain. But Providence has always brought about some good to me by these means'.[20] He now divided his time between Oxford and Senior's house in Kensington.

The prospective editor told the Whatelys that he intended to make his new journal 'an *European* or rather *Cosmopolitan* Review'.[21] Among those he invited to contribute were the *afrancesado* Spanish writer J. M. Maury and Andrés Bello, whom he asked to write an article on political developments in South America. But Bello was preparing to leave England. After eighteen years of obscurity, poverty and dedication to scholarship he had at last received the call, not—as expected—back to his native Venezuela, but to Chile. He was on the threshold of a new life as Chile's uncrowned philosopher king. It was the life of honourable and honoured utility, dedicated to the formation of the youth of a young nation, which Blanco always longed for but was always denied.[22]

The title finally decided on for the new journal was *The London Review*. Its contributors were an odd match of market-place and ivory tower. The Oriel common-room was trawled for talent and Newman provided the first catch: an essay on 'Poetry, with reference to Aristotle's Poetics'. In this, his literary debut, Newman sounded an almost mystical note: 'With Christians, a poetical view of things is a duty—we are bid to colour all things with hues of faith, to see a divine meaning in every event. . . Even our friends around are invested with unearthly brightness'. This is quintessential Newman—the Newman who remembered thinking as a boy that life might be a dream or he an angel, and all this world a deception. The tone of the article displeased the prosaic Whately but captivated Blanco:

> I have read your ms in all the hurry of pleasure. I will read it again with all the composure of a critic, if I can; for you are a treacherous writer, you slip so softly through the critic's fingers. Well then, my dear friend, you must write for me constantly. You want an outlet for your mind and heart, which are running over, where there is no call for their riches. Tell the world at large what you feel and think; talk with the people of England through my journal, and let me have the benefit of their delight. . . Adieu, my Oxford Plato.[23]

Newman's Platonism contrasted oddly with the practical and Benthamite tone of other contributions from Senior's circle of London friends, Broad Churchmen and advocates of social reform. Edwin Chadwick, for example, wrote an important article on 'Preventive Police' which played a decisive part in shaping the modern police system established by Sir Robert Peel.[24] This catholicity was part of Blanco's editorial policy. The role of an editor, he argued, should be to provide readers with the wherewithal for informed and balanced judgement, not to impose his own opinion. Like *Variedades*, *The London Review* aimed to provoke its readers to think for themselves, not just to entertain them or to provide them with ready-made opinions. In his opening article on the state of British journalism, which anticipates much of what Matthew Arnold was later to say in *The Function of Criticism*, Blanco castigated the British public's passive addiction to gladiatorial displays of party spirit. 'There is also a sort of interest allied to the pure spirit of gambling . . . Two dogs cannot worry each other in the street without instantly forming each his party among the crowd'.[25] These were telling points, though difficult to reconcile with the writer's recent polemical contribution to the campaign against Catholic emancipation.

Blanco based his hopes for *The London Review* on the belief that the intellectual climate was changing, and that 'party virulence' was 'gradually retreating to the shelter of parish vestries'. The naive wishfulness of this view was to be cruelly exposed only a month after its publication (January 1829). Ironically, the protagonists on both sides of the coming ideological conflict were drawn from the ranks of contributors to Blanco's journal. *The London Review* brought together for the last time representatives of the two forces which divided Oxford in the next decade: those who, like Newman, defended the values of 'ancestral wisdom' and those who, like Senior, held high the 'torch of intellect'. Coming from outside the system and innocent of political and social undercurrents, Blanco was not the man to bring about a meeting of such disparate minds. He was about to find out that *odium theologicum* was not confined to Spain.

Chapter 12
Snake in the Grass

Mutandae sedes. Non haec tibi litora suasit
Delius aut Cretae iussit considere Apollo
—Vergil, *Aeneid* 3.167–8

Blanco's opposition to Catholic Emancipation—to which he owed his place at Oxford—had been based on the argument that an institution committed to intolerance forfeited the right to toleration. At Oxford, however, under the influence of his new liberal friends such as Whately and Senior he had come to realise that the question had to be considered also in its political and social context. The success of O'Connell's monster protest meetings in Ireland was by now forcing even the Tories to face the fact that further refusal to grant emancipation would lead to civil war in Ireland. At the beginning of 1829 Wellington, in a startling reversal of policy, announced his intention to introduce an emancipation bill. He was supported by the member of Parliament for Oxford University, Robert Peel, who, since he had previously opposed emancipation, now felt obliged to resign his seat and submit himself for re-election. Whately, Hawkins and Shuttleworth were prominent in the Oxford committee in support of Peel, and Senior organised the London end of the campaign. The anti-emancipationists, who could reckon on the vote of the country clergy, put up their own candidate, the evangelical Sir Robert Inglis, and the lines of battle were drawn.

Oriel, like the University at large, was divided. Whately, the leader of 'progressive' opinion, found himself opposed not only, as expected, by the older diehards but also by a youthful resistance group which included his protégé Newman. The issue was, characteristically, more to do with style than with principle. Newman was not opposed to emancipation as such ('I have no opinion about the Catholic Question', he told his sister) but he disliked the tone of its supporters. It was taken for granted by the pro-Peel party that the Inglis camp was made up of the stupid and the benighted. As *The Sun* put it, 'All that is healthy—active—aspiring and tolerant in her [the University's] constitution will be promptly and efficiently put forward in defence of Mr

148

Peel . . . The age is advancing with giant pace towards intellectual maturity, and even now, from its superior moral elevation, looks down with contempt on all those who would arrest its progress'.[1] It was just this airy assumption that Oxford must take its cue from its intellectual betters, from the worldly-wise 'talent' who were in touch with political reality and who knew what was best for their *alma mater*, which touched off the spark of rebellion in Newman and caused him to throw in his lot with the so-called 'stupid' party. 'Better be bigoted', he wrote to his sister, 'than time-serving'. It was now that Newman developed his theory that 'bigotry' might be a providential instrument of good, a preservative against liberalism and infidelity: 'Moral truth is gained by patient study, by calm reflection, silently as the dew falls, unless miraculously given, and, when gained, it is transmitted by faith and by 'prejudice'. Keble's book [*The Christian Year*] is full of such truths; which any Cambridge man might refute with the greatest ease'.[2]

Blanco was disturbed by the divisions opening up within his own college and by the apparent perversity of gifted young men like Newman and Froude in throwing in their lot with the party of reactionary clericalism. Their views were not shared by Pusey, at this stage still a liberal, who was active in canvassing for Peel. Blanco wrote privately to Pusey assuring him of his vote and explaining his apparent *volte-face* on the issue:

> Since the constitutional bulwarks of our Church cannot stand without exposing the country to a civil war and the shedding of blood, we must turn our eyes to that *moral* security which arises from Christian mildness and forbearance. By submitting to the judgement of those who are at the head of public affairs, by yielding without a desperate and unbecoming struggle to the necessity by which they declare themselves compelled, we shall disarm our enemies and gain additional respect to the establishment.[3]

Pusey did not have much difficulty in persuading Blanco that it was his 'duty' to allow this letter to be published in the Peelite cause. The reaction was predictable. The anti-emancipationists were not disposed to take lessons in turning the other cheek from one whom they had regarded as their creature. Blanco was lampooned in squibs and pamphlets as a trimmer. A mock poster advertised a 'menagerie show' which included 'a chameleon, with its keeper Bl★nco Wh★te', an 'exhibition of pictures' featuring 'A Snake in the Grass (from the Cathedral, Madrid)' and a 'play' whose cast included 'Titus Oates, played by Mr Blank Whito'.[4] The acrimony of these personal attacks (described by Newman as 'odious') took Blanco by surprise. He must have been equally dismayed by the sight of Tory Oxford in full cry on the day of the election. 'The violence of the parsons was beyond belief, and far beyond decency', one observer reported; 'they made faces at and abused each other'.[5] The triumph of the anti-Peel party shattered his illusion that Oxford was a haven of tolerance and reason. In his private diary he recorded his apprehension that 'the spirit of Popery' was at work within the Church of England. He began to see it now as an 'Ascendancy Church', which was prepared to involve the nation in civil war rather than abandon its monopoly. On the other hand the passing of the Emancipation Bill left him disorientated: 'I cannot help feeling', he told Newman, 'as a man who, flying from a house in flames, takes shelter in another which shakes under his feet and about his head soon after he has entered it. *Protestantism* has had its day in England. Something better may rise, but I have lived only to see the foundations of that once glorious and splendid structure give way'.[6]

With the publication of its second number, in the spring of 1829, *The London Review* came to an end for lack of support. As the Oxford election had demonstrated, the British public was not in a mood for dispassionate journalism. Blanco came back into residence at Oriel, where his close relationships remained as yet unaffected by recent events. He was a constant companion of Newman that summer, dining with him in hall, assisting him in the services at St Mary's, or riding out to visit his mother and sisters at Horspath. Their companionship was strengthened by their shared love of music. Newman, like Blanco, was a violinist, and with two friends they regularly made up a quartet in the latter's lodgings. Thomas Mozley, who attended one or two of these musical evenings was struck by the contrast between Blanco's 'excited, and indeed agitated, countenance' and Newman's 'sphinx-like immobility' as he 'drew long, rich notes with a steady hand'.[7] In his old age Newman recalled that 'one person played Beethoven as no-one else, Blanco White. I don't know how he learned the violin, but he would seem to have inherited a tradition as to the method of playing him'.[8] Music brought Blanco a peace he never found in religion. After hearing Paganini play in London at about this time he wrote to a friend: 'I was the whole evening in a state of mental intoxication—a perfect optimist, unmoved by the existence of the evils of life, and saw that all would end well'.[9]

In spite of the affective sympathy between Blanco and Newman, intellectually the latter was beginning to distance himself. His brother Frank, who for a time shared the same house with them in Merton Lane, later recalled how discussions would end with Blanco solemnly warning his brother that his train of thought would lead him into 'Catholic error'.[10] Newman had already begun his exhaustive study of the Fathers—a study which began as a search for the origin of 'Romish corruptions' but which was to end—as perhaps Blanco already apprehended—in a conviction that the Church of antiquity was identical with the contemporary Church of Rome. He was already beginning to discover that questions of theology, because of their painful associations, touched off a raw nerve in Blanco's mind. When the latter left the Church of England five years later, Henry Wilberforce wrote to Newman: 'How exactly it bears out the opinion you then expressed to me about his state of mind . . . Do you remember pointing out a black dog shaking all over, nearly opposite St John's gate, and comparing him to it?'.

On the letter, Newman noted, with characteristic attention to time and place: 'This must have been in 1830, I think, in the Long Vacation, near Ogle's house. The dog had the distemper. I meant that Blanco's mind seemed to me so helplessly disorganised'.[11]

Intellectually Blanco felt on safer ground with robuster men like Whately. It was Whately who early in 1830 persuaded him to begin the autobiographical narrative which was to be the basis of the posthumous *Life and Letters*. Blanco had made Whately his literary executor and the narrative was intended to be an advocate's brief for use in defending his posthumous reputation. His incentive was an anxiety to prove himself worthy of Whately's trust: 'Of the many friends for whose kindness in a foreign land I am indebted to Providence, you alone seemed to have an instinctive knowledge of my character. The rest had to study me; you read me without preparation. We understood each other as if friendship had begun at school'.[12]

Outside Oriel, Blanco moved in scientific, as well as musical circles. He attended meetings of the Ashmolean Society, recently founded to promote scientific research, and delivered one of the Society's first lectures, 'On Musical Sounds', demonstrating an experiment now associated with the name of the German physicist Ernst Chladni. Few, if any, dons could match such a range of intellectual interests.[13]

Nevertheless he continued to feel underemployed and unproductive at Oxford. An attempt to find him work with the University Press was blocked by the evangelicals, who had now marked him down as a 'malignant', and his own literary projects failed to come to fruition. So when in the autumn of 1830 Nassau Senior invited him to spend part of the year at his Kensington home, as tutor to his son, he agreed with some relief.[14]

As at Holland House, so at Senior's house in Kensington Gore, Blanco had a ringside view of events at a critical moment in British political history. Wellington had just been replaced by Grey, and the Whigs were preparing to go to the country on a radical manifesto of reform. Unless these reforms could be carried through constitutionally it looked as though violent revolution might ensue. In the period immediately preceding the Reform Bill of 1832 the propertied and privileged classes trembled for their survival. These were the years of the 'grande peur'. Senior now came into his own as a one-man government think-tank, researching and drafting the key social reforms of the new Whig administration. His ability to absorb and process data was prodigious. As soon as the Whigs took office he was commissioned to report on the law of combinations and strikes, but his greatest achievement was to compile almost single-handed, the report which formed the basis of the Poor Law Reform Bill. At Senior's house Blanco found himself in the engine-room of a new order planned on Benthamite lines. He was no mere spectator, as Senior's papers show. His comments and suggestions appear, along with those of Whately, Malthus and the rest, on drafts relating to a range of subjects including the Poor Law and the Irish tithe question. He was also recruited by Senior to write for *The Quarterly Journal of Education*, published by the Society for the Diffusion of Useful Knowledge.[15] He was proud to be usefully associated with utilitarian ventures which appeared to be the realisation of his political dreams. He particularly approved the transfer of poor relief from the Church to the State. In an article entitled 'The Bill of Belial', written two years later, he defended the new Poor Law against its conservative critics. Here, in the form of a parable, he developed the thesis that charity ceased to be charity when it was made legally compulsory, and that the previous system of institutionalised parish relief ('which robs the industrious in order to maintain the indolent') only served to discredit Christianity. These arguments show how far the theoretician in Blanco could lose touch with his own natural instincts. Like his father, he could never refuse a call on his personal charity. His diaries record the agony of remorse he once felt after failing to give something to 'a poor negro in tattered rags' whom he passed in Whitehall. The next day he walked all the way back to find the man and help him. Yet the logic of political economy could make him sound as cold-blooded as Whately. 'Pray suggest in your report on paupers', the latter wrote to Senior in July 1832, 'that any female receiving relief should have her hair cut off. A good head of hair will fetch from 5 to 10 shillings'.[16]

Senior valued Blanco not only for the clarity of his intellect but also for the conscientiousness and warmth he brought to his task as tutor. The children found in the latter a demonstrativeness and affection which their father had sacrificed to his Gradgrindian pursuit of facts. 'I can see him now', Senior's daughter recalled in old age, 'running to meet me with outstretched arms after a short absence'. Mrs R. D. Hampden, who saw much of Blanco at Oxford, confirms the gentleness of character and fondness for children which made him such a welcome guest. She remembered him one day meeting a nurse carrying a baby on the stairs: 'Bending over the child he implored so solemn a blessing over him that the nurse, struck by the unusual manner, returned to tell the mother of it: "He did say it so hearty—it must do the baby good"'.[17]

It was back at Oxford, in the autumn of 1831, that Blanco received a visit from Alberto Lista. It was twenty-two years since their parting at the end of 1809 when Lista had unsuccessfully tried to persuade his friend to remain in Seville. The reunion at first so overwhelmed Blanco that he was speechless. The sight of his oldest friend revived his dearest and most sacred memories. Their friendship emerged from this reunion all the stronger. Back in Paris, Lista wrote to Oriel: 'It is now a necessity for me to continue corresponding, even if it is only to tell you of my affection. Not that I needed to see you to realise this. If it is true that souls are immortal, my attachment to the man I have loved most on this earth and to whom I owe the elevation of my feelings, can never be destroyed. I have been so delightfully uplifted since our meeting that I spend half my time thinking of you'.[18]

Did the meeting prompt Blanco to speculate on what might have been, if, like Lista and Reinoso, he had stayed in Spain? Their collaboration with the French was by now past history, and both had emerged into the kind of useful, dedicated life of public service which had always been their, and Blanco's ideal. Lista had become the most influential teacher of the new generation, and as a poet, critic, and historian kept the classical tradition alive at a time of debased standards.[19] Unlike Blanco he had learned to live with his religious doubts, and while ceasing to practise his priesthood had never renounced it. (He was to end his days as a canon of Seville Cathedral.) Like Blanco he found vulgar ignorance and dogmatic intolerance even more unattractive in their liberal, atheist guise than under the old theocracy. Indeed the pre-war régime of Charles IV, which they had all so despised in their youth, now seemed, in retrospect and by comparison with present Spanish reality, like a golden age of enlightenment.

Reinoso, too, whom Lista considered to be morally and intellectually superior to them all—had proved that good men could be quietly effective in bad times. He had written by far the best defence of the afrancesado position in which, like Blanco in the Español, he had ironically questioned the liberals' claim to a monopoly of political virtue. He had been dissuaded by Blanco from emigrating to England and had stayed to do dedicated work over an extraordinarily wide field, as journalist, teacher, penal reformer, sociologist and canon lawyer, a Benthamite who always remained a devout Catholic.[20] The intellectual as well as personal solidarity between these three—Lista, Reinoso and Blanco—is remarkable. Consistently, throughout their lives, they retained the same breadth of intellectual interests, the same practical concern for social progress and education, the same refinement of literary taste and the same absolute loyalty in personal relations.

Blanco's intellectual reputation in England at this time contrasted sharply with his social insecurity. In December 1831 J S Mill told a French correspondent, Gustave d'Eichtal, that if he wanted to promote his ideas in England, he could not do better than establish contact with Blanco and Whately: 'Any impression made upon these two men will spread far and wide'.[21] Yet at the same period Blanco was considering an invitation from John Allen to apply for the vacant post of organist at Dulwich College, of which Allen was Warden. 'The duties', Allen informed him, 'are to play the organ on Sundays, and instruct the children in music—twelve in number. The emoluments are at present about £160 a year—besides apartments, commons and wine . . . We wish, of course, to avoid common musicians, and to have a man of education, with the manners and feelings of a gentleman'. Blanco's protestation that he was not, in fact, an organist was not seen by Allen as a disqualification: 'I have no doubt that you will learn to play the organ in much shorter time than you mention'.[22] In the event, the scheme did not materialise.

At Oxford Blanco was increasingly ill-at-ease. In the Oriel common room he could not but feel the gathering tensions. Though Newman had helped to elect Hawkins as Provost in 1828, there was now a coolness between them, and Newman resigned from his tutorship on the principle—which Hawkins did not accept—that the tutor should be not just a director of studies but a moral pastor. Whereas Senior and his circle were absorbed in planning the future, their juniors in Oxford were turning their eyes to the past in search of spiritual certainties. Newman was engaged on researching the Arian controversy and discovering an enthusiasm for Athanasius, the hammerer of heretics. Blanco, who was simultaneously planning a history of the Inquisition, was coming to realise that they were moving in diametrically opposite directions. He liked Athanasius, he told Newman, even less than Arius.[23]

At the same time Newman and his associates were feeling their way towards a more spiritual and elevated idea of the church: no longer just a Church English and established, but a Church catholic and universal, the Mother of the Faithful, the Bride of Christ. This was just the kind of mystical language which irritated the rationalist in Blanco and he found he had to watch his tongue for fear of offending the young men's susceptibilities. The anonymous reviewer of *Evidence* had been remarkably prophetic when in 1825 he declared that in choosing Oxford as a place of retirement Blanco had chosen the place 'least fitted to erase from his memory the religion he had originally professed'.[24]

Younger fellows like Thomas Mozley who had earlier taken him up as a curiosity now decided that he was no longer interesting or that they must 'take a stand', and now left him to his own devices. Blanco himself had always been touchy on the question of his status. Mozley relates how one evening, when dining as a guest at Merton, he complimented one of the Fellows on the excellence of the college bread. The result was that a gift of the bread began to arrive daily at

Blanco's rooms, at which he protested at first mildly but as day succeeded day, with gathering resentment at being treated, as he saw it, like a 'common dolesman'. He was driven, comments Mozley, to a violence 'quite alien to his nature'.[25]

This excitability, not so alien to Blanco's nature as Mozley believed, was not what the senior common room was used to. A telling little note survives among Hawkins' papers, written by Blanco to apologise for his 'vehemence' in a discussion the previous night. 'Do never try', he begged Hawkins, 'to dispel the flattering impression which makes you forget that I was not brought up among you'.[26] One can imagine the scene: Blanco betrayed, perhaps by some painful association, into a passionate outburst—the awkward silence at the departure from form—the averted glances—the tactful change of subject. His insecurity was increased by the fact that some Fellows, such as Keble, had always been faintly disapproving. 'The tone of his books', as a later Tractarian wrote primly, 'and—we must add—of his conversation occasionally, was offensive to many, and that licence of profane sarcasm which sceptical literary men have such a tendency to, stamped him in many eyes'.[27]

He was to feel his isolation even more acutely after the departure of Richard Whately from Oxford at the end of 1831, on his appointment to the Archbishopric of Dublin. He poured out his feelings in a letter to Elizabeth Whately. He had now to be cautious in expressing his views to certain 'pious friends', he told her. 'They' (and it was clear whom he meant) 'would purchase the whole stock of the Pope's shop, provided the Pope himself retired from business'. He had been putting his enforced leisure to use by finishing the second part of his Memoirs—in haste, since he now felt that he had not long to live. By way of postscript he added, prophetically, 'Hampden is preaching an excellent course of Bampton Lectures, which will bring him into trouble'.[28]

At the time these Lectures, published under the general title *The Scholastic Philosophy, considered in its relation to Christian Theology*, made little impact in Oxford, for the good reason that no one at Oxford knew anything about scholasticism. It was only in 1836, four years later, when Newman was looking for hard evidence of Hampden's heterodoxy, that he brought the Lectures out of obscurity, picking through them in order to make them the basis of his indictment. It was then suggested that Blanco (by then a Unitarian) was the grey eminence who had supplied Hampden with his ideas and material. Rather than read what was, after all, a rather unreadable book, gossips like Thomas Mozley were reduced to circumstantial evidence such as that 'in the latter part of 1831 and the early part of 1832 (the period when Hampden was working on the Lectures), these two gentlemen saw a great deal of each other'.[29]

It would have been surprising if Hampden, venturing on to such uncharted ground, had not consulted Blanco as being the only man in Oxford likely to be familiar with the subject. Yet the medieval writers on whom Hampden drew—Abelard, Bernard, Duns Scotus, Anselm—were not ones with whom Blanco was familiar. It is when one turns to the spirit of the Lectures that one finds a remarkable unanimity between the two men. Hampden described his undertaking as an attempt to show how the 'simple religion of Christ' had gradually become encrusted and obscured by the formulaic language of speculative theology—a thesis that would not today be much disputed. In the course of separating the scholastic husk from the biblical grain, he repeatedly touched on Blanco's favourite themes: the evils of 'professional' religion; the misuse of theology as an instrument of social control by a priestly caste; the dangers of 'mysticism' and a 'religion of the feelings'; the absurdity of taking antiquity as a touchstone of truth; the conviction that Christ came not to tell mankind what to think, but how to live. 'Strictly to speak,' Hampden declared, 'in the Scripture itself there are no doctrines'. Blanco would have warmly approved this, as also Hampden's warning against the separation of Christianity into two religions: one for the many, and the other a 'way of perfection' reserved for privileged souls.[30]

The fact that Hampden's and Blanco's attitudes, opinions and prejudices coincided does not necessarily mean that they were transmitted from one to another. Hampden's lack of sympathy for contemplative spirituality stemmed from his own stolid preference for virtue rather than holiness, action rather than contemplation, sense rather than sensibility. But Blanco knew by experience what Hampden knew only by report: he had breathed the air of the garden of the soul which was and always would be closed to Hampden. He was therefore valuable to Hampden, as he had been to Whately in the preparation of *The Errors of Romanism*, as a living example of one who, in his own eyes, had been 'led astray into a wilderness of visionary perfection'.[31]

By the spring of 1832 Hampden, Baden Powell and Hawkins were intellectually the only kindred spirits remaining in Oxford. So when the invitation came from Whately to join him in Dublin as tutor to his son Edward, Blanco accepted the offer. The time of his departure was well chosen. That autumn Newman set out on the critical journey to Rome and Sicily from which he returned in 1833 with the conviction that he had been singled out by providence for the task of renewing the Church of England. In the same year Keble preached the Assize Sermon which is generally taken to mark the inauguration of the Oxford Movement, and the first of the *Tracts for the Times* was published. Blanco was to follow these developments with mounting concern, but the attachments of the heart remained. It was Newman to whom he entrusted the task of winding up his Oxford affairs, and their affectionate correspondence continued. From Dublin, in August 1833, Blanco wrote: 'The Oriel quadrangle shows itself vividly to my mind, and in the midst of dear friends leaves there a *desiderium* for those with whom I have passed so many delightful hours. There are dark points in our University, there are men who strongly remind me of monks and Inquisitors, but I never mention the place without calling it *dear Oxford*'.[32]

10. Merton Street, Oxford, from a watercolour by F. Mackenzie, 1851. Blanco was a frequent visitor at Alban Hall (*left*) where Whately was Principal from 1826 to 1831. His own lodgings ('Palmer's') were further down, on the right, opposite Merton chapel.

Chapter 13
The Swan of Redesdale

In montes patrios et ad incunabula nostra
—Cicero, *Marius*, fr. 4

Blanco left Oxford for Dublin in June 1832. En route, he went for a ride on the recently opened Liverpool and Manchester railway, an excursion which he described to Provost Hawkins—back in rail-less Oxford—as 'truly magical': 'The effects of the intoxicating gas are nothing to the feeling of exultation I had when we were moving at the rate of twenty miles an hour . . . No man capable of the pleasures of sublime poetry should be in England a single year without going to Liverpool or to Manchester to drive on the rail road'. Inspired by this transport of delight he wrote a story for children, 'Atmos the Giant', in which young readers were introduced to the excitements of steam by the imp of progress 'Jack Tellall, Universal Messenger to the March of Intellect Company'.[1]

As a representative himself of the March of Intellect, Blanco was nervous of his reception in Ireland. He was, after all, returning to the country of his Catholic ancestors, driven into exile for their faith, as a declared enemy of Catholicism and as an associate of a Protestant archbishop, the spiritual head of the Ascendancy.

Whately's appointment as Archbishop of Dublin had been nothing short of sensational. His name had not even been mentioned in the list of possible candidates. One of the more popular of these had been the King's illegitimate son, the Reverend Lord Augustus Fitzclarence, whose showmanship (inherited from his mother, the Irish actress Mrs Jordan) would have endeared him to the Dublin public.[2] Instead, one of the richest sees in the Kingdom ('£15,000 a year', as a Dublin newspaper put it, 'with a patronage equal to a pair of German principalities') was awarded to an Oxford don without any connection with Ireland and known only for his Whig politics and eccentric manners. The appointment raised a storm of protest from the Irish Protestant clergy, who saw Whately as a dangerous English liberal of doubtful orthodoxy imposed upon them by an infidel government in order to preside over the dismemberment of the established Church.

Whately certainly went to Ireland with radical intentions. He was heard to say that he would be the last Protestant Archbishop of Dublin, and he told Blanco that he was against the representation of bishops in the House of Lords. It was a mystery to his friends why he should have exchanged the satisfactions of academic life for what his daughter later described as a life of 'anxious toil, disappointment, misapprehension—often fruitless labours, only repaid by obloquy—philanthropic efforts met with suspicion'. His renowned eccentricities now had to be curbed in the interests of prelatical dignity. One of his turns had been to show off the tree-climbing feats of his dog in Christ Church meadow. Shortly after his appointment to Dublin was announced, Whately put the dog through its paces for the benefit of a visitor. Asked what he thought of the performance the latter observed, 'I think that some beside the dog, when they find themselves at the top of the tree, would give the world they could get down again'.[3]

The established clergy and their ladies, used to stiff ecclesiastical protocol, were taken aback by Whately's brusque manner and reluctance to suffer fools gladly. They were even more incensed by what they regarded as his betrayal of their interests. The newly emancipated Catholics, under the leadership of O'Connell and the redoubtable James Warren Doyle ("JKL"), the Bishop of Kildare and Leighlin, having grown in confidence, were now refusing to pay tithes to the clergy of an established Church to which they owed no allegiance. Whately was conscious of the injustice of the tithe system, whereby an alien clergy was maintained at the expense of the Catholic peasantry. He was also in favour of the Catholic clergy being paid by the Government, and was prepared to have the necessary funds drawn from the revenue of the established Church and to countenance the suppression of a number of its sees. 'In large districts of Ireland', he told Copleston, 'The Established church is such as, by the help of a map, you might establish in Turkey or China—viz no place of worship, no congregation'.[4] The embattled Protestants were further incensed by Whately's plan for an ecumenical system of national schools in which Protestant and Catholic children would be educated together and even follow a basic agreed syllabus of common religious instruction. The system was resisted by a large section of the Protestant community and Whately was boycotted by some of his own clergy.[5] The opposition to him had its stronghold in Trinity College, the heart of Protestant Dublin.

In academic circles Whately was chiefly known for his *reductio ad absurdum* of empiricism, *Historic Doubts relating to Napoleon Bonaparte*. Neatly turning the tables, the *Dublin University Magazine* of 1835 contained an article which propounded the theory that it was not just Bonaparte who did not exist but the Archbishop of Dublin. Other sections of the press were more vitriolic. The Protestant *Dublin Record* declared: 'If a Jesuit in disguise were filling the office, he could not

labour more assiduously in his vocation, more decidedly for the
honour and exaltation of his master the Pope, than does Dr Whately,
our Protestant Archbishop'.[6] Thus, from the very beginning of his
tenure of the most uncomfortable see in the kingdom. Whately was
brought up against the absolute implacability of the diehards within
his own Church. 'Here', he told Coplestone, *parcere subiectis* is unknown . . . We parade Orange flags and decorate King William's
statue, and play the tunes of insulting songs under the noses of the
vanquished, till they are goaded to madness; and it is curious that they
are more studious to provoke than to disable their enemies; they are
like sportsmen who preserve foxes on purpose to hunt them'. With
Swiftian irony he went on:

> This being the character of the people, I say again that the permanent
> pacification of Ireland through the predominance of Orange spirit must be
> by the *entire* extermination of at least all the adult males of the Roman
> Catholics. If *any* are left, mark my words, there will be, on the one side,
> oppression and vexatious insult: on the other, assassination, burning,
> houghing of cattle, etc till they have, or fancy they have, strength for a
> fresh outbreak—and so on, over and over again, to the end of time.[7]

It might have been Blanco speaking of Spain.

From the beginning Whately saw his responsibility as being to Irish
society as a whole rather than to any one sect. Apart from his
education scheme he was chairman of a monumental royal commission on the condition of the Irish poor which adapted the principles of
his friend Senior to Irish conditions. Political economy and social
welfare were more congenial to him than theological controversy, and
he governed his see rather as Dr Arnold governed Rugby School: with
stern benevolence.

Blanco found in Dublin that he had exchanged one hotbed of *odium
theologicum* for another. He was a pariah to the Catholics and at the
same time cut off from Protestant society which boycotted Whately.
The latter spent as little time as possible in his Palace on Stephen's
Green and took refuge in his country retreat at Redesdale, near
Stillorgan, with its views of Dublin Bay and the Wicklow mountains,
where he could enjoy the pleasures of tree-cutting and romping with
his children. Blanco, for his part, admitted that Dublin beyond the
confines of Stephen's Green was *terra incognita* to him. Even more than
Whately he loved the peace of Redesdale. 'I wish', he wrote to
Newman euphorically, 'I could live for the rest of my days in this quiet
retired spot'. He went out shooting magpies: 'When the sun is very
hot and I feel the pressure of the gun on my arm, I imagine myself for
an instant young again and in Spain'. Five years later, noting a
reference in Michelet's *History of France* to the Flemish predilection for
the swan, he wrote: 'The last swan that has delighted my eyes was, and

probably still is, at Redesdale, the place of my last enjoyments and my last regrets'.[8]

It is further proof of Blanco's isolation in Dublin that he failed to make contact there with his fellow-exile Joaquín de Villanueva, the doyen of Spanish Jansenism and former member of the Cortes who was now settled in Ireland. Blanco had given material assistance to Villanueva when the latter arrived penniless in London in 1824. Villanueva, too, had become involved in religious controversy, attempting unsuccessfully to convert the Irish Church to the principles of Spanish Jansenism and to persuade them to resist papal interference. Though this brought him into conflict with O'Connell and some of the bishops, he maintained contacts on both sides of the sectarian divide. One of the books he published in Dublin was dedicated to the Protestant patriot Archibald Hamilton Rowan, and another (*Ibernia Phoenicea*, an eccentric work of recondite scholarship which set out to prove that the Irish were of Phoenician descent) to the Catholic Archbishop of Dublin, Daniel Murray. He survived Blanco in Dublin, and one of his 'last Spanish poems celebrates the simple pleasures of his cottage in Blackrock: boating in fine weather, and whisky punch by the fireside on wet evenings.[9]

Almost the only record in Blanco's journal of an expedition into the world outside Redesdale and the Palace is that of a visit to the Moravian mission in Dublin. 'I never saw a more quiet and Christian-like meeting', he noted. 'The Love-feast appeared to me not only unobjectionable, but interesting and useful. There was no confusion, no disturbance, while tea and cakes were handed about. The singing of the hymn with which the meeting had begun, went on while this simple repast took place . . . I may say with truth that I never received deeper impressions from any religious meeting'.[10] There could hardly have been a more striking contrast with the ceremonies of Seville Cathedral.

Along with an attraction to simplicity of worship went a resurgence of the old antipathy to established priesthoods. He had come to Dublin with the intention of working on a history of the Inquisition, but found the subject too painful to pursue because of its disturbing relevance: 'Church tyranny, church ambition, church craft are constantly haunting my mind when I think upon my subject. And, as all these evils exist in full activity around me, they cannot be a subject of historical contemplation'. Experience of the ascendancy Church in Ireland for the first time stirred feelings of remorse for his part in the campaign against Catholic Emancipation:

> It grieves me, it humbles me to perceive in what a shocking light I must have unawares presented myself to a great mass of respectable people when I appeared as an auxiliary to the Protestant party such as it exists in this country. . . Self-defence alone—self-defence against *intolerance*—can

justify political *disabilities* (and nothing else) on the ground of religious
opinions. But to say to any man, 'You have inferior rights to national
benefits, because you believe not in what we choose to call *national*
religion' is abominable in my view of religious liberty . . . A national
religion which is not professed by the *whole* nation is a contradiction.[11]

This conversion would have been more admirable if it had been
prompted less by a sense of having offended 'respectable' opinion and
more by a realisation of having done a grave injustice to Irish
Catholics. But Blanco never met any Irish Catholics. He never saw at
first hand the condition of the peasantry which was described so
graphically a few years later by de Tocqueville.

The time devoted to tutoring Edward Whately, the Archbishop's
son, was not enough to occupy Blanco's energies. He made himself
useful by undertaking the translation into English of Clairaut's
Geometry and *Algebra*, for use as textbooks in the new Irish national
school system. This work enabled Blanco to contribute to the realisation in Ireland of the scheme of elementary practical education he
had long ago advocated in Spain. In the Preface he struck a characteristic note: 'Among those whose circumstances do not permit a proper
training of their intellectual faculties, there are many whose usefulness
and comfort might be increased by a *degree of intellectual education*
suited to their occupations; and if there is any branch of knowledge
which can adapt itself to an indefinite variety of circumstances in the
lower ranks of a civilised nation, it is Geometry'.[12] But he had all too
much time to devote to the consideration of the evils of established
religion. He had now come to see the notion of an infallible Bible as a
distortion of Christianity, just as harmful as that of an infallible
Church. Words, he argued to himself, were capable of widely differing interpretations. How, then, could a just God hold men to
account for failing to interpret the Bible correctly? 'In that case no-one
can be saved but those who in the Lottery of theological opinions,
draw the right ticket'. Even the Gospel texts relating to the divinity of
Christ were ambiguous, and for that reason, he concluded, the
acknowledgement of the divinity of Christ could not be one of the
essentials of Christianity. 'Horrible! It may be so; but I see no
alternative between charging God with setting a trap for men, and my
conclusion that he does not demand from them such an explicit
acknowledgement'.[13]

These were not thoughts which Blanco could share with the
Archbishop of Dublin. Yet at the very moment when he could
compare his situation to that of Jonah under the withered gourd,
Blanco was prevailed upon by Whately to come before the public as a
defender of the established religion. The occasion was the publication
in 1833 of Thomas Moore's *Travels of an Irish Gentleman in Search of a
Religion*. Moore's position as an apologist was as ambiguous as that of

Blanco. The son of a Catholic grocer in Dublin, as a young man he had been barred on account of his religion from taking his degree at Trinity, but he had gone on to take London by storm. 'Anacreon' Moore's wit and charm made him the favourite of society hostesses, and he was Byron's trusted friend and executor. Meanwhile, he had acquired *in absentia* the status of Ireland's national poet. The *Irish Melodies* published over a period of twenty-five years between 1807 and 1834 entranced English drawing-rooms with their sweet, romantic melancholy. His visit to Ireland in 1830 was an apotheosis: he was mobbed by wildly enthusiastic crowds wherever he went.[14]

During his long residence in England, Moore had allowed his practice of Catholicism to lapse. He married an English Protestant, and allowed his children to be brought up in their mother's religion. However, although he had become the darling of English society he always regarded it with an ironic detachment, retaining his Irishness and, along with it, an emotional allegiance to the religion of his fathers. He had stood aloof from O'Connell, by whom he had been rebuked for lukewarmness in the political cause. However, now that Emancipation had been achieved and Catholic self-confidence was growing, Moore turned on the Irish Protestant establishment the deadly weapon of ridicule. He was prompted to enter the arena of religious controversy, he told a correspondent, by 'the disgust I feel and have ever felt at the arrogance with which most Protestant parsons assume to themselves and their followers the credit of being the only true Christians, and the insolence with which, weekly, from their pulpits, they denounce all Catholics as idolaters and anti-Christ'. Moore sought to prove the paradox that it was the Irish peasantry, not their lords and masters, who were the heirs of the apostles and of Christian antiquity. Rather surprisingly, he was well-read in theology, or rather in the more curious byways of church history, disreputable and spectacular heretics being his speciality. 'Good company is a good thing', he observed, 'but bad is better'. In 1829 he had written for the *Edinburgh* a review of H. J. Rose's *The State of Protestantism in Germany* and E. B. Pusey's *Historical Enquiry into the Probable Causes of the Rationalist Character*, which he used as an opportunity to compare the 'unwearied industry' of German theologians with the torpor of 'the sleek, somnolent and satisfied divines of the Church of England'. In the same mischievous spirit he set about undermining the Protestant establishment's claim to Christian superiority. His aim was to entertain, and so he chose the form of a novel, interweaving a romantic plot with erudite scholarship.[15]

The hero of *Travels of an Irish Gentleman* is a young Irish Catholic, who is overheard on page one breathing a sigh of relief at the passing of the Catholic Emancipation Bill. Previously he had defended the church out of loyalty to his fellow-countrymen, while secretly harbouring the fear that Protestantism might be true. Moreover, as a young man of social ambition he had felt uncomfortably aware that Catholicism was not a religion for gentlemen. Now that he is free at last to choose a religion for himself, he embarks on a study of the early Church, but as he investigates the Fathers, what he finds—to his surprise—is evidence not of primitive Protestantism but of 'stark, staring Popery'. 'If St Ambrose woke up in Carlow', he concludes, 'he'd be proud to make the acquaintance of Dr Doyle'. Meanwhile he has fallen in love with a Protestant girl, and at her suggestion travels to Germany in order to drink at the source of reformed religion. However, after attending the lectures of the eminent biblical scholar, Professor Scratchenback, he concludes that 'the descendants of those very men who cried up the Bible as everything have now succeeded . . . in degrading the Bible to almost nothing'.[16] The tale ends with the narrator confirmed in his ancestral faith, and with the timely conversion of his *inamorata*.

Though his book was published anonymously, Moore was known to be its author, and this caused him some embarrassment. 'I find I am called in Ireland "Defender of the Faith" and "Father of the Hibernian Church"', he wrote wryly to McVey Napier. Moore's true theological opinions were not, in fact, very different from Blanco's, in so far as he had the same enlightened disdain for anything that savoured of 'enthusiasm'. While in his poetry he idealised the simple religion of the Irish peasant, in private he could write of 'that wretched faith which is again polluting Europe with Jesuitism and Inquisitions, and which of all the humbugs which have stultified mankind is the most narrow-minded and mischievous'.[17] Yet he remained devoted to the 'poetry' of religion, and he found theology 'piquant'. Besides, though his book appeared to be theological, it was essentially political, designed to put heart into his fellow-Irishmen and to puncture Protestant pride.

Whately had the sense to see that Moore had to be met on his own ground and that only Blanco had the wit and erudition to match him. Besides, Blanco had spent a lifetime in search of a religion, and had a fundamental sincerity which Moore—for all his good nature—lacked. As a doubter himself, Blanco had a sure instinct for scenting doubt in others, and he divined the scepticism at the heart of Moore's entertaining sallies. His reply, *Second Travels of an Irish Gentleman in Search of a Religion*, was written in less than twelve weeks. Wisely, Blanco retained the tone of the original novel, of which his work purported to be the sequel. However, while Moore's thrust was political, Blanco's was theological. Moore had dedicated *Travels* to 'the People of Ireland', as a 'Defence of their Ancient and National Faith', whereas Blanco's corresponding dedication read; 'To the People of Ireland, whose virtue, improvement and happiness must depend, not on the *antiquity* or *nationality* but on THE TRUTH of the religion which their great majority shall profess; this attempt to soften their prejudices and to lead them, whether Catholics or Protestants, to a fair and independent examination of the subject most intimately connected with their union as brothers and fellow-countrymen is inscribed by one who fairly loves them'. The call for disinterested enquiry would have been more convincing if it had not been commissioned by the head of the established Church. And someone should have warned Blanco that it is not advisable to start an argument with an Irishman by telling him you are going to 'soften his prejudices'.

The *Second Travels* contains many shrewd blows at Moore, and the 'novel' is continued with an ingenuity which matches that of the original. A gothic note is supplied by a villainous priest who tries to lure the heroine into a convent—a character obviously modelled on the confessor who persuaded Blanco's sister to take the veil. But the author of *Second Travels* defended the established Church by sawing away the very branch on which he was seated. Moore looked to antiquity, to the Fathers, for authentication, but Blanco declared that antiquity was no warrant for truth. Moore pointed to the absence of 'Protestantism' in the early Church, but Blanco argued that the writings of the heterodox had been suppressed by the victorious orthodox, and that in any case 'Protestantism' as a system never existed. Moore based his argument in favour of the authority of Rome on the assumption that the founder of Christianity could not have intended there to be differences of opinion about his teaching, but Blanco maintained that since such differences did and—given the ambiguity of many of the Gospel texts—must exist, Christ not only foresaw that his teaching would be a source of contention but positively willed his followers to exercise intellectual freedom, for he 'did not come to change the laws of human understanding'. Moore asserted that ecclesiastical unity was founded on agreement, but Blanco argued that in practice 'what binds together Churches is not what each *believes* but what each *denies*; not what each *loves* but what each hates'. 'Faith', in other words, was often disguised party spirit. If these were strange propositions with which to defend Protestant orthodoxy, even stranger was Blanco's declaration in the preface that he had 'no distinct or precise idea of any being, either individual or collective to which the name Church of England applies' and therefore that 'nothing whatever adduced as an argument on the authority of the Church of England' could have any weight with him. The Church, in other words, was merely a collective noun. Anticipating objections, Blanco justified his own continuing membership of the Church of England by speaking through his lips of one of his characters, who described the language of the Thirty-Nine Articles as metaphorical: 'I find much in them which *encumbers* Christianity; but nothing that invalidates its spirit and efficiency, and therefore I remain attached to a

Church which has done much good and which, if it were delivered in spiritual matters from the trammels of Parliament, would continue to be a distinguished supporter of Christian revelation'.[18] The ultimate test of the rightness of articles of faith was whether they made an individual more Christlike.

It was hardly to be expected that *Second Travels* would find a hearing among Irish Catholics, and Moore did not pursue the controversy. He seems not to have discovered the identity of the author, remarking to a correspondent that he supposed it must be someone 'who wants to be a bishop'. (One hopes that Blanco would have appreciated the irony.) One who could have enlightened Moore was his friend Lord Holland, who wrote to congratulate Blanco on a 'lively, acute, and in many particulars original work'. The refined and aristocratic Christianity of *Second Travels* may have been to Lord Holland's taste, but it was not likely to appeal to the less privileged. Blanco's *hidalguía* is evident in his contempt for all manifestations of popular piety, and implicit in the way he contrasts the readiness of the Catholic hierarchy to 'pander' to superstition, with Christ's 'disdain' for the 'common herd'. As a whole the book reveals rejection of the social and incarnate dimension of Christianity, and a fastidiousness encapsulated in his remark that 'the general state of the Christian society began at a very early period to be most unsatisfactory'.[19]

Nor did *Second Travels* win the approval of the very people it was supposed to defend—the Protestants of Ireland. The theological implications of the book were certainly not lost on the nascent Tractarian party at Oxford. Keble's Assize sermon, preached in April 1833, which is generally taken to be the starting point of that movement, was provoked by Parliament's proposal to abolish a number of bishoprics in Ireland—which Keble represented as an unjustified interference by the state in church affairs. Since Whately had thrown his authority behind this decision, he was a target for Tractarian indignation, and from now on Whately's words and actions were critically scrutinised by his enemies. Since Blanco was a known associate of Whately, any heterodox statement by Blanco could be used to discredit the Archbishop. Significantly, Blanco's correspondence with Newman faded away after November 1833. Newman had just published his *Arians of the Fourth Century*, and Blanco—whose views about the Fathers were clearly shown in *Second Travels*—did not find it to his taste.

It was at this time that he came across, in translation, the work of the German church historian Johann August Neander, which immediately attracted him with its ideal of a non-institutional, non-dogmatic, 'spiritual' Church. In order to study the work more profoundly he set about learning German—thereby laying the foundations for the final stage of his intellectual life, which was to be so concerned with German philosophy and theology. Meanwhile he and Neander corresponded in Latin, like two Renaissance humanists.[20] In his state of isolation, reluctant to reveal to Whately the full extent of his doubts, Blanco found relief in unburdening himself to Neander and to another correspondent whom he had never met, George Armstrong, once a clergyman of the established church in Ireland and later a dissenting minister in Bristol. Blanco had been in correspondence with Armstrong since 1828, and now turned to him as a confidant in his last and decisive crisis. Writing to Armstrong in August 1834 he tried to clarify his position:

> I do not belong to that class of Divines who are commonly called Unitarians. To the Church of England as a political body, I certainly do not belong . . . I believe that if I were twenty years younger I should be very much inclined to open a chapel of my own, and avoid the giving it any *denomination* besides that of *"Christian"*. But it is evident that my course cannot be far from its end. Whatever powers are left me, I am, however, determined to employ in writing against the spirit of *Orthodoxy*—that bane of the Christian church, which began to corrupt it almost in the time of the Apostles themselves.[21]

In accordance with this resolve, Blanco published in 1834 what is the most concise statement of his views on freedom of expression. It was prompted by an article in the Dublin *Christian Examiner* supporting the principle of the right of government to censor publications hostile to Christianity. In *The Law of Anti-Religious Libel Reconsidered* he simply and incisively stated his conviction that truth needs no law to protect it: *Deorum injuriae dis curae*. Church history, he declared, contained a wealth of horrors to exhibit the dangers of governments taking on themselves the role of truth's guardians. 'No man has a right to prescribe to others what propositions they must never attack as erroneous . . . No man comes to Christ unless the Father draws him'.[22]

He also started work on the work which he intended to be a distillation of his lifelong preoccupation with the question of heresy and orthodoxy. He had always previously discussed his projects with Whately and sought his comments but on this occasion withheld his draft manuscript on the grounds that he did not want to unsettle Whately's mind—even though, as the latter pointed out, the published book was likely to unsettle a far wider readership.

The situation was complicated by the fact that Mrs Whately was also going through, at this time, a period of religious uncertainty. Because of the tension of reconciling these difficulties with her official position as the Archbishop's wife, and because of strains within her marriage (her sister wrote to Blanco of 'those painful scenes which take place between her and the Archbishop'), her health had been declining for several months. She confided her problems to Blanco, and her husband appears to have held the latter responsible for contributing to her unsettled state. It was a charge which Blanco rejected: 'It is a fact which Mrs Whately herself will, I have no doubt, attest, that I never volunteered a single opinion of my own, and that she has always enquired of me upon points which she *before* doubted: that she has repeatedly assured me that were it not for the assistance which at her desire I have given her, she could hardly hope to have supported her Christian faith.[23]

These tensions gradually built up during the last months of 1834. Blanco's journal records the incident which provoked the final crisis. He had given Mrs Whately the manuscript of a pamphlet by Neander on the free teaching of theology, and the Archbishop saw it lying on the breakfast table.

> I expressed my sincere regret that, owing to the desire of putting it in his power, when I publish anything, to say that he had not read it, and consequently is not answerable for any opinions expressed by me, I could not avail myself of his judgment, as I used to do formerly. He answered 'that there was no reason why I should keep my MSS from him, for he had always maintained that the person who consults is not bound to follow the advice given to him'. And then he added, 'But, of course, I should not like you to publish anything too *radical*'.

The words were just such as to inflame one who could not endure the slightest tug on the bridle. 'Must I then reduce myself to publish only what may be allowed (with the utmost latitude of *clerical* liberality) to come out of an Archbishop's Palace? . . . Must I spend the last days of a life devoted to mental independence, under any such restraint? Am I doing my duty? Am I not concealing the ultimate results of my study and experience, just when they may be supposed to have arrived at the utmost maturity of which they may be capable?' Once launched upon this line of reasoning, Blanco took little time to convince himself that he must sacrifice his position in the Archbishop's house in order to preserve his intellectual integrity. 'If a second sacrifice is still demanded by Truth, my heart (I trust in God) will not shrink from it. I shall tear myself from those whose affection has struck roots in my heart.—I shall tear myself from them—and drop them into my grave'.[24]

The overwrought language gives some indication of Blanco's state of mind. Later Whately was to speak of the latter's 'derangement', attested by medical opinion. It is true that the private journals of this date reveal a profound agitation of mind and body. Yet this does not alter the absolute logic of Blanco's position. The last tenuous threads which attached him to the Church of England had over the two previous years been broken one by one. The spectacle of Protestant theocracy in Ireland, and the influence of Neander and Armstrong had simply served to fortify his profound, if long suppressed conviction that, to be genuine, Christianity must be a religion of the spirit free of all institutional shackles. Even the word 'religion' was now intolerable to him. 'Christ came to liberate man from *all religion*, that great source of the worst human evils'.[25]

It was George Armstrong who persuaded Blanco that the last threadbare arguments which kept him in the Church of England were no longer tenable. The latter came to the final decision less as a result of doctrinal difficulties than because of his now overriding objection to the political endowment of religious orthodoxy: 'A Society, under the name of a Christian Church, to which the State appropriates a large portion of the public property, on condition that it shall maintain a certain set of doctrines *as the doctrines of the Gospel*, is a great evil to the country and to mankind at large. If this be not bribing . . . I do not know to what I can give that name'.

Convinced where his duty lay, Blanco told Whately of his final decision by letter on 2 January 1833.

> I am under an imperative conviction that it is my duty to publish the fact that I am a decided anti-Trinitarian . . . The first, the most distressing and most inevitable consequence of the declarations which I intend to make in a Preface to my Letters on Heresy and the Inquisition, is my exclusion from the bosom of your family. To save you from every perplexity between your kindness and the demands of your situation in the Church, I intend to cross over to Liverpool, as soon as I receive an answer from my friend Zulueta, to whom I intend writing this day.[26]

Though the attraction of Liverpool was in part due, no doubt, to the presence there of a strong Unitarian community, it was in the first instance a Spanish connection which prompted the decision. Clemente de Zulueta and his brother Pedro were Cadiz merchants who had been associated with the liberal regime and had been outlawed by the monarchy. Pedro had set up a shipping business in London and Clemente had opened a branch of this business in Liverpool in 1828. A man of literary tastes (the friend of Reinoso as well as of Blanco) he had been in correspondence with the latter for some years, and had confided to him his religious difficulties. It was under the influence of Blanco that he had recovered his faith in Christianity. He did not fail his friend in this time of crisis.[27]

Right up to the time of his departure Blanco confided his turbulent thoughts to his journal. In his own mind he was a martyr. 'Deeply afflicted as I am, I really feel grateful that I have been found worthy to suffer for the CAUSE of truth and mankind . . . I feel it my bounden duty to show, by my sufferings, to the world, how injurious to the cause of religion, of Christian charity, and of humanity itself, that

Church system must be, which makes such sacrifices to *the love of truth* unavoidable to me'.

As he prepared to cross the last of his Rubicons, he made a final poignant entry in his Dublin journal: 'Waiting in anguish for the hour of departure'.[28]

Chapter 14
High Minds and Plain Furniture

'Hitherto, then, I have been in an error', answered Don Quixote.

To the world Blanco had left, Liverpool stood for all that was base and godless in the new industrial England: unconsecrated territory which lay beyond Oxford's pale. A former Oriel pupil, E T Daniell, expressed the general feeling: 'Your "*having taken a house*" sounds very awful . . . What there can be to keep you in that land of steam engines, ships and railroads puzzles me'.[1] But for Blanco, the secularity of Liverpool was one of its main attractions: the fact, as he told Lord Holland, that it was not a *clerical* town.[2]

In 1835 Liverpool was undergoing a phenomenal expansion. The death of William Roscoe four years earlier had marked an important stage in its development. Roscoe, the poet banker, the scholar merchant, author of biographies of Lorenzo de Medici and Pope Leo X, had envisaged his native city as a Florence on the Mersey, a model republic in which the arts and sciences would flourish. Neo-classical buildings such as the Athenaeum and the Royal Institution bore witness to his vision. But the population of the city increased tenfold in Roscoe's lifetime, and this had now created social problems on an unprecedented scale. The increase in shipping, the building of docks, canals and railways, had attracted crowds of unskilled labourers, many of them from Ireland, first-generation city-dwellers who recreated the conditions of rural poverty in the narrow courts and cellars of the new urban slums. Those who could not find work, starved, and only a few inadequate voluntary societies attempted to cope with the social and moral chaos. Herman Melville visited the place as a young sailor in 1839 and in his novel *Redburn* left an unforgettable picture of the degradation he witnessed in 'pestilent lanes and alleys . . . putrid with vice and crime, to which perhaps the round globe does not furnish a parallel'.[3] A vast gulf divided this desperate proletariat from the merchant oligarchs who had recently moved away from the inner city to the elegant houses of Rodney Street, Upper Parliament Street and Abercromby Square.

Roscoe was typical of his class in being a radical in his politics and a Unitarian in his religion. Liverpool's rise to prosperity in the late eighteenth century had been based on the slave trade, and it was Roscoe's achievement to have convinced his fellow-citizens of the righteousness of the abolitionist cause, so that they sacrificed profit to

171

principle. The moral tone was set by the Unitarian community—a cultivated and liberal plutocracy—which throughout the century exercised an influence out of all proportion to its size. Roscoe was succeeded as the leading Unitarian layman by William Rathbone, who established a family tradition of public service and philanthropy which has lasted to the present day. There were two Unitarian chapels, Renshaw Street and Paradise Street, presided over by two young clergymen who were to lead their congregations until almost the end of the century: James Martineau and J. H. Thom.[4] Blanco arrived at a critical moment of change when these two were engaged on transforming the rationalist sect of Joseph Priestley into a transcendentalist High Church open to all men of goodwill. Of the two, Martineau, the minister at Paradise Street, was the more profound thinker. He disliked the term 'Unitarian' as being too dogmatic and divisive, and would have preferred a name which stressed not so much a negative opposition to Trinitarian belief as a positive, purified, churchless Christianity. His God was not a Priestleyan First Cause, operating his created mechanism from without, but an indwelling light to be found within the soul. His colleague at Renshaw Street, J. H. Thom, never became a national figure but exercised the greater influence locally. A later incumbent, L. P. Jacks, who knew Thom in his old age, described him as the greatest preacher Unitarianism had ever produced. In his austere chapel—Jacks described it as 'the spirit of Puritanism turned into stone'—he preached exalted, Platonic sermons which at first puzzled his businesslike congregation, used to practical moral exhortation.[5] Blanco established an immediate rapport with this solemn, refined, rather sacerdotal young man who was to become his disciple and executor. He attended Unitarian worship for the first time two weeks after his arrival in Liverpool and professed himself delighted with its simplicity. 'What a relief it was to me', he told George Armstrong, 'to be able to join in social worship undisturbed by offensive expressions and without the necessity of mental protests and reservations at every step'. 'Sunday after Sunday', he recorded in his journal, 'going alternately to the two Unitarian chapels in this town, I enjoy the most sublime moral and intellectual treat which the purified religious principle can offer to man'.[6]

The scars of the separation from the Whatelys took a long time to heal. A few days after his departure from Dublin, Elizabeth Whately wrote, 'You will not doubt how I of all persons must miss my very kind and dear friend; and therefore I will say little on the subject. Especially as my reason refuses to see anything but evil in the step you have thus hastily taken. The self-devotedness it involves, I suspect, has even tended to mislead your feelings. The purity of your motives could never be doubted. My anxiety is therefore most for others—for the world'. The Archbishop, she added, had ordered one hundred

11. Richard Whately, Archbishop of Dublin.

pounds to be placed to Blanco's account annually to allow him to
maintain a manservant and 'as a pledge that you do not consider our
friendship broken by this change'. It says much for the charity of the
Whatelys that in their affectionate regard they overlooked Blanco's
reply to this letter, which showed him at his self-righteous worst. It
was, he declared, 'extremely painful' for him to receive this 'bounty'.
As to his usefulness, 'it may be diminished for one sort of people; but I
still think it will be increased in regard to others who from their tone of
mind are objects of greater sympathy to me and more likely to have an
influence on those who really belong to the present age of the world'.[7]

To Whately, facing attack from both Protestant Dublin and Tractarian Oxford, Blanco's public abandonment of the Church of England
was an acute embarrassment. Blanco was known to have been his
intimate friend and confidant, and might be presumed to have shown
him the manuscript of the book he was now about to publish in order
to explain his final break with orthodoxy. Whately himself was
accused of holding heterodox views on the Trinity and on Sabbath
observance and knew that his enemies would use the association with
Blanco to accuse him of being a crypto-Socinian.

In his anxiety to tell the world of his state of mind, Blanco ignored the consideration he owed his friend. As an archbishop, he argued, Whately was the prisoner of the system he served and could not be disinterested. Whately protested:

> Do not, I entreat you, let anyone persuade you that every bishop and beneficed clergyman must be presumed to be an intolerant bigot, or hypocritical, or narrow-minded . . . It should not be forgotten that one of the greatest breaches of charity is, rashly and without cause to impute want of charity to another . . . Permit me to warn you, my dear friend, not to judge of each person's freedom from intolerance of spirit by the vehemence with which he censures it, or the readiness with which he imputes it.

He also warned Blanco of the reaction which his rushing into print might provoke:

> I shall probably be told, "Why should he publish, when he cannot be sure that he knows his own mind? What has happened may happen again, or may be taking place now. We have every reason to expect that next year, or next month, he will publish a book declaring that he not only is, but has been all along unconsciously, a Deist or an Atheist, a Quaker, a Swedenborgian or a Papist, and that he has only just met with someone who has removed the flimsy veil which had concealed his real views from himself . . . And judging of the future by the past, we ought not to be surprised if he should tell us a year hence that he never was a believer in Christianity at all, though he had persuaded himself that he was so".[8]

These arguments only served to increase Blanco's resentment, and he was even more agitated by Whately's suggestion that he should delay publication until he had recovered mental equilibrium. Entries in Blanco's journal—which he later shamefacedly crossed out or excised—bear witness to his almost frenzied struggle to resist the pressure being put upon him, and to escape from the shadow of Whately's 'gigantic' intellect.[9]

In his efforts to prevent or at least delay publication, Whately now resorted to devious means. He asked Senior to distract Blanco by writing to consult him as an authority on Political Economy: 'Try *speedily* to occupy his mind with the best thing that comes to hand. It may make the difference of saving his mind from—I don't know what'. Another stratagem shows how thoroughly Whately knew his man. Senior was to write to an old friend of Blanco—evidently a Unitarian and a bore—informing him of the latter's conversion. The friend 'would be likely to communicate with him and bestow some of his tediousness upon him: and I have some little hope that this homoeopathic treatment might recall him and perhaps do good to both!' In a last desperate throw, Whately asked his own publisher to write and propose himself to Blanco as the publisher of the forthcoming book, of which Whately (unknown to the author) would cover the costs. By this means Whately hoped to 'interpose such delay as might at least lessen his [Blanco's] exposure of himself'. All these moves were unsuccessful.[10]

The news of the defection provoked a reaction of horror at Oxford. Newman wrote a letter—unfortunately no longer extant—which Blanco described as 'nothing but a groan, a sigh, from beginning to end'. 'I cannot leave your letter unanswered', he replied, 'lest you should imagine I could receive it with any other feelings than those of affection and gratitude . . . I would give anything in my power to relieve the pain you suffer on my account. But as long as the notion that opinions can decide the fate of immortal souls shall exist, the most excruciating sufferings await the best minds. If I have any strength left, I will employ it in combating that error'.[11] Privately, Newman thought it not impossible that Blanco would come full circle. 'It is difficult to see how it will all end', he wrote to Robert Wilberforce, 'whether he will end his days in infidelity, Romanism or confinement. His personal antipathy to Romanism makes me think it impossible he should go back to it—yet, who knows? he may be like Pentheus'.[12] Pusey, for his part, thought that the fault lay in Blanco's having left the Church of Rome in the first place. To his letter, warning of the dangers of the pride of reason, Blanco replied: 'I should think very unfavourably of anyone who could take offence at your letter. Your kindness and goodness of heart are stamped on every line of it. But I regret that the state of mind it discloses, is quite melancholy to me. I see you perfectly subdued by the principles of Mysticism'. Again Blanco reacted fiercely to the suggestion that some moral weakness must lie at the root of the problem and he also rejected the charge of solipsism: 'No man tolerably acquainted with the Philosophy of the human mind would assert that there is only *subjective* truth: but whoever has examined the matter even slightly must be thoroughly convinced that we can know nothing of the *objective* but through the *subjective*. The nearest approach that any man can make to objective truth is in his own mind'.[13]

When he wrote to inform Provost Hawkins of his move, Blanco asked for his name to be removed from the Oriel books: 'I do not conceive that you, as head of Oriel College, could allow a professed Anti-Trinitarian to be one of its members'. Hawkins was unwilling to provide the martyrdom which Blanco was courting. 'I am not the person to exclude you from this College because I hear of a conscientious change in your Theological views', he declared. However, he too argued against any rushing into print: 'If ever a man had cause to weigh most carefully all his motives, to consider the state of his health, everything in a word which can influence opinions, before he takes a step such as you meditate, you are that man'.[14]

But for Blanco, publication was a 'duty'. In *Observations on Heresy and Orthodoxy* he finally cut loose from Church and dogma. In the preface he explained that though the work had begun as a history of the Spanish Inquisition he had gradually become convinced that every form of orthodoxy, Protestant and English as well as Catholic and Spanish, tended towards intolerance and persecution. The core of the book, clearly and forcefully written, was the declaration that the Gospel could not consist 'in abstract doctrines, about which men of equal abilities, virtue and sincerity are, and always have been, divided . . . The promises of the Gospel must have been attached to a MORAL, not a LOGICAL act. It must be an act in which to fail is blameable; the failure must be not a *mistake*, but a sin'.[15] How, he asked, could salvation depend upon successfully negotiating the theological tightrope in order to reach the approved conclusions? Christianity, he argued, was not a religion for the theologian but for the layman, and the only guide in determining Christian truth was not Church or Bible but the subjective individual mind and conscience.

Newman described *Observations* to his sister as 'as bad as can be. He [B] evidently wishes to be attacked. I hope as far as possible he will be left alone; it will do him most good. He is not content till he is talked about, and he has a morbid pleasure in being abused'.[16] Even before the book appeared, Newman had encouraged Henry Wilberforce to use Blanco's 'defection' as a cautionary example with which to attack the theological liberalism of Whately, Hampden, Senior, Arnold and Hawkins—what Newman called 'the advanced guard of a black host'. In his anonymous pamphlet, *The Foundations of the Faith Assailed in Oxford*, Wilberforce alleged the existence at Oxford of an enemy within, 'a party on whom I think I should hardly lay an unjust censure were I to apply to them the awful name of *Socinian*', a party among whom there existed 'an unequivocal disposition to modify our system by a series of liberal changes tending to make knowledge, rather than moral discipline, the object of our studies, and to cultivate rather the habit of bold and irreverent inquiry, often conducted in the most flippant tone and spirit, and sparing no subject, whether human or divine, for that humility and self-distrust which characterises the true philosopher'. Blanco was presented as one who had simply followed to its logical extreme the liberal philosophy of his friends, and even as one who, 'with all his speculative profaneness, shows far more of heartfelt religious feeling than is betrayed in the writings of Dr Hampden or some others who might be named'.[17]

Rather than counter Blanco's arguments directly, Newman and Hurrell Froude now calculated how the attack might be pressed home in the latter's review of *Observations*. It was decided to adopt a mild tone in relation to Blanco personally, even to the extent of granting that there was much 'force, truth and ingenuity' in his arguments. The real targets were to be Hampden and Whately. 'I mean after praising his [B's] talent and amiable qualities, and alluding to his "interesting history"', Froude wrote, 'to give an analysis of his argument in which to the best of my ability I shall strengthen his arguments and soften his conclusions so as to make the whole appear and indeed be a legitimate development of Protestantism'.[18] It seemed to be Blanco's fate to be manipulated by others for their political, or theologico-political, ends. Unable, or unwilling, to meet Blanco's arguments head-on, his enemies adopted the very English tactic of damning him with faint praise.

Newman's careful orchestration of the campaign against Hampden's appointment as Regius Professor of Divinity the following year shows what a formidable theocrat he would have become if Tractarianism had finally carried the day at Oxford, and if he had remained in the Church of England. If it did nothing else, his conversion to Rome saved him from the temptations of power. His dislike of Hampden—'the most lucre-loving, earthly-minded, unlovely person one ever set eyes on'[19]—amounted to revulsion, and this personal element helped to turn the controversy into a vendetta. Early in 1836 he resurrected Hampden's forgotten Bampton Lectures and combed through them for evidence of heterodoxy. Part of the case then mounted by the Corpus Committee, formed to block Hampden's appointment, rested on the assertion that Blanco—now a self-confessed 'Socinian'—was the begetter of these Lectures. Hampden's guilt was to be imputed by association.

Blanco had been kept in close touch with developments at Oxford by Hawkins and Baden Powell. He could not bring himself to read the Tracts, as he told Hawkins:

> When people have advanced to that stage of mental disease in which the ultimate ground of argument is an act of the Will, it is most distressing to attempt anything like reasoning. Newman, I am convinced, is in that state, and I remember to have perceived the first symptoms when I was at Oxford. He had drawn into the same course the more lively mind of poor Froude, who seemed to me at times to laugh at the extravagance of the conclusions with which he found himself compelled by logical consistency . . . I have loved both these young men for their talents, and their natural kindness, but they are, especially the survivor, very remarkable instances of the poisonous nature of bigotry, and have added two bleeding scars to the many which love, defeated and outraged by what is called Religion, has left in my heart. The close of my life has been fearfully darkened by the very evil which embittered my youth.[20]

As the campaign against Hampden gathered force, so Blanco saw it as melancholy proof of the case he had argued in his recent work on the evils of orthodoxy. Just as Newman was obsessed by Hampden, so Blanco now became obsessed by Newman and his colleagues—'soft-worded bigots' whom he saw in a 'lurid and hellish' light. 'Newman, who has raised himself into a Protestant Pope and who, as sure as he lives would persecute to the death if he had the direction of the civil power for a dozen years,—Newman expresses the utmost tenderness for those who, holding any opinions whatever, will only whisper them, tremblingly, into his ear'. It was as if he saw Newman as the reincarnation of his former spiritual director Father Teodomiro Diaz de la Vega, the priest who attended the *beata ciega* in her last hours. 'I do not exaggerate when I say that the tone of *tenderness* in which they speak of the victim [Hampden] whom they have marked down for as great destruction as it is in their power to inflict, gives me more intolerable pain than any of the sentences of death by the Spanish Inquisition. It is only in this specimen of Protestant persecution that the true nature of Orthodoxy, supported by Law, can be observed'.[21]

For Blanco, the witch-hunt and condemnation of Hampden seemed to show that the danger of theocracy was perhaps even greater in England than elsewhere, since in England the clerical party had the advantages of social and intellectual respectability and organisational efficiency which were lacking to their counterparts on the continent. On 5 May 1836 he recorded in his journal: 'For the first time since my arrival in 1810 I have this morning felt an impulse to quit this country'. Yet in spite of all, he still dreamed of Oriel: 'I am by affection', he told Hawkins, 'a thorough Oriel man. When in my frequently sleepless nights, I amuse myself by frequently walking *in spirit* up and down the quadrangles, hall, library, and looking into your study, my whole heart yearns for you'.[22]

The truth was that his life at Liverpool was one of profound solitude. Clemente de Zulueta, whose presence there prompted his original move, had by now returned to Cadiz. Of the Unitarians, only Thom offered personal friendship, and he was taken up with pastoral and family responsibilities. Hence the feeling of emptiness which underlies the outwardly cheerful account he sent Julia Moore of his Liverpool routine: 'When I return from my daily walk to the Athenaeum and find everything quiet, the house perfectly clean, my plain furniture in the best order, and my books ready to whisper wisdom and peace to my mind, my heart expands with thankfulness and I almost forget I have ever been in trouble'.[23] His affections found an outlet only in correspondence with his brother in Seville, and with old friends such as the Christies, Carletons and Moores, Lord Holland, and the Whatelys and Seniors. He was now at the mercy of housekeepers, of whom as a class he was at once nervous and disdainful. One of them, a Welshwoman, he described to Elizabeth Whately as 'a wilful, deceitful and encroaching woman, with the habits of wandering of an old mountain goat'.[24] Even in furnished rooms in Upper Stanhope Street he was still the hidalgo.

Nevertheless within the Unitarian community Blanco held a place of honour, as is demonstrated by the part he played in setting up the Domestic Mission in Liverpool in April 1836.[25] Inspired by the work of the American Unitarian Joseph Tuckerman in Boston, Thom preached an historic sermon the previous Christmas in which he roused the conscience of his congregation to the social and spiritual deprivation on their doorstep. They were not yet prepared for the idea that they should do this work themselves, or that it should take the form primarily of material relief. The work was to be deputed to a special minister, whose task was to raise the consciousness of the poor, to help them to help themselves. At the inaugural meeting of the Mission, it was Blanco who defined the Minister's duties as being

> to establish an intercourse with a limited number of families of the neglected poor—to put himself into close sympathy with their wants and feelings—to become to them a Christian adviser and friend—to promote the order and comfort of their homes and the elevation of their social tastes—to bring them into a permanent connection with religious influences—and, above all, to promote an affective education of their children and to shelter them from corrupting agencies.[26]

The idea was not the twentieth century one that the middle class should atone for their privilege by sharing the conditions of the poor, but rather that they should elevate the poor to their own moral level. There was much in the scheme to commend itself to Blanco's enlightenment mentality, not least the fact that the Mission was to be non-sectarian and non-proselytising—a novel feature at a time when the soup ticket was inseparable from the bible text. In a letter to William Rathbone on the first anniversary of the Mission, Blanco expressed his satisfaction that the Minister had resisted 'the amiable delusion that Poverty and Misery can be removed by alms' and that he had made it his chief concern to encourage the poor towards self-help. 'To this simple method, the whole Art and Science of doing Good to Mankind is exclusively reduced. The human Being who does not sincerely wish to *help himself* will always be the worse for any external help'. He went on:

> There is an immense difficulty in making most individuals of the uneducated classes conceive that a *Gentleman* who gives them no money, can be their friend. But it is well worth labouring among a multitude of selfish wretches for the sake of discovering a single person who can make the distinction between pecuniary bounty and sincere, brotherly goodwill. I heartily join in the wish of our Minister, to have a room where he may assemble the best disposed among his poor; but I deprecate everything that might give to such a place the formality of a Chapel. Useful reading; Conversation upon what has been read, if anyone present should feel inclined to put a question; Prayer, but not at stated times, which would

soon turn it into a mere ceremony;—in a word, *friendly intercourse* with the best disposed, in a room devoted to such a purpose, could not fail to increase our Minister's powers for good.[27]

The chilliness of the vision is the more remarkable in one who was, in all his personal relations, so warm and generous. One cannot but remember Blanco's description of his own father 'employed till late at night in making the beds of the poor, taking the helpless in his arms, and stooping to such services as even the menials in attendance were often loth to perform'.[28] No doubt the reality of the Liverpool slums would have been too much for Blanco's tender and sensitive heart. The Renshaw Street congregation were fortunate in finding a man with the necessary combination of compassion and stamina to assume the heavy burden on their behalf. The man appointed was John Johns, a Devonian, who now single-handed began his pioneering ministry in a city where laissez-faire ruled. There was no municipal water supply, no sanitation, no control of health or housing. In such circumstances, where only private charity stood between poverty and starvation, it was difficult to retain a belief in the possibility of spiritual and moral improvement. Yet Johns had a faith which survived first hand experience of degradation. He not only taught the poor, he also had the humility to learn from them. In one of his first reports he wrote of the great 'sleeping power of good in the town' and of the lessons of charity that were to be learned in its slums: 'For one kindness that the rich show to the poor, I firmly believe that they show twenty to each other'. These annual reports of his make sombre reading. In one of them he quoted the words of a man he found making a coffin for his grandchild: 'Blood must flow before things mend. The great ones must be frightened, and this can only be done with blood'.[29] Such people, he declared, 'live and die in a Christian land, but neither their lives nor their deaths have anything to do with Christianity'. In the winter of 1846, the year after Blanco's death, the resources of his Mission were put to an even severer test when in the aftermath of the Potato Famine the town was swamped by an influx of three hundred thousand Irish immigrants. It was in one of the ensuing typhoid epidemics, in 1847, that Johns died after contracting the plague while helping a Catholic priest to remove a corpse which the authorities would not touch.

Whately had warned Blanco of the dangers of being lionised by the Unitarians. This did not happen. At first, indeed, Martineau was wary of the new recruit. Nevertheless Blanco had an important influence on Martineau's theology. In his *Rationale of Religious Inquiry* (1836), the latter declared that those who rejected the historicity of the gospel miracles could not continue to call themselves Christians. Blanco disputed the point, and won Martineau over to the view that *reports* of miracles were not adequate grounds for believing in Christianity. This demotion of miracles from their high ranking in the scale of Christian evidences was to be one of Blanco's most important bequests to latitudinarian theology. Now that he had cut free of all institutional restraints his own theology was moving into uncharted waters. He was impatient of those who counselled caution and prudence, or who argued that the destruction of error brought with it a corresponding obligation to be constructive. This he saw as a typically English prejudice. The process of rebuilding, he declared, could only begin when the ground had been completely cleared of the rubble left from the old system: 'While employed in the removal of individual errors, we should be on our guard against the usual bugbear, "Where shall we stop?"—"What will be left?" When we shall have removed what is positively *not* Christianity, then and not till then shall we be able to perceive what *true* Christianity is'.[30]

This was to become a constant theme. As he chided his fellow-Unitarians for their timidity he compared them to Columbus' companions who, 'because they had sailed a *great way* toward the West, were sure that they had gone *too far*', turning back when they were only 'a short distance of the land towards which Protestantism has been constantly tending'.[31] That land receded further and further into the mist as Blanco pressed on. Some of his radical thinking anticipates twentieth-century preoccupations, such as his assertion that parents and teachers should refain from 'indoctrinating' children and respect their mental rights: 'As long as education proceeds as it is promoted at present, I cannot look upon it otherwise than as a system of mental slavery, a spiritual kidnapping exercised by the members of the various hierarchies or priesthoods which unfortunately divide this country, and angrily tolerate each other'.[32] The moderation which he had once praised politically as the English virtue he now scorned theologically as the English vice, and he turned increasingly for support to German philosophy and theology, above all to Fichte's ethical pantheism.

He had two American correspondents also: Andrews Norton of Harvard, and W. E. Channing, the Boston Unitarian from whom Martineau and Thom derived much of their theology. Channing found Blanco's rationalism too extreme: 'You seem to me to make religion too exclusively a product of the reason, and carry your jealousy of the Imagination too far'. When he tried to suggest to Blanco that the Tractarian Movement had its positive side, as offering some resistance to 'the material tendencies of the Age', the latter would have none of it: 'I consider the Imaginative Faculty—that faculty which clothes every idea in matter—as the arch-enemy of . . . truly spiritual enjoyments.—Cleanse the internal sanctuary from idols, if the Deity is to take his seat within it'.[33] This is the language of a mystic *malgré lui*, who is content with nothing less than the absolute, stripped of all that is fleshly and contingent. Answering the charge of Pantheism, he wrote to Norton: 'In regard to the Deity, my mind is necessarily placed between the extremes of Idolatry (in the broadest etymological sense of εἴδωλον) and of Pantheism, or identification of God with the world . . . Both systems are necessarily in contact with gross errors, but I think the coarsest Pantheism less mischievous than the most refined Idolatry, which is the parent of all superstition, Fanaticism, Priesthoods, etc'.[34]

The development of Blanco's literary ideas was all of a piece with this theology. Soon after his arrival in Liverpool, he was asked by J S Mill to write for the new *London* (later *London and Westminster*) *Review*. His contributions show a turning away from the romantic aesthetic of the previous decade to what may be called a utilitarian idealism. In a revealing article on Crabbe, he criticised the poet for his lack of *improving* power, for being content with mere realism, for failing to *elevate*. Merely to describe scenes of degradation was, he believed, to pander to a kind of voyeurism in the comfortable reader, offering him 'the pleasure of curiosity gratified without the pain and trouble of a disgusting experience'. The poet, he declared roundly, had a social responsibility:

> We are persuaded that the period is nearly gone by, during which either poets or critics have been considered as dealers in words. The great concern of social man, his progress as a rational and moral being, must now be the final end of every work of literature and art . . . Poetry in fact is a luxury of language—a mere delicacy of the intellectual feast; and as such it is rejected when we are hungry'.[35]

By 'poetry' in this context he meant poetry that was merely decorative, a dressed up imitation of nature. He developed his idea further in a review for J. S. Mill of the work of the contemporary Spanish dramatist Martinez de la Rosa, in whom he detected—alongside much that was praiseworthy—a lingering subservience to the classical unities. The artist's task, he maintained, was not to reproduce a literal copy of reality, making himself a slave to verisimilitude, but to represent reality in metaphors and symbols, not so much to the eye as to the mind's eye.[36] It was Shakespeare, therefore, who gave him his chief satisfaction and delight during these last years. He had been an admirer of Shakespeare since his earliest days in England, and in *Variedades* had published fine translations into Spanish of speeches from Hamlet and Richard II, but it was only now that Shakespeare became what he called a 'necessity' to him. In a marvellously perceptive essay on *A Midsummer Night's Dream* for *The Christian Teacher*, he wrote of Shakespeare using metaphor as a key to 'the secret ties of Relationship by which nature connects the, apparently, most distant notions', and praised the 'dazzling undercurrent of images which give life and motion to the style in which the larger pictures or conceptions are drawn'.[37] In this passionate preference for the spirit rather than the letter one can see the connection between Blanco the literary critic and Blanco the theologian.

If literature must be directed towards man's 'progress as a rational and social being', then again it was Shakespeare, 'the writer who, of all whom we know, was best acquainted with the mysteries of the human character', who offered the richest source of moral enlightenment and understanding. In his journal Blanco even sketched out the draft of a *Guide for the Young in Reading Shakespeare*, whereby moral education could be achieved without preaching, pedantry or moralising. So far did his enthusiasm lead him that he expressed in *The Christian Teacher* the idealistic hope that the hard-pressed Mr Johns would provide lectures on the subject at his Mission for the Poor: 'May we not hope that the morally and intellectually vivifying spirit of our Bard will prove a most efficient restorer of minds whom the pressure of misery and its general attendant vice had apparently deprived of all chance of being reclaimed to the path of respectability and virtue?'[38] One wonders how Falstaff fitted into this scheme of things.

Blanco found his most lasting satisfaction in the character of his son, 'the most valuable jewel of my heart'. In his letters from India, Ferdinand did not disguise his difficulties. With only an ensign's pay to live on, he soon got into debt trying to keep up with the life-style of his fellow-subalterns. Often, he confessed to his father, despondency drove him to billiards and drink. Why had his father not pushed harder to obtain Lady Holland's influence in his favour? 'I'm no author, it is true', he wrote ruefully, 'nor do I care much about Catholics and Protestants, yet I think her Ladyship might have taken a fancy to me'. His father's reluctance to introduce him, he went on, must have made her think him 'a horrid lubberly boy whom you were ashamed of'. Perhaps Lord Holland might recommend him as an aide-de-camp to Lord Clare, the Governor of Bombay? Or perhaps he might even make him his own secretary? It must have been difficult for him to resign himself to the fact that these were fantasies, but that is what—courageously—he did.

Ferdinand's reaction to his father's removal to Liverpool was characteristically loyal. 'I have ever reverenced you, dear Father, and I venerate you still more for having pursued the path you have done. I have ever held up to myself as an example to follow your fearless integrity and your honourable feelings of independence'. He was able to tell his father of the good opinions he had won from his comrades and superior officers, and of his promotion to adjutant, but he was too much his father's son to identify with the Anglo-Indian ascendancy: 'I am not an East Indian—I hate the country—I hate the Government', he declared. There seemed little prospect of finding the money to buy a captaincy, and without that he saw himself doomed to perpetual bachelorhood. In one of his letters he asked wistfully for 'pretty Mary Carleton': 'Has she yet married the rich old nobleman whom her Mamma so kindly intended for her? I suppose all dangerous and noxious people like subalterns are still solemnly kept away from her?' 'If I live', he declared dramatically, 'I shall be an old man at forty'.[39]

Ferdinand's first home leave in 1838 came at a time when his father's health was rapidly declining. Blanco could not at first face the emotional ordeal of a meeting and wanted to spare Ferdinand the sight of his suffering and it was only after the latter had been in England for five months that the reunion took place. Once it was over, the company of the son gave the father profound pleasure. Within a week the two were studying Italian and the flute together ('You know my determined propensity to *teach*', he wrote to Elizabeth Whately). The parting, when it came, was all the more painful, for both knew it was final. Blanco told Julia Moore,

> I will not conceal that this separation has afflicted me more than any other event in my life. My philosophy is only a guide to me, but it has not steeled my heart against pain. It has taught me to advise Ferdinand to return to India, because I thought it was the best thing in the circumstances; it has enabled me to spare him pain by concealing my own; but as I shook him by the hand on Saturday evening, knowing that I should in all probability never see him again, I could hardly contain my anguish within my bosom.[40]

Blanco's health and spirits were now at their lowest ebb. His state of physical suffering can be seen from a description he gave to Channing in June 1839:

> I do not enjoy a single hour of rest from distress and pain. It is now more than a year since I last stood on my feet. I have totally lost the use of my knee joints, and am constantly compelled to sit the whole day, and to lie on my back the whole night. I am wheeled in a chair from my bedroom to my study, and taken to bed early in the same manner. It is only by means of my hands that I can shift myself from the chair to the bed. There is no prospect whatever of relief; death alone can release me from this thraldom.[41]

There were moments when he appears to have contemplated the possibility of suicide. Yet he was about to rediscover a forgotten self as, by the waters of the Mersey, the *sevillano* in him was born again.

Chapter 15
Promised Land

'Alas! good Sir', replied Sancho, 'do not die, I pray you; but take my advice and live many years; for the greatest folly a man can commit in this world is to give himself up to death without any good cause for it, but only from melancholy'.

In September 1839 Blanco was visited by his cousin Luke Beck, now head of the family firm of Cahill, White and Beck in Seville. The cousins had not met since, thirty years earlier, they had made the dangerous journey together down the Guadalquivir to Cadiz as the French were closing on Seville. Beck had the commercial hard-headedness which Guillermo Blanco and his two sons lacked. By combining marriage to Thomas Cahill's daughter with sheer efficiency he had gained control of the business, supplanting Fernando Blanco who, manoeuvred into a subordinate position, was still, twenty-five years after his father's death, unsure of his legal rights. The visit to Liverpool marked a reconciliation and Beck offered to put up the money which Ferdinand White needed to purchase his captaincy. He also brought with him a presentation copy of the second edition of Lista's poems which now included the latter's translation of *Night and Death*. The meeting and the gift affected Blanco deeply. The entry in his journal for 6 October 1839—a week later—reads significantly: 'Began to write in Spanish'.[1]

For over thirteen years Blanco's creative powers had been stifled by his obsessive preoccupation with theology. 'Scarcely do I begin to enjoy the delights of philosophy and literature', he recorded ruefully, 'when Theology, like some spectre to which I had pledged my first love, in total ignorance of its nature, interposes itself between me and the interesting objects by which I began to be absorbed'.[2] He had, it is true, written some excellent criticism for his own and J. S. Mill's *London Reviews*, but his spasmodic attempts at creative writing had been left unfinished. The most interesting of these was 'The Priest's Return to Spain; or Second Part of Doblado's Letters' (1833) in which the author vicariously retraced his steps to Spain, not as the ex-dignitary Doblado but as an unknown music teacher, Neve. Encouraged by Clemente de Zulueta, Blanco intended to make this the framework for a series of *novelas* taken from Spanish history and literature and including the story of the rise and fall of Pablo de Olavide. The only fragment which survives is a description of the exile's return by sea to Cadiz. For the first time, the satire is directed not at Spanish superstition but at English complacency, incarnated in Neve's fellow-traveller, the pompous clergyman Dr Allcrust.[3]

The reunion with his relatives and the reading of Lista's poems had suddenly given him back the power to write in his mother tongue, to speak with his original voice. He began to write a novel in which, at last, Blanco took his revenge on White. It represented the rebellion of his unregenerate Spanish self against the assumed English character to which he had so painfully accommodated himself for thirty years. The closer he came to the end of his life, he told the reader, the more memories and impressions of his youth crowded in upon him:

> Even my dreams, which for many years have been in my adopted language, so to speak, began to take on an admixture of Spanish. Since then I have felt a keen desire to see if heaven may grant me, in the short space of my life which remains, the satisfaction of leaving to Spain a little work which may afford her sons some profit as well as pleasure . . . The desire to speak for the last time to the people of Spain seems to take possession of me. Behold me, then, giving way to a sort of inspiration which, if it be not a sign of madness, will I trust sustain me in what I see as no small undertaking.[4]

As in his poetry, so in this unfinished novel—however imperfect—Blanco escaped from the rationalisations and self-justifications of auto-biography and allowed his deeper instincts freer expression. The subject is the plight of the emigré, personified in the young heroine, whose father, Miguel de Bustamante, an *afrancesado*, is forced to seek political asylum in London, where he dies in poverty. The description of the reduced circumstances of the noble family in their sordid lodgings in Clerkenwell, and of the death of Luisa's parents, is drawn from life. The London of these chapters is the London which had so shocked Blanco on his arrival there in 1810, and which, a decade later, dismayed the exiles of Somers Town: a city of fog, dirt and moral squalor, divided between east and west, between ostentatious wealth and desperate poverty. Luisa, left alone in this Babylon, has to find work as a governess, and the narrator accompanies her to a tea party where she is to meet her prospective employers, Mr and Mrs Chub. The Chubs personify all the vulgarity, the Philistinism, the complacent and patronising self-righteousness of the prosperous evangelical milieu, and in venting his spleen on them Blanco topples over from satire into farce. The 'Saints' assembled in the Chubs' drawing-room include Mr Chub the stockbroker, Mrs Chub the stockbroker's wife, and the Reverend Ezechiel Paunch, 'the English Tartuffe', an oleaginous clergyman who does the round of tea and bible parties in order to ogle pious spinsters. The ill-bred children of the house misbehave, the tea table is upset and Miss Rollikin (the pious spinster) has the vapours. Luisa is unwise enough to laugh, thereby drawing down the affronted wrath of Mrs Chub, who does not let the Spanish Papist go without handing her a tract, in the hope that it may save her from the 'whore of Babylon'. (One is tempted to speculate whether the tract might not have been Blanco's own *Preservative against Popery*).

After this scene—likely to confirm the Spanish reader in his secret conviction that the Englishman's superior airs conceal a vulgar hypocrite—Luisa obtains a post as companion to a colonel's lady who is about to sail for India. Their ship catches fire in the Channel, and Blanco, drawing on real events, shows dramatic skill in describing the scenes of confusion and heroism which attend the disaster and ship-wreck. Luisa is saved, but the last completed chapters find her back in England, in imminent moral danger from the attentions of Lord Ford, a spectacularly wicked Irish peer who, tired of playing with the affections of marchionesses and countesses, now 'like an Oriental sultan, must have a perpetual succession of fresh rosebuds which would suggest without fully revealing the beauty concealed within their tender leaves'. Lord Ford is last seen in an elegant bordello, cynically laying plans to inveigle Luisa to his remote Irish estate, ostensibly as a governess but in reality to become the latest victim of his lusts.

Though Blanco in his preface protested his innocence of any intention to inflame national prejudice, *Luisa de Bustamante* can only have reinforced a certain Spanish stereotype of English society. To compare it with the *Letters from England* of fifteen years earlier is to see just how far Blanco's anglophilia had abated. The Lord Ford episode is preceded by a lurid exposé of London's underworld of vice, ranging from body-snatching to organised prostitution, by way of the commercial exploitation of broomsellers from Saxony and organ-grinders from Piedmont. The English genius for businesslike and systematic organisation and method extended, the author maintains, even to their vice. England is a country in which money is king. English luxury is implicitly contrasted with Spanish simplicity, English materialism with Spanish humanity, English stiffness with Spanish spontaneity, English vulgarity with Spanish dignity. From his new position on the fringe of polite society, ostracised by the Church and King establishments which he had once helped to support, Blanco was now voicing the inevitable disenchantment of the convert who discovers that his idol has feet of clay. He claimed to have been cured at last of his thirst for the absolute. 'The experience of a long life', he declared in the introduction to *Luisa de Bustamante*, 'has convinced me that unmixed good and unmixed evil are not to be found in this world. There is no nation so degraded that it does not present some virtues, no class so perverted that it does not contain some individuals deserving of respect'.[5] But unable to sustain such qualified caution for long, he went on a few lines later to express the conviction that it would not be long before all national rivalries and hatreds were dispelled by the spread of 'knowledge and civilisation and above all the decline of religious fanaticism':

> Even in Ireland, that lovely but ill-starred country, in which religious passions are unfortunately fed by political interests, yes even in Ireland party feelings are gradually abating, and would soon be extinguished altogether were it not for the ambition and pride of the Protestants, who are accustomed to regard the native Catholics as a class of Helots.

Though written from a Spanish point of view, *Luisa de Bustamante* anticipates the attacks on moral pretension and hypocrisy which were to be made by a whole series of native English novelists. The Reverend Ezechiel Paunch was a more crudely drawn forerunner of Mr Pecksniff, or Charlotte Bronte's Mr Brocklehurst, or George Eliot's Mr Bulstrode. The social criticism to be found in Blanco's novel was already being voiced in unexpected quarters. Only a year later a reviewer in *The Christian Teacher*, the organ of Liverpool Unitarianism, looking for a spiritual and cultural model to set against the materialism and cant of Protestant England, found it in—of all places—Catholic Spain. The reviewer drew a satirical contrast between the ugly commercialism of Gibraltar, redolent of English 'purse-pride', and the artistic and spiritual richness to be found in the churches and cathedrals of Andalucia: 'One cannot but respect that sentment of a good Catholic—the origin, no doubt, of this splendour—that nothing is too good to be offered unto God'.

What appealed to the writer was the way in which, through its paintings, sculptures and ceremonies, the Catholic Church spoke to the heart and imagination as well as to the mind of all her children, educated and uneducated alike. 'We think too little of the infinite worth of the imagination, that divine attribute of our nature . . . We are without doubt the vulgarest nation upon the face of the earth'.[6]

It is ironic that some Unitarians should have been seeking to reinstate the imagination and casting envious glances in the direction of Catholic worship just when their new recruit was insisting more fiercely than ever that the imagination was the 'arch-enemy' of purified rational religion. The nation he now looked to as a model of social and religious hygiene, was Germany. 'Happiness', he announced confidently in a review for *The Christian Teacher*, 'is diffused among the Prussians in as large a proportion as the progress of mankind at this moment can enable a government to bestow it upon a nation at large. But it is a happiness which has its foundation not in the senses but in the mind. Cheap *rational* pleasures are placed within the reach of all'.[7]

Intellectually Blanco may have been attracted by this bleak (and imaginary) landscape of the reason, but emotionally he was increasingly drawn back to Spain. Luke Beck's visit to Liverpool was followed by that of his daughter Maria Ana, who stayed for ten months. Her vivacious and tender companionship brought him back to emotional life. As she talked or sang, in the familiar Andalucian tones, her young voice revived the distant sounds and rhythms heard in early childhood. He began to write Spanish verse again—not, as before, in Italian neo-classical metres, but the *redondillas* and *seguidillas* popular in Seville, which gave his poetry a new freedom and simplicity. For three months, between December 1839 and February 1840, the inspiration flowed unchecked, bringing a pleasure not unmixed with pain. The Stoicism which he had cultivated as a protective shell proved to be no defence against disturbing images from the past:

> Leave me, you treacherous memories I must reject,
> Of peace, of love, of a mother's tenderness!
> Do not expose the wounds
> Misfortune had begun to heal in me.
> Image of my beloved mother, depart from hence!
> Do not unman a heart which must be steeled
> Against that bitter hour of pain
> Which I await in trembling and in fear.[8]

The poetry is shot through with images of music and of the child at his mother's breast. In these dreams Blanco was visited by friends as well as parents. In one of the most moving, addressed to Alberto Lista, he asks, like Hamlet, why he should not put an end to his sufferings. The prison door is open: why not take it?

> Why? Because a loving friend
> Takes living shape to bar the way
> And, weeping, bids me 'Wait!'

Another poem is addressed to his nephew and namesake José María Blanco y Olloqui, whom he now looked to as his spiritual heir in Spain, who would carry on the struggle against the forces of darkness:

> You would lead a life of usefulness?
> Then shun the priesthood,
> Shun those who, with fanatic zeal,
> Aim to be more than men, and finish less.[9]

The horror of priestcraft did not diminish with age. 'The priesthood do not care about our *belief*', he noted in his journal; 'what they want is our *assent*'.[10]

Baden Powell and Hawkins kept him in touch with the affairs of Oxford, now dominated by those whom they and their friends called variously 'Rabbinists', 'Intolerants', 'Judaizers', or 'Tractites'. Of all the Noetics, only Baden Powell continued to sustain the tradition of free enquiry in a now hostile environment. Hampden and Whately's wings had been clipped by their acceptance of high office. Even Shuttleworth had at last got his bishopric and was glad to escape to Chichester from an Oxford in which he had long been ill-at-ease. Like his patron Lord Holland, he was a bemused survivor from the eighteenth century. 'Our undergraduates, I fear', he reported to Holland House, 'are much bitten by the self-mortifying spirit of Newman and Pusey; both of them really good men, but sadly wanting in discretion and fitter for the Thebaid or the top of a pillar than for England in 1836'.[11] But Baden Powell continued to advocate pluralism and tolerance when they were in short supply at Oxford. He remained a loyal friend of Blanco in spite of significant disagreements. Unlike the latter he remained a believer in natural theology and thought that the Liverpool Unitarians were as misguided as the Tractarians in making their own subjective ideas and feelings, rather than external 'evidences', the basis of their philosophy of religion.[12]

Blanco had a personal link with the younger generation at Oxford. He had used his influence at Oriel to obtain a place there for Albany Christie, the nephew and ward of his old friend James Christie and boyhood companion of his own son Ferdinand. Now the young man had become a disciple of Newman and was living in Pusey's 'monastery' in St Aldate's. It must have been from information derived from him that Newman told a friend that Ferdinand White 'came home on leave a Christian and returned to India [as a result of his father's influence] an unbeliever'.[13]

In April 1840 Christie wrote to tell Blanco he had been elected a Fellow of Oriel, and explained his reason for not writing before: 'I have been afraid to do it. I am very young, and though you may wish not to influence others, you cannot help doing it; in fact, I never feel more perplexed than when I have been with you, and it cannot be right for me, so unprepared, to expose myself to what I do feel so dangerous'. One may detect the hand of another behind this—a curiously ingenuous letter to come from a twenty-three year old Fellow of an Oxford college. For Blanco it was 'a melancholy exhibition of the morally perverting influence of Orthodoxy'. He had, he told Hawkins, 'scrupulously abstained from anything that might disturb Christie's mind', restricting himself only to the advice 'not to bind himself to any party till he had by patient study made himself competent to judge'. It should be added that the young man's affection later got the better of his scruples, and he made the journey to see Blanco in Liverpool shortly before he died.[14]

Ferdinand, writing from India, excused his old friend on the grounds that he could not think otherwise than he did, being 'at that Sorbonne, Oxford'. Evidently Ferdinand himself had something of a reputation in garrison society for being 'not quite orthodox'. In one of his letters home he criticised the author of a novel he was reading for converting the hero 'from a free-thinker into a no-thinker, which means having a lot of gentlemen educated at the virtuous seminaries of learning, Oxford and Cambridge, to think for him'. Ferdinand did not conform to type. He must have been the only officer in the Indian army to carry a copy of Ariosto with him on campaign, and though he was evidently a popular and brave soldier he had his own views about the cause he was fighting for. In the summer of 1840 he marched north with his regiment on a punitive campaign into Baluchistan and Afghanistan. 'I fancy it will be a war of extermination', he told his father; 'such has been our career in the East and so it ever must be—occupation of territory without leave and massacring to keep it'. Blanco must have been gratified by this evidence of moral independence. Ferdinand was able to mock his own world-weariness. 'The best part of my life is gone', he lamented. 'Like the French *belles* who become *dévotes* when their beauty fades, I would become the *savant*'. Nevertheless he wrote his father a vivid account of the assault on Khelat, in which he took part. Before the battle he read in the *Aeneid* Evander's prayer for his son Pallas, one of Blanco's own favourite passages, and was deeply affected by its appropriateness.[15]

In August 1840 Maria Ana Beck returned to Seville and soon afterwards, on his doctor's recommendation, Blanco moved out to the rural surroundings of a cottage in Toxteth Park. There his isolation was even more complete, and only correspondence with old friends brought consolation. From Italy, Francis Carleton wrote: 'I have long wished to tell you, my dear Blanco, that you are as fresh in our memory and as dear to our hearts as when twenty years ago we used to chat and fiddle and laugh at Gaddesden'. 'I lose sight of the suffering body', his wife added, 'and only see in you a noble spirit that God is calling to himself by dissolving all earthly ties'. On the last day of December 1840 Blanco recorded in his journal: 'The only blessing I can hope for is Death: my only prayer that it may be a gentle one'.[16]

As death approached so he became increasingly preoccupied with the spiritual testament he was to leave to the world at large. He went back over his journals and autobiographical writings of earlier years noting his embarrassment at the strained sentiments of orthodoxy expressed by his younger self. This revisionist task involved not just editing his intellectual history to prove that he had been a Unitarian all along, but also establishing his moral blamelessness. The lesson he wanted posterity to learn from his life was that heterodoxy was the result of a difference of opinion, not of any moral flaw. The demonstration of this truth in his own life involved Blanco in an increasing tendency to self-justification, a determination to prove that, if he had strayed in the past from the path of rectitude, he had been more sinned against than sinning. The bleakness of his tone dismayed Elizabeth Whately, who told Edward Hawkins she had received from Liverpool

> a sort of take-leave letter—the most painful I ever received in my life. It seemed to me to exlude even the lowest view of Christianity—it spoke not even the common general language of human hope. It spoke of the happy consciousness of a well-spent life as the only good to be sought and expected. The chill one felt on reading it is not easily to be forgotten. I thought this indeed is death—the death of a friend.[17]

However weak in body, in mind he remained active, planning a History of the Inquisition, reading Aristophanes, corresponding with Dr Channing. Restless to the last, he entertained the wild project of moving to a sanatorium in Hamburg, or to the warmer climate of Jamaica. More practical, but vain, attempts were made to convey him to a place where he would be among old friends: to the Whatelys, the Moores or the Bishops. Fernando Blanco wanted to have his brother brought back to Seville, and in this he had the support of Alberto Lista. Juan Sintierra, the latter argued, had long been forgotten there, and if the name of Blanco White still aroused controversy, it was not in Spain that it did so, but in England. Looking back at his brother's career, Fernando was inclined to attribute his and his companions' infidelity to the sins of the flesh. This Blanco categorically rejected. 'It is perfectly true that such *was not* my case. Nor was it true of our excellent and pure friend Reinoso'. When 'forced into disbelief', he protested, he was leading a 'pure inoffensive life . . . Thirty years and more I lived in England, and more than eight and twenty of them have passed without my having to reproach myself for any indulgence to my animal passions'. He went on to warn his brother, however, of the folly of trying to protect his adolescent son from sexual experience, 'unless you make him as disgusting as the young saints who grew around me . . . My dear brother, be not offended if I tell you that you have grown too retiring and reserved. Your melancholy tendency is deeper than mine, indeed I doubt whether I ever had any proper melancholy in my disposition'. Alberto Lista also disagreed with Fernando's analysis. His verdict carried the authority of Blanco's oldest and most intimate friend, whose affection did not diminish his perceptiveness. 'When we meet', he told Fernando, 'I shall disabuse you of the false notion you have of Pepe and his "misspent" youth. This is not true. You must know that Pepe, as he is physically and morally constituted, and happiness, are and always have been mutually exclusive. He was born to be the plaything and the victim of his immediate feelings'.[18]

Removal, however, was by now out of the question. When Elizabeth Whately ventured to offer the consoling thought that at Liverpool he was, at least, among friends, Blanco corrected the illusion:

> You are totally mistaken in regard to the moral ties which Liverpool has offered me. Mr Thom alone has obtained my confidence and affection. But Mr Thom married three years ago a very amiable young lady with a number of relations all of whom claim her husband's attentions and it is long since our intercourse has been limited to half-an-hour perhaps in a fortnight which my good friend snatches away from his occupations. From Unitarians *as such* I might say that I have received more proofs of indifference (perhaps dislike) than of attachment. Mr Martineau, with the greatest politeness, cut off all intercourse with me as soon as he removed to a distance of three miles . . . It is the character of this place: mercantile coldness and selfishness appear in everything.[19]

It would be unwise to attach too much importance to the last letters of an old man in pain. In fact, in his final weeks Blanco had cause for nothing but gratitude to Unitarian friends, above all to the Rathbones. On 23 February 1841 he was taken in a sedan chair to William Rathbone's own house at Greenbank.[20] There he celebrated on 3 March the thirty-first anniversary of his arrival in England. For three months—to use his own words—he 'lingered in the face of death', unable to move from his chair and yet still wrestling aloud with the questions which had been his lifelong concern. J H Thom, who with Mrs Rathbone and other friends attended him in these months, kept a record of what he called 'the solemn grandeur of his last days'. Thus Blanco was enabled to die an early Victorian death—a death which would make a fitting conclusion for Thom's posthumous biography. It was, at the end, the death of a Stoic philosopher who yet professed a Christian faith. A few days before, he had made his own the words "My God, into thy hands I commend my spirit", adding 'God to me is Jesus, and Jesus is God—of course, not in the sense of Divines'.

'He remained some days longer', Thom recorded, 'chiefly in the state of one falling alseep, until the morning of the 20th, when he awoke up, and with a firm voice and great solemnity of manner, spoke only these words:—"Now I die". He sat as one in the attitude of expectation, and about two hours afterwards—it was as he had said'.[21]

At the funeral service in Renshaw Street Chapel on 24 May the address was given by James Martineau, and the service was followed by interment in the adjoining burial ground.[22] When the news reached Fernando Blanco in Seville, he had a requiem mass celebrated in the family parish church, the Sagrario, for the repose of his brother's soul.

Chapter 16
Blanco Redivivus

And he said to me, 'Son of man, can these bones live?'
Ezekiel, 37.3

Outside Liverpool, Blanco's death went almost unnoticed. To his former patrons he was now an embarrassing memory. Coplestone, Bishop of Llandaff, wrote to Hawkins, his successor at Oriel: 'Of poor Blanco White's release I was not sorry to hear. He had long been lost to his best friends, and his example, instead of being encouraging to our endeavours and hopes against the Romish cause, was at last adverse to them'.[1] Coplestone was wrong if he thought that the ghost had been finally laid.

At Liverpool Blanco had altered his will to make Thom his literary executor in place of Whately. Thom began his promotion of the cause with a controversial tribute published in *The Christian Teacher*. Though careful not to claim Blanco as a Unitarian prize ('He revolted from all orthodoxies, wherever they might appear, and having emancipated himself from older and more imposing authorities he was not likely to yield himself up to Unitarian standards'), he represented him as a victim of orthodoxy, a 'venerable confessor' who had sacrificed everything—family, friends, security, comfort—for the sake of Truth: 'From an archbishop's palace he went forth, a lonely man, to contented obscurity and neglect'.[2] Whately strongly objected to the implication that Blanco had been cast out by his friends, given that he had left Dublin of his own accord and had continued to receive their financial and moral support. On Whately's behalf, Henry Bishop wrote to protest at the injustice which Thom, in his concern to discredit what he termed the 'orthodox system', had done to Blanco's friends among the Anglican clergy.[3] Consequently, when Thom wrote asking them to release their correspondence for use in the forthcoming *Life and Letters*, Whately and Bishop refused to co-operate. The former justified his refusal on the grounds that, in his opinion and in that of medical authorities, Blanco had in his last years been in an unsound state of mind, and that 'no memoir not adverting to this fact . . . could be correct or could fail to convey erroneous impressions'.[4] He demanded not only that Thom should return all his correspondence but that he should cut out of the biography every passage relating to him and his family. Thom refused to accede to the second part of this peremptory request. Baden Powell was the only one of Blanco's Oxford friends to co-operate, and he dissociated himself from Whately's imputation of mental derangement.

Thom's *Life*, or to give it its proper title, *The Life of the Rev Joseph Blanco White, written by himself; with Portions of his Correspondence, edited by John Hamilton Thom in three volumes*, published in 1845, falls into three distinct parts. The first volume contains two autobiographical memoirs: a 'Narrative of His Life in Spain', written at Oxford for Richard Whately, and a 'Sketch of his Mind in England', an apologia written at Liverpool and designed to defend himself against the charge of inconsistency by showing that his abandonment of the Church of England was only the culmination of a lifelong struggle against orthodoxy. The rest of the work consists of extracts from correspondence and journals, concentrating almost entirely on the last nine years of Blanco's life. This imbalance gives the *Life* a disproportionately Unitarian and theological flavour. Family correspondence was completely omitted, and since the editor knew no Spanish, the literary and political dimension of Blanco's life was largely neglected. The lack of correspondence with family and intimate friends (with the exception of the Moores) also means that the reader sees too little of the affectionate and playful side of Blanco's character and too much of the self-doubting diarist. As Thom himself admitted, 'The happiest and most vigorous times of his mind have often no record here . . . and it is right that those who had constant intercourse with him should openly witness that he describes himself as at times more morally disaffected by pain and distress than they ever knew him to be'.[5]

The nakedness of the self-revelation in the *Life* set a new precedent in Victorian biography. Hurrell Froude's *Remains*, published a few years before, had been thought morbid, but they look almost robust compared with Blanco's records of mental anguish and physical pain, interspersed with notes on an astonishingly wide range of reading, critical insights, theological speculation and antiquarian asides. Distress, whether of body or mind, seems to have acted as a stimulus rather than an obstacle to Blanco's intellectual activity. Whately reacted violently to what he called the 'indelicacy' of the publication, which he described in a letter to his publisher as 'an indecent exposure of the private memoranda of an invalid in a diseased state of mind'. He even went on to impugn Thom's motives: 'Still more disgusting is the sordid and heartless avarice of those (so-called) friends who are eager to turn a penny by pandering to this depraved appetite and as it were digging up the corpse of a friend, and selling it to be dissected and exhibited in a school of anatomy'. The contents of this letter became

public knowledge and further embittered the dispute between Thom
and Whately, which even continued after the latter's death when a
truncated version of the letter was published in Jane Whately's biography of her father.[6] The violence of Whately's language may be
explained by a plain man's natural distaste for morbid introspection,
but Thom may have had some reason in attributing it to a deeper
unease. Why did Whately become so agitated on the subject of
Blanco's Memoirs? he asked. Did it remind him of his failure to follow
through, as Blanco had done, the logic of his principles?

The book made a profound impression on the reading public—and
not the one which Whately had predicted. He told Mrs Thomas
Arnold that he was 'much annoyed' at the general reaction to the
work:

> Since it appears that some not ill-disposed persons can read it without
> disgust and mortification, I conclude that there will be great danger from
> it. Some will be convinced that free inquiry must, in the end, be fatal to
> Christian belief, and that, one by one, all doctrines will be overthrown by
> it; and hence, part will be led to shun and deprecate inquiry and resolve to
> shut their eyes and 'believe all that the holy Church believes', while
> another part will make short work another way and believe no religion at
> all.[7]

In fact, the autobiography would not have touched off so deep a
resonance if it had not articulated thoughts which were already latent,
but suppressed, in many early Victorian minds. As one reviewer put
it, 'The revelation in the volumes before us contain, we are persuaded,
the secret history of thousands who have felt the same doubts and been
urged towards the same conclusions but who have buried them in
prudent silence or put them down by main force at the bidding of a
worldly authority'.[8] It was as if Blanco, by casting himself out and
then by dying, had taken on himself the burden of others' secret
doubts. The record of his struggles was a source of strength especially
to women readers, who in early Victorian England suffered most
from the pressures of conformity. He spoke to them, as few Englishmen could, with that candour and sympathy which once had
enabled him to bring spiritual comfort to troubled souls in the
convents of Seville. Sara Coleridge, for instance, was inspired by what
she called Blanco's 'determined, far-going, all-sacrificing truthful-
ness' and by the Christian faith and hope he manifested on his
deathbed. It was not that he loved Christianity too little, she wrote to
F. D. Maurice: he loved it too much to endure to hear half-truths and
make-believes pressed into its service.[9]

Others, too, contrasted the uncompromising integrity of the
Spaniard with the pusillanimity of English intellectual life. This was
the lesson drawn by the scientist Sir Charles Lyell from what he called

'the confessions of Saint Blanco the Martyr'. The reaction of the poet W. S. Landor was even more ecstatic. 'I heartily wish', he told a friend, 'that no gentle man at either of our Universities could take a bachelor's degree before he had been examined in this book'. For him it 'opened a California: all gold below and all salubrity above'. In his journal he recorded his admiration for Blanco's passionate but disinterested love of truth, dialectical power and a 'purity and elevation' of critical sensitivity which placed him 'utterly above the rabble of magazine men'. 'Is it not incredible', he asked, 'that a Spaniard should be a critic?'[10]

For others, the reading of the *Life* was equally catalytic but more painful. One such as A. H. Clough, who found to his distress that he 'could not but believe much the same' as Blanco. For a time it attracted him towards Unitarianism though ultimately he rejected this as satisfying neither his reason nor his need to believe.[11]

Whately proved to be more accurate in his prediction that the *Life* would strengthen the orthodox in their attachment to authority. Such readers subjected the book to intense scrutiny in order to detect the chink in Blanco's moral armour and to discover the flaw of character which might explain his tragedy. Gladstone, in *The Quarterly Review*, wrote with magnificent solemnity, as if his own salvation depended on solving the riddle. For him the book was one 'which rivets the attention and makes the heart bleed'. He diagnosed Blanco's problem as one of disconnection: 'The natural relation between his speculative and his practical life' had been 'violently and fundamentally disturbed'. His religion had put down no roots in his life: 'No assimilating process had mixed it with the courses of his nature. The internal and experimental evidences which familiarity supplies, and the rooted persuasion which it thus engenders, had no existence for him'. He went on to trace the fundamental discord in Blanco to

> the total want of moral choice in the determining action of his life . . . The moral consequences of maintaining a Christian profession for eight years upon a basis of Atheism—the Breviary on the table and the anti-Christian writers of France in the closet—may have been fatal to the solidity and consistency of his inward life thereafter . . . We cannot with impunity thus tamper with the fearful and wonderful composition of our spiritual being.[12]

Though the effect which the *Life* had on Gladstone was one of horror—'at that dreadful process by which faith is eaten out of the soul'—he wrote of its author with sympathy and insight. J. B. Mozley, in *The Christian Remembrancer* adopted a more dismissive and sarcastic tone. 'We do not think that nature intended Mr Blanco White for a theologian', he declared at the start, arguing that Blanco's mind lacked the balance and the serenity needed for the task: his thinking was clear but narrow, penetrating but not lateral, impatient of qualification or reserve. On Blanco's compulsive tendency to revise earlier, in the light of later, opinions, he commented sardonically: 'The very act of reflexion is itself reflected upon. The very autobiography itself becomes an animal and begins to move, and the very narrative turns narrator. The extended trunk that we are sitting on begins to creep'. He characterised Blanco's theology as based on a total rejection of incarnation, and of any sort of medium between God—a God of pure, characterless spirit—and man, and contrasted the bleakness of this pantheism with the warmth of Blanco's human affections. He saw Blanco, along with all rationalist theologians as grasping at shadows: 'They want a truth bodiless: they cannot have it. Nothing is without a body here, and truth is not. Resolve to have it without body: a hopeless work is before you'.

Pressing home his investigation Mozley directed his attention to Blanco's assumption of the role of martyr to truth and his insistence on the *sufferings* he had endured in its cause, suggesting that the suffering was accompanied in his case by a sense of satisfaction, and pleasure in representing himself to himself and to the world as a victim. This was the 'sin of intellect'—less easily identifiable but more dangerous than the 'sin of sense'—which Mozley thought he had at last tracked down in the labyrinth of Blanco's spiritual life. On a more general note, he concluded with a critique of the whole 'philosophy of search' upon which Blanco's life was based. Blanco seemed to him to be obsessed not so much with truth as with the idea of truth, to be more interested in the journey than the goal. 'The fact is, that the love of truth in fallen man is a corrupted affection, just as natural love is. It betrays the selfish element. His mind annexes truth to itself and not itself to truth'. In the case of the faithful disciple of Christ, he concluded, 'Truth finds him out, and not he It'.

Though Mozley's review is by far the most penetrating critique of the *Life* written from the orthodox point of view, it is marred by a lack of imaginative sympathy, a patronising and sometimes sneering tone and a proprietary attitude to Christian revelation. If Mozley was one of those who had been sought out by Truth, Charity was not a fellow-caller. The style reveals the man, as in the passage where he predictably uses Blanco to question Whately's orthodoxy: 'We must say, what gives us the deepest pain to say, that the theory which dominates in him [viz Sabellianism in Whately] does not in principle differ from the Socinian one'.[13] The pre-emptive use of the first person plural is characteristic, as is the mealy-mouthed tone reminiscent of the housemaster about to administer corporal punishment.

One voice was, in public at least, noticeably silent. In April 1845, Newman was living in monastic seclusion at Littlemore. Oxford, though only an hour's walk away, was now alien territory to him, a part of the past, as he hovered on the brink of his Rubicon. Blanco's *Life* was instrumental in bringing him to the point of decision. It was, he wrote to Henry Wilberforce,

> the most dismal possible work I ever saw . . . His biographer actually calls him a *Confessor*—Confessor to what? Not to any opinion, any belief whatever, but to the search after truth, ever wandering about and changing, and therefore great to the end of his life? Can there be a greater paradox than this? But what a view does it give one of the Unitarians and *id genus omne*! They really do think it is no harm whatever being an Atheist, so that you are sincerely so, and do not cut people's throats and pick their pockets!

The book, he went on,

> shows more and more that one knows the *lie of the country*. It is an additional testimony to the fact that to be consistent one must believe more, or less, than we are accustomed to believe . . . For years I have an increasing intellectual conviction that there is no medium between Pantheism and the Church of Rome. If intellect were to settle the matter, I should not now be where I am. But other considerations come in, and distress me. Here is Blanco White, honest but sincere. He gives up his country, and then his second home—Spain, Oxford, Whately's family— all for an idea of truth, or rather for liberty of thought. True, I think a great deal of morbid restlessness was mixed with his sincerity, an inability to keep still in one place, a readiness to take offence and to be disgusted, an unusual irritability, and a fear of not being independent, and other bad feelings. But then the thought forcibly comes upon one, why may not the case be the same with me? I see Blanco White going wrong, yet sincere— Arnold going wrong, yet sincere. They are no puzzle to me. I can put my finger on this or that fault in their character and say, There was the fault. But they did not know the fault, and so it comes upon me, How do I know that I too do not have my weak points which occasion me to think as I think? How can I be sure I have not committed sins which brings this unsettled state of mind on me as a judgment?[14]

Blanco's *Life*, therefore, made Newman's decision at once easier and more difficult. Easier, because it confirmed his conviction that there was 'no medium between Patheism and the Church of Rome'. More difficult, because he saw Blanco's life as illustrating the insufficiency of reason divorced from experience. That may be why he hesitated for a further six months before taking the final step. He was already intellectually convinced of the Roman claims, but the example of Blanco—and in particular of Blanco's precipitate abandonment of the Church of England in 1835—confirmed him in his instinct that intellectually reasoned conclusions were unreliable as a guide to action unless they were what he called 'realised'—worked out and assimilated emotionally in all their personal implications. The exercise of reason, he believed, had to be preceded and accompanied by a rigorous self-purification and self-examination, 'searching all the hidden places of the spirit to detect sources of illusion, of false attitudes'.[15] Twenty years earlier at Oriel he had, in a letter to Blanco, admitted to uncertainty about whether there was a connection between 'speculative error' and 'bad ethos'. Now, after reading Blanco's *Life*, he was in no doubt.

The *Life* also affected Newman in a more personal way. He was at once touched by what it revealed of Blanco's feeling for him in the past, and dismayed by the contrast between the youthful self it depicted—the Newman of nearly twenty years before—with the burnt out and middle-aged failure (for that is what he felt himself to be) at Littlemore. 'I am nearly the only person he speaks with affection of in it [the *Life*] among his English friends', he continued, '—at least he says more about me than anyone else . . . I say to myself, is it possible I was this? And then a second set of feelings succeeds. It is over—my spring, my summer, are over, and what has come of it? It seems Blanco White thought so and so of me,—others, then, I suppose thought in a degree the same; but what has come of it? . . . Now my prime of life is past and I am nothing'.

One of those who followed Newman into the Church of Rome six months later was Albany Christie. When he wrote to Provost Hawkins to resign his Oriel fellowship, Christie revealed the part played by Blanco, as well as Newman, in his decision: 'I must, to be consistent, be a Catholic or an Infidel. The books which my poor benefactor Mr White lent me to read were incapable of reply on Protestant grounds'. Another of the Tractarians for whom Blanco acted as a catalyst was W. G. Ward, who made his decision to join the Church of Rome in the course of writing a review of the *Life*. These and other reactions confirm the view of H. G. Liddon, Pusey's biographer, that Blanco's most lasting effect on the English Church was to intensify in the Tractarians 'that reasoned and sensitive resistence to even incipient Rationalism which characterised all their writings'.[16]

Yet the impact of Blanco's *Life* was short-lived. His controversial works rapidly sank into oblivion. When in 1851 Newman reviewed the contemporary situation of Catholics in England he devoted a section of his lectures to a survey of anti-Catholic 'witnesses', including Blanco, of whom he spoke with remarkable justice:

> I admired him for the simplicity and open-ness of his character, the warmth of his affections, the range of his information, his power of conversation, and an intellect refined, elegant and accomplished . . . He was certainly most bitter-minded and prejudiced against everything in and connected with the Catholic Church; it was nearly the only subject on which he could not brook opposition; but this did not interfere with the confidence I placed in his honour and truth.

He then went on to contrast the fate of Blanco's *Evidence* with that of the scurrilous anti-Catholic 'revelations' of Maria Monk: 'Whatever the one said was true, as often as he spoke to facts he had witnessed, and was not putting out opinions or generalising on evidence; whatever the other said was, or was likely to be, false . . . Yet the truth spoken against us by the man of character is forgotten, and the falsehood spoken against us by the unworthy woman lives'.[17] Of all Blanco's controversial writings, only *The Poor Man's Preservative against Popery* survived to promote, after his death, the Protestant cause which he had abandoned in life. The critique of dogmatic Christianity which made such an impact on readers of the *Life* in the late 1840s was soon overtaken by the more disturbing challenge of science. By the end of the century Blanco White was remembered principally in his adopted country as the author of a sonnet which Coleridge had once pronounced to be the finest in the language.

Another, more lasting, resurrection awaited Blanco in his native country but it had to wait more than a century. The only man of the next generation in Spain to appreciate his worth was the dissident scholar Luis Usoz del Rio, whose life and character offer an illuminating comparison. Usoz, the younger man by thirty years, was a convert to evangelical Christianity and a friend of George Borrow and Benjamin Wiffen. Through Wiffen, whom he first met on a visit to England in 1840, he became acquainted with the Society of Friends and though he never formally became a member he spent the rest of his life as a Quaker in spirit. His working life was dedicated to the recovery and publication, with Wiffen's collaboration, of the works of the Spanish Protestant reformers of the sixteenth century—including that remarkable group of heterodox theologians—Cipriano de Valera, Antonio del Corro, Cassiodoro de Reina—who originated from the Hieronymite monastery of San Isidoro at Seville. Usoz was, if anything, more fierce than Blanco in his denunciation of the immorality and hypocrisy which permeated Spanish society, and he agreed with him in identifying the lack of religious freedom as their root cause: 'This whole country is enveloped in darkness. There is frightful idolatry, irreligion, superstition, idleness, sinfulness of every kind, ignorance of all that is good and useful, invincible depravity. This is the general state of Spain'. Unlike Blanco, however, he maintained a strict and lonely independence of all parties. He never formally became a Quaker because membership of what was regarded as an English sect would have compromised him in Spanish eyes, and made a point of refusing English subsidies for his great publishing venture: 'No Spaniard should accept English money if he is to avoid the possible accusation of having been bought for British gold'. Eschewing proselytism, he went his single-minded way in almost complete social isolation.

Usoz and Blanco had much in common: passionate sincerity and a bitter anti-clericalism only matched by the distaste for the 'ignorance and immorality' of Spanish liberals. But when he read Thom's *Life*, Usoz could not help regretting Blanco's failure to appreciate the Quaker spirituality of writers such as Barclay and Fox which might have helped him to avoid the 'exclusive and extreme rationalism' of his later years. The fact is that while Blanco admired the purity of the Quakers' religion, his eighteenth-century mind recoiled from the evidence he found in them of mystical 'enthusiasm'.[18]

In the later years of the nineteenth century Blanco's memory in Spain was only just kept alive by the occasional publication of his poetic fragments, but the facts of his life were now encrusted by myth. It was confidently asserted that he had left Spain with a woman, that he had fathered four children and ended as a canon of St Paul's[19] . . . His real personality was too elusive, his range too vast and his *oeuvre* too scattered to be tracked down by any but the most erudite and patient investigator. The discovery was at last made by the prodigious polymath Marcelino Menéndez y Pelayo, whose massive *Historia de los heterodoxos españoles* is a monument to his belief in the identity between Spanish nationhood and Catholic religion: 'Spain the evangelizer of half the planet: Spain the hammer of heretics, the light of Trent, the sword of the Pope, the cradle of St Ignatius. This is our greatness and our glory: we have no other'.[20] For Menéndez, Blanco was the archetypal *déraciné*, who in abandoning his faith had betrayed his country and lost his identity:

> Thus he passed his life of pain and sorrow, like a pilotless ship in a storm . . . doubting each day what he had asserted the day before. No sturdy thought or steady emotion had ever crossed his existence. The renegade of every sect, the outcast of every party, he made his way to the grave without even a faith in his own doubt, apprehensive of the very thing he denied, abhorred in Spain, despised in England, pursued by the cries of his Irish victims and even haunted by nightmares in which he seemed to see the grim shadow of his own death.[21]

Yet in spite of his violent antipathy to Blanco as a renegade, Menéndez was the first Spanish literary historian to recognise his importance. It was he who rediscovered *Letters from Spain*, describing its scene-painting as 'beyond praise', and it was also he who first appreciated Blanco's gifts as a critic.

The black legend established by Menéndez y Pelayo condemned Blanco to another half-century of ostracism. Only a few voices were raised in opposition, notably that of Mario Méndez Bejarano. The tide began to turn in the early sixties, mainly due to the efforts of Vicente Llorens whose personal experience of political exile gave him a key to the understanding of Juan Sintierra. He began the task of reconstruction by patient scholarship, but the wider promotion of Blanco White as the voice of an alternative Spain was due to the novelist Juan Goytisolo. As a member of the immediate post-Civil War generation Goytisolo had experienced the stultifying effects of the Franco regime on intellectual life. Under Franco, the Menéndez y Pelayo thesis was enshrined as the official version of Spanish cultural history, and writers such as Blanco who had deviated from the party line were either ignored or denigrated. Menéndez had at least read *Letters from Spain*, but his satellites simply repeated his judgments at second-hand. To discredit Blanco's work it was enough to revive the old cry of 'Cherchez la femme!' If the régime sought to justify its intolerance it only had to cite the authority of Menéndez y Pelayo himself, who argued that intolerance was simply the mark of a healthy society confident of its values.

In Blanco's 'Portrait of the Artist as a Young Man'—a story of youthful idealism, doubt, guilt, struggle and rage—Goytisolo recognised himself and his generation.

> Blanco's pen has the miraculous effect of confronting the reader with his own life. For anyone who knew the Spain of the forties, his memoirs again and again recall a series of experiences and traumas which they would prefer to have forgotten. This man whose voice from beyond the grave sounds so intimate, is their brother. For if time stands still for Spain, it stands still for Blanco too: his work has aged not a jot . . . The exceptional value of his experience stems from the fact that he embodies the life story of thousands upon thousands of his fellow-countrymen—an unwritten story, locked away in the sanctuary of their hearts; a story of past, present and (I fear) future.[22]

In 1972 Goytisolo published in Buenos Aires a translated selection of Blanco's English writings, prefaced by a long, coruscating attack on the national myth fostered by Menéndez y Pelayo, now built into the monolith of Catholic Church and Falangist State. Again and again he discovered that Blanco's experience had anticipated his own. He too had been the object of an official campaign of denigration and denounced by the régime as a traitor, and he too had come to feel ashamed of being Spanish on its terms. If he identified with Spain, it was with an alternative Spain of outsiders, pariahs and victims—Jews, Moriscos, Lutherans, *afrancesados*, anarchists—of whom Blanco was the spokesman and symbol. (The list, it will be noticed, excludes Carlists.) Blanco's analysis of the abuse of spiritual power to achieve social and even political control, seemed to Goytisolo to have a relevance far beyond the situation of late eighteenth-century Seville. Above all he responded to Blanco's analysis of the corrupting effects of censorship and repression upon public language, which had been reduced by its political masters to a catalogue of sycophantic formulas:

'We can speak of an occupied language in the same way that we speak of an occupied country'.[23]

Goytisolo's essay is a brilliant piece of iconoclastic special pleading. 'In speaking of Blanco White', he admitted, 'I have been speaking of myself'. Nevertheless, his Blanco White caught the imagination of a generation of intellectuals looking for an alternative model of Spanish society. The Blanco White who championed toleration and pluralism was a leading candidate for a new canon of heterodox saints. So his rehabilitation gathered pace. The first Spanish translation of *Letters from Spain* was published in Madrid in 1972—one hundred and fifty years after its first English edition—and became a best seller.[24] In his native Seville, its author emerged from obloquy into belated fame and even adulation. In May 1984 the Mayor of Seville led a delegation to Liverpool to unveil a commemorative plaque on the site of Blanco's grave in the old Unitarian cemetery in central Liverpool—now converted into the anonymity of a municipal garden. A group of dissident Andalucian intellectuals established in 1982 a 'Blanco White prize' to be awarded annually for heterodox writing. What the man himself would have thought of these attentions, and attendant distortions, is a matter for speculation. He might have felt more at home with Marcelino Menéndez y Pelayo, on the principle that the old enemy offers at least the comfort of familiarity.

Perhaps the last word should be left to Henry Bishop, one of Blanco's oldest and most loyal friends, who when J. H. Thom seemed to be laying exclusive claim to the dead man's memory, ventured to doubt whether there was any theological moral to be drawn from Blanco's life. Its true value, he suggested, lay in the fact that 'his single-mindedness and intrepidity were rewarded by his holding fast, without a single exception, the attachment of every individual whom he could value or whose friendship he had ever possessed'.[25]

Appendix

'The Finest Sonnet in the Language'

In Ocober 1825 Blanco ceased to be the editor of *Variedades*. He saw his resignation as marking the end of his career as a Spanish writer and his definitive adoption of the English language. Two months later, without any thought of publication, he made his first hesitant steps as an English poet in some verses which recorded the pangs of this death and rebirth. The poem, 'On my attempting English Verse',[1] for all its infelicities, reveals Blanco's inner mood at this crucial juncture in his life. The emphasis is, significantly, more on death than on resurrection, more on the pains of loss than on the joys of gain. The rather insistent professions of unworthiness to take up 'the British lyre' are less convincing than the nostalgic evocations of the 'Castilian muse' whom he had abandoned only because of her faithlessness:

> For pressed and soiled her lips had been
> By lordly priest and monk obscene.

In spite of his protestations of admiration for England:

> I thought of thee till my fired brain
> Bade me to thee be born again

his rebirth is described in bleak terms:

> Can any pain be more refined
> Than that which has in it combined
> The ills which wait around the womb
> For man, and those that haunt his tomb?
> 'Tis worse than death the bands to part
> Which knit our country to our heart.

A few lines further on Blanco reveals that though an idealised England might be his rational home, the real England was a place in which spiritually and emotionally he would always be an alien. All his resentment at being patronised by the complacent finds expression in the lines:

> Oh looks of strangeness and disdain!
> Oh schooling from the vulgar vain!

Oh struggles of the humbled mind
By restive words her thoughts confined!
Oh feelings of the heart suppressed
Or met with laughter when expressed!

When therefore in the final couplets the poet announces his resolve to 'change his soul' for love of his adopted country, the humility sounds forced and unconvincing:

Painful the change: yet high the prize
Thus in the scale of life to rise.
A transient death endures the worm
And wakes endued with nobler form.

The time would come when this particular worm would turn.

On 19 December 1825, three days after writing these lines and leaping at one bound from the faintly absurd to the altogether sublime, Blanco wrote a sonnet dedicated to Samuel Taylor Coleridge, whom he had met for the first time the previous July. Some time in the following year he sent the text of the sonnet, 'Night and Death', to Coleridge, who wrote belatedly on 28 November 1827 to acknowledge 'the finest and most grandly conceived sonnet in our language, —(at least it is only in Milton's and in Wordsworth's sonnets that I recollect any rival,—and this is not my judgment alone, but that of the man κατ᾽ ἐξοχήν φιλοκαλοῦ, John Hookham Frere)'.[2] Due to an oversight on Coleridge's part, the manuscript of the sonnet found its way with other papers to the desk of the editor of *The Bijou*, who printed it in his 1828 number, much to Coleridge's embarrassment since Blanco had never intended it for publication.[3]

A few months before its composition Blanco had written to Robert Southey to acknowledge a presentation copy of the latter's *A Tale of Paraguay*, a poem which also attempted to come to terms with the mystery of death and ended on a similar note of acceptance. 'The strain of pure feeling and sublime morality which runs through it', he declared, 'is just what I want to find in poetry. My heart has been too long a prey to agitating feelings to find pleasure in the artificial storms of passion which the writers of the day are exclusively employed in raising'.[4] Blanco's own sonnet is characterised by just those qualities he admired in Southey's poem. It is noticeable, incidentally, that though it concludes with the hope of a future life, there is nothing explicitly Christian in this resolution. Geoffrey Tillotson sees it as belonging 'to the great deistic utterances of the eighteenth century: its purpose is to enlarge and ennoble the human mind and to calm it, to calm it into a marmoreal repose'.[5]

In its structure the sonnet fits the model which Blanco outlined years later:

I have always compared the Sonnet to a Cameo or Gem. If the artist cannot suit his drawing to the natural veins and colours of the substance, his labour is thrown away . . . But when the matter is suited to the form, when the poet has been struck with a thought which will naturally develop itself within the first portion of the composition and then close, strikingly, at the end of the nicely-disturbed external frame of verse and rhyme,—a sonnet is one of the most charming compositions in poetry. It is, I must repeat it, a perfect Cameo or Gem which you may carry in the memory, as you have the Gem on your finger, and look at it for ever, and ever receive fresh delight from the sight.[6]

Blanco was a compulsive tinkerer with his own work, and in making copies of 'Night and Death' for his friends he took the opportunity to make changes, not always for the better. There are at least four extant versions. The original version reproduced below was published in *The Bijou* and later in the *Gentleman's Magazine*.[7] The better-known version, however, (Q) is that which Blanco copied out for a friend in October 1838 and which was included in Thom's *Life* and, many years later, in the Quiller-Couch *Oxford Book of English Verse*.[8] The relative merits of these two versions were the subject of a perceptive critique by the Reverend Richard Perceval Graves (an ancestor of the poet Robert Graves, who became acquainted with Blanco in Dublin) which convincingly demonstrated the superiority of the original.[9] Blanco copies out at least two other versions, one for his friend Alberto Lista, (L), on which the latter based his Spanish rendering, and the other (H) for Mrs Hawkins, the wife of the Provost of Oriel.[10] In both these, Blanco replaced the famous opening, 'Mysterious Night!', with the rather jejune 'Oh Night!'. Since these versions were made late in Blanco's life, it may be suspected that the alteration was made out of a rationalist distaste for mystery. The same thinking may lie behind the replacement of 'Weak man! Why, to shun Death, this anxious strife?'—which the author may have found too redolent of the pulpit—by other, less striking, versions. It is odd that in all these recastings Blanco should have continued to overlook the tautology implicit in the phrase 'fly and leaf and insect', especially as 'fly' lent itself so easily to substition by 'flow'r'.[11]

Blanco's only other published sonnet, written three months after 'Night and Death' and entitled 'On hearing myself for the first time called an Old Man, aet. 50' was published by John Murray in 1829. It is concerned with the same theme, and though it lacks the symmetry and the steady development of its more famous partner, its conclusion is memorable:

Gone Youth! Had I thus missed thee, nor a hope
Were left of thy return beyond the tomb,
I could curse life:—but glorious is the scope
Of an immortal soul.—Oh Death, thy gloom,

Short, and already tinged with coming light,
Is to the Christian but a summer's night.[12]

It is 'Night and Death', however, which is deservedly remembered
as Blanco's epitaph. Leigh Hunt, who knew the author, wrote of it
that 'in language, some little imperfections are discernible, which do
not detract, however, from its singular merits even in that respect,
especially considering that the author was not young when he came
into England and that he then spoke English like a foreigner. In point
of *thought* the sonnet stands supreme, perhaps above all in any
language. Nor can we ponder it too deeply, or with too hopeful a
reverence'.[13]

Night and Death

Mysterious Night! when the first man but knew   1
    Thee by report, unseen, and heard thy name,
    Did he not tremble for this lovely Frame,
    This Glorious canopy of Light and Blue?
Yet 'neath a curtain of translucent dew,   5
    Bathed in the rays of the great setting Flame,
    Hesperus with the Host of Heaven came,
    And lo! Creation widened on his view.
Who could have thought what darkness lay concealed
    Within thy beams, O Sun! or who could find,   10
    Whilst fly and leaf and insect stood revealed,
    That to such endless Orbs thou mad'st us blind!
Weak man! Why, to shun Death, this anxious strife?
    If Light can thus deceive, wherefore not Life?

19 December 1825

1   When our first Parent knew (Q)
     Oh Night! When yet unseen the first man knew (H, L)
2   from report divine (Q)
8   in Man's view (Q): in their view (H): in his view (L)
9   such darkness (Q)
12   countless Orbs (Q)
     To worlds of worlds thy splendour made us blind (H)
13   Why do we then shun Death with anxious strife (Q)
     Why then oh Man with Death such anxious strife (H)

Notes

Abbreviations

BAE	Biblioteca de Autores Españoles
BH	Bulletin Hispanique
BHS	Bulletin of Hispanic Studies
BL	British Library, London
BN	Biblioteca Nacional, Madrid
BSS	Bulletin of Spanish Studies
CT	The Christian Teacher
EBW	'Examination of Blanco by White' (LUL III/56)
EE	El Español, Londres 1810–14, 8 vols.
ER	Edinburgh Review
Evidence	J. Blanco White, Practical and Internal Evidence against Catholicism, 1825 (2nd edn 1826)
Goytisolo	Obra Inglesa de D. José María Blanco White, con un prólogo de D. Juan Goytisolo, Buenos Aires 1972
Lambeth	Lambeth Palace Library, London, Whately papers
LFS	Letters from Spain, by Don Leucadio Doblado, 1822 (2nd edn 1825)
Life	The Life of the Rev. Joseph Blanco White, ed J. H. Thom, 1845, 3 vols.
LR	The London Review
LUL	Liverpool University, Sydney Jones Library, Blanco White papers
MB	Mario Méndez Bejarano, Vida y obras de José María Blanco y Crespo
MCO	Manchester College, Oxford: Blanco White papers
NLD	J. H. Newman, Letters and Diaries
NLI	National Library of Ireland, Dublin
NLW	National Library of Wales, Aberystwyth
NMM	New Monthly Magazine
OHO	Observations on Heresy and Orthodoxy
Oriel	Oriel College, Oxford, Letter books
PRO	Public Records Office, London
PUL	Princeton University Library, Blanco White papers
QR	Quarterly Review
SP	Semanario Patriótico

Preface

1. W. E. Gladstone, 'The Life of Mr Blanco White', QR vol. 76 (1845), pp. 167–203, reprinted in Gleanings of Past Years, 1879, vol. 2, pp. 1–63.
2. Jane Welsh Carlyle, A Selection of her Letters, ed. Trudy Bliss, 1969, p. 169 (letter to Thomas Carlyle of 28 September 1845).
3. The four works which I classify here as apologetic are Letters from Spain (1822); Practical and Internal Evidence against Catholicism (1825); The Poor Man's Preservative against Popery (1825); 'Despedida de los americanos', in Variedades, vol. 2 (1825), pp. 299 ff.

Chapter 1

1. See Francisco Aguilar Piñal, Historia de Sevilla: Siglo XVIII, 2nd edn (Sevilla, 1982).

2. Quoted in G. L. Vazquez, 'Juan Pablo Forner and the Formation of the New History in Spain', *Iberian Studies*, 7 (Autumn, 1978).

3. See Francisco Aguilar Piñal, 'Sevilla en 1791', *Archivo Hispalense*, nos 132–3 (1965), pp. 95–105.

4. Joseph Townsend, *A. Journey through Spain in the Years 1786 and 1787*, 2nd edn (1792), vol. 2, p. 312ff.

5. See Maria José Alvarez Pantoja, 'Nathan Wetherell, un industrial inglés en la Sevilla del antiguo regimen', *Moneda y Credito*, no 143 (December, 1977). Nathan's son, John Wetherell, a friend of BW, was a pioneer of archaeological studies in Seville. He left his collection of Mexican antiquities to the British Museum, from which it passed to the Museum of Mankind, London.

6. F Aguilar Piñal, op. cit., p. 128; Joseph Townsend, op. cit., vol. 2, pp. 318–19.

7. For a good general account of Olavide, see Douglas Hilt, 'Pablo de Olavide: Spirit of an Age', *History Today* (December, 1978), pp. 793–802.

8. For BW's recollections of the event, see EE vol. 3, pp. 38–41 (English version in *Letter upon the Mischievous Influence of the Inquisition*, 1811, pp. 8–14). On the harrowing and lurid details of the *auto*, see D[on] J[osé] M[aria] M[ontero de] E[spinosa], *Relación histórica de la Judería de Sevilla, establecimiento de la Inquisición en ella, su estinción y colección de los autos que llamaban de fé celebrados desde su erección* (Sevilla: Imprenta de El Porvenir, 1849), pp. 182–209 (copy in the Wiffen Collection, Wadham College, Oxford). The fact that this work was published on a nineteenth century liberal press may be thought to cast doubt on its objectivity, but the details correspond to those in the contemporary account cited by F. Aguilar Piñal (op. cit., p. 367, n 424).

9. Joseph Townsend, op. cit., vol. 2, p. 345ff.

10. The Bodleian possesses a contemporary MS copy of Olavide's *Plan de estudios para la universidad de Sevilla*, 1768. On the theatre, see F. Aguilar Piñal, *Sevilla y el teatro en el siglo XVIII* (Sevilla, 1974).

11. *Relación de las suntuosas exequias celebradas en Sevilla el día 8 de junio de ·1793 . . . por el alma de Luis XVI rey christianísimo de Francia* (Sevilla, 1793), p. x (copy in Menéndez y Pelayo library, Santander). The contributors to the enormous mausoleum erected for the occasion in the crossing of the Cathedral included the Whites and the Wisemans.

12. *Evidence*, p. 3.

13. See W. McDonald, 'Irish Colleges since the Reformation: Seville', *Irish Ecclesiastical Record* IX, (1872–3), pp. 208–221; J. J. Silke, 'The Irish College, Seville', *Archivium Hibernicum* XXIV (1961).

14. Earl of Ilchester (ed.), *The Spanish Journal of Elizabeth Lady Holland* (1910), p. 60.

15. On BW's connection with Justino de la Neve, see his letter to Lord Holland of 13 March 1833 (BL Add MSS 51845, ff 195–6). On Felipe de la Neve, see Hubert Howe Bancroft, *History of the Pacific States of North America* (1884), vol. 13, pp. 220–387, 446–48. In the last two years of his life, Don Felipe was Commandant General of the Provincias Internas—a position second only to that of Viceroy. Bancroft describes him as an enlightened, humane and able administrator. BW's maternal uncle Antonio Crespo y Neve also served in America. He died in New Orleans at the age of 24, leaving a volume of poems dedicated to Don Bernardo Gálvez.

16. LFS, 2nd edn (1825), pp. 60–61.

17. On the rise and fall of the family firm, see María José Alvarez Pantoja, 'Comerciantes irlandeses en la Sevilla del siglo XVIII: White, Plunket y Cía, 1737–1769' (forthcoming).

18. *Life* I, p. 6.

19. LFS, pp. 231–2.

20. George Santayana noted, 'This is even more Spanish than Italian: a

domestication of the heart in religion, and being tender in small things, rather than coldly despising them and confining religion to morality or to great tragic and cosmological vistas' (*Persons and Places*, 1944, p. 244). Santayana's autobiography takes on an added resonance when read alongside BW's.

21. Jos. Townsend, op. cit., vol. 2, p. 364.
22. LFS, pp. 61–2.
23. *Life* I, p. 24.
24. BW's experience was echoed a century and a half later by the Sevillan poet Luis Cernuda, who recalled the effect on him, as a boy, of a book of Greek myths: 'Those pages revealed to you a world in which poetry transmuted reality, kindling it to life. How sad your own religion then appeared. You did not dispute or question it—that would have been too difficult for a child—but into your deep and rooted convictions there crept, if not a rational objection, then the awareness of an absent joy. Why did they teach you to bow your head before deified suffering when in other ages man's happiness was such that he worshipped beauty, in all its tragic fullness?' (Translated from 'El poeta y los mitos', in Luis Cernuda, *Ocnos*, ed. D. Musacchio, Barcelona, 1977, pp. 50–1.)
25. *Life* I, pp. 7–8.
26. On the university, see F. Aguilar Piñal, *La universidad de Sevilla en el siglo XVIII. Estudio sobre la primera reforma universitaria moderna*, (Sevilla, 1969).
27. EBW, pp. 14–15.
28. For Lista, see Hans Juretschke, *Vida, obra y pensamiento de Alberto Lista*, (Madrid, 1951). On Reinoso there has been nothing of substance published since the biographical account by Antonio Martín Villa in his *Obras de D. Felix José Reinoso*, vol. 1, (Sevilla, 1872). See also N. Pastor Diaz, *Galería de españoles celebres*, vol.7 (1845), pp. 97–196. On

the Academia de Letras Humanas, see V. Lloréns, 'Una academia literaria juvenil', in *Studia Hispánica in honorem R. Lapesa* (Madrid, 1972), vol.2, pp. 281–95. For Reinoso's own 'Historia de la Academia de Letras Humanas desde su establecimiento (1793) hasta el 10 de mayo 1799' see *Archivo Hispalense* II (1886).

29. *Alexis. Drama pastoral . . . por el P. Andres Friz, S. J., traducido en castellano por D.J.M.B.y C.* (Sevilla, 1795). The copy presented by the author to the Academia de Letras Humanas is in the Menéndez y Pelayo library, Santander.
30. The poem is reprinted by V. Lloréns in his *José María Blanco White: Antología de obras en español* (Barcelona, 1971), pp. 78–81. It echoes the sentiments in Forner's own *Contra la falsa sabiduría* (BAE 63, p. 345).
31. On Forner and Cadalso, see M. Jiménez Salas, *Vida y obras de D. Juan Pablo Forner y Segarra* (Madrid, 1944); Nigel Glendinning, *Vida y obra de Cadalso* (Madrid, 1962).
32. *Poesías de una Academia de Letras Humanas de Sevilla* (Sevilla: por la viuda de Vázquez y Compañía, 1797); LFS, p. 105. I owe the expression *ivresse de savoir* to J. Sarrailh, *L'Espagne éclairée de la seconde moitié du 18e siècle* (Paris, 1954), p. 147.
33. EBW, p. 8.
34. *Evidence* (1825), p. 4.
35. Frederick Augustus Fisher [*vere* Christian August Fischer], *Travels in Spain in 1797 and 1798, translated from the German* (London: Longman and Rees, 1802), pp. 300–1. After a visit in 1809, Byron was equally effusive: 'Cadiz—sweet Cadiz!—it is the first spot in creation . . . The beauty of its streets and mansions is only excelled by the loveliness of its inhabitants. For with all national prejudice I must confess that the women of Cadiz are as far superior to the English women in beauty as the Spaniards are inferior to the English in every quality that dignifies the name of man'. (*In My Hot Youth. Byron's Letters and*

Journals, vol. 1, ed. Leslie A. Marchand, 1973, pp. 216–17.)

36. *Life* I. pp. 32–4.
37. EBW, p. 12. C. A. Fischer's description of the Cadiz theatre suggests that Guillermo Blanco's fears were not without foundation. Its chief attraction was 'the little comedies called *saynetes,* which are somewhat licentious, and the lascivious dances called *voleros*; the former containing the chronicles, as it were, of scandal, and the latter portraying the mysteries of love'. Once seen, the bolero made all other Spanish spectacles—including the bullfight — seem 'tame and inexpressive' (op. cit., pp. 302–4).
38. *Life* I, pp. 50–1.
39. *Life* I, pp. 35–48. The whole passage anticipates James Joyce's description of the school retreat in *Portrait of the Artist.*
40. *Life* I, p. 55.
41. See the MS 'Pruebas de las legitimidad, limpieza de sangre, nobleza y demas circunstancias de D. José Ma Blanco pretendiente de una beca teóloga del colegio mayor de Sta Ma de Jesús, Universidad de Sevilla, que vulgarmente llaman de Maese Rodrigo' [1797], Seville University Library. On BW's academic career, see F. Aguilar Piñal, 'Blanco White y el Colegio de Santa María de Jesús, *Archivo Hispalense* LVIII (1975), pp. 1–54.
42. BW to his brother Fernando, 11 July 1816 (PUL 7/2).
43. *Life* I, p. 63.
44. EBW, p. 19. Blanco's statements on this subject are supported by Byron: 'I beg leave to observe that Intrigue here [Andalucia] is the business of life. When a woman marries, she throws off all restraint, but I believe their conduct is chaste enough before' (op. cit., pp. 218–21).
45. EBW, p. 21.
46. 'Epístola a Albino' (1798), in *Poetas líricos del siglo XVIII,* BAE 61 (Madrid, 1875), pp. 227–8.
47. Guillermo Blanco to BW, 7 July 1798 (PUL 7/5).
48. *Life* I, pp. 63–4.
49. J. H. Newman, *Lectures on the Present Position of Catholics in England,* 1851, pp. 141–60.
50. LFS, pp. 108–9.

Chapter 2

1. LFS, p. 110.
2. *Life* I, pp. 67–8. For the story of Maria Francisca Barreiro, see *Evidence,* pp. 285–88. The theme of the reluctant nun (LFS, p. 157) was treated by the contemporary playwright Leandro Fernández de Moratín in his play *La Mojigata,* and by the satirical writer Sebastian Miñano y Bedoya in his *Cartas de Don Justo Balanza.* (I owe the reference to Moratín to Professor Nigel Abercrombie).
3. *Obras de D. Felix José Reinoso,* ed A. Martín Villa (Sevilla 1872), vol.1.
4. *Life* I p. 76. The plague and exposition of the *Lignum Crucis* are described in LFS, p. 171 ff.
5. Justino de Matute, quoted in F. Aguilar Piñal, op. cit., p. 113.
6. On Blanco's membership of the Escuela (still in existence) see Francisco Sanchez-Castañer y Mena, 'José Mª Blanco White y Alberto Lista en las Escuelas de Cristo Hispalenses', *Archivo Hispalense* XLII (1985) pp. 229–248. For Blanco's rather lurid account of the spiritual exercises at La Cueva (with details of self-flagellation designed to titillate Protestant ears), see *Life* I, pp. 85–92. It was for this church, decorated with paintings by Goya, that Haydn had recently written his sacred oratorio *The Seven Last Words on the Cross.*
7. *Life* I, pp. 92–107.
8. On Spanish 'Jansenism' (an inaccurate term, used by the opponents of the reform movement in order to discredit it), see Jean Sarrailh, *La Crise Religieuse en Espagne à la fin du XVIIIe siècle* (Oxford 1951); J. Marichal, 'From Pistoia to Cadiz: A. Generation's Itinerary, 1786–1812', in *The Ibero-American Enlighten-*

ment, ed A. Owen Aldridge (University of Illinois, 1974) pp. 97–110; W. J. Callahan, *Church, Politics and Society in Spain, 1750–1874* (Harvard 1984), pp. 309–10.

9. *Discurso sobre si convendría restablecer el método de predicar de los santos padres; presentado a la Academia de Letras Humanas de Sevilla para optar el premio mayor de Elocuencia propuesta por la Academia* (1799), MS in the Seville University Library. On the place of preaching in the 'Jansenist' programme, see Joël Saugnieux, *Les jansénistes et le renouveau de la prédication dans l'Espagne de la seconde moitié du XVIIIe siècle* (Lyon 1976). The author has some interesting observations on the continuity between the Spanish Erasmists of the 16th and the Jansenists of the 18th century. He describes the latter as 'professeurs nés', characterised by 'le goût pour l'utile et l'efficace'.

10. LFS, pp. 75–76.
11. *Life* I, p. 287.
12. *Evidence*, pp. 9–10.
13. *Life* I, p. 33.
14. *Sermon predicado en la función solemne que consagró la Real Brigada de Carabineros a su patrono San Fernando en su Santa y Real Capilla de Sevilla el dia 13 de julio de 1802* (Sevilla: Viuda de Hidalgo y Sobrino, 1804). Copy in the Menéndez y Pelayo library, Santander. The text of the sermon, without the introduction, is reproduced in V. Lloréns, *Antología*, pp. 115–138.
15. EBW, p. 30. For the text of other sermons of this period, see MB, pp. 298–340.
16. *Evidence*, p. 142.
17. *Life* I, p. 124.
18. *Evidence*, p. 130.
19. EBW, pp. 36–37.
20. EBW, p. 34.
21. *Life* I, pp. 112–13.
22. ibid., p. 116.
23. LFS, p. 110.
24. See the strictures of Joaquín de Villanueva on the Seville clergy in his *Vida Literaria* (London 1825), vol. I, p. 214.

25. *Don Juan Calderón* (London 1855), p. 24. The value of this autobiography (addressed to Calderón's friend Benjamin Wiffen) for the history of the late 18th and early 19th century Spanish church has not been fully appreciated.
26. LFS, p. 56.
27. 'I never felt proud of being a Spaniard, for it was as a Spaniard that I found myself mentally degraded. For many years did I feel that a sentence of banishment, would be a blessing to me' (*Life* I, p. 141).
28. 'The Life of Mr Blanco White', QR LXXVI (1845), pp. 167–203, reprinted in *Gleanings of Past Years*, vol. 2 (1879). When in the final number of *El Español* (May–June 1814) Blanco made a last plea for religious toleration, he eloquently recalled the rage and despair of his young manhood: 'It can truly be said of this oppression, this torture, that it shares the house of the sufferer, it follows him when he goes out, it sits down with him at table, it allows him no rest when he lies down on his bed, it dogs his steps in the city, it follows him to the country, it eats up his youth and embitters his last years'. (EE vol. 8, p. 304). There is an echo here of Cicero, *Pro Archia* vii.16.
29. *Evidence*, p. 132.
30. EBW, p. 40.
31. BW to Fernando Blanco 27 June 1803 (PUL 7/2). See also the letters in V. Lloréns, *Antología*, pp. 313–14.
32. His most famous work was the anticlerical satire *Lamentos del pobrecito holgazán* (Madrid, 1821). The distinguished 19th century scholar Eugenio de Ochoa was almost certainly his illegitimate son. See Donald A. Randolph, *Eugenio de Ochoa y el romanticismo español* (Berkeley, Ca. 1966).
33. See F. Aguilar Piñal, op. cit., pp. 238, 358 (n. 305).
34. *Prospecto y plan de una clase de humanidades que establece la Real Sociedad de Sevilla*, Sevilla 1804 (Extract in MB, pp. 294–97).

35. This is the line taken in BW's anonymous article on 'Education in Spain' in the *Quarterly Journal of Education* (published by the Society for the Diffusion of Useful Knowledge) vol. I (1831), pp. 225–239. Cf. his letter to Reinoso of 26 January 1816 (Menéndez y Pelayo Library M 542). Reinoso took over the course after the war and wrote to Blanco for advice.

36. EBW, p. 42 (text legible beneath deletion).

Chapter 3

1. 'Recollections of a Night at Sea', MS poem in blank verse (MCO III/8), lines 77–79. The poem is printed by A. Garnica in his article, 'La poesía inglesa inédita de Blanco White', in *Homenaje a Don Esteban Pujals* (Oviedo 1981).

2. J. M. Sotelo to Reinoso, 7 July 1807 (original MS in Menéndez y Pelayo Library, Santander, M540), quoted by V. Lloréns in his article 'Blanco White en el Instituto Pestalozziano', *Homenaje a Antonio Rodriguez-Moniño* (Madrid, 1966), pp. 349–65.

3. On this crucial period, see Richard Herr, *The Eighteenth-Century Revolution in Spain* (Princeton, 1958); Carlos Corona Baratech, *Revolución y reacción en el reinado de Carlos IV* (Madrid 1957).

4. LFS, p. 335.

5. Ibid., p. 223.

6. Ibid., p. 333–4.

7. *Variedades* I (October 1824), p. 476.

8. Letter of 16 August 1806, in V. Lloréns, *Antología*, pp. 315–16. On Tavira, see Joël Saugnieux, *Un prélat éclairé: Don Antonio Tavira* (Toulouse, 1970).

9. *Life* I, p. 129.

10. EBW, p. 44. BW's first lodgings in Madrid were at Caba de San Miguel 18–19, near the Plaza Mayor. The house is still standing. He later moved to c/de Silva 8, then to c/ Escorial 15. All the correspondence between BW and his father at this time is in PUL 7/5–6.

11. Quoted in V. Lloréns, art. cit., p. 349.

12. See Albert Dérozier, *Manuel Josef Quintana et la naissance du libéralisme en Espagne* (Annales littéraires de l'Université de Besançon no. 95) 2 vols, Paris 1968–70.

13. For the expurgated version of this poem, see V. Lloréns, *Antología*, pp. 91–8, and M. V. de Lara, 'Nota a unos manuscritos de J. M. Blanco White', BHS XX (1943), 110–20, 196–214. The missing lines are supplied in Brian Dendle, 'A Note on the First Published Version of the Epístola a D. Manuel José Quintana by J. M. Blanco', BHS LI (October 1974), pp. 365–71. The similar poem by Jovellanos is among his *Sátiras* (BAE 46, pp. 35–6). On the humanitarian theme in the Spanish pre-romantics, see E. Allison Peers, *History of the Romantic Movement in Spain* (Cambridge 1940), vol. 2. pp. 290–1.

14. M. de Godoy, *Memorias*, ed C. Seco, BAE II, no. 89, p. 237. Amoros is an interesting specimen of the period of transition from enlightenment to liberalism. Under Joseph Bonaparte he served as governor of Santander and chief of police, and then fled to France where he achieved some fame as a pioneer of gymnastics and physical education, his methods being adopted by the French army. His grave in Montparnasse bore the inscription: 'Ci-gît le colonel Amoros, mort avec le regret de n'avoir pas assez fait pour le gymnastique'. See C. J. B. Amyot, *Histoire du Colonel Amoros, de sa méthode d'éducation physique et morale et de la fondation de la gymnastique en France* (Paris, 1852); A. Morel-Fatio, 'Don Francisco de Amoros', BH XXVI (1924), pp. 207–40, 339–68; XXVII (1925), pp. 38–78.

15. See Edward J. Sullivan, *Goya and the Art of His Time*, Meadows Museum, Southern Methodist University, Dallas, 1982, pp. 62–3. A copy of the

complete painting, probably by Agustín Esteve, survives in the Academia de San Fernando, Madrid.

16. 'Noticias sobre el Instituto de Yverdun con algunas reflexiones sobre el método de Pestalozzi', LUL III/54.

17. J. M. Blanco y Crespo, *Discurso sobre si el metodo de ensenañza de E. Pestalozzi puede apagar el genio y especialmente el que se requiere para las artes de imitación* [Madrid] 1807 (reprinted in V. Lloréns, *Antología*, pp. 139–58). Blanco's own copy of the *Discurso*, with his note of 23 July 1821 explaining why at an earlier date he excised his name from the title page, is in MCO II/7. When it was acceptable to do so, BW paid a warm tribute to Godoy in his article 'Godoy, Prince of the Peace', *London and Westminster Review* III (1836), pp. 28–60. In this review of Godoy's memoirs, he wrote that the Prince 'unquestionably exerted himself in promoting mental freedom' (p. 46), and did justice to the 'kindness and benevolence of his natural disposition'. He was also warm in his praise of Charles IV (pp. 36–8). Lord Holland, who knew Godoy well, wrote of him in similar vein (*Reminiscences*, ed Henry Edward, Lord Holland, 2nd edn 1851, pp. 132–8).

18. EBW, p. 50. The poem 'La Verdad: Oda al Sereníssimo Señor Principe de la Paz, Generalísimo Almirante, Protector del Real Instituto Militar Pestalozziano. Leida . . . el 1 de enero 1808' was published by Miguel Artigas at the end of his article 'El soneto *Night and Death* de Blanco White', BSS I (1924), pp. 3–12. The original autograph MS is in the Menéndez y Pelayo library, Santander. In her article 'Nota a unos manuscritos de J. M. Blanco White II', BSS XX (1943), pp. 207–09, M. V. de Lara reproduces the MS of a poem, now in Liverpool University Library, which is substantially identical to 'La Verdad' except that it has been topped and tailed of the stanzas specifically relat-

ing to the Prince of the Peace. There is a close correspondence in imagery and phraseology between 'La Verdad' and the sonnet 'Night and Death' composed by BW nearly twenty years later (see Appendix 1). Other examples of adulatory poems addressed to Godoy by contemporaries are given in C. Corona Baratech, *Revolución y reacción en el reinado de Carlos IV* (Madrid, 1957), pp. 274–5.

19. *Manifesto de D. Antonio de Capmany en respuesta a la contextación de D. Manuel Quintana* (Cadiz: Imprenta Real, 1811). A copy is in the BN, Gomez Imaz collection R 60167. Arjona's 'Pindaric ode' is reproduced in M. Méndez Bejarano, *Historia política de los afrancesados* (Madrid, 1912), pp. 207–10. Arjona defended his conduct by claiming that it was not he who made the adaptation, but his friend José Marchena, another *esprit fort*. See BAE 63, p. 516.

20. EBW, p. 44. The autograph MS of the poem, *El incordio: Poema epigálico en un canto*, annotated by the author, is in the library of the Hispanic Society of America, where it forms part of the collection originally belonging to the Marqués de Jerez de los Caballeros. See A. Rodriguez-Moniño and Maria Brey Mariño, *Catálogo de los MSS poéticos castellanos . . . en la biblioteca de The Hispanic Society of America* (N.Y. 1965), vol. 1, xciii. The text was published, with a short introduction, by Antonio Garnica in *Rara Avis* nos. 2–3 (Sevilla, 1987), pp. 63–72.

21. *Life* I, p. 132; BW to Fernando Blanco, 2 September 1816, PUL 7/2. The letters of Felipa Esquaya to Fernando are in PUL 10/1. The most notorious sneer is that which disfigures the often perceptive study of BW by M. Menéndez y Pelayo: 'Que siempre han de andar faldas de por medio en este negocio de herejías' ('There's always a woman involved when it comes to heresy'), *Histo-*

ria de los heterodoxos españoles, Madrid, 1932, vol. 7, p. 184.

22. For what follows, see C. Corona Baratech, op. cit., pp. 329–88.

23. LFS, pp. 346–52. The description of the Escorial in BW's account illustrates his skill in satisfying his English readers' taste for Gothic gloom: the palace is 'sullen', its vaults 're-echo', 'monkish' tapers 'glare', the surrounding woods are 'stunted', etc.

24. LFS, pp. 358, 360.

25. Ibid., pp. 364–5.

26. Ibid., p. 375. Cf. EBW, p. 49: 'I conceived the most visionary hopes from the interference of the French'.

27. *Life* I, p. 142. BW's recent public act of homage to Godoy would have rendered him suspect both to the loyalists in Seville and the afrancesados in Madrid, but he was more liable to danger in Madrid where memories of the adulatory ode were fresher. This consideration, it need hardly be said, is not mentioned by BW.

Chapter 4

1. LFS, pp. 381–8.

2. *Oda a la instalación de la Junta Central de España* (Madrid: Gomez Fuentenebro y Cía, 1808. Copy in BL). Later, in his own copy of this published ode, BW characteristically altered the title in his own hand, replacing the words 'Instalación de la Junta Central' by 'Reunión de las Provincias' (LUL VI/1). No doubt he was embarrassed at being confronted by printed evidence of his earlier support for an institution (the Junta Central) which after its collapse in January 1810 was generally discredited.

3. Lord Holland, *Reminiscences*, ed. Henry Edward Holland, 2nd edn, 1851, pp. 143–4.

4. See the licentiate thesis by Juana María Ridao Lopez, 'Blanco White: Capellán Real de San Fernando', University of Seville, 1985.

5. Quoted in Leslie Mitchell, *Holland House*, 1980, p. 226.

6. *The Spanish Journal of Elizabeth, Lady Holland*, ed. Earl of Ilchester, 1910, p. 376.

7. William Thomas, 'Lord Holland', in *History and Imagination: Essays in Honour of H. R. Trevor-Roper*, 1981, p. 306. Other English travellers who met BW in Seville were the architectural writer Henry Gally Knight, the naturalist J. G. Children, and Lord Dudley. See John William Ward, 1st Earl of Dudley, *Letters to the Bishop of Llandaff*, 1840, p. 357; A[nna] A[tkins], *Memoir of J. G. Children*, 1853, pp. 90, 109. Gally Knight's contribution to the war effort was a 'fragment of an Epic Poem in three parts', *Iberia's Crisis*, published on his return to England in 1809. As it progresses, the poem is gradually submerged under a rising tide of footnotes.

8. *Manifiesto de D. Antonio de Capmany en respuesta a la contextación de D. Manuel José Quintana*, Cadiz: Imprenta Real, 1811, p. 14.

9. *Semanario Patriotico*, no. 16, 11 May 1809, pp. 28–9; no. 26, 20 July 1809, p. 187; no. 22, 22 June 1809, p. 128. I owe these references to M. André Pons. On the *Semanario*, see also V. Lloréns, 'Jovellanos y Blanco', *Nueva Revista de Filología Hispánica* XXX, Mexico, 1961, pp. 261–78.

10. Correspondence in *Life* III, pp. 318, 320–1.

11. Lord Holland, *Reminiscences*, pp. 144–6.

12. *Obras . . . de D. Gaspar Melchor de Jovellanos*, ed. Miguel Artola, BAE, Madrid, 1956, IV, pp. 376, 380.

13. John Allen to BW, 16 May 1809, LUL I 1/42.

14. *Life* I, p. 149.

15. Ibid., p. 151.

16. Ibid., p. 146.

17. 'Dictamen sobre el modo de reunir las Cortes de España', in *El Español*, no. 2, May 1810, pp. 83–98.

18. William Jacob, *Travels in the South of Spain written A.D. 1809 and 1810*, 1811, p. 145.

19. *Life* I, p. 158. For Lista's conduct, see H. Juretschke, *Vida, obra y pensamiento de Alberto Lista*, Madrid, 1951, pp. 50ff.
20. *Evidence*, p. 11.
21. *Life* I, p. 162.

Chapter 5

1. This stormy voyage later took on an allegorical importance in BW's memory, and was the subject of two poems: 'Recollections of a Night at Sea', written in 1826 (published by A. Garnica in 'La poesia inedita de Blanco-White', *Homenaje a Don Esteban Pujals*, Oviedo, 1981), and 'Una tormenta nocturna en alta mar', written in 1839 (V Lloréns, *Antología*, pp. 105–8).
2. *Life* I, pp. 165–6.
3. *Variedades* no. 1 (January 1823), p. 16.
4. *Life* I, pp. 169–70. Carlton House was then the residence of the Prince of Wales.
5. *Variedades*, no. 1, pp. 23–3; no. 2 (January 1824), pp. 120–30. For Children see Chapter 4, n.7.
6. *Life* I, p. 173; Variedades, no. 1, p. 17.
7. BL Add Mss 51951 (Holland House dinner book).
8. *Life* III, p. 322. In a letter of 28 April 1810 (BL Add Mss 51645, f. 66) BW's old colleague Isidoro Antillón expressed surprise that he should consider collaborating with Abella.
9. On the *Español*, see p. 256 for the thesis by M. André Pons. For a short, but incomplete, account see V. Lloréns, '*El Español* de Blanco White; primer periódico de la oposición', *Boletín informativo del Seminario de Derecho Político*, Princeton, March 1962, pp. 3–21.
10. Hamilton to Vaughan, 12 May 1810, Vaughan Papers, All Souls, C 48/6 (OB 128). Though careful to distance himself publicly from the *Español*, Wellesley from an early stage made available to Blanco relevant Foreign Office papers and

correspondence. See, for instance, BW to John Allen, 5 September 1810 (BL Add Mss 52193, f. 218).
11. Add MSS 51645, f. 67.
12. Add MSS 51621, ff. 30–32. On the other hand, BW's attack on the politicians of Cadiz went down well with their enemies, particularly among the military. The Marqués de la Romana had the article on the Junta Central reprinted and distributed at Badajoz (ibid. ff. 76–77).
13. See P. Michael McKinley, *Prerevolutionary Caracas: Politics, Economy and Society 1777–1811*, Cambridge, 1985, pp. 146–174.
14. EE Vol. 1 (30 July 1810), pp. 312–20. In a postscript (p. 323) BW sought to reassure his Spanish readers about the non-separatist intentions of the Americans by reporting pledges personally given him by Bolívar and Luis López Méndez, who had arrived in London in June to seek British recognition and support. On BW's American policy, see Manuel Moreno Alonso, 'La independencia de las colonias americanas y la política de Cádiz (1810–1814) en *El Español* de Blanco White', *Jornadas de Andalucia y America*, Sevilla 1986, vol.1, pp. 83–128.
15. On the Spanish view of English policy, see the introduction by José Alberich to his *Bibliografía Anglo-Hispánica 1801–1850* (Dolphin Press, Oxford, 1978).
16. EE Vol.1, pp. 369–77.
17. *Life* III, pp. 326–9.
18. The article 'Reflexiones generales sobre la revolución de España' was reprinted in nos. 4 and 5 (March–May 1819) of *El Colombiano* and subsequently in the *Gaceta de Caracas*. See the facsimile reprints: '*El Colombiano*' de F. de Miranda (Caracas 1952), pp. 52–56, 68–79; *Gaceta de Caracas 1808–1810* (Caracas 1960), vol. 2, p. 35.
19. Text in EE vol.2 (February 1811), pp. 342–3.
20. *El Observador*, nos 10, 12 (Cadiz, 7 and 14 September 1810). Copies in BN, Gómez Imaz R 60362. See also

Denunciación de D. José Blanco (Cadiz: Imprenta Real, 1810). BW's reaction to Lord Holland in *Life* III, pp. 334–5.

21. J. B. Arriaza, *Poesías patrióticas* (Londres: T. Bensley, 1810), pp. vii, xxii; *Breve registro de los seis numeros que hasta ahora se han publicado del periódico intitulado El Español. Es carta de un patriota español residente en Londres a un amigo suyo en la peninsula* (Londres: Vogel y Schulze, 1810). The author's presentation copy to Francisco de Saavedra is in the Saavedra archive in Granada (Facultad de Teología).

22. *Manifiesto del Duque de Alburquerque acerca de su conducta con la Junta de Cadiz, y arribo del exercito de su cargo a aquella plaza* (Londres: R. Juigné, 1810). The Simancas archives (Estado 8320) contain a copy of the Junta's printed riposte as well as the report of the French emigré doctor who attended the Duke. This states (confirming the account given by BW in *Life* I, pp. 191–8) that he died of the consequnces of 'un chagrin violent—une âme très exaltée, une sensibilité outrée'. On the funeral, see also *The Times*, 4 March 1811.

23. Simancas, Estado 8173, ff 17–19 (letter from the Secretary of the Regency, Bardaxí, to the Ambassador, Ruiz de Apodaca, 2 June 1810; report on BW dated London, 2 April 1811). The writer of the report compared BW with the emigré Brazilian journalist Hipólito da Costa, whose journal *Correio Brasiliense*, also edited in London under the patronage of the Duke of Sussex, provoked the Portuguese by advocating the right of the Brazilians to self-government. On BW the report declared: 'Su misma divergencia de ideas, su mala coordinación y su banalidad lo harán al fin de poca importancia'.

24. *Life* I, pp. 198–9.

25. Letter of BW to Wellesley, 25 September 1810 (PRO FO 72/104 ff 308–11). BW's Spanish draft of this letter is reprinted in V. Lloréns,

Antología, pp. 316–18); Lord H. to BW, 26 September 1810 (LUL II/1 229/6).

26. *Life* III, p. 326.

27. Lord H. to BW, 20 October 1810 (LUL II/1 229/6).

28. *Life* III, pp. 333–4.

29. For BW's correspondence with Bentham at this period, see J. Bowring (ed) *The Works of Jeremy Bentham* (Edinburgh 1838–41), vol.10, pp. 456–7; Pedro Schwartz and Carlos Rodriguez Braun, 'Cartas españolas de J. Bentham', *Moneda y Crédito*, no. 165 (June 1983). In EE nos. 6 and 7 (September–October 1810), BW for the benefit of the Cortes published extracts from the rules of parliamentary debate in Bentham's *Tactique des Assemblées Politiques*. Bentham's influence in Spain was strongest during the liberal triennium of 1820–3. See J. R. Dinwiddy, 'Liberal and Benthamite Circles in London 1820–29' in *Andrés Bello: The London Years*, ed. John Lynch (1982), pp. 119–36. Prominent among Spanish Benthamites was BW's friend Reinoso, who attempted to reconcile utilitarianism with Catholic belief.

30. 'Juan Sintierra al Editor del Español, Carta 2a', EE vol. 3 (April 1811). BW exemplifies his own contention that Spanish writers come most to life when they are attacking each other. It is indicative of his political *volte-face* that the satirical epithets he uses to describe the radicals in the Cortes—'matemáticos', 'filósofos', 'secretaristas', 'petimetres', 'mozalbetes', etc—are those used against them by the conservative and clerical opposition in Cadiz, led by the Dominican P. Francisco Alvarado, who wrote under the pseudonym 'el filósofo rancio'. The profusion at Cadiz of periodicals, squibs and pamphlets with such colourful titles as *The Robespierre, The Hobgoblin, The Civic Catechism, The Imp*, etc, is satirised in the amusing *Diarrea de las imprentas. Memoria sobre la epidemia de esta nombre que reina*

actualmente (Cadiz 1811. Copy in BN Madrid, Gomez Imaz collection R60167/1).

31. *Diario de las Cortes* for 24 May 1811. The debate is reported in EE vol. 3 (30 July), pp. 165–79. For the bogus letter and BW's reactions to it, see EE vol. 3 (30 April), pp. 69–72; ibid. (30 June), pp. 253–6.

Leigh Hunt recorded his impressions of BW at this time, when he was 'suffering under the calumnies of his countrymen . . . Though of extremely gentle manners in ordinary, he almost startled me by suddenly turning round and saying, in one of those incorrect foreign sentences which force one to be relieved while they startle, "If they proceed more, I will go mad"'. Hunt's description of BW's physical appearance brings him to life: 'Though English by name and origin, he was more of the Spaniard in appearance, being very unlike the portrait prefixed to his *Life and Correspondence* . . . He had a long, drooping nose, anxious and somewhat staring eyes, and a mouth turning down at the corners. I believe there was not an honester man in the world, or one of an acuter intellect, short of the mischief that had been done it by a melancholy temperament and a superstitious training . . . But perhaps there was something naturally self-tormenting in the state of Mr White's blood' (*Autobiography*, ed. J. E. Morpurgo, 1949, p. 228).

32. EE vol. 3 (April 1811), p. 35.

33. Southey to J. G. Lockhart, 2 January 1826, in K. Curry (ed.), *New Letters of Robert Southey*, vol. 2 (N.Y., 1965), p. 297.

34. *Life* I, p. 178; letter of BW to his parents of 24 September 1812 (V. Llorens, *Antología*, pp. 323–41).

35. K. Curry, op. cit., p. 2. For the correspondence between BW and Southey, see *Life*, passim; G. M. Murphy and A. Pons, 'Further Letters of Blanco White to Robert Southey', *BHS* vol. 62 (1985),

pp. 357–72; V. Lloréns, 'Blanco White and Robert Southey: Fragments of a correspondence', *Studies in Romanticism* 11 (1972), pp. 147–52. On Southey's politics, see Geoffrey Carnall, *Robert Southey and his Age: The Development of a Conservative Mind* (Oxford, 1960). For an ironic deflation of Southey's hispanomania, see *Edinburgh Review* vol. 22 (January 1814), pp. 447–54.

36. For the articles inspired by Arriaza, see *The Times* of 1 February, 13 February, 9 May, 9 July, 18 October 1811. Most are translations of attacks on BW in the Cadiz press. Arriaza was also responsible for the pamphlet *Observaciones sobre el systema de guerra de los aliados en la peninsula* (Londres: T. Bensley, 1811), an attack on British strategy in Spain. For Crabb Robinson's intervention, see Edith J. Morley (ed.) *Henry Crabb Robinson on Books and their Writers* (1938), vol. 1, p. 42; V. Llorens art. cit., pp. 147–8. For Lord Holland's view of Arriaza's conduct, see BL Add MSS 51645, f. 102.

37. K Curry, op. cit., 1965, p. 16.

Chapter 6

1. See Asa Briggs, *The Age of Improvement 1783–1867* (1959), pp. 172–75.

2. *Evidence* (1825), p. 13. On this conversion, see V. Lloréns, *Literatura, Historia, Política* (Madrid, 1967), pp. 167–86.

3. EE vol. 3 (July 1811), p. 308.

4. *Obras de D. Gaspar Melchor de Jovellanos*, ed. M. Artola, BAE 4 (Madrid, 1956), pp. 477–8; *Cartas de Jovellanos y Lord V. Holland sobre la guerra de independencia* (Madrid, 1911), vol. 2, pp. 406, 545.

5. BW was kept *au fait* with American affairs by personal friends in London such as Andrés Bello (the secretary to the Venezuelan envoy), Colonel Juan Murphy (whose firm Gordon and Murphy carried on an extensive

trade with Spanish America), Fray Servando de Mier, the Marques de Apartado (who had influential correspondents in Mexico). In addition the Foreign Office supplied him with press reports and intelligence from Caracas, Cartagena, Lima, Buenos Aires, etc (PRO FO 72).

6. EE vol. 3 (July 1811), p. 303; vol.4, (October 1811), p. 50.

7. EE vol. 5 (July 1812), p. 162. *Cartas de Jovellanos y Lord Vassall Holland sobre la guerra de las independencia 1808–11*, ed. Julio Somoza Garcia-Sala (Madrid, 1911), vol. 2, pp. 545–604.

8. On Mier, see David Brading, *Los orígines del nacionalismo mexicano*, 2nd edn (Mexico, 1980) pp. 59–148. His *Historia de la revolución de la Nueva España antiguamente Anáhuac* (2 vols, London 1813) was published under the pseudonym José Guerra.

9. EE vol. 4 (October 1811), pp. 296–309; ibid (April 1812), pp. 409–425; vol.5 (August 1812), pp. 274–285.

10. Fray Servando de Mier y Noriega, *Caras de un americano* (London, 1811–12; Mexico, 1976), pp. 11–50, 137.

11. EE vol.5 (August 1812), p. 285.

12. EE vol.5 (October 1812), pp. 424, 472.

13. 'The Present State of the Spanish Colonies', QR VII (1812), pp. 235–64; Southey to John Murray, 14 August 1812, in K. Curry, op. cit., p. 38. The QR article marked Blanco's début as an English writer. His earlier *Letter upon the Mischievous Influence of the Spanish Inquisition as it actually exists in the Provinces under the Spanish government* (London: J. Johnson, 1811), was translated by Belgrave Hoppner from the article in EE vol. 3 (April 1811), pp. 36–48. This was an attempt to counter the indulgent press which the contemporary Inquisition had recently been receiving from English writers (*eg* William Jacob), by describing the effects of its censorship on the moral and intellectual life of the nation's youth. The Inquisition might have ceased to use flames and torture, he

explained, but was just as dangerous under its 'mask of gentleness and kindness'. This little work contains the first seed of BW's later autobiography.

14. EE vol.3 (April 1811), p. 52ff; vol. 4 (April 1812), p. 489; vol. 5 (August 1812), p. 248. Cf. vol. 3 (May 1811), pp. 154–9.

15. Draft of a letter to Andrés de la Vega, MCO II/7 (quarto commonplace book 1812–22).

16. Vaughan papers, All Souls College, OB 37/1. On what follows, see G. M. Murphy and A. Pons, 'Further Letters of Blanco White to Robert Southey', BHS LXII (1985), pp. 362–4.

17. PRO FO 72/133, ff. 183–6. After the liberation of Seville, the British did in fact sponsor a daily news-sheet there in 1813 which was favourable to their cause, defending Wellington against attacks on his strategy and rebutting allegations that the British were supporting the rebels in America. Copies of this journal, *Los Ingleses en España* (nos 1–18), and its successor, the *Gazeta Diaria de Londres en Sevilla* (nos 1–18) are preserved in the Saavedra archive in the Jesuit faculty of theology at Granada. In his seventh number (undated, but c.July 1813) the editor of the *Gazeta Diaria* defended BW against attacks on him in the Cadiz press. The references to Wellington are adulatory in the extreme: in no.2 of *Los Ingleses en España* he is compared with Q. Fabius, Alexander, Scipio, Hercules, Bayard and Jugurtha.

18. BW to Southey, 31 October 1812, in G. M. Murphy and A. Pons, art.cit. In giving BW an indirect subsidy, the Foreign Office was applying the method it already used to support J. G. Peltier, the editor of the French-language anti-revolutionary newspaper journal *L'Ambigu*, which also had a circulation in America. The relationship between the two editors was close, and for a time they shared the same office in Duke

Street. See Hélène Maspéro-Clerc, *Un journaliste contre-révolutionnaire, Jean-Gabriel Peltier, 1760–1825* (Paris, 1973).

19. art. cit., p. 371, n. 40.
20. *Life* I, p. 207.
21. V Lloréns, *Antología*, p. 324.
22. Guillermo Blanco to BW, 7 November 1812, PUL 7/7.
23. F. J. Reinoso to BW, 7 November 1812, in MB pp. 75–8. On Arjona's tergiversations during the war, see H. Juretschke, *Los â francesados en la guerra de independencia*, Madrid 1962, p. 225.
24. BW to his parents, 4 October 1812, MB p. 81; EE vol.4, November 1811, p. 147. The terms *liberales* and *serviles*, to describe the opposing factions, were by now in general use.
25. BW's earliest account book (Liverpool MSS III 57/263) has an entry for 20 January 1814 recording the payment to a Mrs Ottley of a school bill for the previous quarter, under the name 'Ferdinand White junior'. The boy must therefore have reached London by the autumn of 1813. The arrangements were made by BW's friend Juan Gualberto González.
26. Private Journal 1812–20, LUL III/56 262, entry for 4 October 1812 (extracts in *Life* I, pp. 241–3). For BW's later, painful self-examination on this matter, see EBW, pp. 62–5.
27. EE vol. 5 (December 1812), p. 558.
28. EE vol. 6 (January 1813), p. 1–19. BW's conversion from jacobin to monarchist mirrors that of Wordsworth and Southey.
29. EE vol. 6 (March 1813), p. 177–194.
30. EE vol. 8 (January-February 1814), pp. 3–23; ibid (May-June 1814), pp. 213–22.
31. EE vol. 7, no. 40 (August 1813), pp. 126–37; ibid (September 1813), pp. 182–203. BW's choice of the dialogue form may possibly owe something to the influence of Erasmus, whose *Colloquia* include two dialogues on celibacy: 'Virgo μισόγαμος' and 'Virgo Poenitens'.

He later included a translation of the former in *Evidence*, pp. 267–80. For another use of the dramatic dialogue form, cf. 'Conversaciones americanas sobre España y sus Indias' in EE vol. 5 (30 May 1812), pp. 1–77—a more fully realised and imaginative essay in the genre.

32. *Bosquejo*, etc (Londres: Ellerton y Henderson, 1814). The Cambridge University Library has the copy of this work which was presented by BW in 1840 to the Institut d'Afrique, Paris, on the occasion of his being made an honorary vice-president. It includes a short MS account by BW on the 'nature and origin' of the work (Camb. UL Syn 5 81 90). Two hundred copies of the edition were ordered by the British Minister in Madrid for propaganda purposes in trying to influence the Spanish government towards abolition. See David R. Murray, *Odious Commerce: Britain, Spain and the Abolition of the Cuban Slave Trade*, Cambridge 1980, p. 61.
33. EE Vol. 8 (January-February 1814), 'Reflexiones sobre los asuntos de España', pp. 86–87. The narcissism of the Cortes is illustrated by the declaration of the deputy for Seville that Cadiz was to the Spanish nation what Noah's ark had been for the human race.
34. BW to Vaughan, 14 December 1813, Vaughan papers, All Souls College, OB 37/2.
35. EE vol. 8 (January-February 1814), p. 96.
36. EE vol. 8 (May-June 1814), 'Conclusión de esta obra', pp. 296.
37. BL Add MSS 51621, ff. 91–6.
38. *Variedades* vol.1 (January 1824), p. 119.

Chapter 7

1. Antonio Orozco Acuaviva, *La gaditana Frasquita Larrea* (Cadiz, 1977), pp. 118–21. Nicholas Böhl de Faber was important later as a Spanish interpreter of Schlegel's ideas on

romanticism. He and his wife were the parents of the novelist Fernán Caballero.

2. Alfredo Martinez Albiach, *Religiosidad hispana y sociedad borbónica* (Burgos, 1969), p. 577. At the request of the Foreign Office, BW published a translation of the principal documents relating to the counter-revolution: *Some Documents reflecting the History of the Late Events in Spain being (1) A plain exposition of the reasons which occasioned the journey of Ferdinand VII to Bayonne in April 1808 by J. de Escoiquiz (2) Remarks on the preceding work by . . . P. de Ceballos (3) A full abstract of a petition addressed to King Ferdinand VII by sixty-nine members of the Cortes* (London, Longman, Hurst, 1815). He continued to carry out commissions for the Foreign Office until the autumn of 1814 (PRO FO 72/169 fols. 237–8, 258–9; 72/170 fol. 111; 71/171 fols 177–80).

3. *Relación historica de la Judería de Sevilla, &c.* (Sevilla: El Porvenir, 1849), pp. 47–53. In 1814 BW was still nominally a Royal Chaplain, he and the rest of the chapter having been restored to the positions of which they were deprived by Joseph Bonaparte. He did not resign officially until 1815.

4. BW to RS, 14 October 1816. See G. M. Murphy and A. Pons, art. cit., pp. 364–5.

5. *Life* I, pp. 287–8.

6. PRO FO 72/168, fols. 123–4. Hamilton offered BW the post of Chaplain to the Embassy in Rio de Janeiro (*Life* I, p. 208).

7. Shuttleworth kept a benevolent eye on Henry Fox during his residence at Oxford. He was 'acquainted with all the young scions of the literary aristocracy of England, and when they came up to Oxford he was their patron and their friend'. (Frederick Oakeley in *Reminiscences of Oxford*, ed. L. M. Quiller-Couch, Oxford Historical Society, vol. XXII, 1892, pp. 316–17). As Warden (1822–1840) he strove manfully to reform New College and deserves better

than to be remembered simply as the inventor of the mechanical device which conveys the port from one side of the senior common room fireplace to the other. His services to the Whig party were belatedly rewarded by his elevation to the see of Chichester in 1840. To the Tractarians he was Erastianism incarnate—to the extent that his death in 1842 was interpreted by Pusey as 'a token of God's presence in the Church of England'. (H. P. Liddon, *Life of Pusey*, vol. 2, p. 294).

8. *Life* I, p. 217.

9. Hastings Rashdall and Robert S. Rait, *New College*, 1901, p. 249; *New College, Oxford, 1379–1979*, ed John Buxton and Penry Williams, 1979.

10. *A Correct Account of the Visit of HRH the Prince Regent* (Oxford, 1814).

11. Elizabeth Grant of Rothiemurchus, *Memoirs of a Highland Lady 1797–1827*, ed. Angus Davidson, 1950, pp. 91–100. For a mordant satire on contemporary Oxford, see the anonymous novel *Rhydisel: The Devil in Oxford*, 2 vols, 1811. Its hero, by odd coincidence a young visitor from Seville, 'Don Juan Vincentio de Morla', is taken on a bird's eye tour of the town's follies by the resident devil.

12. MB, pp. 115–16.

13. M. L. Amunátegui, *Vida de Don Andrés Bello* (Santiago de Chile, 1882), p. 137.

14. See *Andrés Bello: The London Years*, ed. John Lynch, p. 198. On Bello's relations with BW, see also S. Fernández Larrain, *Revista Mapocho* 4 (Santiago de Chile, 1965), pp. 288–308.

15. 'Perhaps if a man's bowels are treacherous, he cannot trust anything else'. (George Santayana, *Selected Critical Writings*, ed. N. Henfrey, Cambridge, 1968, vol. 1, pp. 285–6).

16. *Life* I, p. 288.

17. *Letters of Sydney Smith*, ed Nowell C. Smith (Oxford, 1953), no. 254; BM Add MSS 51645 f. 112–122.

18. EBW, p. 70 (text deleted but legible). Blanco later published his schoolroom 'lectures': *Preparatory Observations on the Study of Religion in eight lectures delivered before the children of a family in high life, by their tutor, a clergyman of the Church of England* (Oxford: J. Parker, 1817). Southey congratulated the author on a work which was not 'the less remarkable for the place where it has been written'. (*Life* I, p. 310).

19. Sir Henry Holland (no relation), quoted in Sonia Keppel, *Sovereign Lady*, 1974, p. 249. Cf. Leslie Mitchell, *Holland House*, 1980, p. 22.

20. BW to Fernando Blanco, 12 June and 9 July 1817 (PUL 7/2). The addiction to incense seems to have been passed on from Holland House to Woburn Abbey. Lord Frederick Hamilton who visited Woburn later in the century recalled how 'at the conclusion of dinner, the groom of the chambers walked round the dining-room, solemnly swinging a large silver censer. This dignified thurifer then made the circuit of the other rooms'. (*The Days before Yesterday*, 1920, p. 325).

21. Holland House dinner-books, BL Add MSS 51951–3.

22. *Life and Letters of Lady Sarah Lennox 1745–1826*, ed. Countess of Ilchester, 1901, vol. 2, p. 278.

23. *Variedades*, vol. 1, no. 3 (April 1824), pp. 305–09.

24. 'A Journey to the Trossachs in 1816', autograph MS, LUL III 5/23.

25. LUL III 56/262.

26. BW to Lady Holland, 15 January 1817, BL Add MSS 51645 fol. 127–42; Journal entry of 10 February 1817, LUL III 56/262; Lord H. to BW 27 June 1817, BL Add MSS 51645 fol. 39–40. Henry Fox, who succeeded to his father's title, was received into the Roman Catholic church before his death in 1859.

27. *Life* I, pp. 302–3.

28. For the dismissal of Bello by William Hamilton, see BW's journal for 10 March 1817 (LUL III/56) reproduced, with the names omitted, in

Life I, p. 303. BW recommended Bello (who had a wife and family to support) as his successor, but the man appointed was the Revd Matthew Marsh.

Chapter 8

1. Private journal (LUL III 56/262) entries for 21 December 1817 and January 1818.

2. Journal entry of 11 December 1817 in *Life* I, pp. 316–317. As early as June 1815 Blanco wrote to William Wilberforce asking to see him 'in connection with a subject which under Providence may be of transcendental utility. I imagine that an opening presents itself for the spreading of the seeds of a religious reformation in South America'. (Bodleian Library, MSS Wilberforce d. 14 f. 348). Another 'prospect of doing good in a tropic climate' tempted him when he was invited in 1816 by a representative of the King of Haiti, Henri I, 'to accept a professorship in the university which his most black Majesty is establishing'. (BW to his brother, 27 May 1816, PUL 7/2).

3. See *Life* I, p. 335; III, pp. 346–47, 350–53. In the privacy of his journal BW vented his indignation at the Colonial Secretary's 'strange liberality' in sanctioning the appointment of a Roman Catholic vicar apostolic: 'Thus this government are to aid the Pope and his agents in keeping the Spanish population in Trinidad . . . in ignorance of everything but what their clergy wish them to know'. For his *arrière-pensées* on this affair, see EBW, p. 72.

4. 'Carta del americano al autor de las Observaciones sobre los inconvenientes del celibato de los clerigos traducidas del francés, e impreso en Londres este año de 1815', in J. E. Hernández y Davalos, *Colección de documentos para la historia de la guerra de independencia de Mexico 1808–21*, vol. VI, Mexico 1882, pp. 865–68. (cf. pp. 682, 686, 758, 805, 834). The

work for which BW wrote his controversial prologue and epilogue was a translation of Jacques Gaudin (not Servin, as Mier stated), *Inconvénients du célibat des prêtres prouvés par des recherches historiques*, Geneva 1781. I have not been able to locate a surviving copy of the Spanish translation, despite enquiries in Argentina, but for firm evidence of the controversy it aroused there, see Guillermo Gallardo, *La política religiosa de Rivadavia*, Buenos Aires 1962, p. 177. BW's additional material is omitted from the later *Extracto de la obra francesa intitulada Inconvenientes del celibato eclesiástico* (Mexico, 1833), of which there is a copy in the BL. On Pazos Kanki, see Charles Harwood Bowman, *Vicente Pazos Kanki: un boliviano en la libertad de America*, La Paz 1975. As editor of the *Gaceta de Buenos Aires*, before coming to London, Pazos had reprinted several articles from *El Español* and supported its 'moderate' line. During a second long stay in London (1825–49) he translated St Luke's Gospel into his native Aymara for the British and Foreign Bible Society, and published some disappointingly unrevealing *Memorias histórico-políticas* (Londres 1834). Mier's difference of opinion with BW did not diminish his affection and regard. In his last letter from his Mexican prison in 1827 he asked Bello to assure BW of his 'unaltered and profound friendship'.

5. *Life* I, p. 339.
6. *ibid* pp. 348–49.
7. *Rousseau juge de Jean-Jacques. Dialogue. D'après le manuscrit de M. Rousseau, laissé entre les mains de M. Brooke Boothby* (Lichfield: J. Jackson, 1780). For a modern edition, see that by Michel Foucault (Paris 1962).
8. LUL III 56/262.
9. *Life* I, pp. 356–59.
10. M. L. Amunátegui, *Vida de Don Andrés Bello*, Santiago de Chile 1882, pp. 138–39, 141. When Bello later lost his job as tutor to the Hamiltons, BW tried to have him appointed as his successor at Holland House. See *Life* I, p. 303, where Bello's name is suppressed. For the correspondence between BW and Bello, see Sergio Fernández Larrain, *Cartas a Bello en Londres 1810–1829*, Santiago de Chile 1968; 'Correspondencia inédita de Bello', *Revista Chilena* XIII (1929), pp. 656–60. See also Carlos Pi Sunyer, *Patriotas americanos en Londres*, Caracas 1978; Pedro Grases, *Tiempo de Bello en Londres 1810–1829*, Caracas 1962; John Lynch (ed.), *Andrés Bello: The London Years*, London 1982.

11. *Life* III, p. 356. In this published version Bello appears as 'Mr B'. In view of what is said here, it seems likely that Bello is the 'South American' who is referred to in the footnote to *Life* I, p. 128. There BW asserts that Meléndez Valdes was the only Spaniard he had ever known 'who, disbelieving Catholicism, had not embraced Atheism. He was a devout Deist'. In the footnote he adds, 'I subsequently knew a South American in the same state'.

12. There are two copies of this MS, dated 10 January 1819, one in Liverpool (LUL III/56 262) and one in Santiago de Chile (in the Fernández Larrain collection of Bello papers). *Habent sua fata libelli.*

13. *Life* III, pp. 359–61.
14. BW to his brother, 5 February 1819, in Lloréns, *Antología*, pp. 331–33.
15. Carleton correspondence in MCO I B6.
16. BW to his brother, 21 April 1819 and 31 January 1820, PUL 7/2. Cf. the undated letter of Mary Christie to BW, LUL I 17.49.
17. Retrospect in *Life* I, pp. 372–74. BW's revision of Antonio de Alvarado's *Liturgia Inglesa o el Libro de la Oración Común* (1707) was first published in *The Book of Common Prayer in Eight Languages*, London: Samuel Bagster 1821. The Blanco-Bello edition of the Scio Bible was first published by the British and Foreign Bible Society in 1821.

18. BW to Lord H., 4 April 1820, BL Add MSS 51645, ff. 152–53.
19. BW to his brother, 23 May 1820, PUL.
20. Private journal of 28 April 1820 (LUL III 6/41).
21. BW's letter is reprinted in Llorens, *Antología*, pp. 333–42; Quintana's reply in M. V. de Lara, 'Nota a unos manuscritos de J. M. Blanco White—I', BHS XX (1943), pp. 114–15.
22. C Cottu, *De la administración de la justicia criminal en Inglaterra*, Londres: Carlos Wood 1824, pp. v–xv.
23. Both letters in M. V. de Lara, art. cit., pp. 116–18.

Chapter 9

1. Diary for 17 December 1820, LUL III 6/41.
2. LFS, pp. 423–4. For BW's views on the Spanish recourse to masquerade, see *Life* II, pp. 307–08.
3. LFS pp. 8, 59. A German translation of LFS, *Briefe aus Spanien*, was published at Hamburg in 1824, dedicated to Dr Ludwig Tieck, the German translator of *Don Quixote* and friend of Coleridge and Southey. The translator, Esther Domeier, added some illuminating, and occasionally sharp, notes of her own. She remarked that while the colourful parts of the book delighted English readers, the criticism of Spanish society provided them with the more doubtful pleasure of *schadenfreude*. On this, see Klaus-Dieter Ertler, *Die Spanienkritik im Werk J. M. Blanco Whites*, Frankfurt-am-Main, 1985, p. 200.
4. *Ibid.*, p. 58. The first use of the word 'autobiography' is credited by the OED to Southey, writing in QR I, p. 283 (see A. J. Cockshut, *The art of Autobiography in 19th and 20th century England*, Yale 1984, p. 3). Previous Spanish writers had written accounts of their lives, but none of these can compare with BW in self-revelation. The most intimate of these autobiographers was the Salamanca jack-of-all-trades Diego de Torres Villaroel (1693–1770), but he was not the kind of company BW would have wanted to be seen in. His *Vida* is a picaresque and frankly exhibitionist account of the author's life on the academic fringe. (I am grateful to Professor Nigel Glendinning for this reference.) On BW's 'literary bashfulness', see LUL III 14/197; Goytisolo, pp. 13–14.
5. *The Letters of Sydney Smith*, ed Nowell C. Smith, Oxford, 1953, no 417.
6. A. L. Amunátegui, *Vida de Don Andrés Bello*, Santiago de Chile, 1882, pp. 142–3 (and in V. Llorens, *Antología*, pp. 348–50).
7. *Journal of Hon H. E. Fox 1818–1830*, ed Earl of Ilchester, 1923, entry for 1 May 1822. Cf. entry for 8 October 1821.
8. MB, p. 152.
9. G. M. Murphy and A. Pons, 'Further Letters of Blanco White to Robert Southey', BHS LXII (1985), p. 365. Southey's 'excessive eagerness and partiality' for Spain and Spaniards, the Edinburgh Reviewer wrote maliciously, 'has to us, we will confess, something of a ludicrous character; and appears so entirely without any reasonable cause that we have sometimes been tempted to ascribe it to two very slight and rather unsatisfactory motives;—one, the circumstance of Mr Southey having been accidentally for a few months in that country, in the early part of his life;—and the other, *our* having unluckily presumed to speak dispraisingly and despondently of a race that had been honoured by such a visit'. (ER XXII, January 1814, pp. 447–54.) Southey was not the last hispanophile to give the impression that he had a copyright on Spain.
10. *Supplement to the Fourth, Fifth and Sixth Editions of the Encyclopaedia Britannica*, vol.6, Edinburgh, 1824, pp. 508–33. On this, see María Teresa de Ory Arriaga, 'José Blanco White:

Spain', in *Archivo Hispalense* LX (1977), pp. 67–87.

11. Initially in a series of articles for the *New Monthly Magazine*: 'Prince Carlos of Spain and his father Philip II', vol. 5 (1822), pp. 231–6, 352–9; 'Peranzules: A Spanish Historical Fragment', vol.8 (1823), pp. 300–04; 'Studies in Spanish History, I. Aragon', vol.10 (1824), pp. 1–10; 'Studies in Spanish History, II. Prince Don Juan Manuel and his book El Conde Lucanor', vol. 11 (1824), pp. 97–103.

12. See Robert Johnson, 'Letters of Blanco White to J. H. Wiffen and Samuel Rogers', *Neophilologus* LII (Amsterdam, 197), pp. 138–48. J. H. Wiffen's younger brother Samuel was to become, with his collaborator Luis de Usóz y Río, the leading authority on the Spanish Protestant reformers of the sixteenth century. His papers, at Wadham College, Oxford, contain much of interest on BW, including his annotated and supplemented copy of LFS entitled 'Cosas de España'. BW's letters to Douce are in the National Library of Scotland and LUL I/21; for those to Garnett, see LUL I/69, 96, 98.

13. For BW on David Roberts, see *Life* II, pp. 313–14.

14. *Blackwood's Edinburgh Magazine* XII (December 1822), pp. 730–40. Some of the arguments for BW's authorship of *Vargas* are set out in MB pp. 439–44.

15. On the novel *Cornelia Bororquia*, see Juan Ignacio Ferreras, *Los orígines de la novela decimonónica*, Madrid, 1973, pp. 268–82. The first edition was probably published in 1801. Two later editions are in the Wiffen Collection: *Cornelia Bororquia*, segunda edición, revista corregida y aumentada, Paris, 1802; *Historia verídica de la Judit española, Cornelia Bororquia, escrita por el presbítero Doctor Don Fermin Araujo . . . tercera* [sic] *edición corregida y aumentada por Don D[iego] A. C[orrea] y G. Reimpresa en Londres* [E Justins] *en 1819*. The real

author was almost certainly Luis Gutierrez, an ex-Trinitarian friar and *afrancesado*, executed as a spy at Seville in 1809. In the Godoy years the novel was evidently circulated secretly among anti-clericals in manuscript form. (See item 95 in J. L. Gili's Dolphin catalogue 50, Oxford, 1976).

16a. 'Claims of the Spanish refugees to public benevolence. To Edward Hawke Locker FRS'. In *The New Times*, 10 January 1825.

16b. Thomas Carlyle, *The Life of John Sterling*, 1871, p. 56. On this emigration, see V. Lloréns, *Liberales y románticos*, 2a edición, Madrid, 1968. See also Count Pecchio, *Semi-serious observations of an Italian exile during his residence in England*, 1833, pp. 150–6.

17. 'Cartas de un emigrado español residente en Londres', in *Ocios de Españoles Emigrados* III (1825), pp. 320, 402–05, 484–7; IV, pp. 27–32, 115–20, 521–2; V (1826), 276–83.

18. 'Don Esteban', QR no. 65 (December 1825), pp. 205–27; 'Sandoval', QR no. 68 (September 1826), pp. 488–506. For Alcalá Galiano's reply, see *Westminster Review* VI (1826), pp. 278–303. For Llanos' own reply, see *Letter from a Spaniard (the author of Don Esteban) to the Editor of the Quarterly Review*, (London, 1826). For other Spanish reactions, see *Ocios* V (1826), pp. 214–36 (probably by José Canga Arguelles) and 379–87 (Pablo Mendíbil).

19. BL Add MSS 51645 ff. 92–3 (November 1810).

20. John Ford, *Ackermann 1783–1983*, London 1983, pp. 84–8, 231–2; idem, 'Rudolph Ackermann: Culture and Commerce in Latin America 1822–1828', in *Andrés Bello: The London Years*, ed John Lynch, London, 1982, pp. 137 ff. For BW's ideas on elementary education, see EE vol.8 (1814), pp. 218–19. In *El Español* BW also advocated the Bell and Lancaster education system (ibid. pp. 10–23) which was later adopted by Bolívar in Caracas. On

the textbook project, see *Variedades* I (1824), p. 459.

21. *Life* I, pp. 224–5. BW to Bello (November 1822) in *Revista Chilena* XIII (1929), pp. 656–60.

22. *Repository of Arts*, January 1823, p. 61.

23. 'Bosquexo de la historia del entendimiento en España', *Variedades* I (January 1824), pp. 104–19.

24. 'Sobre el placer de las imaginaciones inverosímiles', *Variedades* I (October 1824), pp. 413–18. On this article, see V Llorens *Liberales y románticos*, 2a edición, pp. 386–398.

25. 'El Alcázar de Sevilla', in *No Me Olvides*, 1825, pp. 3–27 (English version in *Forget-Me-Not*, 1825, p. 31 ff.). On this, see V. Lloréns, op. cit., pp. 239–43. The Spanish version is reprinted in Lloréns, *Antología*, pp. 295–310. BW heard García sing in *The Barber of Seville*. This was the year in which García's daughter María Felicia—later known as La Malibrán—made the London début which resulted in what Fanny Kemble called an 'absolute conquest of the nation'. Her sister Pauline, also a singer, became the wife of the French art critic Viardot and, more famously, the companion of Turgenev. BW described the meeting in a letter to his brother of 6 October 1924 (MB pp. 170–1).

26. M. L. Amunátegui, *Vida de Don Andrés Bello*, pp. 253–4.

27. V. Lloréns, *Antología*, p. 355.

Chapter 10

1. RS to BW, 26 April 1825, *Life*, I, p. 414.

2. RS to BW, 28 June 1822, *Life* I, p. 381.

3. *Earlier Letters of J. S. Mill 1812–1848*, ed Francis E. Mineka, Toronto 1963, pp. 82–3. Cf Macaulay's review of Southey's *Vindiciae Ecclesiae Anglicanae* in ER vol.50 (January 1830), pp. 528–65.

4. BW to RS, 10 July 1812, in G. M. Murphy and Pons, BHS LXII (1985), pp. 361–2.

5. RS to BW 28 June 1822, *Life* I, p. 381. On the ensuing controversy, see Sheridan Gilley, 'Nationality and Liberty: Robert Southey's *Book of the Church*', *Studies in Church History* 18, ed Stuart Mews, Oxford 1982, pp. 409–32.

6. *The Life of Robert Southey*, vol. 5, p. 137.

7. RS to BW, 26 April 1825, *Life* I, p. 412. For BW's account of the origins of *Evidence*, see *Life* I, pp. 226–29.

8. First edition (London: John Murray), 1825; Second edition, revised and enlarged, 1826. An American edition was published by J. C. Dunn of Georgetown D.C. in 1826. For the German version see J. B. White, *Beleuchtung der römisch-katholischen Glaubens*, Dresden: Arnold, 1826.

9. *Evidence*, 1825, p. 192.

10. RS to BW, 22 May 1825, *Life* I, p. 415.

11. C Butler, *Vindication of the Book of the Roman Catholic Church*, 1826, pp. xxxii–xxxiii.

12. Full text in *The Truthteller*, vol. 2, no. 20 (25 February 1826), and in *The Catholic Miscellany*, vol.5 (1826), pp. 96–100.

13. J. B. White, *A Letter to Charles Butler on his Notice of Practical and Internal Evidence &c*, 1826, pp. 24–25.

14. BL Add MSS 51645, ff 172–3; *Life* I, p. 416.

15. Letter of 21 July 1825, LUL I/51.

16. *The Poor Man's Preservative* (London: Rivington, 1825) went into many subsequent editions in England, Ireland and the United States and became a powerful weapon in the armoury of the Protestant Truth Society. It even reached Spain, after BW's death, in a translation by J. J. de Mora: *Preservativo contra Roma*, Edinburgo: Constable, 1856. For a Catholic reply, see F. C. Husenbeth, *Defence of the Creed and Discipline of the Catholic Church*, London, 1826. A letter of Nicholas Wiseman to Husenbeth of 10 July 1830 (Ushaw College, Wiseman correspondence 774) sheds inter-

esting light on BW's connection with the Wiseman family and on his later reputation in Seville.

17. *A Few Observations on the Evidence against Catholicism by the Revd J. B. White*, 1825, p. 22.

18. BL Add MSS 51645, ff. 176–77. BW's state of mind is revealed in his letter to Southey of 18 May 1826 (G. M. Murphy and A. Pons, BHS LXII (1985), pp. 367–68). One of those who rallied to BW's defence was S. T. Coleridge, who attacked 'Smooth Butler, who says grace at slander's feast' in his poem 'Sancti Dominici Pallium'. This was first published anonymously in *The Standard* of 21 May 1827 under the title 'A Dialogue written on a blank page of Butler's Book of the Roman Catholic Church'. Cf. *Life* I, pp. 439–40.

19. *Life* I, p. 434.

20. 'Consejos importantes sobre la intolerancia dirigidos a los hispano-americanos', *Variedades* II, pp. 95–100.

21. 'Cartas sobre Inglaterra IV–V, Sobre el estado moral y religiosa de Inglaterra', *Variedades* I (1824), pp. 406–12; II (1825), pp. 35–42.

22. See [J. Egaña], *Memoria política sobre si conviene en Chile la libertad de cultos . . . Reimpresa . . . con una breve Apologia [by Ignacio de Moreno] del art. 8 de la Constitución politica del Perú de 1823 . . . en que . . . se responde a los argumentos del Sr J. M. Blanco en favor de la tolerancia y libertad de cultos en sus Consejos a los Hispano-Americanos*, Lima, 1827. This work was reprinted at Bogotá in 1828. For BW's comment on the Chilean constitution, see *Variedades* II, pp. 5–22.

For a conservative reaction in Mexico, see *!Atención! Que los apóstatas quieren variar nuestra religión*, (Mexico: imprenta del ciudadano Alejandro Valdes, 1825). This provoked a reply by the liberal journalist José Joaquín Fernandez de Liznardi ('El Pensador'), *Dentro de seis años o antés hemos de ser tolerantes*, [Mexico]: ofi-

cina del feriado Ontiveros, 1825. In January 1826 the Mexican Congress, under liberal control, passed a resolution formally thanking BW for his efforts in the cause of religious freedom. In his accompanying letter Vicente Rocafuerte, the Mexican minister in London, wrote: 'Let it be a consolation to you that the inhabitants of the New World acknowledge you as the champion of that justice which certain ultramontane fanatics, debasing the sublimity of the Christian religion by their servility, have vainly tried to deny them'. (LUL III/6).

Bolivar had wanted the Colombian constitution to include a clause allowing for religious freedom, but was forced to give way on the issue, which remains contentious in Spanish America to this day.

23. *Variedades* II (1825), p. 300.

24. 'Despedida del autor a los hispano-americanos', *Variedades* II (1825), p. 299 ff.

25. *Collected Letters of S. T. Coleridge* ed. Earl L. Griggs, vol. 5, Oxford 1971, no. 1503, p. 528. See also nos 1474, 1476, 1480, 1501, 1503 and *Life* I, pp. 417–20, 422–23.

26. S. T. Coleridge, *Marginalia*, ed George Whalley, Princeton 1980, p. 503 (STC's note on *Letters from Spain*). Coleridge's copies of *Evidence* and *The Poor Man's Preservative* (now in the BL), presented to him by BW, contain many interesting annotations.

27. Thomas Carlyle, *Life of John Sterling*, 1871, pp. 46–54.

28. BW's English poems have been published collectively by Antonio Garnica in his two articles 'Blanco White, poeta inglés, *Filología Moderna* 56–58 (1975–76), pp. 79–90; 'La poesía inédita de Blanco White', *Homenaje a Don Esteban Pujals*, Oviedo 1981.

29. See the letter of BW to Rogers, 13 June 1839, in Robert Johnson, 'Letters of Blanco White to J. H. Wiffen and Samuel Rogers', *Neophilologus*, L11 (1968), p. 145.

30. Minutes of the Hebdomadal Board, 24 April 1826.
31. Lloyd of Christ Church wrote to his former pupil Sir Robert Peel the same day: 'Coplestone proposed the degree and told me the University was unanimous. He desired that BW's attack on the Church of Rome should be stated as the great ground of the proposition—I tell you fairly, that had I not been assured that the University was unanimous I should have opposed it, as I do not think we were called upon for any such demonstration'. (BL Add MSS 40342, f. 341).
32. BW to his brother, 24 August 1826, PUL 7/2.

Chapter 11

1. *Life* III, p. 128.
2. Llorens, *Antología*, pp. 356–7. BW sent the books via José María, the brother of his deceased friend Manuel de Arjona, but they were never delivered. Reports on BW's part in the Catholic Emancipation controversy had now reached Seville, perhaps through the Irish community, and Arjona may have thought it imprudent to associate himself with his name.
3. E. Jane Whately, *Life and Correspondence of Richard Whately, DD.*, 1866, vol. 1, p. 55.
4. Richard Whately, *Use and Abuse of Party Feeling*, Oxford, 1822. The *Letters of an Episcopalian* which advocated disestablishment were published by Whately anonymously. On the liberal Anglicanism of the Noetics, see Richard Brent, *Liberal Anglican Politics: Whiggery, Religion and Reform 1830–41*, (Oxford, 1987).
5. Baden Powell, *Rational Religion Examined*, London, 1826. See Pietro Corsi, *Science and Religion: Baden Powell and the Anglican Debate 1800–60* (Cambridge, 1988).
6. R. D. Hampden, *The Scholastic Philosophy, considered in its relation to the Christian Theology*, 2nd edition, 1837, p. 374.
7. Thomas Mozley, *Reminiscences of Oriel College and the Oxford Movement*, 1882, vol. 1, p. 58.
8. Arthur Milman, *Henry Hart Milman, A Biographical Sketch*, 1900, pp. 106–07. Milman wrote that BW expressed himself 'with force and fluency such as one rarely hears from a native Englishman, with the slightest tinge of foreign accent'.
9. Sermons, MCO III/1. There was little danger of Romanism at Burford, where the Low Church curate-in-charge, Alexander Dallas, had rearranged the pews so that the congregation had their backs to the chancel, facing a pulpit at the west end of the nave. See R. H. Gretton, *The Burford Records*, Oxford, 1920, pp. 121–22.
10. R Whately, *The Errors of Romanism traced to their Origin in Human Nature*, 1830.
11. *Life* I, p. 439.
12. E. B. Pusey, *An Historical Enquiry into the Probable causes of the Rationalist Character lately predominant in the Theology of Germany*, London, 1828.
13. BW to EBP, 10 June 1828, Pusey House MSS.
14. Thomas Mozley, op, cit., p. 226.
15. JHN to Samuel Rickards, 19 March 1827, in NLD vol. 2, p. 9, cf. p. 5. On BW's relations with Newman, see G. M. Murphy, 'Blanco White y J. H. Newman: un encuentro decisivo', *Boletín de la Real Academia Española* LXIII (1983), pp. 77–116.
16. JHN to BW, 1 March 1828, in NLD vol. 2, pp. 59–60. BW's letters of 24 February and 9 March in Robert Wilberforce papers, Birmingham Oratory. On this exchange, see David Newsome, *The Parting of Friends*, London, 1966, pp. 86–90.
17. *Life* I, p. 419. For BW's thoughts on disposition of heart as the precondition of assent, see his letter to A. Bello of 22 October 1824, in Amunategui, *Vida*, pp. 253–4.
18. JHN to BW, 4 July 1828, NLD vol. 2, pp. 79–80.

19. There had been a Professor of Modern Languages since the early eighteenth century, but his duties were confined to the delivery of one lecture per term. The first teacher of Spanish at the university was not appointed until 1858. This was Lorenzo Lucena (1806–1881), like BW an Andalucian convert to Anglicanism, later honorary canon of Gibraltar. See C. H. Firth, *Modern Languages at Oxford 1724–1929*, Oxford, 1929, p. 41.

20. BW to JHN, 14 October 1828, in NLD vol.2, p. 101 (extract from text of full letter in Newman papers, Birmingham Oratory).

21. BW to E. J. Whately, Lambeth, ff 214–15.

22. BW to AB, 1 September 1828, in *Revista Chilena* XIII (1929), p. 659.

23. BW to JHN, 8 November 1828, NLD vol. 2, p. 105. On *The London Review*, see *The Wellesley Index to Victorian Periodicals*, ed W. E. Houghton, 1972, vol.2, pp. 522–6 and V. Llorens, 'El fracaso de The London Review de 1829', in *Liber Amicorum Salvador de Madariaga*, Bruges, 1966. Houghton identifies the contributors to the LR, and his appreciation of it is a valuable corrective to the one-sided verdict of J. H. Newman in *Essays Critical and Historical*, vol.1, 1871, pp. 24–9.

24. See S. E. Finer, *Sir Edwin Chadwick*, London, 1952, pp. 29–30.

25. *The London Review*, no. 1 (January 1829), pp. 1–9. The Review also contained two excellent literary contributions by BW himself, an acerbic review of Robert Pollok's neo-Miltonic poem *The Course of Time* (pp 233–51), and the brilliant 'Spanish Poetry and Language' (pp 388–403). The editor made a point of stressing his non-partisan approach in the preliminary 'advertisement': '*The London Review* belongs to no party. To Tories it will probably appear Whig, and to Whigs, Tory. Having for its chief object the investigation of TRUTH, the intended journal will decline all support for party feelings . . . the pages of *The London Review* will never be stained by acrimonious controversy, harsh invective or calumnious misrepresentation'.

Chapter 12

1. *The Sun*, 26 February 1829, Bodleian B 421.

2. JHN to Jemima Newman, 4 March 1829, LD II, p. 127; to his mother, 13 March 1829, ibid. pp. 129–31.

3. BW to E. B. Pusey, 14 February 1829, Oriel Treasurer's Muniments ETC Al. For the published version, see *Letter from the Rev. J. Blanco White to a Friend in Oxford*, Oxford 1829 (Bodleian B 421/39).

4. Bodleian Library, Bliss Collection B 421/40. The reference to 'A Snake in the Grass' was topical. The painting of that name by J. Gebaud had been the sensation of the 1828 season when it fetched a record price at Christie's.

5. *Earl of Ellenborough, Political Diary 1828–1830*, 1881, vol. 1, p. 366.

6. *Life* I, pp. 457–60; BW to JHN, 9 February 1829, Birmingham Oratory MSS.

7. Thomas Mozley, *Reminiscences &c*, vol. 1, pp. 247–8.

8. Edward Bellasis, *Coram Cardinali*, 1916, p. 8. As an Oratorian, Newman might have been surprised to learn that BW learned his technique in the orchestra of the Seville Oratory. Though Beethoven and Mozart were for BW the 'sun and moon of the musical firmament', Haydn was his first love. See his article 'En la muerte de Haydn', SP XXIX (10 August 1809), in Lloréns, *Antología* pp. 277–78.

9. BW to Julia Moore, *Life* I, p. 476.

10. F. W. Newman, *Contributions chiefly to the Early History of the late Cardinal Newman*, 1891. Cf. *Our Memories: Shadows of Old Oxford*, ed. H. Daniel, Oxford 1893, pp. 1–4, for other unreliable recollections of BW

by Frank Newman. The BW he describes sounds like a Frankenstein: 'His head was of a remarkable shape like that which is ascribed to North American Indians, very narrow on the level of the eyes but very lofty above them, and in appearance sloping up, almost like the gable of a house'.

11. H. Wilberforce to JHN, 25 March 1835, in NLD vol.5, p. 52.

12. *Life* I, p. 2.

13. The MS of the lecture is in LUL III/19. For eyewitness accounts, see *Our Memories*, ed. H. Daniel, Oxford, 1893, pp. 70, 81. The experiment involves spreading sand over a plate and running a violin bow over the edge: the resulting vibrations produce symmetrical patterns analogous to the harmonic tones. BW's demonstration anticipated that performed by Sir Charles Wheatstone at one of the early meetings of the British Association.

14. Senior's list of friends and correspondents reads like a *Who's Who* of nineteenth century liberalism: Grote, Mill, Malthus, de Tocqueville, Renan, Cavour and Thiers. See S. Leon Levy, *Nassau W. Senior 1790–1864*, 2nd edition, Newton Abbot 1970. For a more personal account, see the unpublished *Victorian Meridian, being an intimate biography of Nassau William Senior* by Mrs St Loe Strachey, preserved in MS along with the Senior papers in the National Library of Wales. (As the grand-daughter of Nassau Senior and the mother of John Strachey, Mrs St Loe Strachey linked the radical reformers of 1832 with those of 1945.) The family claimed to be descended from Abraham Señor, a Spanish Jew from Segovia who held high office at the court of the Catholic Kings.

15. NLW Senior papers C496, 511, 515; NLI MS 21286; J. B. White, 'Education in Spain', *The Quarterly Journal of Education*, vol.1 (1831), pp. 213–224.

16. 'The Bill of Belial: A Political Allegory', *New Monthly Magazine* vol.37 (1833), pp. 412–17; *Life* III, pp. 349–50; NLW Senior papers C503.

17. M. C. M. Simpson [née Senior], *Many Memories of Many People*, 1898, p. 10; Henrietta Hampden, *Memorials of R. D. Hampden*, 1871, p. 23.

18. MCO I B. 3 (27 October 1831). Cf. H. Juretschke, *Vida, obra y pensamiento de Alberto Lista*, Madrid 1851, pp. 595–96.

19. See the tribute of his pupil Eugenio de Ochoa quoted in J. C. J. Metford, 'Alberto Lista and the Romantic Movement in Spain', BSS vol.16 (1939), pp. 84–103.

20. On Reinoso, see N. Pastor-Díaz, *Galería de españoles célebres*, Madrid 1845, vol.9, pp. 97–196; Antonio Martín Villa, *Obras de D. Felix-José Reinoso*, Sevilla, vol.1 (1872), introduction (see pp. cxcvi–cc for Lista's tribute). A. modern study of this fascinating figure is overdue. For an assessment of Reinoso's apologia, *Examen de los delitos de infidelidad a la patria*, Auch (1815), see Carmelo Viñas-Mey, 'Nuevos datos para la historia de los afrancesados', BH XXVII, pp. 97–130.

21. *Earlier Letters of J. S. Mill 1812–1848*, ed Francis E. Mineka, Toronto 1963, p. 92.

22. *Life* I, pp. 471–75 (cf. p. 227, n.).

23. BW to JHN (24 August 1832), NLD, vol.3, p. 85.

24. *A Few Observations on the Evidence against Catholicism by the Reverend J. B. White*, 1825, p. 14.

25. T Mozley, *Reminiscences* etc, p. 60.

26. Oriel 124.

27. J. B. Mozley, *Essays Historical and Theological*, vol.2 (1874), p. 107.

28. BW to EJW (12 April 1832), Lambeth Palace Library, Whately MSS 222. Cf. BW's letter to Hawkins of 11 April 1836, after the 'Hampden controversy' had broken, Hawkins correspondence, Oriel f. 108.

29. T Mozley, *Reminiscences*, pp. 352–61; W. Tuckwell, *Pre-Tractarian Oxford* (1909), p. 18. This *leyenda*

negra was canonised by H. P. Liddon in his *Life of Edward Bouverie Pusey* (1893), pp. 315, 380.

30. R. D. Hampden, *The Scholastic Philosophy* etc. (1832), p. 388.

31. See Pietro Corsi, *Science and Religion: Baden Powell and the Anglican debate 1800–60* (Cambridge, 1988), p. 100. This important work shows that Hampden's Lectures developed ideas already touched on not only by other Noetics but by earlier High Churchmen such as van Mildert.

32. BW to JHN, 24 August 1832, NLD vol. 3, p. 85.

Chapter 13

1. BW to EH, 4 June 1832, Oriel no. 192; *Life* I, pp. 485–87. 'Atmos the Giant' in Lady Mary Fox (ed), *Friendly Contributions for the Benefit of three Infant Schools in the Parish of Kensington*, 1834. Blanco's first story for children had been published the previous year in a volume edited by Mrs Whately. See 'Norval' in [E Jane Whately], *Reverses: or, Memoirs of the Fairfax Family*, London 1833, pp. 190–216.

2. *Dublin Evening Post* of 18 August, 1 September 1831.

3. E Jane Whately, *Life and Correspondence of Richard Whately*, 1866, vol. 1, pp. 100–101. There is now a modern biography: Donald H. Akenson, *A Protestant in Purgatory: Richard Whately, Archbishop of Dublin*, Hamden, Conn. 1981.

4. *Ibid*, p. 112.

5. Donald H. Akenson, *The Irish Education Experiment*, 1970.

6. Quoted in W. J. Fitzpatrick, *Memoirs of Richard Whately*, 1864, vol. 1, pp. 283–84.

7. E. J. Whately, op. cit., vol. 1, pp. 127–28.

8. BW to JHN, 13 June, 4 July 1832, Newman archive, Birmingham Oratory; *Life* III, p. 72. Redesdale is now St Ann's House, Upper Kilmacud Road. The former town house of the Archbishops of Dublin survives at no. 16, St Stephen's Green.

9. *Poesias escogidas de D. Joaquín Lorenzo Villanueva*, Dublin: T. O'Flanagan, 1833, p. 164; J. L. Villanueva, *Ibernia Phoenica &c*, Dublini: R. Graisberry, 1832.

10. *Life* I, pp. 497–500.

11. Ibid, pp. 493–94, 496.

12. *Elements of Geometry for the Use of the Irish National Schools*, Dublin: M. Goodwin, 1836 (reprinted 1845, 1846). Edward Whately recalled his former tutor in *Personal and Family Glimpses of Remarkable People*, 1889, pp. 114–22. For the recollections of his sister Henrietta, see *E. J. Whately: Reminiscences of her Life and Work. By her sister*, 1894, pp. 9–10. Henrietta later devoted herself to the Spanish Evangelization Society, working on the mission at Puerto S. Maria and at Seville, where she distributed bibles at the Feria.

13. *Life* II, pp. 19–21.

14. Stephen Gwynn, *Thomas Moore*, 1905, pp. 137–41; H. H. Jordan, *Bolt Upright: The Life of Thomas Moore*, Salzburg 1975, vol. 2, pp. 526–33; W. F. P. Stockley, 'The Religion of Thomas Moore', in *Essays in Irish Biography*, Cork 1933, pp. 35–93.

15. *The Journal of Thomas Moore*, ed. P. Quennell, 1964, entry for 2–9 November 1835; T. Moore, *Travels of an Irish Gentleman in Search of a Religion*, 1832, p. 124; ER LIV (1831), pp. 238–255.

16. *Travels*, pp. 41, 278 ff.

17. W. S. Dowden (ed.) *The Letters of Thomas Moore, 1793–1847*, Oxford 1964, vol. 2, no. 1030. Cf. nos 978, 1028, 1033, 1059. Lord John Russell (ed.), *The Diary of Thomas Moore*, 1853, vol. 2, p. 73. Blanco had actually met Moore at Holland House in 1822, in the company of Washington Irving (see his journal for 2 May 1922, MCO II/1).

18. *Second Travels of an Irish Gentleman in Search of a Religion*, Dublin 1833, vol. 2, p. 55. BW speaks through his *alter ego*, the Rev Joseph Fitzgerald. This character, like his creator an ex-RC priest converted to the Church of England, reveals on his

deathbed that he had been a fellow-student in Coimbra with Bishop Doyle. BW was well informed. Doyle had indeed studied in Portugal, where his course was interrupted by his service as an agent for Wellington. See W. J. Fitzgerald, *The Life of James Warren Doyle*, 1861, vol. 1, pp. 22–34.

19. Lord John Russell, *The Diary of Thomas Moore*, entries for 8 March, 21–25 April 1834; *Life* II, pp. 36–37; *Second Travels*, vol. 2, pp. 95, 99.

20. For this correspondence, see LUL I/130–133. Neander prefaced the fifth volume of his *Kirchengeschichte* (1840) with a long tribute to BW. For his later assessment, see August Neander, *Ueber das Leben des Joseph Blanco White*, Berlin: Wilhelm Besser, 1846.

21. *Life* II, pp. 49–53. For Armstrong's letters to BW, see Robert Henderson, *A Memoir of the late Rev George Armstrong*, 1859, pp. 25–40.

22. *The Law of anti-Religious Libel Reconsidered in a Letter to the Christian Examiner in answer to an article in that periodical against a pamphlet entitled Considerations &c, by John Search*, Dublin 1834. The 'article' to which BW's work was a riposte had been written by Thomas Elrington, the Bishop of Ferns. 'John Search' was the pseudonym of the Congregationalist minister Thomas Binney.

23. Journal entries for 30 December 1834, LUL III 59/277; letter to BW from Charlotte Pope (n.d., but *circa* January 1835), MCO I B 6. Charlotte Pope, Elizabeth Whately's sister and soon to become the wife of Baden Powell, was a staunch supporter of BW. In the same letter she wrote: 'My mind on religious subjects has been fortified and cheered by the diligent search and meditation to which I was led by you . . . I look with gratitude to your counsel and example as having released my mind from the slavish fears to which orthodoxy binds us'.

24. *Life* II, pp. 56–57, 60.

25. *Life* II, pp. 38–9. The thought was prompted by BW's reading of Karl Immanuel Nitzsch's pamphlet, *Ueber den Religionsbegriff der Alten*. For a medical opinion on BW, see Sir Henry Holland, *Reminiscences of Past Life*, 1872, pp. 254–55.

26. *Life* II, pp. 65, 71–2.

27. Clemente de Zulueta had been in correspondence with BW since 1824 (see LUL I/33, 87, 116; MCO I B. 4/31–2). For his Spanish translation of 'Night and Death' see LUL V/25. Pedro de Zulueta, Clemente's brother, also became an Anglican but his son (who married into the P. and O. Line) returned to the Church of Rome under the influence of Newman, and his daughter was the mother of Cardinal Merry del Val. (Information from Sir Philip de Zulueta.)

28. *Life* II, pp. 74–76, 78.

Chapter 14

1. *Life* III, pp. 178–80. The tone of the letter is further proof of BW's power to inspire affection even in the most conventional and unintellectual of his pupils.

2. BW to Lord Holland, 31 May 1835, in *Life* II, pp. 127–8.

3. Herman Melvile, *Redburn*. De Tocqueville, who passed through Liverpool in July 1835 (and was given an introduction to BW by their mutual friend Nassau Senior) recorded that there were 50,000 living in its cellars. See A. de Tocqueville, *Oeuvres Complètes* vol. 5, Paris 1958, p. 84.

4. See J. Drummond and C. B. Upton, *Life and Letters of James Martineau*, 2 vols, 1902; R. K. Webb, 'John H. Thom: Intellect and Conscience in Liverpool', in *The View from the Pulpit: Victorian Ministers and Society*, ed. P. T. Phillips, Toronto 1980, pp. 211–244. There is a brilliant, if acerbic, portrayal of the Unitarian transcendentalists in the Oxford B. Litt. thesis by Ian Sellers, *Social and Politi-*

cal Ideas of Representative English Unitarians 1795–1850 (1956).

5. L. P. Jacks, *The Confession of an Octogenarian*, 1942. Jacks described Thom in his old age as 'a stately figure clothed in immaculate broadcloth under a broadbrimmed silk hat, and needing only an apron and gaiters to make him the perfect Bishop'. By that time, Thom had retired and was a member of the congregation himself. Rathbone, tongue in cheek, once suggested that Jacks should startle Renshaw Street by preaching on the text 'Howl, ye rich!', but Jacks recorded, 'I never tried the experiment . . . I could not bring myself to the point of asking Mr Thom to howl'. (p. 141).

6. *Life* II, pp. 101, 124.

7. Whately papers, Lambeth Palace Library, nos 230, 232.

8. E Jane Whately, *Life and Correspondence of Richard Whately*, 1866, vol. 1, pp. 266–7, 284–5.

9. LUL III 58/277, entries for January–April 1835.

10. NLW, Senior papers C 530, 531, 535–7, 543.

11. *Life* II, pp. 101, 124.

12. Newman to Robert Wilberforce, 30 August 1835, NLD vol. 5, 1981, pp. 133–4. His view was shared by Hawkins: 'If he returns to the bosom of any Church, so much the creature of feeling he is, and so desirous of repose from suspense of mind, I almost suspect he will die a Romanist'. (Oriel, Hawkins correspondence no 1108).

13. BW to Pusey, 23 April, 5 May 1835, MS in Pusey House Library, Oxford.

14. BW to Hawkins, 27 January 1835; Hawkins to BW, 29 January 1835 (Oriel no 100a); Hawkins to BW, 19 February 1835 (MCO I B 6).

15. *Observations on Heresy and Orthodoxy*, 1835, pp. 13–14.

16. JHN to Jemima Newman, 9 August 1835, in NLD vol. 5, pp. 122–3.

17. JHN to Henry Wilberforce, 23 March 1835, in NLD vol. 5, pp. 50–51; [H Wilberforce], *The Foun-*dations of the Faith assailed in Oxford: A Letter to His Grace the Archbishop of Canterbury*, 1835, pp. 8, 31, 34. The pamphlet contains a revealing statement of what the Tractarians saw as the function of the University: 'Is it not to be the nursery of the Church of England, whence a succession of men may constantly issue who, with minds well-stored with the wisdom of former times and with characters moulded after the pattern of those worthies whose histories and whose works have been their study and delight, may go forth into the world each to fill some important sphere of action and to diffuse into the surrounding mass, less favoured than himself, with the blessings of education, a sincere admiration for the achievements of former times, an earnest attachment to the principles whence they sprung and a resolute purpose of adhering to them at whatever hazards?' Newman was the true author of this work.

18. R. H. Froude to JHN, 15 November 1835, in NLD, vol. 5, p. 162. Cf pp. 153–5, 155–6, 190–2, for the careful orchestration of the attack by Froude and Newman. Froude's review appeared in *The British Critic*, XIX (January 1836), pp. 204–05. See E. R. Houghton, 'The British Critic and the Oxford Movement', in *Studies in Bibliography* XVI, Charlotteville Va., 1963.

19. JHN to S. L. Pope, 3 March 1836, NLD, vol. 5, p. 251.

20. BW to EH, 9 May 1836, Oriel, Hawkins correspondence, no 109.

21. *Life* II, pp. 213, 222–3, 230–2. BW's view of Hampden's persecutors was widely shared. *The Morning Chronicle* of 18 March 1836 published 'Alma Mater's Call to her Zealous Sons', which concludes:

> Then, Oxford, hail the glorious day,
>   Enjoy the exhibition:
> In Hampden's grand auto-de-fé
>   Revive the Inquisition!'

22. *Life* II, p. 230; BW to EH, 14 March 1837, Oriel no 111.

23. *Life* II, p. 169. BW's lodgings in Liverpool were at 56 Seel Street (de Zulueta's house), 25 Upper Parliament Street, 5 Chesterfield Street and 22 Upper Stanhope Street.

24. BW to EW, 31 August 1837, Lambeth Palace Library, Whately MSS 259.

25. On the Domestic Mission, see Ann Holt, *A Ministry to the Poor*, Liverpool 1936; Margaret Simey, *Charitable Effort in Liverpool in the Nineteenth Century*, Liverpool 1951.

26. Margaret Simey, op. cit., p. 36.

27. *Life* II, pp. 356–360.

28. LFS, p. 62.

29. *The Christian Teacher*, vol. 2 (1840), pp. 110–118; R. K. Webb, art. cit. p. 236; Anne Holt, op. cit., pp. 20–49.

30. 'Portion of a Letter to the author from the Revd J. Blanco White'. Appendix to J. Martineau, *The Rationale of Religious Enquiry*, 4th edn 1853, pp. 102–126.

31. See the MS 'Fear of Going too Far' (1836), LUL III 17/200; *Life* II, pp. 239–40.

32. *Life* III, p. 377–8, 439–42. Moral education, according to BW, consisted in awakening the child's awareness of his dependence, and moral conscience.

33. *Life* III, pp. 118–23.

34. Letter of 28 December 1837, PUL 7/11.

35. 'On Crabbe's Life and Works', *The London Review*, vol. 1 (1835), pp. 76–93. What BW missed in Crabbe, he found in Samuel Rogers' *Italy*: 'a spirit of refined, benevolent Humanity'. See Robert Johnson, 'Letters of Blanco White to Samuel Rogers', *Neophilologus*, vol. 53, pp. 144–5/

36. 'Recent Spanish Literature', *The London Review*, vol. 1 (1835), pp. 76–93. BW's contributions to J. S. Mill's *London Review* between 1835 and 1836 also include 'Lamb's Specimens of English Dramatic Poets' (vol. 2, p. 51–69); 'Guizot's Lectures on European Civilization' (vol. 2, pp. 306–336); 'Godoy, Prince of the Peace' (vol. 3, pp. 28–60). He took advantage of the last to do justice to his former protector.

37. 'A Midsummer Night's Dream', *The Christian Teacher*, vol. 2 (1840), pp. 42–53. Cf. 'The Pictorial Shakespeare', CT vol. 1 (1839), pp. 322–32, 469–81; 'Notes on Hamlet', *ibid* pp. 573–80.

38. *Life* II, pp. 289–91; CT vol 1 (1839), p. 450.

39. Ferdinand White to BW, 28 April 1831, 3 June 1835, 16 August 1835, MCO I A 2.

40. BW to Julia Moore, *Life* III, p. 65.

41. *Life* III, p. 67.

Chapter 15

1. *Life*, p. 102.

2. MS 'Fear of Going Too Far', LUL III 17/200.

3. LUL III 58/277; 14/197.

4. *Luisa de Bustamante, o la huérfana española en Inglaterra*, ed Ignacio Prat, Barcelona 1975, pp. 26–77.

5. *Ibid* p. 28. For another revisionist comparison of the English with the Spanish character, see BW's review, 'Stories of Spanish Life', in CT vol. 1 (1839), pp. 214–55.

6. *The Christian Teacher*, vol. 2 (1840), pp. 431–9. I have not been able to identify the reviewer, 'M', but suspect it may have been Harriet Martineau, who was a contributor to *The Christian Teacher* at this time. (See Francis E. Mineka, *The Dissidence of Dissent*, University of N. Carolina, 1944).

7. Review of John Strang, *Germany in MDCCCXXXI*, CT vol. 1 (1839), pp. 91–104.

8. 'Seguidillas', 'Una tormenta nocturna en alta mar', 'A María Ana Beck', 'Recuerdos y esperanzas', 'Poder del recuerdo de mi amigo Lista', in Lloréns, *Antología*, pp. 104–112. The translation of excerpts is mine.

9. 'Al joven Don José María Blanco White y Olloqui, su tío paterno Don José María Blanco White, de Liverpool', in MB pp. 421–3.

10. *Life* III, p. 66.
11. BL Add MSS 51597 f. 135.
12. In his last years BW was a merciless critic of the complacencies of natural theology. See his demolition of William Buckland's version of the argument from design in CT vol. 5 (1843), pp. 137–55. Even crocodiles, in Buckland's Mickawberite theology, were an example 'of the well-regulated workings of a consistent plan in the economy of animated nature under which each individual, while following its own instincts and pursuing its own good, is instrumental in promoting the general welfare of the whole family of its contemporaries'. 'The eaten', Blanco commented ironically, 'are devoured for their own good'. (pp 151–2).
13. Thomas Mozley, *Reminiscences* &c (1882), vol. 1, p. 62.
14. *Life* III, p. 184; BW to Hawkins, 28 April 1840, Oriel 120. Albany Christie followed Newman to Littlemore in 1845 and was received into the Catholic Church there, nine days after Newman. In 1847 he became a Jesuit. See Richard F. Clarke, *A short Sketch of Father Albany James Christie S. J. Reprinted from 'The Month'*, 1891.
15. Letters from Ferdinand White to BW, MCO I A 2. Ferdinand married in 1842 and died, a Lieutenant-Colonel, in 1856. His son George Ferdinand White, born in 1850, was educated at Wellington College, but nothing is known of his subsequent career. The eminent divorce lawyer George Rivers Blanco White, QC (1883–1966), believed himself to be a descendant of BW but his son G. R. Blanco White, QC, doubts the connection.
16. C. and F. Carleton to BW, 2 May, 14 June 1840, MCO I B/6; *Life* III, p. 230.
17. EJW to Edward Hawkins, Oriel 228.
18. BW to FB, 22 September 1840, PUL 7/4; Lista to FB, 29 March 1841, in MB pp. 213–14.
19. BW to EJW, 26 December 1840, Lambeth 291.

20. Others who benefited from Rathbone's charity included Robert Owen, Dorothea Dix (the American lunatic asylum reformer), Lady Byron and the Irish temperance campaigner Father Mathew. ('If the visitor happened to be obscure, or in bad health, or regarded with suspicion by the rest of the world, or a faddist, his welcome was all the more sure'—Eleanor Rathbone, *William Rathbone: A Memoir*, 1905.)
21. *Life* III, p. 310.
22. The funeral address is included in the 1877 edition of OHO.

Chapter 16

1. Oriel 124, note.
2. 'Joseph Blanco White', CT vol. 3 (1841), pp. 285ff.
3. Thom-Bishop correspondence in MCO III 8.
4. E Jane Whately, *Life and Correspondence of Richard Whately*, 1866, vol. 2, p. 33.
5. *Life* I, pp. vii–viii.
6. E. J. Whately, op. cit., pp. 32–4. Thom published the full version of the letter (which he was shown by its recipient, Edward Fellowes) in his article 'Archbishop Whately and the Life of Blanco White', *Theological Review*, vol. 4 (January 1867), pp. 82–120.
7. E. J. Whately, op. cit., pp. 122–3.
8. J. J. Tayler, in *The Prospective Review*, vol. I (1845), pp. 465–496. This is one of the most perceptive reviews of the *Life*, and perhaps the most objective. It was Tayler who described BW memorably as, at the end, 'adrift, a lonely voyager, on the vast ocean of thought'. Cf. *Earlier Letters of J. S. Mill 1812–1848*, ed. Francis E. Mineka, Toronto 1963, vol. 2, p. 666.
9. *Memoir and Letter of Sara Coleridge*, edited by her daughter, 1873, vol. 2, pp. 24–5. See also pp. 185–6 for her poem 'Blanco White', inspired by BW's *Life*.
10. John Forster, *W. S. Landor: A Biography*, 1869, vol. 2, pp. 515–23.

11. Evelyn Barish Greenberger, *A. H. Clough: The Growth of a Poet's Mind*, Harvard University Press 1970, pp. 101–04.

12. W. E. Gladstone, 'The Life of Mr Blanco White', QR vol. LXXVI (1845), pp. 167–203; *Gleanings of Past Years*, vol. 2, 1879. See also Gladstone's note of June 1845, BL Add MSS 44735.

13. 'Blanco White', Christian Remembrancer vol. X (1845), pp. 144–212, reprinted in J. B. Mozley, *Essays Historical and Theological*, 1878, vol. 2, p. 68ff.

14. Letter to Henry Wilberforce of April 1845, quoted in Wilfrid Ward, *The Life of John Henry Cardinal Newman*, 1912, vol. 1, pp. 80–82.

15. JHN to A. P. Perceval, NLD vol. 5, p. 196.

16 Albany Christie to E. Hawkins, 19 October 1845, Oriel 709; Wilfrid Ward, *W. G. Ward and the Oxford Movement*, 1889, p. 356; H. G. Liddon, *The Life of E. B. Pusey*, 1893, vol. 1, p. 315.

17. J. H. Newman, *Lectures on the Present Position of Catholics in England*, 1851, pp. 141–60.

18. See letters of Usóz to J. B. Wiffen of 4 February 1943 and 22 October 1845, Wiffen papers, Wadham College, Oxford, H 4 14. For an appreciation of Usoz, see Domingo Ricart, 'Notas para una biografía de Luis Usóz y Río', *Studia Albornotiana* vol. XIII (Publicaciones del Real Colegio de España 1973), pp. 437–532. BW's comments on the Quakers are to be found in *Life* II, pp. 217–22; III, pp. 366–70.

19. Some of these stories can be traced back to BW's contemporary Bartolomé José Gallardo, who wrote the short biography of BW which prefaces vol. 67 of the BAE (1875). For further elaborations, see Angel Lasso de la Vega, *Historia y juicio crítico de la Escuela poetica sevillana en los siglos XVIII y XIX*, Madrid 1876, pp. 135–51; Leopoldo de Cueto, introduction to *Poetas líricos del siglo XVIII*, BAE 61, Madrid, 1869, pp. ccviii–ccxi; Julio Cejador y Frauca,

Historia de la lengua y literatura castellana, Madrid 1917, vol. 6, pp. 293–5. The most inventive of all the mythographers of BW was the historian of Venezuela who described him as 'an ex-Dominican friar, former tutor of the Prince of the Asturias and protégé of Godoy who, charged with a scandalous offence, abandoned the white habit from which he derived the name Padre Blanco, and turned freemason' (C. Parra-Pérez, *Historia de la primera república de Venezuela*, Caracas 1959, vol. 2, p. 398).

20. Quoted by Sir Raymond Carr in his *Spain 1808–1939*, Oxford 1966, p. 355.

21. Marcelino Menéndez y Pelayo, *Historia de los heterodoxos españoles*, Madrid 1882, vol. 3, pp. 347–83.

22. J Goytisolo, *Obra inglesa de D. José María Blanco White*, Buenos Aires 1972, pp. 17, 21.

23. *Ibid*, p. 72. Hence Goytisolo went so far as to speak of the need for a 'decolonisation' of the language (p. 98).

24. BW had prophesied, in *Letters from Spain*, that 'ages must pass before they can see the light in Spain'. (LFS, second edn, p. 66).

25. H Bishop to J. H. Thom, 1842, MCO III/8.

Appendix

1. MCO III/8. The text was published by Antonio Garnica in his article 'La poesía inédita de Blanco White', *Homenaje a Don Esteban Pujals*, Oviedo, 1981. See also, by the same author, 'Blanco White, poeta inglés, *Filología Moderna* 16 (1975–76), pp. 79–90. I owe much to the study by V. Lloréns, 'Historia de un famoso soneto' in *Homenaje a Casalduero*, ed. R. Pineus Sigele y Gonzalo Sobejano, Madrid, 1972, pp. 299–315.

2. *Life* I, p. 439. J. H. Frere, diplomat, classical scholar and poet, first met BW during his time as British envoy to the Junta Central at Seville in

1808–09. His Latin epitaph for the Duke of Alburquerque was translated into Spanish by BW in EE XII (March 1811), p. 498. He is best known as a translator of Aristophanes.

3. See *Collected Letters of S. T. Coleridge*, ed. Earl L. Griggs, vol. V, Oxford, 1971, no 1608.

4. BW to Southey, 25 August 1825, in G. M. Murphy and A. Pons, BHS LXII (1985), pp. 366–7.

5. G Tillotson, 'Newman's Essay on Poetry', *Newman Centenary Essays*, 1945, pp. 178–200.

6. *The Christian Teacher*, vol. I (new series), 1839, pp. 178–82.

7. *The Bijou*. 1828, p. 16; *The Gentleman's Magazine* , May 1835, p. 529.

8. *Life* III, p. 48; *The Oxford Book of English Verse*, ed. Sir Arthur Quiller-Couch, new edition, 1939, p. 685. The sonnet was not included by Helen Gardner in her *Oxford Book of English Verse* of 1972.

9. See D. M. Main, *A Treasury of English Sonnets*, Manchester, 1880, pp. 398–9.

10. For the version sent to Lista, see M. Artigas, 'El soneto *Night and Death* de Blanco White', BSS I, no. 4 (September 1924), pp. 3–12. For Lista's rendering into Spanish, 'El Sol y la Vida', see BAE I, vol. 67, Madrid, 1837, p. 319. Among other Spanish versions may be mentioned those by Jorge Guillen (in *Obra inglesa de D. José María Blanco White*, ed. Juan Goytisolo, Buenos Aires, 1972, pp. 330–1), and Rafael Pombo (in A. Gómez Restrepo, *Historia de la literatura colombiana*, vol. 4, Bogotá, 1946, p. 175). See Joaquín de Entrambasaguas, 'La traduccíon del famoso soneto de B.-W.', *Revista de Literatura* VI (1954), pp. 337–49. For the version sent to Mrs Hawkins, see Oriel Correspondence no 125. With it, BW enclosed the French rendering by his friend J. M. Maury (in H. Juretschke, *Vida . . . de D. Alberto Lista*, Madrid, 1951, p. 663).

11. Yet another version was published in *The Academy*, no 1010 (12 September 1891). Lloréns (art. cit.) gives good grounds for doubting its authenticity.

12. *Life* I, pp. 430–1; *The Casket, A miscellany consisting of unpublished poems*, 1829, p. 253.

13. *The Book of the Sonnet*, ed. Leigh Hunt and S. Adams Lee, vol. I, 1867, p. 258.

Select Bibliography

I *Manuscript Sources*

At Blanco's death, the papers, notebooks and correspondence in his possession passed to his literary executor, the Reverend John Hamilton Thom. The greater portion of this collection was bequeathed to the then University College, Liverpool, in 1894, probably by the Rathbone family, with whom Thom was connected by marriage. The collection lay unsorted and unlisted until 1942, when a catalogue was prepared by Anne D. Holt, given 'the importance now attached to Hispanic studies in the University'. A rather smaller, but important, portion of papers had meanwhile found its way to the Unitarian College at Manchester and was transferred to Oxford when that institution moved there in 1888 to become Manchester College, Oxford. A handlist of this collection was prepared by H. John McLachlan in 1951. Some of BW's theological books, annotated by their owner, are in the Sydney Jones Library at Liverpool University, along with the papers, but an interesting collection of Spanish books belonging to BW passed to the Liverpool Athenaeum, of which he was a member.

The family papers of Fernando Blanco y Crespo, BW's brother, handed down through the generations, were made available earlier in this century by General Mariano Blanco y Valdenebro, Fernando's great-grandson, to the historian D. Mario Méndez Bejarano, who used them extensively in his book on BW published in 1920. After the Second World War they were purchased from the widow of D. José María Blanco de Quintana, the general's son, by Professor Vicente Llorens, who deposited them in the library of Princeton University. This archive, which has recently been catalogued, contains family papers covering a period of two and a half centuries, from the arrival of the Whites in Spain at the beginning of the eighteenth century until after the Spanish Civil War. The genealogical section of the archive is of much interest not just for the Whites, but also for the Gough, Morrogh and Olloqui families with whom they were connected by marriage. By far the largest portion of the letters and papers in the collection belonged to BW's brother, Fernando, and chart his activities for almost half a century (1803–1848) as family man, businessman and university teacher. The importance of the archive for the student of BW is that it contains his manuscripts, poems and letters mainly dating from the first thirty-five years of his life, before his emigration to England. The documents of most importance to the biographer are BW's letters to and from his parents and brother. The correspondence between the brothers is of particular value: BW's side of it recalls his intimate and least guarded thoughts over a period of forty years (1798–1810, 1816–1841). The archive also contains the manuscripts of BW's last Spanish poems, written just before his death, presumably sent to Seville by J. H. Thom.

Professor Llorens published a full bibliography of BW's published and unpublished works in his *Antología* (pp. 51–60). Since then other sources have come to light which are included in the list which follows.

ABERYSTWYTH

National Library of Wales

Two letters of BW to Nassau Senior, and a note (Senior papers C8 22–23; C515). Some of the letters from Richard Whately to Senior covering the period 1830–1835 are of much value in relation to BW.

BIRMINGHAM

The Birmingham Oratory

Letters of BW to J. H. Newman, 1828–1835. The library also contains Newman's annotated copies of *Evidence, The Poor Man's Preservative* and *Life*.

DUBLIN

National Library of Ireland

Draft of Senior's *Letter to Lord Howick* (1831), with MS comments in the margin by BW, Malthus and Samuel Hinds (MS 21286).

DURHAM

Ushaw College

Letter of 10 July 1830 from Nichols Wiseman to F. C. Husenbeth, re BW. (Wiseman papers no 774).

EDINBURGH

National Library of Scotland

Six letters from BW to J. G. Lockhart, Robert Southey, Captain Basil Hall, Henry Colburn and Miss Yates.

LIVERPOOL

SYDNEY JONES LIBRARY, UNIVERSITY OF LIVERPOOL

The collection has been divided as follows:

I.   Letters. Correspondents include John Allen, Andrés Bello, Thomas Campbell, W. E. Channing, J. D. Coleridge, E. Coplestone, E. Hawkins, Lord and Lady Holland, E. H. Locker, Francis Douce, John Murray, the Moore family, A. Neander, McVey Napier, Baden Powell, Manuel Quintana, Vicente Rocafuerte, Robert Southey, Richard Whately, William Wilberforce.
II.   Correspondence relating to *El Español*, 1810–13.
III. Autograph MSS of BW. These include diaries for 1816, 1819, 1821, 1823, 1825, 1833–35, 1836–39; Private Journals 1812–20; account book for 1813–30; MSS of articles and books; MS poems.
IV.   Other manuscripts, including family documents, not in the hand of BW.
V.   Notebooks and commonplace books in the hand of BW.
VI.   Printed pamphlets and newspapers belonging to BW.

LONDON

British Library

Holland House papers, Add MSS 51645 (correspondence of BW with Lord and Lady Holland); 52194–52196 (correspondence with John Allen); 51621–51622 (correspondence between Lord Holland and the Duke of Infantado, Manuel Quintana, A. de Capmany, etc); 51626 (Abella and Quintana). Add MSS 44735 contains Gladstone's notes of June 1845 on his reading of BW's *Life*.

Chelsea Public Library

Letter of 9 June 1826 to the Vice-Chancellor of Oxford University.

Dr Williams' Library

Letter of BW to H. Crabbe Robinson, 1812.

Lambeth Palace Library

Whately papers (MS 2164). Correspondence of BW with Richard and Elizabeth Jane Whately, 1830–41.

Public Record Office

Correspondence of BW with Foreign Office Ministers; reports, press abstracts and translations prepared by him, 1810–14. PRO FO 72/104, ff.308–

11; 72/123, ff.172–77; 72/124, ff.93–100, 161–65, 173–84; 72/133, ff.183–86; 72/138, ff.102–07, 108, 220–21, 245–46; 72/139, ff.127–28; 72/140, ff.255–62, 331–40; 72/141, ff.217–18; 72/151, ff.157–58; 72/152, ff.95–100, 51–54; 72/154, f.14; 72/155, ff.ff.184–92; 72/156, ff.15–24; 72/166, ff.32–35, 144–45; 72/167, ff.163–64; 72/168, ff.39–40, 123–24; 72/169, ff.68–85, 237–38, 258–59; 72/170, f.111; 72/171, ff.177–80.

University College, London

Seven letters of BW to Sir Edwin Chadwick: six of 1829, one of 1839.

MADRID

Archivo Histórico Nacional

Letter of BW, 6 December 1811, to Luis de Iturribarria (Consejos no. 6036).

Biblioteca Nacional

Letter of William Walton to B. Wiffen re the authorship of *Vargas* (U/8795), dated 3 October 1855.

NEW YORK

Hispanic Society of America

Nine poems by BW in MS, catalogued in A. Rodríguez-Moñino and María Brey Mariño, *Catálogo de los MSS poéticos castellanos . . . en la biblioteca de The Hispanic Society of America*, New York 1965, Vol.1, p.xciii.

OXFORD

All Souls College

Letters of BW to Andrés de la Vega and Charles Vaughan, and relevant leters of Vaughan, John Allen, William Hamilton and A. de la Vega (C 9/2, 9/5; OB 37/1–2, 38/1–3, 126, 128, 134).

Bodleian Library

Letters of BW to William Wilberforce (MS Wilberforce), R. Southey, R. Douce, E. H. Locker, E. Hawkins, E. Coplestone, Wm Napier. The letters to Southey have been published in G. M. Murphy and A. Pons, 'Further Letters of Blanco White to Robert Southey', BHS LXII (1985), pp. 357–71.

Keble College

The library contains S. T. Coleridge's annotated copies of *Letters from Spain,*
A Letter to Charles Butler, Evidence and *The Poor Man's Preservative.*

Manchester College

The collection of BW's papers has been arranged as follows:

Ia) Family letters (in Spanish) to BW from his father, brother and other
relatives, 1815–42; (in English) from his son Ferdinand White, 1831–41.

Ib) Letters from various correspondents, including Alberto Lista, A. de la
Vega, Leandro Fernández de Moratín, Juan Antonio Llorente, Valentín
Llanos, Pablo Mendíbil, Joaquín María Sotelo, Agustín de Yturbide,
Clemente de Zulueta, Nicolas García Page, J. M. Maury, Alvaro
Agustín de Liaño, José Muñoz de Sotomayor, Joaquín Uriarte, Dioni-
sio Capaz, E. J. Whately, John Allen, Francis and Charlotte Carleton,
Charlotte Pope (later Mrs Baden Powell), E. Hawkins, George
Armstrong, Charles Dickinson, etc.

II. Notebooks and Diaries. Journals for 1822, 1835, 1838–39;
Commonplace Books for 1831–32, 1837, 1839, 1812–22, 1824.
The last-mentioned contains the MS of poems written in English
by BW 1825–26.

III. Manuscripts and Articles by BW. These include Henry Bishop's collection of BW's occasional articles and other souvenirs; BW's sermon
notes, 1826–30.

IV Miscellaneous documents, including the probate copy of BW's will,
dated 26 March 1841, and certificates of his degrees and diplomas from
the Universities of Seville and Osuna.

Oriel College

Correspondence of BW with Edward Hawkins, 1828–41. There are other
relevant letters to Hawkins from J. H. Thom (no. 124), R. Whately (nos.
187, 208, 214, 216, 223), E. J. Whately (nos. 208, 209), E. Coplestone (no.
214). See also Hawkins' letter to R. Whately of 13 October 1835 (no. 1108),
and BW's letter to Mrs Hawkins (no. 125), enclosing a version of the sonnet
'Night and Death' with a translation into French by J. M. Maury.

BW's letter to E. B. Pusey of 14 February 1929 is in Oriel College
Treasurer's Muniments ETC A1.

Pusey House

Letters of BW to E. B. Pusey, 1828–9 and 1835.

Taylorian Library

Letter of BW to Robert Southey, 25 August 1825 (MS Sp BW1) published in
G. M. Murphy and A. Pons, art. cit.

Wadham College

Letters of BW to J. H. Wiffen, 1822–23, published in Robert Johnson, 'Letters of Blanco White to J. H. Wiffen and Samuel Rogers', *Neophilologus* 52 (1968), pp. 138–48.

PRINCETON, NEW JERSEY

University Library

The collection has been classified as follows:

I.   MS works by BW. These include sermons and sermon notes, c. 1800–1802; the unfinished novel *Luisa de Bustamante*; last poems, 1839–40; Spanish translations of *Letters from Spain* and part of *Life*, perhaps by BW's brother.

II. MS works by others, mainly by Fernando Blanco y Crespo. The most important of these are Fernando's diaries covering the years 1808–1814 (the years of his military service and imprisonment in France), 1817, 1820–48. These, like the correspondence between the brothers, were written in English, no doubt for security reasons.

III. Correspondence.

    A. Letters to and from José María Blanco White. These include well over 100 letters (1798–1841) from BW to his brother Fernando, and drafts of Fernando's replies; about 90 letters of BW to his parents, principally his father (1798–1816), and drafts or copies of replies; letters from BW to various correspondents, including Michael Faraday (1), Edward Hawkins (1), Harriet Moore (5), Andrews Norton (1); letters to BW from John Allen (1), Manuel de Arjona (1), Richard Whately (1).

    B. Letters to and from Guillermo Blanco y Morrogh (BW's father).

    C. Letter to José Blanco y Morrogh (BW's uncle).

    D. Letters to and from Guillermo Blanco y Nangle (BW's grandfather).

    E. Letters to and from José María Blanco y Olloqui (BW's nephew).

    F. Letters to and from Mariano Blanco y Valdenebro (BW's great-nephew).

    G. Letters to and from Fernando María Blanco y Crespo (BW's brother). These include about 200 letters to and from his father (1803–15); 7 letters from Ferdinand White (1826–39); 11 letters from Felipa Esquaya (1816–25), the sister of BW's mistress. This section is the largest in the collection. ction.

    H. Letters to and from Fernando María White y Crespo and Juana María Olloqui y Estrada, his wife.

    I. Miscellaneous correspondence.

IV. Documents.

    A. José María Blanco y Crespo: Ecclesiastical and academic documents and certificates.

    B. Documents relating to BW's father and grandfather.

    C. Documents relating to BW's brother.

D. Genealogical papers relating to the Gough, Morrogh, Farvaeques, Olloqui, Estrada and White families.
V.   Accounts and Expenses.
VI. Printed Materials (official documents and newspaper clippings).

SAN MARINO, CALIFORNIA

Huntington Library

Letters of BW to E. H. Locker, 1823–28.

SANTANDER

Menéndez y Pelayo Library

Letters of BW, his brother Fernando, and Joaquín María Sotelo to Felix-José Reinoso.

SEVILLA

Biblioteca Universitaria

MS poems and one discourse read by BW to the Academia de Letras Humanas; Documents proving BW's *limpieza de sangre*, from the archive of the Colegio de Santa María de Jesús.

SIMANCAS

Correspondence (1810–11) between Secretary Bardaxí and Admiral Ruíz de Apodaca, Spanish ambassador in London, relating to BW (Estado 8173, ff.17–19); documents relating to the funeral of the Duke of Alburquerque, 1811 (Estado 8320).

II   *Published Works by Blanco White*

(i) Contemporary

Alexis. Drama pastoral compuesto en prosa latina por el P. Andres Friz, de la Compañía de Jesús. Traducido en verso castellano por D. J. M. B. y C. Sevilla: Vázquez y Cía, 1795.
Poesías de una Academia de Letras Humanas de Sevilla. Sevilla: por la viuda de Vázquez y Compañía, 1797. (Contains 17 poems by BW).

El triunfo de la Beneficencia. Oda leída el dia 23 de noviembre de 1803 en la Junta Publica de la Real Sociedad Económica de Sevilla (in *Memorial Literario* V, 1806, pp. 369–76).

Sermón predicado en la función solemne que consagró la Real Brigada de Carabineros a su patrono San Fernando en su Santa y Real Capilla de Sevilla el día 13 de julio de 1802, por el Magistral de ella Don—, Colegial Mayor de Santa María de Jesús de Sevilla, Examinador Sinodal de los Obispados de Córdoba y Cádiz, &c. Sevilla: Viuda de Hidalgo y Sobrino, 1804.

Prospecto y Plan de una clase de Humanidades que establece la Real Sociedad Económica de Sevilla. Sevilla: Viuda de Hidalgo y Sobrino, 1804.

Poems published in *El Correo de Sevilla*, between February 1804 and May 1806, signed 'Alfesibeo', 'ALBN', 'Albino' or with the author's real name: 'En la partida de Elisa de Sevilla', 'En los días de Elisa', 'A Elisa, cantando al fortepiano', 'Canción de la alborada, traducción libre de Gessner', 'Dafnis, idilio de Gessner, traducido libremente', 'El Mesías, égloga', 'Los placeres del entusiasmo'.

'Contestación al juicio sobre el poema de *La inocencia perdida*', in *Variedades de Ciencias, Literatura y Artes*, Madrid, año 2o, vol. 1 (1805), pp. 164–184, 241–252.

Discurso sobre si el método de enseñanza de Enrique Pestalozzi puede apagar el genio, y especialmente el que se requiere para las artes de imitación. Por Don José María Blanco, Magistral de la Real Capilla de San Fernando de Sevilla e individuo de la Real Comisión de Literatos del Real Instituto Militar Pestalozziano. Madrid: Gómez Fuentenebro y Compañía, 1807.

Oda a la instalación de la Junta Central de España por Don Josef María Blanco. [Madrid]: Gómez Fuentenebro y Cía, 1808.

Articles in *Semanario Patriotico*, Sevilla, 4 May to 31 August 1809.

El Español, London April 1810 to June 1814. 8 volumes.

A Letter upon the mischievous influence of the Spanish Inquisition as it actually exists in the Provinces under the Spanish government. Translated from El Español &c. London: J. Johnson & Co., 1811. (Translation by Belgrave Hoppner).

Letter to *The Times* of 13 February 1811, prompted by an article of 1 February.

'Present State of the Spanish Colonies', QR VII (1812), pp. 235–64.

Bosquexo del comercio en esclavos, y reflexiones sobre este tráfico, considerado moral, política y cristianamente. Londres: Ellerton y Henderson, 1814.

Some documents respecting the history of the late events in Spain being: 1) A plain exposition of the reasons which occasioned the journey of Ferdinand VII to Bayonne in April 1808 by J. de Escoiquiz; 2) Remarks on the preceding work by . . . P. de Ceballos; 3) A full abstract of a petition addressed to King Ferdinand VII by sixty-nine members of the Cortes. London: Longman, Hurst, 1815, (Translation and introduction by BW).

Observaciones sobre los inconvenientes del celibato de los clerigos. Londres: 1815. (Prologue and epilogue by BW. See n. 4, p. 223).

Preparatory Observations on the Study of Religion, by a Clergyman of the Church of England. Oxford: J. Parker, 1817.

Revision of the Spanish translation of the Book of Common Prayer (by Antonio de Alvarado) in *The Book of Common Prayer in Eight Languages*. London: Samuel Bagster, 1821.

La Biblia o El Antiguo y Nuevo Testamento traducidos al Español de la Vulgata Latina por el Rmo P. Phelipe Scio de San Miguel, de las Escuelas Pias, Obispo electo de Segovia. Londres: B. Bensley, 1821. (Joint edition by BW and Andrés Bello).

Letters from Spain, by Don Leucadio Doblado. London: Henry Colburn and Co., 1822. Second edition, 1825. (Originally published serially in the *New Monthly Magazine,* April 1821—April 1822). German translation: *Briefe aus Spanien, von Leucadio Doblado. Aus dem Englischen uebersetzt von E. L. Domeier . . . mit einem Briefe an dem Herrn Dr Tieck in Dresden.* Hamburg: A. Campe, 1828.

Vargas, A Tale of Spain. London: J. Baldwin, 1822.

'Prince Carlos of Spain and his father Philip II', *New Monthly Magazine* V (1822), pp. 231–36 and 352–59.

'Spain', QR no.57 (April 1823), pp. 240–76. (Review of Michael J. Quin, *A Visit to Spain,* 1823).

'Peranzules. A Spanish Historical Fragment', NMM VIII (1823), pp. 300–304.

'Spain', in *Supplement to the Fourth, Fifth and Sixth Editions of the Encyclopaedia Britannica,* vol. 6, Edinburgh, 1824, pp. 508–33.

Variedades, o Mensagero de Londres. Periódico trimestral, por el Rev. Joseph Blanco White. Londres: R. Ackermann, 1823–25 (2 vols. The first number is dated January 1823; nos 2–8 are from January 1824 to October 1825).

gubernativo inglés. Obra escrita en francés por M. [Charles] Cottu; traducida al castellano por el autor de El Español y de las Variedades. Londres: C. Wood, 1824.

Londres: C. Wood, 1824.

'Studies in Spanish History. I. Aragon', NMM X (1824), pp. 1–10.

'Studies in Spanish History. II. Prince Don Juan Manuel and his book El Conde Lucanor, with the history of Count Don Rodrigo the Liberal and his Knights', NMM XI (1824), pp. 28–35.

'The Dean of Santiago: A Tale from the Conde Lucanor', NMM XI (1824), pp. 97–103.

Practical and Internal Evidence against Catholicism, with occasional strictures on Mr Butler's Book of the Roman Catholic Church: in six letters addressed to the impartial among the Roman Catholics of Great Britain and Ireland. London: John Murray, 1825. (2nd edition, revised and enlarged, 1825). American edition, Georgetown D.C.: J. C. Dunn, 1826. German edition: *Beleuchtung der romisch-katholischen Glaubens.* Dresden: Arnold, 1826. The autobiographical section of the book is also included in *Zwey Briefe durch die jüngst zu Dresden erschienene Schrift: Die reine katholische Lehre, veranlasst. Nebst Mollard-Lefevre's und Joseph Blanco's Berichten von ihrem Übertritte zur evangelischen Kirche,* herausgegeben von Dr H. G. Tzschirner. Leipzig, 1826, pp. 117–37.

'Claims of the Spanish Refugees to public benevolence. To Edward Hawke Locker FRS', in *The New Times,* 10 January 1825.

'Don Esteban', QR no.65 (December 1825). A review of the novel by Valentín Llanos.

William Paley, *Evidencias del cristianismo,* London: 1825. Translation attributed to José Muñoz de Sotomayor, but in fact by BW (see Life I, pp. 337–9, and III, p. 353).

'El Alcázar de Sevilla', in *No Me Olvides*, Londres: J. Ackermann, 1825, pp. 3–27. (English translation in *Forget Me Not*, 1825, p. 31ff).

A Letter to Charles Butler Esq on the notice of the 'Practical and Internal Evidence against Catholicism' by the Rev. Joseph Blanco White MA of the University of Oxford. London: J. Murray, 1826.

The Poor Man's Preservative against Popery: addressed to the lower classes of Great Britain and Ireland. London: Rivington, 1825. There are various editions of this work. For the Irish edition of 1834, BW modified the title to *The Poor Man's Preservative against the Errors of Romanism: addressed to the lower classes of Great Britain and Ireland . . . Corrected and considerably altered by the author* (Dublin: Richard Milliken, 1834). Spanish edition: *Preservativo contra Roma* (translated by J. J. de Mora), Edimburgo: Constable, 1856.

A Letter to Protestants converted from Romanism. By the Rev. Joseph Blanco White. Oxford: W. Baxter, 1827.

'Night and Death', in *The Bijou*, London, 1828, p. 16.

The London Review. London, 1829. (Only two numbers published.)

'On hearing myself called an Old Man', in *The Casket*. London: J. Murray, 1829.

Letter from the Rev. J. Blanco White, MA, of Oriel College, to a Friend in Oxford. Oxford, 1829.

'Education in Spain', *The Quarterly Journal of Education*, vol. 1 (1831), pp. 213–224.

'Norval', in [E Jane Whately], *Reverses: or, Memoirs of the Fairfax Family*. London, 1833, pp. 190–216.

'The Bill of Belial', NMM no.148 (April 1833), pp. 413–17.

Second Travels of an Irish Gentleman in Search of a Religion. with notes and illustrations. Not by the author of 'Captain Rock's Memoirs'. Dublin: R. Milliken, 1833, 2 vols.

'Guizot's History of Civilization', *Dublin University Review*, vol. 2 (November 1834), pp. 259–277.

'Inglis' Spain in 1830', *ibid.*, pp. 296–317.

The Law of anti-religious Libel reconsidered, in a Letter to the editor of the Christian Examiner, in answer to an article of that periodical against a pamphlet entitled 'Consideraions &c' by John Search. By the Rev. Joseph Blanco White, MA, of Oriel College, Oxford. Dublin: R. Milliken, 1834.

An Answer to some Friendly Remarks on 'The Law of Anti-Religious Libel Reconsidered'. With an Appendix on the true meaning of an Epigram of Martial, supposed to relate to the Christian Martyrs. Dublin: R. Milliken, 1834.

'Atmos the Giant', in Lady Mary Fox (ed.), *Friendly Contributions for the benefit of three infant schools in the parish of Kensington*. London, 1834.

Observations on Heresy and Orthodoxy. London: J. Mardon, 1835. (2nd edn, 1839).

'Thoughts on Baptism', *The Christian Teacher*, vol. 1 (1835), pp. 581–90.

'Recent Spanish Literature', *The London Review*, vol. 1 (1835), pp. 76–93.

'On Crabbe's Life and Works', *ibid.*, pp. 316–41.

'Lamb's Specimens of English Dramatic Poets', *London Review*, vol. 2 (1835–6), pp. 51–69.

'Guizot's Lectures on European Civilization', *ibid.*, pp. 306–36.

Elements of Geometry for the Use of the Irish National Schools. Dublin: M. Goodwin, 1836 (reprinted 1845, 1846).

'Godoy, Prince of Peace', *London and Westminster Review*, vol. 3 (1836), pp. 28–60.

'A Fragment of Philosophy', *The Christian Teacher*, vol. 2 (1837), pp. 640–47.

'Historians of Germany', CT vol. 1 (new series), pp. 37–54.

'The causes of the intenser zeal in fanatics than in liberals', CT vol. 1 (1839), pp. 80–82.

'Germany in 1831', CT vol. 1 (1839), pp. 91–104.

'The Sonnet', CT vol. 1 (1839), pp. 178–82.

'Stories of Spanish Life', CT vol. 1 (1839), pp. 214–25.

'Mental signs of the times', CT vol. 1 (1839), pp. 589–93.

'The Pictorial Shakespeare', CT vol. 1 (1839), pp. 322–32, 469–81.

'Notes on Hamlet', CT vol. 1 (1839), pp. 573–80.

'A Midsummer Night's Dream', CT vol. 2 (1840), pp. 42–53.

'On the Christian Rule of Faith', CT vol. 3 (1841), pp. 98–108.

'On Inspiration and Miracles', CT vol. 4 (1842), pp. 333–53.

'The argument from design', CT vol. 5 (1843), pp. 137–55.

(ii) Posthumous editions

The Life of the Rev. Joseph Blanco White, written by himself, with portions of his correspondence. Edited by John Hamilton Thom. London: John Chapman, 1845, 3 vols.

Spanish poems published in *Revista de Ciencias, Literatura y Artes*, vol. 4 (1858), pp. 702, 762; vol. 5 (1859), pp. 169–71; BAE vol. 67 (1875); *Archivo Hispalense* vol. 1 (1886), pp. 44–46; Angel Lasso de la Vega, *Historia y juicio crítico de la Escuela poética sevillana en los siglos VIII y XIX.* Madrid, 1876, pp. 135–51; Mario Méndez Bejarano, *Vida y Obras de D. José Ma Blanco y Crespo*, Madrid, 1920, pp. 411–29, 523–36.

'*Dos cartas autógrafas e inéditas de Blanco White* . . . Por D. Manuel Gómez Imaz, de la Real Academia de Buenas Letras de Sevilla. Sevilla: E. Rasco, 1891.

M Méndez Bejarano, *Vida y obras de D. José Ma Blanco y Crespo.* Madrid, 1920. Contains the text of unpublished sermons, letters and poems.

Vicente Llorens (ed.), *José Maria Blanco White: Antología de obras en Español.* Barcelona: Editorial Labor, 1971.

Obra inglesa de D. José María Blanco White . . . *con un prólogo de D. Juan Goytisolo.* Buenos Aires: Ediciones Formentor, 1972. (Contains a translation into Spanish of excerpts from the *Life, Letters from Spain* and other works).

Cartas de España. Introducción de Vicente Llorens. Traducción y notas de Antonio Garnica. Madrid: Alianza, 1972.

Luisa de Bustamante, o la huérfana española en Inglaterra. Costumbres húngaras . . . Intrigas venecianas o Fray Gregorio de Jerusalén . . . El Alcázar de Sevilla. Edición a cargo de Ignacio Prat. Barcelona: Editorial Labor, 1975. An unfinished novel, and three stories.

Autobiografía de Blanco White. Edición, traducción, prólogo y notas de Antonio Garnica. Sevilla: Universidad, 1975 (2nd edn 1988). A translation of the section of the *Life* relating to Spain.

'El incordio: Poema epi-galico en un canto', ed. Antonio Garnica, in *Rara Avis*, nos. 2–3 Sevilla 1987, pp. 63–72.

III   *Published works relating to Blanco White*

An Address to the Flocks of the Reverend Approvers of Blanco White's Internal Evidences against Catholicism (Baltimore: Fielding Lucas Jun., 1826).

Aguilar Piñal, Francisco, *La Universidad de Sevilla en el siglo XVIII* (Sevilla, 1969), p. 503, n.167.

Aguilar Piñal, Francisco, 'Blanco White y el Colegio de Santa María de Jesús', *Archivo Hispalense* (Sevilla, 1975), vol. 58, pp. 1–54.

Akenson, Donald H., *A Protestant in Purgatory: Richard Whately, Archbishop of Dublin* (Hamden, Conn., 1981).

Alberich, José, *Bibliográfica Anglo-Hispánica 1801–1850* (Oxford: Dolphin Books, 1978).

Alcalá Galiano, Antonio, 'Literature of the 19th Century: Spain', *The Athenaeum*, April–June 1834.

Amunátegui, Miguel Luis, *Vida de Don Andrés Bello* (Santiago de Chile, 1882), pp. 136–143.

Apología de la Inquisición. Respuesta a las reflexiones que hacen contra ella el Semanario Patriótico y el periódico intitulado El Español (Cadiz, 1811; Mexico, 1811).

Arriaza, Juan Bautista, *Poesías patrióticas* (Londres: T. Bensley, 1810), pp. vii, xxii.

Arriaza, Juan Bautista, *Breve registro del periódico intitulado El Español* (Londres: Vogel y Schulze, 1810).

Arroyo Lameda, Eduardo, 'Un desengañado de España y un buen amigo de América', in *Motivos hispanoamericanos* (Paris, 1930).

Artigas, Miguel, 'El soneto Night and Death de Blanco White', *Bulletin of Spanish Studies*, vol. 1 (1924), pp. 3–12.

Atención! Que los apóstatas quieren variar nuestra religión (Mexico: Imprenta del ciudadano A. Valdés, 1825).

A[tkins], A[nna], *Memoir of J. G. Children* (1853), pp. 90, 109.

Bellasis, Edward, *Coram Cardinali* (1916), p. 8. Cardinal Newman's memories of BW as a musician.

Bello, Andres, 'Correspondencia inédita', *Revista Chilena*, vol. 13 (1929), pp. 656–60. Five letters of BW.

Blunt, Reginald, *Paradise Row* (1906).

Bolívar, Simón, *Carta de Jamaica* (Kingston, Jamaica, 1815; facsimile edition, Caracas, 1965), p. 26.

Brading, David, *Los orígines del nacionalismo mexicano* (Mexico, 1980).

Buceta, E., 'La opinión de Blanco White acerca del autor de La Celestina', *Revista de Filología Española*, vol. 7 (1920), pp. 372–74.

Butler, Charles, *Vindication of 'The Book of the Roman Catholic Church' against the Reverend George Townsend's 'Accusations of History against the Church of*

Rome': with notice of some of the charges brought against 'The Book of the Roman Catholic Church' in the publications of Doctor Philpotts, the Rev. John Todd, the Rev. Stephen Isaacson, the Rev. Joseph Blanco White (London: John Murray, 1826).

Cameron, Rev. Charles Richard, *A Letter in Reply to the Letters of the Rev. J. Blanco White and Mr Peel's Committee* (Oxford, 1829).

Capmany, Antonio de, *Manifiesto de D. Antonio de Capmany en respuesta a la contextación de D. Manuel José Quintana* (Cádiz: Imprenta Real, 1811).

Carlyle, Jane Welsh, *A Selection of her Letters*, edited by Trudy Bliss (London, 1949), p. 169.

Carpenter, J. Estlin, *James Martineau: Theologian and Teacher* (London, 1905), pp. 161–63.

Castro, Adolfo de, *Historia de los protestantes españoles* (Cádiz, 1851), pp. 449–57.

Catholic Miscellany, vol. 5 (January–June 1826), pp. 96–100, 283–87, 326–33, 405–09; vol. 6 (July–December 1826), pp. 267–71; vol. 9 (January–June 1828), pp. 50–51, 250–51, 326–27. English Catholic ripostes to BW's polemics.

Catholic Spectator, or Catholicon, 3rd series, vol. 4 (1826), pp. 94–95. This periodical, like the last, was edited by W. E. Andrewes.

Cejador y Frauca, Julio, *Historia de la lengua y literatura castellana* (Madrid, 1917), vol. 6, pp. 293–95. Mythologically inventive.

Chorley, Henry F., *Memorials of Mrs Hemans* (1836), p. 105.

Clayden, P. W., *Rogers and his Contemporaries*, 2 vols (London, 1889).

Clough, Arthur Hugh, *Correspondence*, edited by Frederick L. Mulhauser (Oxford, 1957), vol. 1, pp. 155–58.

Cockshut, A. O. J., *The Art of Autobiography in 19th and 20th Century England* (1984).

Coleridge, Samuel Taylor, *Table Talk* (Oxford, 1917), p. 114. Entry of 7 June 1830.

Coleridge, Samuel Taylor, *Collected Letters*, edited by Earl L. Griggs, vol. 5 (Oxford, 1971), nos. 1474, 1476, 1480, 1501, 1503; vol. 6 (Oxford, 1971), nos. 1607, 1608, 1639, 1645, 1658.

Coleridge, Samuel Taylor, *Marginalia*, edited by George Whalley (Princeton, N.J., 1980), p. 503.

Coleridge, Sara, *Memoir and Letter . . . edited by her daughter* (1873), vol. 2, pp. 24–25, 185–86.

Correio Brasiliense, vol. 8 (London, 1812), pp. 161–64, 630–35; vol. 9 (1812), pp. 252–53. On BW's debate with Mier.

Corsi, Pietro, *Science and Religion: Baden Powell and the Anglican Debate 1800–1860* (Cambridge, 1988).

Cox, G. V., *Recollections of Oxford*, 2nd edition (1870).

Cross, Tony, *Joseph Blanco White: Stranger and Pilgrim* (Liverpool, 1984).

Cueto, Leopoldo Augusto de, *Poetas liricos del siglo XVIII*, BAE 61 (Madrid 1869), pp. ccviii–ccxi. See also BAE 67 (1875), pp. 649–50, 652–53.

Curry, Kenneth (ed.), *New Letters of Robert Southey*, vol. 2 (New York, 1965), pp. 2, 9, 16–18, 37–9, 251, 301, 427.

Dendle, Brian J., 'A Note on the first published version of the "Epístola a D. Manuel José Quintana" by José María Blanco', *Bulletin of Hispanic Studies*, vol. 51 (1974), pp. 365–71.

Denunciación de D. José Blanco, autor del periódico que se publica en Londres con el título del Español (Cádiz, 1810).

Dérozier, Albert, *Manuel Josef Quintana et la naissance du libéralisme en Espagne* (Paris, 1968).

Diccionario de Historia Ecclesiástica de España, edited by Q. Aldea Vaquero et al. (Madrid, 1972), vol. 1, p. 265. Repeats the *leyenda negra*.

Dinwiddy, J. R., 'Liberal and Benthamite Circles in London 1820–1829', in *Andrés Bello: The London Years*, edited by John Lynch (1982), pp. 119–136.

Domergue, Lucienne, 'Blanco White, ou l'éxil d'un dissident', in *L'Espagne face aux problémes de la modernité. Actes du colloque international de Toulouse* (1978), pp. 27–47.

Drummond, James, and Upton, C. B., *The Life and Letters of James Martineau*, 2 vols (London, 1902).

El Español Libre, no.4 (Cádiz, 21 July 1813). The whole number consists of 'Un pasa-gonzalo. Al Editor de *El Español* esclavo en Londres, en defensa de *El Español* libre de Cádiz'.

Egaña, Juan, *Memoria política sobre si conviene en Chile la libertad de cultos, reimpresa en Lima, con una breve apología del art. 8 y 9 de la Constitución política del Perú, y con notas y adiciones en que se esclarecen algunos puntos de la memoria y apologia, y en que se responde a los argumentos del Señor Don José María Blanco a favor de la tolerancia y libertad de cultos, en sus consejos a los hispanoamericanos.* (Lima, 1827).

Entrambasaguas, Joaquín de, 'La traducción castellana del famoso soneto de Blanco White', *Revista de Literatura*, vol. 6 (Madrid, 1954), pp. 337–49.

Ertler, Klaus-Dieter, *Die Spanienkritik im Werk J. M. Blanco Whites* (Frankfurt-am-Main, 1985).

Esclarecimiento de una calumnia. Véase el no. XIII del Español fol.69 (Cádiz: Antonio de Murguía, 1811). On the controversy aroused by the forged letter of Antonio Joaquín Pérez, sent to BW by a hoaxer.

Fernández Larrain, Sergio, *Cartas a Bello en Londres* (Santiago de Chile, 1968), chapter 5.

Fernández Larrain, Sergio, 'José María Blanco White y Andrés Bello', *Revista Mapocho*, vol. 4 (Biblioteca Nacional, Santiago de Chile, 1965), no.3, pp. 288–308.

A Few Observations on the Evidence against Catholicism by the Rev. J. Blanco White (London, 1825).

Ford, John, 'Rudolph Ackermann: Culture and Commerce in Latin America 1822–28', in *Andrés Bello: The London Years*, edited by John Lynch (London 1982).

Ford, John, *Ackermann 1783–1983* (London, 1983).

Forster, John, *W. S. Landor, A Biography* (London, 1869), vol. 2, pp. 515–23.

[Froude, Richard Hurrell], 'Mr Blanco White's Heresy and Orthodoxy', *The British Critic* (January 1836), pp. 204–25.

Garnett, Richard, *The Philological Essays of the late Richard Garnett, edited by his son* (London, 1859), pp. vi–ix. Excerpts from 4 letters of BW.

Garnica, Antonio, 'Blanco en Cádiz', *Archivo Hispalense*, no.176 (Sevilla, 1974), pp. 1–40.

Garnica, Antonio, 'Los sonetos de Blanco-White (a propósito del soneto "bíblico": "El despertar de Adán")', in *Palabra y Vida: Homenaje a José*

Alonso Díaz en su 70 cumpleaños (Universidad Pontificia Comillas, Madrid, n.d.), pp. 433–38.

Garnica, Antonio, 'La poesía inglesa inédita de Blanco-White', in *Homenaje a D. Esteban Pujals* (Oviedo, 1981).

Garnica, Antonio, 'La poesía inglesa inédita de Blanco-White', in *Homenaje a* no.198 (Sevilla, 1982), pp. 25–40. The text of a lecture delivered by Professor V. Llorens at Seville on 11 July 1975 with introduction.

Garnica, Antonio, *Autobiografía de Blanco White*, 2nd edition (Sevilla, 1988). A translation of the section of the *Life* relating to Spain, with introduction and notes.

Gladstone, W. E., 'The Life of Mr Blanco White', *The Quarterly Review*, vol. 76 (1845), pp. 167–203. Reprinted in *Gleanings of Past Years*, vol. 2 (London, 1879).

Gómez Imaz, Manuel, *Los periódicos durante la guerra de independencia (1808–1814)* (Madrid, 1910).

Gómez Imaz, Manuel (ed.), *Dos cartas autógrafas e inéditas de Blanco White* (Sevilla: E. Rasco, 1891).

Goytisolo, Juan, *Obra inglesa de D. José María Blanco White* (Buenos Aires, 1972).

Grases, Pedro, *Tiempo de Bello en Londres y otros ensayos* (Caracas, 1962).

Greenberger, Evelyn Barish, *A. H. Clough: The Growth of a Poet's Mind* (Harvard, 1970), pp. 100–1.

Hampden, Henrietta (ed.), *Some Memorials of Renn Dickson Hampden* (London, 1871).

Harrod, G. R., 'Blanco White on Spanish Literature', BHS, vol. 24 (1947), pp. 269–71.

Holland, Sir Henry, *Recollections of Past Life* (1872), pp. 254–5.

Hunt, Leigh, *Autobiography*, edited by J. E. Morpurgo (1949), p. 228.

Ilchester, The Countess of, *Life and Letters of Lady Sarah Lennox 1745–1826* (1901), vol. 2, p. 278.

Ilchester, The Earl of (ed.), *The Spanish Journal of Elizabeth, Lady Holland* (1910).

Ilchester, The Earl of (ed.), *Elizabeth, Lady Holland to her Son, 1821–1845* (1946).

Ilchester, The Earl of (ed.), *Journal of the Hon Henry Richard Fox 1818–1830* (1923).

Ilchester, The Earl of, *The Home of the Hollands 1605–1820* (1937).

Jacob, William, *Travels in the South of Spain written A.D.1809 and 1810* (London, 1811), p. 145.

Johnson, Robert, 'Letters of Blanco White to J. H. Wiffen and Samuel Rogers', *Neophilologus* (Amsterdam, 1968), vol. 52, pp. 138–45.

Jovellanos, G. M. de, Letters to Lord Holland 1809–1811, in *Obras*, vol. 4, edited by Miguel Artola, BAE (Madrid, 1956).

Jovellanos, G. M. de, *Cartas de Jovellanos y Lord Vassall Holland sobre la guerra de la independencia 1808–1811*, edited by Julio Somoza-García (Madrid, 1911).

Juretschke, Hans, *Vida, obra y pensamiento de Alberto Lista* (Madrid, 1951).

Lara, Maria Victoria de, 'Nota a unos manuscritos de José María Blanco White', BHS, vol. 20 (1943), pp. 110–20, 196–214.

Lardizabal, J. de, *Contestación a la falsa e injuriosa idea que el papel numero 12 titulado El Español da de la memorable acción del 5 de marzo en los campos de Chiclana* (Cádiz, 1811). Denounces 'el atrabiliario Blanco'.

Lasso de la Vega, Angel, *Historia y juicio crítico de la escuela poética sevillana en los siglos XVIII y XIX* (Madrid, 1876), pp. 135–151.

Liddon, Henry Parry, *Life of Edward Bouverie Pusey*, 2 vols (1893).

Lista, Alberto, 'De la moderna escuela sevillana de literatura', *Revista de Madrid*, vol. 1 (1838), pp. 251–276.

Llorens, Vicente, 'Moratín y Blanco', *Insula*, no.161 (Madrid, April 1960). Reprinted, with additions in *Literatura, historia, política* (Madrid, 1967).

Llorens, Vicente, 'Jovellanos y Blanco', *Nueva Revista de Filología Hispánica*, vol. 30 (Mexico, 1961), pp. 261–78. Reprinted in *Literatura, historia, política* (Madrid, 1967), pp. 89–119.

Llorens, Vicente, '*El Español* de Blanco White, primer periódico de oposición', *Boletín informativo del Seminario de Derecho Político* (Princeton, March 1962). Reprinted in *Aspectos sociales de la literatura española* (Madrid, 1974), pp. 67–103.

Llorens, Vicente, 'Los motivos de un converso', *Revista de Occidente*, 2a epoca, vol. 2 (1964), no.13, pp. 44–60.

Llorens, Vicente, 'El fracaso de *The London Review*', *Liber Amicorum Salvador de Madariaga* (Bruges, 1966), pp. 253–261.

Llorens, Vicente, 'Blanco White en el Instituto Pestalozziano', *Homenaje a Antonio Rodríguez-Moniño* (Madrid, 1966), vol. 1, pp. 349–65.

Llorens, Vicente, 'Moratín, Llorente y Blanco White. Un proyecto de revista literaria', in *Literatura, historia y política* (Madrid, 1967), pp. 57–73.

Llorens, Vicente, 'Historia de un famoso soneto', in *Homenaje a Casalduero* (Madrid, 1972), pp. 299–313.

Llorens, Vicente, *José María Blanco White: Antología de obras en español* (Barcelona, 1971).

Llorens, Vicente, 'Blanco White and Robert Southey: Fragments of a Correspondence', *Studies in Romanticism*, vol. 11 (1972), pp. 147–52.

Llorens, Vicente, 'Una academia literaria juvenil', in *Studia Hispánica in honorem R. Lapesa* (Madrid, 1972), vol. 2, pp. 281–95.

Llorens, Vicente, *El romanticismo español* (Madrid, 1979).

Llorens, Vicente, *Liberales y románticos*, 3rd edition (Madrid, 1979).

Llorens, Vicente, 'En busca de Blanco White' (Sevilla, 1982). See under Garnica, Antonio (ed.).

Locker-Lampson, Frederick, *My Confidences* (London, 1896).

Lockhart, J. G., review of *Vargas* in *Blackwood's Edinburgh Magazine*, vol. 12 (December 1822), pp. 730–40.

[López de Cepero, Manuel], 'Nueva impugnación al periódico intitulado El Español que se publica en Londres', *El Observador de Cádiz*, no.12 (14 September 1810). Signed M. de C.

Lyell, Sir Charles, *Life, Letters and Journals* (London, 1881), vol. 2, pp. 92, 94, 168.

Lynch, John, 'Great Britain and South American Independence 1810–1830', in *Andrés Bello: The London Years* (London, 1982), pp. 7–24.

[McCombie, Alexander], 'Blanco White and Brownson', *British Quarterly Review*, vol. 4 (1846), pp. 38–80. A review of *Life* by an Aberdeenshire farmer–journalist, representative of moderate dissent.

Martín Villa, Antonio, *Obras de D. Felix José Reinoso* (Sevilla, 1872), vol. 1, pp. xviii, xxix, xxxi, xl, lix, cxcviii–cxcix.

Martineau, James, 'Protestant and Catholic Popery', *The London and Westminster Review*, vol. 3 (1836), pp. 425–49.

Martineau, James, *The Rationale of Religious Enquiry*, 4th edition (1853), pp. 102–126. Contains an important letter of BW.

Martineau, James, 'Funeral Address' (1841), in the 1877 reprint of BW's *Observations on Heresy and Orthodoxy*.

Méndez Bejarano, Mario, *Historia política de los afrancesados* (Madrid, 1912).

Méndez Bejarano, Mario, *Vida y obras de D. José María Blanco y Crespo (Blanco White)*, (Madrid, 1920).

[Mendíbil, Pablo], 'Dos palabritas más en respuesta a un artículo inserto en el número LXV del *Quarterly Review*', *Ocios de Españoles Emigrados*, vol. 5 (London, 1826), pp. 379–87.

Menéndez y Pelayo, Marcelino, *Historia de los heterodoxos españoles* (Madrid, 1965), vol. 6, pp. 173–212.

Menéndez y Pelayo, Marcelino, *Historia de las ideas estéticas en España* 2a edición (Madrid, 1904), vol. 6, pp. 164–66. On BW's defence of Reinoso's 'La inocencia perdida'.

Menéndez y Pelayo, Marcelino, *Orígenes de la novela* (Santander, 1943), vol. 3, pp. 257, 271, 280, 409. On BW and *La Celestina*.

[Mier, y Noriega, Servando de], *Carta de un americano a El Español sobre su núm.XIX* (Londres: W. Lewis 1811); *Segunda carta de un americano a El Español* (Londres, 1812).

Mill, John Stuart, *The Earlier Letters of J. S. Mill 1818–1848*, edited by Francis E. Mineka, 2 vols (Toronto, 1963), vol. 1, pp. 82–83, 92, 248–49, 264, 268, 270; vol. 2, p. 666.

Milman, Arthur, *Henry Hart Milman: A Biographical Sketch* (1900), pp. 106–07.

Mitchell, Leslie, *Holland House* (1980), pp. 231–55.

Monegal, E. R., *El otro Andrés Bello* (Caracas, 1971).

Montoto, Santiago, *Fernán Caballero* (Sevilla, 1969).

Moreno Alonso, Manuel, 'La independencia de las colonias americanas y la política de Cádiz (1810–1814) en "El Español" de Blanco White', *V Jornadas de Andalucia y America* (Sevilla, 1986), tom.1, pp. 83–128.

Moreno Alonso, Manuel, 'Lord Holland y los orígenes del liberalismo español', *Revista de Estudios Políticos*, no.36 (Madrid, 1983), pp. 181–218.

Moreno Alonso, Manuel, 'Las ideas políticas de "El Español"', *Revista de Estudios Políticos*, no.39 (Madrid, 1984), pp. 65–106.

Morley, Edith, *Henry Crabbe Robinson on Books and their Writers*, 3 vols (London, 1938).

Mozley, James B, 'Blanco White', *Christian Remembrancer*, vol. 10 (1845), pp. 144–212. Reprinted in *Essays Historical and Theological*, 2 vols (1878).

Mozley, Thomas, *Reminiscences, chiefly of Oriel College and the Oxford Movement*, 2 vols (1882), vol. 1, pp. 9, 53–62, 246–50, 352–61, 440.

Murphy, G. Martin, 'Blanco White: An Anglicised Spaniard', *History Today* (January 1978), pp. 40–46.

Murphy, G. Martin, 'Blanco White y J. H. Newman: Un encuentro decisivo', *Boletín de la Real Academia Española*, tom. 63 (1983), pp. 77–116.

Murphy, G. Martin, 'España perseguidora, Irlanda perseguida: un aspecto de la vida de Blanco White', *Archivo Hispalense*, vol. (Sevilla, 1982), pp. 115–138.

Murphy, G. Martin, 'Blanco White's Evidence', *Recusant History*, vol. 17 (May 1985), pp. 254–73.

Murphy, G. Martin, and Pons, André, 'Further Letters of Blanco White to Robert Southey', BHS, vol. 62 (1985), pp. 357–72.

Murray, David R., *Odious Commerce: Britain, Spain and the Abolition of the Cuban Slave Trade* (Cambridge, 1980), p. 61.

Neander, August, *Ueber das leben des Joseph Blanco White* (Berlin: Wilhelm Besser, 1846).

Newman, Francis W., *Contributions chiefly to the early history of the late Cardinal Newman. With comments by his brother* (1891).

Newman, Francis W., recollections of BW in *Our Memories: Shadows of Old Oxford*, edited by H. Daniel (Oxford 1893), no.1 (December 1888), no.5 (June 1889), no.12 (November 1891), no.14 (February 1892).

Newman, John Henry, *Lectures on the Present Position of Catholics in England* (1851), pp. 141–60.

Newman, John Henry, *Apologia pro Vita Sua* (1864), edited by Martin J. Svaglic, pp. 65, 69, 118–19. (Oxford, 1967), pp. 21, 23, 53–4.

Newman, John Henry, *Essays Critical and Historical* (1907), vol. 1, pp. 27–29. On the *London Review*.

Newman, John Henry, *The Letters and Diaries*, edited by Ian Ker and Thomas Gornall, vol. 2 (Oxford, 1979), vol. 3 (1979), vol. 4 (1980), vol. 5 (1987), vols.2–5 (Oxford 1979–81).

Newsome, David, *The Parting of Friends* (1966), pp. 66–67, 86–90. On BW's early Oriel friendships.

Odgers, J. C., 'Joseph Blanco White. A Newly Discovered Portrait', *The Inquirer* (London, 11 August 1906).

Ory Arriaga, María Teresa, 'J Blanco White: "Spain"', *Archivo Hispalense*, vol. 60 (Sevilla, 1977), pp. 67–87.

Orozco Acuaviva, Antonio, *La gaditana Frasquita Larrea* (Cádiz, 1977), pp. 118–21.

Palencia, Ceferino, 'Las Cartas sobre España de Blanco White', *Cuadernos Americanos*, vol. 115 (México, 1961), pp. 179–63.

Parra-Pérez, C, *Historia de la primera república de Venezuela* (Caracas, 1959), vol. 2, pp. 398–402.

Piñeyro, Enrique, 'Blanco White', *Bulletin Hispanique*, vol. 12 (1910), pp. 71–100, 163–200.

Pi Sunyer, Carlos, *Patriotas americanos en Londres* (Caracas, 1978), pp. 290–93, 319.

Pons, André, 'Recherches sur Blanco White et l'indépendance des colonies espagnoles d'Amérique. Analyse et critique des nos 1 à 16 de *El Español* (avril 1810–juillet 1811). Thèse pour le doctorat du 3ème cycle (Université de la Sorbonne Nouvelle, Paris, 1974).

[Powell, Baden] 'Life of the Rev. Joseph Blanco White', *The Westminster Review*, vol. 44 (1845), pp. 273–325.

Q[uintana], M[anuel] J., 'A los editores', *Memorial Literario*, vol. 5, no.8 (Madrid, 20 March 1806), pp. 365–68. Requesting the publication of BW's poem 'El triunfo de la beneficencia'.

Quintana, Manual José, *Obras Completas* (Madrid, 1898), vol. 3, pp. 126, 240, 283–84. On his trial and imprisonment in 1814.

Rathbone, Eleanor, *William Rathbone, A Memoir* (1905).

Redding, Cyrus, *Literary Reminiscences and Memoirs of Thomas Campbell* (London, 1860), vol. 1, pp. 187–89.

Redding, Cyrus, *Personal Reminiscences of Great Men*, vol. 3 (1867), pp. 173–92.

Sánchez-Castañer, Francisco, 'José María Blanco White y Alberto Lista en las Escuelas de Cristo hispalenses', *Archivo Hispalense*, 2a época, vol. 47 (1965), pp. 229–47.

Schwartz, Pedro, and Rodríguez Braun, Carlos, 'Cartas españolas de Jeremias Bentham', *Moneda y Crédito*, no.165 (Madrid, June 1983), pp. 59–69. Includes a letter of 25 October 1810 to BW.

Seco Serrano, Carlos, 'José María Blanco White y la revolución atlántica', in *Comunicación y sociedad: Homenaje al Profesor Beneyto* (Universidad Complutense, Madrid, 1983), pp. 219–43.

Sieveking, I. Giberne, *Memoir and Letters of F. W. Newman* (London, 1909).

Simpson, M. C. M, *Many Memories of Many People*, 3rd edition (London, 1898).

Smith, Sydney, *Letters*, edited by Nowell C. Smith (Oxford, 1953), nos. 254, 417.

Socias Albaladejo, María Antonia, 'La estética y la crítica literaria de J. M. Blanco White'. Tesina presentada a la Universidad de Palma de Mallorca, junio 1980.

[Southey, Robert], *Edinburgh Annual Register for 1810* (Edinburgh, 1812), vol. 3, Part 1, pp. 354, 382, 483, 505; *Edinburgh Annual Register for 1811* (1813), vol. 4, Part 1, p. 298.

Southey, Robert, *History of the Peninsular War*, vol. 1 (1823), p. 271ff.

S[tephen], L[eslie], *Dictionary of National Biography*, vol. 21 (1909), pp. 63–67.

Tagart, Edward, *A Discourse . . . occasioned by the Rev. J. B. White's recent profession of Unitarian Christianity* (London, 1835).

[Tayler, J. J], *Prospective Review*, vol. 1 (1845), pp. 465–96. The best review of the *Life* by a Unitarian.

Thom, John Hamilton, 'Archbishop Whately and the Life of Blanco White', *Theological Review*, vol. 4 (1867), pp. 81–120.

Tillotson, Geoffrey, 'Newman's Essay on Poetry', in *Newman Centenary Essays* (London, 1945), pp. 178–200.

Truthteller, The, vol. 2, no.20 (London, 25 February 1826). Contains the text of the denunciation of BW by Eneas McDonnell at a meeting of the British Catholic Association, 31 January 1826.

Tuckwell, W, *Pre-Tractarian Oxford. A Reminiscence of the Oriel 'Noetics'* (London, 1909), chapter 8.

Varela Bravo, Eduardo, 'Blanco White, periodista politico', tesis doctoral de la Universidad de Sevilla (1987).

Varela Bravo, Eduardo, 'Un periodista radical: Blanco White en el *Semanario Patriótico*', *Archivo Hispalense*, no.215 (Sevilla, 1987), pp. 127–42.

V[ásquez y] R[uíz], J[osé], 'Carta del presbítero D. José Ma Blanco a D. Alberto Lista', *Archivo Hispalense*, 1a epoca, vol. 1 (1886), pp. 44–46.

[Wake, Henrietta], *E. J. Whately, Reminiscences of her Life and Work* (1894), pp. 9–10.

Ward, John William, 1st Earl of Dudley, *Letters to the Bishop of Llandaff* (London, 1840), p. 357. Writing to Edward Coplestone, the author praises LFS, whose author he met in Spain.

[Ward, W. G], 'Autobiography of the Rev. Joseph Blanco White', *Dublin Review* vol. 20 (1846), pp. 346–86.

Ward, Wilfrid, *W. G. Ward and the Oxford Movement* (1889), p. 356. How WGW, the author's father, was converted to Catholicism while writing the *Dublin Review* notice of BW's *Life* (see preceding item).

Ward, Wilfrid, *The Life of John Henry, Cardinal Newman* (London 1912), vol. 1, pp. 80–82.

Ward, W. R., *Victorian Oxford* (1965), p. 70.

Webb, R. K, 'John H. Thom: Intellect and Conscience in Liverpool', in *The View from the Pulpit: Victorian Ministers and Society*, edited by P. T. Phillips (Toronto, 1980), pp. 211–44.

Whately, Edward, *Personal and Family Glimpses of Remarkable People* (London, 1889), p. 117.

Whately, E. Jane, *The Life and Correspondence of Richard Whately*, 2 vols (1862).

Whately, Richard, *The Errors of Romanism traced to their Origin in Human Nature* (1830). This first edition is dedicated to BW.

[Wilberforce, Henry], *The Foundation of the Faith assailed in Oxford* (London, 1835).

Woods, John, O.S.D., *Remarks on the Rev. Blanco White's Practical and Internal Evidence against Catholicism and his Poor Man's Preservative against Popery* (1830).

Zavala, Iris, 'Forner y Blanco. Dos vertientes del XVIII', *Cuadernos Americanos*, vol. 25 (1966), pp. 128–38.

IV Background reading

Aguilar Piñal, Francisco, *Historia de Sevilla, Siglo XVIII*. 2a edición (Sevilla, 198).

Aguilar Piñal, Francisco, 'Sevilla en 1791', *Archivo Hispalense* nos 132–33 (Sevilla, 1965), pp. 95–105.

Amyot, C. J. B., *Histoire du Colonel Amoros, de sa méthode d'éducational physique et morale, et de la fondation de la gymnastique en France* (Paris, 1852).

Bancroft, Hubert Howe, *History of the Pacific States of North America*, vol. 13 (1884), pp. 220–387, 446–48.

Bernhardt-Kabisch, Ernest, 'Southey in the Tropics: *A Tale of Paraguay* and the Problem of Romantic Faith', *The Wordsworth Circle*, vol. 5 (Spring 1974), pp. 97–104.

Bowman, Charles Harwood, *Vicente Pazos Kanki: Un boliviano en la libertad de America* (La Paz, 1975).

Brent, Richard, *Liberal Anglican Politics: Whiggery, Religion and Reform 1830–41* (Oxford, 1987).

Briggs, Asa, *The Age of Improvement 1783–1867* (1959).

Buxton, John, and Williams, Penry (ed.), *New College, Oxford, 1379–1979* (1979).

Calderón, Juan, *Don Juan Calderón* (London, 1855).

Callahan, William J, Church, *Politics and Society in Spain 1750–1874* (Harvard, 1984).

Carlyle, Thomas, *The Life of John Sterling* (1871).

Carnall, Geoffrey, *Robert Southey and His Age: The Development of a Conservative Mind* (Oxford, 1960).

Carr, Sir Raymond, *Spain 1808–1939* (Oxford, 1966).

Clarke, Richard F, *A Short Sketch of Father Albany James Christie S. J. Reprinted from 'The Month'* (1891).

Colson, Percy, *A Story of Christie's* (1950).

Corona Baratech, Carlos, *Revolución y reacción en el reinado de Carlos IV* (Madrid, 1957).

Crawley, C. W., 'French and English Influences in the Cortes of Cadiz 1810–1814', *Cambridge Historical Journal* (1939), pp. 176–206.

Cueva de Guzman, J. M., Duque de Alburquerque, *Manifiesto . . . acerca de su conducta con la Junta de Cádiz, y arribo del exercito de su cargo a aquella plaza* (Londres: R. Juigné, 1810).

Davis, H. W. C., *The Age of Grey and Peel* (1929).

Finer, S. E., *Sir Edwin Chadwick* (1952).

Firth, C. H., *Modern Languages at Oxford 1724–1929* (Oxford, 1929).

Fisher, Frederick Augustus [*vere* Fischer, Christian August], *Travels in Spain in 1797 and 1798, translated from the German* (London: Longman and Rees, 1802.

Forrester, D. W. F., 'The Intellectual Development of E. B. Pusey 1800–1850', Oxford D.Phil.thesis, 1967.

Furlong, Guillermo, 'Diego Leon Villafañe y sus cartas referentes a la revolución argentina', *Boletín de la Academia Nacional de la Historia*, año 37 (Buenos Aires, 1960), p. 194.

Gallardo, Guillermo, *La politica religiosa de Rivadavia* (Buenos Aires, 1962).

Gilley, Sheridan, 'Nationality and Liberty, Protestant and Catholic: Robert Southey's Book of the Church', *Studies in Church History*, vol. 18, edited by Stuart Mews (Oxford, 1982), pp. 409–32.

Glendinning, Nigel, *A Literary History of Spain: The Eighteenth Century* (1972).

Glendinning, Nigel, 'Spanish Books in England 1800–1850', *Transactions of the Cambridge Bibliographical Society*, vol. 3 (1959), pp. 70–92.

Gobbi, Claire, 'The Spanish Quarter of Somers Town: An Immigrant Community 1820–30', *Camden History Review*, no. 6 (1978), pp. 6–10.

Grant, Elizabeth, of Rothiemurchus, *Memoirs of a Highland Lady 1797–1827*, edited by Angus Davidson (1950).

Halévy, Élie, *A History of the English People in the 19th Century*, vol. 1, 2nd edition (1949).

Hampden, Renn Dickson, *The Scholastic Philosophy, considered in its relations to Christian Philosophy* (1832).

Henderson, Robert, *A Memoir of the late Rev. George Armstrong* (1859).

Hernández y Davalos, J. E. (ed.), *Colección de documentos para la historia de la guerra de independencia de México de 1808 a 1821*, tom. 6 (Mexico, 1882).

Herr, Richard, *The 18th Century Revolution in Spain* (Princeton, 1958).

Holland, Henry Edward, Lord, *Lord Holland's Reminiscences*, 2nd edition (1851).

Jacks, L. P., *The Confessions of an Octogenerian* (1942).

Johns, John, Report on the Liverpool Domestic Mission in *The Christian Teacher*, vol. 2 (1840), pp. 110–18.

Jordan, Hoover H, *Bolt Upright: The Life of Thomas Moore*, 2 vols (Salzburg, 1975).

Juretschke, Hans, *Los afrancesados en la guerra de la independencia* (Madrid, 1962).

Kamen, Henry, *The Spanish Inquisition* (1975).

Levy, S. Leon, *Nassau W. Senior 1760–1864* 2nd edition (Newton Abbot, 1970).

Machin, G. I. T., *The Catholic Question in English Politics 1820–30* (1964).

McKinley, P. Michael, *Pre-revolutionary Caracas: Politics, Economy and Society 1777–1811* (Cambridge, 1985).

Marichal, J, 'From Pistoia to Cadiz: A Generation's Itinerary, 1786–1812', in *The Ibero-American Enlightenment*, edited by A. Owen Aldridge (Urbana, 1971).

Marillier, H. C., *Christie's* (1926).

Méndez Bejarano, Mario, *Diccionario de Escritores Naturales de Sevilla* (Sevilla, 1922–25).

Moore, Thomas, *Travels of an Irish Gentleman in Search of a Religion* (1832).

Moore, Thomas, *Memoirs, Journal and Correspondence of Thomas Moore*, edited by Lord John Russell, 8 vols (1853).

Moore, Thomas, *The Letters of Thomas Moore*, edited by W. S. Dowden, 2 vols (Oxford, 1964).

Moore, Thomas, *The Journal of Thomas Moore 1818–1841*, edited by P. Quennell (1964).

Morange, Claude, 'Sebastian Miñano y Bedoya 1779–1845', Mémoire pour le diplome d'Études Supérieures, Faculté de Lettres de Paris, Institut d'Études Hispaniques, 1959.

M[ontero] de E[spinosa], José M, *Relación histórica de la Judería de Sevilla, establecimiento de la Inquisición en ella, su estinción, y colección de los autos que llamaban de fé celebrados desde su erección* (Sevilla: Imprenta de El Porvenir, 1849).

Morel-Fatio, A, 'Don Francisco Amoros', *Bulletin Hispanique*, vol. 26 (1924), pp. 209–40, 339–68; vol. 28 (1925), pp. 36–78.

Oakeley, Frederick, Memoirs in *Reminiscences of Oxford*, selected by L. M. Quiller-Couch (Oxford Historical Society, 1892), vol. 22. Reprinted from *The Month*, vols 3–4 (1865–66).

O'Connell, Marvin, *The Oxford Conspirators—A History of the Oxford Movement 1833–45* (London, 1969).

Pastor Díaz, N, *Galería de españoles célebres*, vol. 9 (Madrid, 1845), pp. 97–196. On Reinoso.

Pattison, Samuel R. (ed.), *The Brothers Wiffen* (1880).

Pattison, Mark, *Memoirs*, with introduction by Jo Manton (Fontwell, 1969).

Pecchio, Count, *Semi-serious Observations of an Italian Exile during his Residence in England* (1833). On the Spanish exiles in London.

Pendle, George, *A History of Latin America* (1963).

Pfandl, Ludwig, 'Southey und Spanien', *Revue Hispanique*, vol. 28 (1913), pp. 1–315.

Rashdall, Hastings, and Rait, Robert S, *New College* (1901).

Rhydisel; or, The Devil in Oxford, 2 vols (London, 1811).

Ricart, Domingo, 'Notas para una biografía de Luis Usóz y Rio', *Studia Albornotiana*, vol. 13 (Bologna, 1973), pp. 437–532.

Sarrailh, Jean, *L'Espagne éclairée de la seconde moitié du XVIIIe siècle* (Paris, 1954).

Sarrailh, Jean, *La crise religieuse en Espagne à la fin du XVIIIe siècle* (Oxford, 1951).

Saugnieux, Joël, *Un prélat éclairé: Don Antonio Tavira y Almazán, 1737–1807* (Toulouse, 1970).

Saugnieux, Joël, *Le jansénisme espagnol du XVIIIe siècle: Ses composantes et ses sources* (Oviedo, 1976).

Saugnieux, Joël, *Les jansénistes et le renouveau de la prédication dans l'Espagne de la seconde moitié du XVIIIe siècle* (Lyon, 1976).

Sellers, Ian, 'Social and Political Ideas of Representative English Unitarians, 1795–1850', Oxford B.Litt.thesis, 1956.

Simey, Margaret, *Charitable Effort in Liverpool in the 19th Century* (Liverpool, 1951).

Simmons, Jack, *Southey* (1945).

Solís, Ramón, *El Cádiz de las Cortes* (Madrid, 1958).

Sullivan, Edward J, *Goya and the Art of His Time* (Meadows Museum, Southern Methodist University, Dallas, 1982).

Thomas, William, 'Lord Holland', in *History and Imagination: Essays in honour of H. R. Trevor-Roper* (1981), pp. 296–310.

Tocqueville, Alexis de, *Oeuvres Complètes*, vol. 5: *Voyages en Angleterre, etc* (Paris, 1958).

Tocqueville, Alexis de, *Journeys to England and Ireland*, edited by J. P. Mayer (1958).

Townsend, Joseph, *A Journey through Spain in the years 1786 and 1787*, 2nd edition (1792).

Trollope, T. Adolphus, 'Recollections of Archbishop Whately', *Lippincott's Magazine*, vol. 14 (Philadelphia, 1874), pp. 103–112.

Vásquez, G. L., 'Juan Pablo Forner and the Formation of the New History in Spain', *Iberian Studies*, vol. 7, no. 2 (Autumn 1978).

Villanueva, Joaquín de, *Vida literaria*, 2 vols (Londres: Dulau y Cía, 1825).

Viñas-Mey, Carmelo, 'Nuevos datos para la historia de los afrancesados', *Bulletin Hispanique*, vol. 26 (1924), pp. 52–67, 323–38; vol. 27 (1925), pp. 97–130.

Vincent, E. R., *Ugo Foscolo, An Italian in Regency England* (Cambridge, 1953).

Walgrave, J. H., *Newman the Theologian* (1960).

Wellesley Index to Victorian Periodicals, edited by W. E. Houghton et al., vols 1–4 (Toronto, 1966–87).

Young, G. M., *Portrait of an Age*, edited by G. Kitson Clark (1977).

Index